BEYOND ECONOMIC EFFICIENCY IN UNITED STATES TAX LAW

ASPEN ELECTIVE SERIES

BEYOND ECONOMIC EFFICIENCY IN UNITED STATES TAX LAW

David A. Brennen
Dean
University of Kentucky College of Law

Karen B. Brown
Donald Phillip Rothschild Research Professor of Law
George Washington University Law School

Darryll K. Jones
Associate Dean for Academic Affairs and
Professor of Law
Florida A&M University College of Law

Wolters Kluwer
Law & Business

ISBN 978-1-4548-1004-9

Library of Congress Cataloging-in-Publication Data

Brennen, David A.
   Beyond economic efficiency in United States tax law / David A. Brennen, Dean, University of Kentucky College of Law, Karen B. Brown, Donald Phillip Rothschild Research Professor of Law, George Washington University Law School, Darryll K. Joones, Associate Dean for Academic Affairs and Professor of Law, Florida A&M University College of Law.
      p. cm.
   ISBN 978-1-4548-1004-9 (alk. paper)
   1. Taxation—Law and legislation—United States. I. Brown, Karen B., 1954- II. Jones, Darryll K. (Darryll Keith), 1961- III. Title.

KF6289.B75 2013
343.7304—dc23

2013021345

About Wolters Kluwer Law & Business

Wolters Kluwer Law & Business is a leading global provider of intelligent information and digital solutions for legal and business professionals in key specialty areas, and respected educational resources for professors and law students. Wolters Kluwer Law & Business connects legal and business professionals as well as those in the education market with timely, specialized authoritative content and information-enabled solutions to support success through productivity, accuracy and mobility.

Serving customers worldwide, Wolters Kluwer Law & Business products include those under the Aspen Publishers, CCH, Kluwer Law International, Loislaw, ftwilliam.com and MediRegs family of products.

CCH products have been a trusted resource since 1913, and are highly regarded resources for legal, securities, antitrust and trade regulation, government contracting, banking, pension, payroll, employment and labor, and healthcare reimbursement and compliance professionals.

Aspen Publishers products provide essential information to attorneys, business professionals and law students. Written by preeminent authorities, the product line offers analytical and practical information in a range of specialty practice areas from securities law and intellectual property to mergers and acquisitions and pension/benefits. Aspen's trusted legal education resources provide professors and students with high-quality, up-to-date and effective resources for successful instruction and study in all areas of the law.

Kluwer Law International products provide the global business community with reliable international legal information in English. Legal practitioners, corporate counsel and business executives around the world rely on Kluwer Law journals, looseleafs, books, and electronic products for comprehensive information in many areas of international legal practice.

Loislaw is a comprehensive online legal research product providing legal content to law firm practitioners of various specializations. Loislaw provides attorneys with the ability to quickly and efficiently find the necessary legal information they need, when and where they need it, by facilitating access to primary law as well as state-specific law, records, forms and treatises.

ftwilliam.com offers employee benefits professionals the highest quality plan documents (retirement, welfare and non-qualified) and government forms (5500/PBGC, 1099 and IRS) software at highly competitive prices.

MediRegs products provide integrated health care compliance content and software solutions for professionals in healthcare, higher education and life sciences, including professionals in accounting, law and consulting.

Wolters Kluwer Law & Business, a division of Wolters Kluwer, is headquartered in New York. Wolters Kluwer is a market-leading global information services company focused on professionals.

SUMMARY OF CONTENTS

TABLE OF CONTENTS

ACKNOWLEDGMENTS

Any project worth doing is a collective effort. As we near the end of this wonderful collaboration, we would like to heartily thank each of the contributors to this book. Each one is not only an exceptional scholar, but also a wonderful, warmly regarded colleague. We are so grateful for their contributions because they have made this book a tremendous success.

We would also like to thank our respective institutions, University of Kentucky College of Law, George Washington University Law School, and Florida A & M College of Law, for support throughout the process of bringing this book to publication. In addition, we want to express sincere appreciation to Carol McGeehan, Darren Kelly, and Kenny Chumbley, part of the Wolters Kluwer team, for support and encouragement.

Finally, on a personal note, the editors offer the following notes of appreciation:

David dedicates the book as follows: To my partner, Kimberly, and our three boys, Andrew, Spenser, and Clarence. Thanks for your support throughout this project.

Karen expresses love and appreciation to family and friends for their support over the years, especially Leon, to whom she dedicates this book and who will never be forgotten (à mon âme soeur, il y a longtemps que je t'aime, jamais je ne t'oublierai).

David A. Brennen
Karen B. Brown
Darryll K. Jones

INTRODUCTION

BEYOND ECONOMIC EFFICIENCY

David A. Brennen, University of Kentucky College of Law

Karen B. Brown, The George Washington University Law School

Darryll K. Jones, Florida A&M University College of Law

This book is inspired primarily by two events occurring over the past couple of decades. The first was the birth of the critical tax theory movement in a series of conferences initiated in 1995 by Professor Nancy Staudt and colleagues.[1] The original participants chose the name "critical tax theory" because they shared a common dissatisfaction with the traditional way of viewing tax law solely along an equity–efficiency axis, with a narrow construct of equity subordinated to notions of efficiency. The initial conferees presented papers that, without entirely eschewing the equity–efficiency dichotomy, analyzed tax law from perspectives explicitly acknowledging the influence of gender, race, sexual orientation, and other social constructs. Except for a three-year break between 1997 and 2000, tax scholars continue today to organize similar annual critical tax theory conferences throughout the United States on or around April 15, the traditional due date for individual tax returns in the United States. Although many of the papers presented at critical tax theory conferences do not explicitly involve critical legal analysis of tax law, the impetus for the series of conferences was to inject critical legal studies principles into the study of tax law. *Taxing America* (edited by Karen B. Brown and Mary Louise Fellows) (New York University, 1997), a collection of original essays authored by many who participated in the early Critical Tax Theory conferences, was an important milestone because it was the first effort to publish, in book form, a coherent volume of contributions to the critical tax theory debate.

---

1. The critical tax theory conferences have been held at the following law schools: State University at Buffalo (1995 and 1997); University of Wisconsin (2000); Washington University in St. Louis (2001); Tulane University (2002); University of Michigan (2003); Rutgers University at Newark (2004); Seattle University (2005); Mercer University (2006); University of California — Los Angeles (2007); Florida State University (2008); Indiana University — Bloomington (2009); Santa Clara Law School (2010); Saint Louis University (2011); Seton Hall University (2012); U.C. Hastings (2013).

The second impetus for this book was the publication of two other books by Professor Robin Paul Malloy in the early part of the twenty-first century: *Law and Market Economy: Reinterpreting the Values of Law and Economics* (Cambridge University, 2000) and *Law in a Market Context: An Introduction to Market Concepts in Legal Reasoning* (Cambridge University, 2004). Together, Malloy's books lay out a theoretical approach to legal reasoning that challenges many of the long-standing approaches to the type of legal analysis commonly advanced by the law and economics movement. One of the most significant challenges to law and economics is to the notion that rational self-interested behavior inexorably drives markets toward efficient outcomes. Instead, critics of traditional market analysis recognize that many factors — including race, gender, sexual preference, and dominant–subservient relationships in international relations — motivate market actors. Contemporary critics of market analysis, such as Malloy and others, claim that morality, racial construct, social acceptance and political affinity, for example, are often more important to people than maximizing market gains.[2] This more complex view of human beings offers a richer perspective from which to analyze modern society. Thus, while accepting the relevance and importance of traditional economic analysis of law, alternative approaches to legal analysis must be used in order to understand law fully in its market context.

Given the increased prominence of the belief (in the academy, and beyond, for example, in the quarters of the Occupy USA and similar social justice movements) that the merit of the tax system, as well as that of the larger legal framework of rights and obligations, must be judged by reference to concepts of social justice and equality, we felt that it was time for *Beyond Economic Efficiency in U.S. Tax Law*. This is an edited collection of original essays by twelve critical tax theory legal scholars[3] that looks at ways in which reliance on the goal of efficiency in various areas of tax law, without appropriate consideration of other equally important principles, undermines tax law analysis. In particular, scrutiny of the efficacy of a given tax provision without increased consideration of concerns such as fairness, redistribution, anti-discrimination, or subordination invariably reinforces the status quo and forecloses study of the significant ways in which a number of efficiency-based federal and state tax code provisions, left unchallenged, contribute to and perpetuate social and economic inequality. The topics covered in *Beyond Economic Efficiency* are nonprofit taxation, state and local taxation, wealth transfer taxation, retirement and savings, health care, international taxation and redistribution, housing, taxation as regulation, and the normative underpinnings of tax policy discourse.

We begin this exploration of alternatives to traditional analysis in tax law by providing an overview exposing the inadequacy of "classic" analysis by

---

2. This finding, that people are not always motivated by self-interest, is consistent with ideas espoused by scholars who advance the idea of behavioral law and economics as an evolved notion of traditional law and economics. *See, e.g.,* Cass R. Sunstein, *Behavioral Law & Economics* (Cambridge University, 2000).

3. Many authors in *Beyond Economic Efficiency in U.S. Tax Law* also published reprints of prior work in Bridget J. Crawford (Author), Anthony C. Infanti (Editor), *Critical Tax Theory: An Introduction* (Cambridge University, 2009).

detailing the incoherence of the efficiency trope. According to the author, Professor Neil Buchanan, an understanding of the limited usefulness of the concept of Pareto efficiency can only serve to "sharpen analysis of the real issues at stake in any assessment of tax policy." Although the term "efficiency" carries a "powerfully positive connotation," it is deeply value-laden, possessing normative content. Dependent upon a market measuring the amount one is willing to pay for a good or service, Pareto efficiency seeks a market equilibrium in which persons in society are made "better off," while others are not made "worse off." Yet the relative values to which efficiency analysis clings are not reliable, being influenced by a number of variables that cannot be confidently determined. While a so-called efficient market would eschew governmental intervention to reach a correct allocation of resources, market proponents fail to acknowledge the influence of the status quo and the potential need for a governmental role and other types of interventions to guarantee fairness. Buchanan, a Harvard-trained economist who is also a law professor, dismantles the perceived neutrality of efficiency analysis in order to move in the direction of measuring the effects of given tax policy choices on decisions of various actors. His overview provides a template for consideration of the chapters that follow.

Closely related to the issues explored in Buchanan's essay, Professor Sagit Leviner's chapter on the normative underpinnings of tax discourse makes the point that the federal tax system is founded upon a range of normative claims that are often presented in the form of self-evident truths. Yet when issues of social justice are interjected into tax policy debates, they are frequently dismissed as inappropriate. Principles of fairness and redistribution are viewed as outside of legitimate policy discussions, because they are matters of personal preference that have no bearing on the construction of an efficient, welfare-maximizing tax system. Leviner explores the degree to which fundamentals in taxation are built upon subjectivity by reference to three political theories — the theory of natural entitlement, the utilitarian doctrine, and Rawls's theory of justice as fairness. She concludes that a correct elaboration of normative perspectives and the way in which they apply to taxation would lead to a better understanding of society and the tax system.

The next chapter, by Professor James Charles Smith, concerns an issue that arises in the multijurisdictional tax arena: state and local tax. Professor Smith examines the efficiency of the system of market valuation in the U.S. property tax regime, examining contemporary property tax reform proposals. Noting that most property tax battles focus on the connections between raising taxes and the way government spends tax dollars, Professor Smith's chapter takes the debate one step further by considering the justification for modern American property tax systems. He questions whether a property tax system that depends upon fair market valuation is efficient or equitable by reference to a number of templates, including whether a given property tax is progressive, regressive, or proportionate.

The next chapter examines federal tax-exemption law: those income, gift, and estate tax laws that exclude income from taxation by exempting the income as it is earned. Dean David A. Brennen explains how widely accepted efficiency rationales do not fully explain why we have tax laws that exempt charities from the obligation to pay income tax. The Supreme Court explains this efficiency rationale by suggesting that the exemption is a way for the government to compensate nongovernmental entities for providing public goods to society. Tax scholars typically explain the efficiency rationale by suggesting either that charities are exempt by necessity or that the charitable tax exemption is payment to charities for their lack of access to capital markets. In either case, tax exemption is thought necessary to overcome "market failure," an idea steeped in efficiency theory and very nearly oblivious to notions of equity, fairness, or the elimination of disadvantages arising from immutable human characteristics. Both traditional explanations for charitable tax exemption, though seemingly elegant as far as they go, neglect important qualitative aspects of the exemption. As this chapter explains, these elusive qualitative aspects of the charitable tax exemption form the heart of the exemption and are what distinguish mission-driven tax-exempt charities from profit-driven taxable organizations. Dean Brennen's chapter proposes an alternative diversity rationale for the charitable tax exemption that accepts efficiency but also asserts greater relevance of other rationales that account for the fairness and justice aspects of charitable entities. By illustrating that the real world is not nearly as elegantly ordered as efficiency proponents would have us believe, Brennen, too, exposes the much more chaotic and complex world to which tax law ought to respond.

The next three chapters, by Professors Lucinda Jesson, Amy B. Monahan, and Roberta Mann, concern the controversial subsidy of economic activity provided by the government's use of tax expenditures. They explore two "hot button" issues: health care and housing. Congress's decision in recent years to continue to encourage provision of health care by maintaining significant tax benefits for employer-sponsored insurance instead of opting for a single-payer system remains a source of heated debate.

Noting the health care subsidy the federal tax code provides to employers (in the form of salary deduction) and employees (in the form of the exclusion from income), Professor Lucinda Jesson critiques the system as highly inefficient. The benefit disproportionately subsidizes high-income families and creates incentives for overuse, which drives costs higher. Jesson alternatively considers the way in which the tax code can be used to discourage unhealthy activity through so-called "sin taxes" on certain foods and drinks, such as junk food and sodas, or by denying business expense deductions for advertising relating to these products. She also urges reconsideration of the longstanding tax exemption afforded hospitals that do not provide charitable care, suggesting that the size of the government subsidy may not be justified by the benefits to community members and other recipients of care. Finally, Jesson examines the political origins of the 2010 health care legislation known as the Patient Protection and Affordable Care Act (PPACA, or "Obamacare"), which was enacted largely as a result of the efforts of the Obama administration. While the new legislation moves the system "ever so slightly" in the direction of efficiency and fairness, it does not cure the problems of overconsumption of health care and disproportionate benefits to employees of large and medium-size employers (versus those of small businesses). In Jesson's view, adoption of a system like the much-maligned single-payer system or a tax deduction or credit system for workers (eliminating the exclusion for employees and deduction for employers) would have had greater potential to address tax inequities more completely.

Professor Amy Monahan's chapter looks at the complex relationship between health insurance and taxes. Despite the major overhaul in 2010, the tax subsidy for employer-provided health coverage, critiqued as inefficient and unfair, remains in place as the cornerstone of the PPACA. Monahan's essay explores the innovative provisions enacted by the PPACA, critiques them on efficiency grounds, and moves beyond efficiency concerns to consider broader policy issues. These include affordability, access to health care, fairness, and social solidarity. Monahan finds that the PPACA takes a significant step toward addressing the challenges presented by health care reform. She finds it likely to enhance efficiency. Beyond efficiency concerns, Monahan finds substantial improvements in insurance and medical care affordability for low and moderate income individuals. In addition, she finds that the PPACA improves social solidarity, simplifies insurance decision making, and advances fairness and equity. On balance, although retention of the preference for employer-provided coverage creates an inequity between individuals based on employment status, Monahan suggests that individual insurance market reforms may alleviate some of the inequity.

Assuming that homeownership provides useful societal benefits, Professor Roberta Mann's chapter explores the ways in which the tax system could create incentives for homeownership but avoid the problems of the qualified residence interest (QRI) deduction. Homeownership has long been viewed as a social good, but the QRI deduction has faced criticism, including that it is inconsistent with the structure of the income tax system; it is economically inefficient, skewing investment towards private residences; it is inequitable, discriminating against low-income people (a group that may disproportionately include people of color) and certain religious minorities; and it is environmentally unsound, encouraging sprawl, excessive energy use, and inefficient transportation choices. Mann's essay examines alternatives, including adding a homeownership benefit to the standard deduction, creating a refundable housing credit, providing a deduction for contributions to a housing savings account, and including a shelter credit available for renters and homeowners alike.

Professor Reuven S. Avi-Yonah's chapter on taxation as regulation looks at three different types of tax — the carbon tax, the health care tax, and the bank tax — in order to examine the use of the tax system to achieve regulatory goals, including subsidizing activities the government wishes to promote and penalizing activities it wishes to discourage. Avi-Yonah notes that despite the considerable controversy concerning the tax expenditure budget, Congress nonetheless continues to use the tax code to encourage conduct or to discourage it. He believes that regulation is a legitimate goal of taxation. In particular, concerning climate change, Avi-Yonah demonstrates that a carbon tax collected by the Internal Revenue Service (IRS) is preferable to other approaches, such as "command and control" regulation or a cap-and-trade regime. He finds a value added tax a better vehicle for revenue-raising and the individual income tax to be the best means to achieve redistribution. A proposed bank tax — imposed on a small number of taxpayers with enough sophistication to deal with the complexity, and broadcasting a clear regulatory goal — would be effective, because, as designed, it would deter banks from taking excessive risks. On the other hand, the individual health care mandate contained in the PPACA, although upheld by the U.S. Supreme Court, is ill-advised because it is complex, imposed on a large number of taxpayers, and falls disproportionately on the poor.

The next two chapters examine the connection between taxation and wealth in the retirement income security and transfer tax arenas. The first, written by Professor Regina T. Jefferson, focuses on the recent trend of using defined contribution plans (instead of defined benefit plans) as primary retirement savings vehicles, which goes far beyond a mere substitution by the employer of one type of plan for another. A shift from a traditional defined benefit plan promising fixed amounts to beneficiaries determined by reference to account balances upon retirement, though arguably more efficient, exposes a retiree to the risk of losses that may lead to inadequate resources during the retirement years. Notwithstanding the large tax subsidy accorded the private pension system, it is increasingly more likely that retirees will need additional governmental assistance in their old age. Thus, significant changes to pension law are necessary both to ensure that workers receive the retirement benefits they expect, as well as to justify the large amounts of tax revenue the Treasury forgoes each year in connection with preferential treatment of retirement plans. Jefferson's proposals include mandated investment advice to employees and a guaranteed minimum benefits option.

The second, by Professor Mary Louise Fellows, draws lessons from the work of economist Adam Smith and novelist Jane Austen that inform the estate tax debate in which both proponents and opponents are tied to conventional economic arguments. Fellows's chapter offers the Bush Administration's repeal of the estate tax as a motivation for reexamination of the federal transfer tax system. She points to the need to "dislodge the conventional economic arguments" in order to consider the ways in which the tax system can contribute to building a strong civil society by reference to other equally important values, such as justice, beneficence, and prudence. Fellows maintains that in the current political environment, where wealth-maximization has talismanic dimensions, so long as estate tax opponents can plausibly argue that the tax produces inefficiencies and interferes with economic growth, their arguments have political salience. From the writings of Smith and Austen, Fellows draws the understanding that pursuit and retention of wealth are part, but not the whole, of what society should judge as virtuous conduct. After concluding that government should have a role in instilling justice, beneficence, and prudence into civil society by resort to some type of wealth transfer tax, this chapter offers alternatives to the current regime.

The final two chapters consider the international dimension of the allocation of resources, including the role of redistributional goals in the reform of international tax policy and the importance of multiactor input into the design of international tax systems. In the first of these chapters, Professor Karen B. Brown details the importance of the interjection of redistributional norms into international tax policy reform. The "welfare maximizing" strategies employed by high-income nations over the past several decades were not available to poorer nations that could not effectively compete for valuable investment dollars. The competitive strategies adopted by the poor nations to attract the interest of multinational firms were condemned as unfair. Yet, in response to an increasingly weak global economy, high-income nations have resorted to similar competitive strategies, including drastic tax rate reductions, in order to attract larger shares of a declining pool of resources. Brown's chapter urges that high-income nations overhauling their tax systems to address recent economic hardship maintain a concern for the impact of their regimes on the economies of poorer, developing nations. The richer nations, having benefited from the privilege of hierarchy, have an obligation to consider the interests of the developing world in the future design of the international tax system.

Professor Diane Ring's chapter focuses on the international dynamics of international taxation. She shifts attention from establishing desired policy goals to achieving such goals. The chapter brings into focus the core reality of much of international tax: it is not a solitary national endeavor. The behavior, action, and interests of others (including nonstate actors) are significant factors in the actual outcomes from tax policy. As efficiency concerns in tax policy led analysts to delve into economics, questions regarding the international dynamics of designing, implementing, and enforcing international tax policy should lead to international tax relations. Looking at international relations literature and theory, the chapter considers the consequences of resorting to such work to evaluate international tax. This includes how such an inquiry would affect one's view of various international organizations, shape one's research agenda, and impact the debates regarding harmonization and independence of tax systems. Ring demonstrates that analysis must extend beyond the traditional consideration of what is good tax policy based on economic efficiency rationales to encompass study of the full complement of actors influencing design of international systems.

Inspired by the development of the critical tax theory movement and alternative approaches to traditional economic analysis in law in general, *Beyond Economic Efficiency* sheds new light on the understanding of traditional economic analysis and suggests that it is not the sole mechanism for examining the merits of the U.S. tax system. The original chapters in this book — written from a number of different perspectives — inject into the growing debate about the legitimate contours of the tax system the need for resort to a broader range of analytical tools. In particular, *Beyond Economic Efficiency* demonstrates that reference to efficiency, at times a helpful starting point, cannot capture the essential determinants of a just, equal, and progressive society.

THE LIMITATIONS OF EFFICIENCY ANALYSIS

CHAPTER 1

THE ROLE OF ECONOMICS IN TAX SCHOLARSHIP

Neil H. Buchanan, George Washington University Law School

One of the fundamental tenets of modern tax policy analysis is that we should be concerned with so-called economic efficiency. Along with equity and administrability, efficiency is widely held to be a desirable and important goal. Indeed, to some analysts, efficiency is the most important of those goals, and perhaps the *only* appropriate goal of tax policy. Even for those who still take seriously non-efficiency concerns, however, efficiency is at least a central element of tax policy analysis, to be weighed against the other two goals (and, perhaps, some others).

All tax policy proposals are thus scrutinized to determine whether they enhance or reduce the economy's efficiency. If economic efficiency were a coherent concept, it would indeed be extremely useful in the analysis of tax policy, as well as in many other areas of the law. Unfortunately, there is no substance underneath the often impressive superstructure of efficiency analysis. This makes it not just unwise, but in fact affirmatively misleading, to base academic analysis of taxation — in whole or in part — on attempts to measure and maximize efficiency.

These assertions are likely to strike some readers as surprising, if not shocking. So much modern scholarly analysis takes for granted the usefulness of efficiency analysis that legal scholars might not stop to think about whether efficiency means anything at all. Efficiency is simply something that everyone thinks they understand. As I will argue in this chapter, however, there is "no there there" when it comes to efficiency analysis. Efficiency is ultimately nothing more than a seductive guise behind which unexamined assumptions and normative preferences hide.

This does not, however, mean that we must throw out everything that we think we know about using economics in analyzing tax policy. Knowing that efficiency is an empty concept does not mean that all bets are off — that there are no principled ways in which to analyze tax issues. It does mean that we can no longer pretend that there is a "clean answer" that is untouched by a scholar's judgment, values, and choices. Therefore, what we gain by confronting the emptiness of the efficiency trope is the opportunity to sharpen our analysis of the real issues at stake in any assessment of tax policy.

EFFICIENCY ANALYSIS AND ITS MORE SOPHISTICATED EXTENSIONS

"Efficiency" is a word with multiple meanings. It often implies something as simple as turning out the lights when one leaves the room. In academic analysis, however, efficiency is a much more freighted concept. Also known as "economic efficiency" or "Pareto efficiency" (in honor of Vilfredo Pareto, the nineteenth-century economist who was central to developing the concept), "efficiency" as used by modern economic scholars purports to measure something much more subtle and important than whether an item is "inexpensive" or "cheap."

Because of that important distinction, it is necessary to use a consistent label to describe economists' nonintuitive notion of efficiency. Therefore, I will use "Pareto efficiency" consistently throughout this chapter to distinguish what economists mean by "efficiency" from what non-economists might imagine that the word implies.

This distinction is, moreover, not merely a matter of agreeing upon a common vocabulary. The word "efficiency," despite its vagueness, carries with it a powerfully positive connotation. Describing something as inefficient is tantamount to condemnation, while being efficient is much to be desired. It would be foolish, therefore, to allow scholars to take on the mantle of being "in favor of efficiency" when their analyses lead them to make policy recommendations that are anything but objectively desirable.

The definition of the word "efficiency" is also important because so many economists put great weight on the claim that their analyses are "value-neutral," being merely a matter of cold calculation not taking into account anyone's views on morality or philosophy. Describing something as "efficient," therefore, ultimately relies on the familiar (but misleading) distinction between "positive" analysis and "normative" analysis, where positive analysis supposedly takes no position regarding matters of values and morality, while normative analysis allows an analyst to insert her own views about what is good and bad.

Pareto efficiency is generally held out as a positive concept, with no normative content. If that were true, Pareto efficiency would arguably be an improvement upon a world in which disagreements were mere matters of opinion. While one can readily see why such an approach is appealing, it is unfortunately not possible to remove normative concerns from supposedly positive analyses. Indeed, as I will discuss below, Pareto efficiency is ultimately based on very strong, but usually unstated, normative assumptions.

THE STANDARD DEFINITION OF EFFICIENCY

But what does Pareto efficiency mean? The standard definition is usually phrased as follows: "A situation is Pareto efficient if it is not possible to make anyone better off without making someone else worse off." The basic idea, therefore, is that Pareto efficiency analysis involves comparing gains and losses caused by putting people in different situations, with a Pareto efficient situation representing the maximum amount of "well-offness" in the society in question.

How do we measure how well-off people are? Doing so requires choosing a theory of value — that is, a basis to determine how much something is worth, and a metric by which to measure that value. Pareto efficiency analysis, as currently understood, takes as its theory of value the so-called willingness-to-pay principle. This means that value can be measured by asking how much someone would be willing to pay for something, and comparing it to how much people would be willing to pay for something else.

Once we can measure value, we can then compare the values of putting people in different situations. If a person possessed, say, five lamps and ten hats, then we could compare the value of that person's situation with having seven lamps and eight hats — or, for that matter, with having neither lamps nor hats, but having twenty bottles of wine.

This definition of value, therefore, purports to take individual preferences and personal sovereignty seriously. Rather than imposing an external measure of value on people, willingness-to-pay measures value by watching people put their money where their mouths are. Value is, therefore, determined subjectively but measured objectively.

Pareto efficiency analysis involves applying this method of measuring value to alternative possible realities. From any starting point, an economist asks, is it possible to rearrange things so that no one is worse off than they are now, and at least one other person is better off than she is now? If so, then the current situation is not Pareto efficient. We would only stop when we have reached the situation in which no further rearrangements are possible without leaving someone worse off.

Applying this concept to tax policy has become numbingly familiar in modern tax analysis. We measure the gains from any possible change in policy against the losses from such a change and declare a situation Pareto efficient when all possible changes from that situation involve greater losses than gains. If gains are possible, then achieving Pareto efficiency would require us to capture those gains by changing the tax laws.

In the simple graphs used for standard tax analysis, the shortcut for determining whether a situation is Pareto efficient is to look for the existence of so-called "deadweight loss triangles." In the typical analysis, there is only one point on the price/quantity graph at which there is no deadweight loss triangle, making that point the Pareto efficient point.

MARKET SOLUTIONS

One of the most important theoretical claims in modern economics is that "properly behaved" markets will reach a Pareto efficient equilibrium on their own, without any need for planning or guidance on the part of the government (or any other extra-market entity). This claim is, therefore, simply a modernized version of Adam Smith's famous "invisible hand," in which a well-defined market allows self-interested individuals to act on their own behalf, seeking out advantage in transactions in a way that guarantees that every good and service ends up being consumed by the person who values it most highly.

If that is true, then it necessarily follows that any change in tax policy (which, in this simplified world, means the introduction of any tax or subsidy) would disturb a market's Pareto efficient outcome, creating deadweight loss where none had existed before. This means that the government's decision to tax or subsidize *anything* must reduce the total well-offness generated by a market, compared to a market in which the government has not intervened.

In short, the standard economic analysis ends up being a brief for nonintervention by the government in markets — that is, for a *laissez-faire* approach to governing. If self-interested transactions end up maximizing value, then there is simply no need to undertake policies to try to make people happier. Not only will such policies by definition fail (because aggregate happiness is already at its maximum), but they will inevitably make matters worse.[1]

WHEN ARE TAXING AND SPENDING BENEFICIAL?

Of course, any competent economist would readily acknowledge that the analysis above is absurdly simplified, and that there are often situations in which it is possible for the government to engage in policies that will make people better off in the aggregate. Entire areas of scholarly analysis are based on exploring such possibilities. The key, of course, lies in the term "well-behaved," as in the description above.

Using taxes to reduce pollution, for example, can (under very defensible assumptions) be shown to move from a non–Pareto efficient situation to a Pareto efficient one. If we recognize that there are costs and benefits that are not borne by the people who make decisions — that is, if there are externalities — then we can improve the way such a market behaves by adopting any of a number of approaches to forcing people to face the full consequences of their decisions.

Similarly, if we are concerned that not everyone acts in the cold, calculated, self-interested ways required by standard economic theory, then there might be a number of ways in which we can improve market outcomes by assisting people in overcoming various cognitive biases. Or, when we acknowledge that not all markets allow for the kind of competition that is presumed by the standard theory — as when a firm monopolizes a market and excludes new entrants — then we have opened up the possibility that the government can improve matters by creating or restoring the kind of competition required by standard economic theory.

Each of these possibilities, as noted, not only is well understood but also forms the basis for specialized study within economics. Behavioral economics,

---

1. There is a serious problem with the very notion of aggregating preferences — that is, with being able to add together the amount of well-offness that different people feel. This problem is generally assumed away, with "well-behaved" economic models requiring that people's individual happiness generally be unaffected by changes in other people's happiness. For example, standard models generally assume away both altruism and malevolence. This set of problems is fundamentally important, but a discussion of them in any detail would require a technical diversion not appropriate here.

industrial organization, public finance, and other fields of specialization are dedicated largely to understanding when and how real-world markets diverge from the theory that supports *laissez-faire* economics. More sophisticated analyses confront the question of whether it might still be better to leave things alone, despite being in a non–Pareto efficient situation, because of the likelihood that any intervention might (or might not) make matters still worse.

Many of the chapters in this volume dedicate serious efforts along these lines, taking into account real-world considerations that enrich the analysis beyond the basic anti-tax presumption that otherwise emerges from standard economic theory. Such analyses demonstrate that, even thinking within the confines of standard economic analysis based on Pareto efficiency, there remains important uncertainty with regard to a wide range of possible policy interventions.

THE FUNDAMENTAL PROBLEM WITH PARETO EFFICIENCY ANALYSIS

None of the discussion in the previous section, however, addresses the central claim of this chapter, that Pareto efficiency is a fundamentally empty concept that ultimately fails to advance our understanding of tax (and other legal) analysis. Indeed, it might appear that the standard approach is supple and sophisticated, allowing scholars to extend a fundamental model beyond its elements, to include an impressively wide range of possible issues to be analyzed under a common rubric. This is, however, a mirage. The supposed expansiveness of the economic approach is actually its downfall, making the approach either a veil for unstated assumptions and norms or an undisciplined analytical method that can lead to any conclusion at all.

WHAT IS WRONG WITH FOLLOWING PROFESSIONAL NORMS?

As a strategy of advancing understanding and sustaining a productive argument, it is understandable that scholars would seek to extend rather than reject established analytical frameworks. Rather than disagreeing on the most fundamental bases of any question, it is often helpful to accept *arguendo* the majority of the assumptions of another's analysis, and then tweak those assumptions to demonstrate that a different outcome follows. This might be especially true for legal scholars, who are adept at pulling together insights from many disciplines, but who typically are not in the business of changing how any of those disciplines work.

When working within a discipline, of course, it is generally necessary to build upon the structure that has already been built. Many budding economists are tempted during their undergraduate or early graduate studies to try to tear the entire structure of economic theory down to its foundations in an attempt to start over and reinvent modern economics. Their advisors sensibly tell them that this is not how knowledge accumulates, suggesting that the better path is to become conversant in the discussion that has been established in the profession, and then to add to that discussion at the margins.

Unfortunately, this combination of incentives facing various scholars — both non-economists who are understandably hesitant to engage in deep critiques of established economic theory (if, for no other reason, because they do not feel competent in the nuances of a highly technical field) and economists who must accept the basic presumptions of their field — creates a dynamic in which the deep assumptions underlying economic analysis are generally ignored or suppressed. Even so, a great deal of important work has been done along these lines, but it is nonetheless true that the vast bulk of economics-oriented analysis (both inside and outside of economics departments) continues to be based on a theoretical framework that has been shown to be incoherent.

THE BASELINE PROBLEM

An essential assumption behind Pareto efficiency analysis is that there is a neutral starting point that forms the baseline for measuring the consequences of people's economic interactions. That is, when we say that people compete fairly in markets, engaging in mutually beneficial trades that reflect their own assessments of their desires and priorities, we act as if the constraints that shape people's decisions are somehow neutral.

In standard microeconomic analysis, for example, each person is assumed to be trying to maximize her well-being based on her preferences, her income, and her assets, as well as on the prices that she faces as she considers making purchases. Each person is thus constrained by her circumstances, and she does the best that she can under those constraints. Nothing in Pareto efficiency analysis, therefore, is understood to mean that people are in some objective sense happy or well-off, but only that people are in the aggregate as happy as they can be, *while operating under the constraints that the world imposes upon them.*

But what is the nature of those circumstances that constrain people, and how do those circumstances become the baseline used to measure Pareto efficiency? The most obvious issue, of course, is the distribution of income and assets. It is widely known that if one starts from a baseline in which one person possesses all of the productive assets in a society, there is a perfectly valid Pareto efficient outcome in which that one wealthy person keeps everything and maximizes his happiness, while others starve.

One common response to this extreme possibility is to say that the aggregate happiness in society will go up when other people are made less miserable, because the marginal loss to the person who possessed everything must surely be smaller than the marginal gain to those who had nothing. While that seems likely to be true as an empirical matter, one cannot say that it is definitely true. If it is not, then Pareto efficiency would still coexist with severe human misery.

We could, of course, simply assume that transferring resources from rich to poor will increase aggregate happiness. Doing so would allow us to label a redistributive tax system as "achieving Pareto efficiency" rather than "creating deadweight losses," but only because we are willing to make an empirical assumption in the absence of evidence.

One of the fundamental baselines of Pareto efficiency analysis, therefore, is the initial distribution of resources that people possess when they enter the marketplace. If we change the initial distribution, then that new distribution of resources can just as easily be used as the baseline for analysis as any other.

In other words, there is nothing about the current distribution of resources that should give it analytical priority over any imaginable alternative. If, in Situation A, a person would start with one million dollars in assets, while in Situation B, that person would start with zero dollars in assets, then there is no consistent way to assess (from a Pareto efficiency standpoint) a policy that takes one million dollars away from that person. Viewed from Situation A, this would amount to taking away his rightful endowment, leading to Pareto inefficient results. Viewed from Situation B, however, this restores the person to his rightful initial endowment, guaranteeing Pareto efficient results. Even something in between, such as a 50–50 split, does not save the analysis, because the question is what baseline to use when measuring Pareto efficiency. There is no neutral way to elevate one endowment over any other.

The larger point, therefore, is that it is always possible to criticize as Pareto inefficient the same policy that, from a different baseline, enhances Pareto efficiency. The choice of baseline itself, however, is not based on any overarching principle.

THE LEGAL BASELINE PROBLEM

While the baseline of income and assets is the most intuitively obvious area in which a theory based on "willingness to pay" (and, therefore, on ability to pay) falters, the question of defining a baseline ultimately implicates even more fundamental issues of ownership and rights.

Recall that the basic idea behind any measurement of Pareto efficiency is that people will buy and sell goods and services in "free markets." What is generally unacknowledged is the wide range of possible rules under which such "free" markets might operate. Even the freest of markets operates in the shadow of the law.

The basic presumptions behind buying and selling, after all, are that a person possesses the legal right of ownership for something, and that she is capable of transferring that right of ownership to someone else. The rules of property law, therefore, are fundamental in determining what people can and cannot do in the marketplace. The classic scam of selling the Brooklyn Bridge to unsuspecting tourists captures this notion in its extreme form, with a party purporting to be able to sell to another person something that the seller does not even own.

Even short of such outright fraud, however, the nature of ownership is deeply problematic and contingent. The possible rules of property law are so diverse as to defy the possibility of defining a presumptive baseline set of property rules (with all other possible property rules thus defined as Pareto inefficient). Consider, for example, the range of rules regarding land ownership that have existed in England and the United States over their histories.

In most jurisdictions, even a legally recognized owner can be deemed to have lost ownership in the property by "adverse possession," a rule that allows the state to sanction acquisition by a second person who has occupied the land without adequate contest by the nominal owner. Each jurisdiction, however, must set the rules determining what a current owner must do to contest another's adverse possession adequately: the number of years can vary, the nature of "open and notorious" possession is contestable, and so on.

One might argue that even having a law recognizing adverse possession under any circumstances is a violation of the proper baseline. If a person owns property, then we could say that she will continue to own property unless she sells it, gives it away, or dies. Even to take that position, however, at least requires recognizing that an underlying property rule that currently exists nearly everywhere is "not the proper baseline." That would necessarily imply that measuring Pareto efficiency against the baseline of current legal rules is invalid. We would, instead, need to know what people would be willing to pay for all of their various goods and services if there were no adverse possession laws.

Arguing that such a minor law could not affect a large number of transactions is an insufficient response, especially because so many different current laws can be described as violating a proper baseline. Even if none individually appears to be significant, the totality of the arguable violations of the proper baseline cannot be so easily dismissed.

Moreover, even if it were possible to agree that ownership is extinguished only by sale, gift, or death, each of those issues raises its own set of baseline questions. Tax scholars know as well as anyone how difficult it is even to define when something is a gift. When is an arrangement merely a loan? Allowing a person to use property does not necessarily amount to giving a gift, nor necessarily a sale, either.

Sales, of course, move us from the realm of property law into the realm of contract law, which presents its own set of arbitrary choices of what counts as a valid agreement and what does not. Some laws prevent people from selling what they own (including those that prevent parents from selling their children—or themselves—into slavery), making the concept of ownership much more complicated than it initially appears.

In short, legal rules define all of the limits of what can be bought and sold in open markets. There is no "natural" baseline for any of those rules. It might be tempting, however, to imagine that most of these property and contract rules are so well established, and are so unlikely to change, that we can confidently take them in their current form as the baseline. Making such an assumption, one might argue, would not allow us to measure Pareto efficiency perfectly, but we could at least closely approximate a proper baseline.

Even here, however, the reality is that these basic legal rules are changing all the time. Intellectual property laws define entire categories of nonphysical items that can be bought, sold, and owned. A law that would lengthen or shorten the number of years of copyright or patent protections would most definitely change a person's willingness to pay for any particular piece of intellectual property and, as a direct consequence, would also change their ability to buy other goods and services with the money that they earn from their intellectual property. Congress regularly legislates in these areas, and regulatory agencies must fill in gaps in those laws. Each such decision changes the baseline against which one would measure Pareto efficiency, with owners of property viewing the lengthening or strengthening of property rights merely as an affirmation of their natural ownership rights, whereas others are equally justified in viewing legal changes to shorten or weaken such rights as merely a move toward a different (and arguably better) baseline.

Finally, consider the complications involved in the rules governing property at death. Even setting aside the tax consequences of estate planning, the rules of succession must include line-drawing decisions affecting—among a wide variety of other issues—those who die intestate, the rules available to challenge the validity of wills, and any prohibitions against disinheriting spouses or minor children. Even the most notorious doctrine in all of property law, the Rule Against Perpetuities, has recently been abandoned by some jurisdictions, while being retained in modified form in others.

With all of those moving parts, therefore, it is simply impossible to define a neutral baseline against which we could say that a Pareto efficiency analysis of all market decisions must be based. A person's willingness to pay for goods and services under one set of laws will necessarily differ—and could certainly differ substantially—from one's willingness to pay under another set of laws, even if the differences in the two sets of laws appear to be minor on the surface.

TAXES AND THE GOVERNMENT

One important implication of the baseline problem was recently developed in a notable book, *The Myth of Ownership*, by the legal philosophers Liam Murphy and Thomas Nagel. They primarily focused not on the range of possible laws that a government might pass to define the baseline of market transactions, but rather on the variety of ways in which that government might finance itself. Levying taxes on one or a combination of tax bases (income, estates at death, property more generally, sales, wages, and so on) enables a government to determine after-tax incomes in a way that cannot be evaluated meaningfully from the standpoint of Pareto efficiency. Decisions by governments to levy taxes are thus as consequential for the baseline question as are decisions about property laws, contract laws, criminal laws, and so on.

What is now commonly referred to as "the Murphy/Nagel" point is that it is not coherent even to refer to someone's before-tax income, because the level and type of taxes collected will inevitably affect the government's decisions and ability to pass and enforce its laws, which in turn will affect how much money a person can earn (and in many cases even the types of businesses in which she might work). Saying, "I would have had this much money *if there were no government,*" in other words, is to engage in a meaningless hypothetical exercise.

The concept on which the Murphy/Nagel point is built, however, is that the government itself defines and enforces the rules that make market transactions possible. Without guarantees of ownership, respect for the rules of transactions, and so on, there is no commerce. Commerce, therefore, logically requires government and taxes, because economic transactions presume the existence of a government that enacts and enforces the rules by which people transact.

PARETO EFFICIENCY AND VALUE JUDGMENTS

In the end, it might be tempting to dismiss all of the analysis above as needlessly complicating a simple situation. Sure, one might say (as I have actually heard people say), there are many different legal rules that we might adopt, but we are stuck with the ones that currently exist. We should thus use current reality as the baseline, and leave the possible alternative worlds to philosophers and science fiction writers.

As much as that argument might sound like an attractive form of pragmatism, however, it actually misses the entire point of all tax analysis and, indeed, of all legal analysis. No one argues that the current set of laws is perfect. Those who use Pareto efficiency as a way to evaluate policy make the claim that certain policy changes will move us toward a superior situation (that is, a situation that has smaller or nonexistent deadweight loss triangles) because the preferred policies would "correct" some "imperfections" in the market that are currently preventing the market from achieving a Pareto efficient outcome.

As the analysis above makes clear, however, one person's imperfection is another person's baseline law. Taking away something that benefits one person, based on the belief that it is an unnatural deviation from Pareto efficiency, can be justified only if the thing that is being taken away is not part of the background of laws and regulations that allow us to determine Pareto efficient outcomes in the first place. Because there is no hierarchy of laws that allows us to determine which are required and which are optional, however, there is no meaning to the statement: "This policy would improve Pareto efficiency." Even a more careful statement, such as "Under the baseline assumptions on which I am relying, this policy would improve Pareto efficiency," is nonetheless unhelpful, because the ready retort is: "Yes, and under other baseline assumptions, this policy would increase Pareto *in*efficiency."

As a result, those who make evaluative statements about Pareto efficiency are (usually unconsciously, as far as I can tell) generally making value judgments—normative assessments—but cloaking them in the language of efficiency and thus the supposed neutrality of positive analysis. By including within the baseline the values that one holds dearest (for example, views about what the employment laws should say about gender and race discrimination), one is then able to characterize the policies that one does not like as unnatural and economically wasteful.

AN EXAMPLE: WHEN IS A NEW LAW EFFICIENT?

Given the relatively abstract nature of so much of the above analysis, a specific example might be especially helpful to clarify the point. An economist friend of mine used to remind me constantly that the notion of Pareto efficiency is quite broad, because what counts as "well-offness" is in the eyes of all of the various people whose welfare we are trying to maximize in the aggregate. Because there is no accounting for tastes, he argued, one must not fall into the trap of describing outcomes as Pareto inefficient merely because of disagreements over the specific transactions that take place in a market. If enough people love auto racing, then profit-seeking media outlets will cover auto racing. If people love opera, then the government has no business banning or limiting the performance of operas.

The idea, therefore, is not just that markets act through the invisible hand to maximize well-offness, but that we can determine what people care about by what they buy and do not buy. People would then petition the government to make sure that the laws comported with their own preferences, to allow the laws to reflect their values and maximize their ability to use markets to achieve happiness.

This economist was, however, incensed one day when he learned that his state government had jailed a person for committing an extreme act of animal abuse. His argument was that this was "not Pareto efficient." I asked how one could possibly know that this did not maximize the aggregate of human happiness (by, for example, allowing people to know that animal cruelty would be somewhat reduced, offsetting the cost of incarcerating abusers). In the new legal regime that included stricter laws against animal abuse, one could argue that the regime was now accurately reflecting people's preferences or, just as plausibly, that the new regime changed the baseline and thus moved us away from Pareto efficiency. Without a clear baseline, one could not draw a conclusion either way.

This is not, moreover, merely a problem of not being able to measure people's true preferences, because "true preferences" are themselves defined by the nature of the laws. People who lived in a world where bear-baiting was a regular activity could be described as having a "preference" for bear-baiting, but those who live in other places and times apparently do not.

Moreover, one cannot simply say that what the people decide through their government is presumptively the Pareto efficient rule—at least, not without completely undermining the entire enterprise of making policy assessments. Many economists frequently inveigh against what the people desire, saying, for example, that minimum wage laws and rent controls (passed by democratically elected bodies) are Pareto inefficient. The nature of Pareto efficiency analysis requires us to be able to say that some laws are unwise, even if they were passed by a legitimate government, because they do not maximize aggregate happiness. On the other hand, a presumption that all laws are presumptively inefficient is equally baseless, because some laws are necessary to create the baseline in the first place.

My economist friend, therefore, presented what was really nothing more than his normative judgment that animal abuse is not serious enough to warrant jail time as a positive statement about Pareto inefficiency, even though he was otherwise keenly aware that Pareto efficient outcomes can be ones that particular individuals find quite unwise.

More generally, therefore, the "baseline problem" described here undermines claims that one can engage in amoral assessments of market outcomes, describing some outcomes as Pareto efficient even if one personally might dislike the result of market transactions. Because Pareto efficiency analysis requires knowing and agreeing on the proper baseline, which cannot be known, it is incoherent to describe something as Pareto efficient in either an absolute or a comparative sense.

ECONOMICS IS USEFUL, IF WE UNDERSTAND ITS LIMITATIONS

Having offered such a counterintuitive thesis, it is essential to be clear about its limits. Because so many scholars tend to think of "economic analysis" and "efficiency analysis" as synonymous, it would be tempting to imagine that this chapter represents an attack on "economic thinking." It most definitely is not. Any competent analysis of taxation must certainly address issues that are commonly thought of as "economic issues." The point of this chapter, while important, is nonetheless quite limited: The Pareto efficiency criterion is not a coherent or meaningful way to assess laws or policies.

That statement still leaves plenty of room for the use of "economic tools" to assess policies. The most important of these is the simple but powerful question of how people respond to incentives. This is especially potent in tax policy analysis, but it is useful in any assessment of public policies.

Consider, for example, the problem of health care costs. The primary economic question currently confronting the United States regarding health care is how to reduce the rising costs of such care. While one could imagine engaging in an analysis that attempts to determine whether any particular policy change enhances Pareto efficiency, in an attempt to determine the optimal level of health care, the analysis above demonstrates that the outcome of any such analysis would not provide useful guidance.

On the other hand, we can make important strides in understanding the path of health care costs by looking at the nature of the incentives in the health care system. One of the most notable aspects of our current system, for example, is that health care providers are generally reimbursed on a per-treatment basis. This means that doctors and other providers make more money when they perform more procedures, no matter whether those procedures actually help the patients. A different reimbursement model would create different incentives and thus lead to different behavior and potentially lower costs.

This suggests that thinking about the economics of the health care market is essential, even though Pareto efficiency need not (indeed, should not) be part of that analysis. Simply analyzing—and, most importantly, trying to measure—the effects of various policies and rules on people's decisions allows us to gather information that we can then use in forming policy judgments.

Similarly, analysis of tax issues is enriched when scholars try to predict how people will react to changes in the law. Will the amount of money donated to charities fall if the marginal tax rate on millionaires is decreased? Will employers lay off workers if the unemployment insurance tax is increased? Will businesses shut down if the estate tax is increased?

The core of good scholarly analysis of tax law, therefore, involves thinking through how changes in the law will change behavior, and assessing the consequences of those changes. While Pareto efficiency analysis purports to do just that, it is ultimately nothing more than an elaborate superstructure that actually requires (but hides) value judgments, without offering any independent or positive insights that are not otherwise available.

As long as value judgments must be made, it is far better to own up to those judgments up front, rather than hiding them behind an incoherent notion of efficiency. The common strength of the remaining chapters in this volume is that the authors confront the real issues, including the moral choices facing policymakers, and draw careful conclusions based on thorough analysis.

THE NORMATIVE UNDERPINNINGS OF TAX DISCOURSE

CHAPTER 2

THE NORMATIVE UNDERPINNINGS OF TAXATION[†]

Sagit Leviner, SUNY Buffalo Law School and Ono Academic College Faculty of Law, Israel

Questions about the appropriate rules and mechanisms of taxation are first and foremost questions concerning the nature of society. What can be taxed, what may not, and for what purpose, when, and how are all matters that go to the heart of society and, in particular, concern society's underlying beliefs and values vis-à-vis the meaning and attainment of justice. A modern society is required to consider these underlying beliefs and values when contemplating how best to allocate the fruits of social cooperation, including income, wealth, power, and opportunity.[1] This allocation is determined in each societal order by its major institutions.[2] One such key institution is the system of taxation.[3]

In reality, much of the tax scholarship generally suggests that questions of justice cannot form an integral part of the tax debate. The concept of justice, the argument goes, is a matter of personal preference, and to argue about these matters "is to reduce the discussion . . . to the level of ethics or aesthetics."[4] Notwithstanding the merit of this perspective, a decision-making process that

---

[†]. The majority of research for this chapter was accomplished while the author was pursuing her S.J.D. degree at the University of Michigan Law School. The author is grateful for the support and guidance of her S.J.D. advisers: Professors Kyle D. Logue, Reuven S. Avi-Yonah, and James R. Hines Jr. She is also thankful for the generous financial support provided by the University of Michigan Law School, and she owes special thanks to Ilan Ben-Shalom, David Gliksberg, David M. Hasen, Yoram Margalioth, Daniel N. Shaviro, Joel B. Slemrod, the participants of the 2011 Society of Legal Scholars Annual Conference (Cambridge, UK), the 2008 American Law Schools Association Annual Conference Tax Section (New York, NY), the 2004–05 New York University Tax Policy and Public Finance Colloquium (New York, NY), and the 2005 Association for the Study of Law, Culture, and the Humanities Annual Conference (Austin, TX) for useful comments and discussions on earlier drafts. This chapter previously appeared with the Nevada Law Journal 13(1) Nev. L. J. 95 (2012). Excellent editorial assistance was provided by former University of Michigan law student Jessica Berry and University at Buffalo law student Kinsey O'Brien.

1. John Rawls, *A Theory of Justice* (rev. ed., Harvard University, 1999), 7 (advocating equal access to the fruits of social cooperation).

2. *Id.* at 4–7.

3. *Cf.* John Stuart Mill, *The Principles of Political Economy* (1848; Batoche Books, 2001), 227–28 (discussing the methods used by society to redistribute property).

4. Henry C. Simons, *Personal Income Taxation: The Definition of Income as a Problem of Fiscal Policy* (1938), 18; *see also* Charles R. O'Kelley Jr., *Rawls, Justice, and the Income Tax*, 16 Ga. L. Rev. 1, 5

falls short of soliciting discussions on the meaning and attainment of justice leads to de facto acceptance of the prevailing socioeconomic order and its pretax distribution, luring us to believe that they are just or equitable.[5] By so doing, this approach diverts attention from possible transgressions in fiscal policy and hinders the development of society and its system of taxation.

As a practical matter, it is challenging to elaborate clearly the meaning and attainment of justice and, for that matter, to prove the validity of any one normative theory.[6] Normative perspectives are often subjective in nature and can be presented as self-evident truths.[7] It is nonetheless possible to discuss competing arguments of moral judgment meaningfully by elaborating on the basic beliefs and values about society and its mechanisms for achieving justice.[8] In fact, even a very preliminary examination of the current tax discourse reveals it is already grounded in profound normative claims. Often, when inheritance tax is debated, for example, a person's right to transfer her assets to the next generation is invoked.[9] Similarly, when citizens

---

(1981). *Cf.* Thomas Nagel, *Comments: Individual Versus Collective Responsibility*, 72 FORDHAM L. REV. 2015, 2019 (2004) ("The concern for social justice seems to have almost disappeared from the nation's political discourse").

5. *See, e.g.*, Liam Murphy and Thomas Nagel, *The Myth of Ownership: Taxes and Justice* (Oxford University, 2002), 7–8 (criticizing the frequent acceptance of the societal status quo as a basis for tax debate and policies). *See generally infra* notes 169–71 and accompanying text.

6. Charles Fried, *The Laws of Change: The Cunning of Reason in Moral and Legal History*, 9 J. LEGAL STUD. 335, 341–45 (1980) (justifying a theory "of moral causation as an account of legal change"); Deborah H. Schenk, *Foreword: Colloquium on Wealth Transfer Taxation*, 51 TAX L. REV. 357, 361 (1996) (addressing the pragmatic implications of diverse normative perspectives and concluding that "when it comes to tax system design . . . there is much room for disagreement . . . as to what constitutes 'the best we can be'").

7. *But see infra* notes 24–36, 80–85, 132–35, 192–98 and accompanying text (discussing underlying rationales of the theories explored in this chapter).

8. William D. Andrews, *Fairness and the Personal Income Tax: A Reply to Professor Warren*, 88 HARV. L. REV. 947, 950 (1975) ("Matters of fairness are not generally subject to logical demonstration from independent premises. All that reason can do is elaborate the implications of plausible hypotheses in order to facilitate an informed choice among them"). There are several useful examples of scholarly discussions that explore normative arguments for the meaning and attainment of justice in taxation. *See, e.g.*, Donna M. Byrne, *Progressive Taxation Revisited*, 37 ARIZ. L. REV. 739 (1995) [hereinafter Byrne, 1995]; Donna M. Byrne, *Locke, Property, and Progressive Taxes*, 78 NEB. L. REV. 700 (1999) [hereinafter Byrne, 1999]; Yoseph M. Edrey, *Al Huka Deklerativit V' Huka Constitutivit [A Declarative and a Constructed Constitution—The Right for Property Under the Israeli Constitutional Law and Its Location on the "Constitutional Rights" Scale]*, 28 MISHPATIM L. REV. 461 (1997) [in Hebrew]; Marjorie E. Kornhauser, *The Rhetoric of the Anti-Progressive Income Tax Movement: A Typical Male Reaction*, 86 MICH. L. REV 465 (1987); Marjorie E. Kornhauser, *The Rise of Rhetoric in Tax Reform Debate: An Example*, 70 TUL. L. REV. 2345 (1996); Marjorie E. Kornhauser, *Equality, Liberty, and a Fair Income Tax*, 23 FORDHAM URB. L.J. 607 (1996); Jeffrey A. Schoenblum, *Tax Fairness or Unfairness? A Consideration of the Philosophical Bases for Unequal Taxation of Individuals*, 12 AM. J. TAX POL'Y 221 (1995); Linda Sugin, *Theories of Distributive Justice and Limitations on Taxation: What Rawls Demands from Tax Systems*, 72 FORDHAM L. REV. 1991 (2004).

9. *See, e.g.*, Lily L. Batchelder, *Taxing Privilege More Effectively: Replacing the Estate Tax with an Inheritance Tax*, THE HAMILTON PROJECT, June 2007, at 5 (proposing replacement of the estate tax with an inheritance tax based on efficiency as well as equity considerations). *See also* Lily L. Batchelder, *What Should Society Expect from Heirs? The Case for a Comprehensive Inheritance Tax*, 63 TAX L. REV. 1, 7 (2009); Michael J. Graetz and Ian Shapiro, *Death by a Thousand Cuts: The Fight over Taxing Inherited Wealth* (Princeton University, 2005), 7; Edward J. McCaffery, *The Uneasy Case for Wealth Transfer Taxation*, 104 YALE L.J. 283, 304 (1994). *Cf.* Eric Rakowski, *Can Wealth Taxes Be Justified?*, 53 TAX L. REV. 263, 372–73 (2000) ("Wealth might prove a burden for some, a warm blanket for most others. But the choice to retain rather than spend is not one for which society or less fortunate persons can impose a charge, because it is not a benefit to the saver for which the state, or the congeries of social forces, or an unfair nature can claim due").

complain about high tax rates, they generally argue against what is, from their perspective, an unjust appropriation.[10] However, the extent to which the existing normative tax discourse is based on anecdotes and used to advance self-serving interests rather than a well-defined framework of principles and rationales is striking.

A candid and comprehensive tax discourse will allow society a more accurate and meaningful understanding of its tax system than what currently exists. Such a discourse may also further the development of taxation in a manner consistent with society's normative aspirations alongside the more commonly debated pragmatic constraints. This chapter promotes developing a broader normative tax discourse by returning to fundamentals and reexamining three relevant political theories and how they shed light on taxation: the theory of natural entitlement, utilitarianism, and Rawls's theory of justice as fairness. The chapter explores the perspectives of these theories on fiscal policy, particularly with respect to one question: What can taxpayers expect to receive in fair return for their expended labor and capital? The chapter opines that under all three political theories taxpayers can generally expect to receive only a net return on labor and capital — gross return on their investments less the sum needed for maintenance of the existing societal order. In an unjust, or suboptimal, societal order (however this measure is conceived by the three theories), further taxation can be expected to rectify this condition. Importantly, such additional taxation becomes a plausible scenario under each of the theories explored, supporting some form of redistributive mechanism.

The next section of this chapter presents the entitlement theory and addresses the concept of natural or divine law. The succeeding section discusses utilitarianism, its aim to increase aggregate utility, and the social welfare function as a modern interpretation of utilitarianism that has come to dominate the contemporary, especially professional, tax discourse. Finally, a third section explores the Rawlsian doctrine of justice as fairness. While each section examines possible implications of the three theories on taxation, in its summary and conclusions the chapter seeks to offer a broader normative undertaking. Due to the scope of this chapter, as well as space limitations, the chapter does not address the advantages and disadvantages of utilizing the tax system to advance redistributive ends, nor does it explore the theory of optimal taxation to a meaningful extent. These issues are left for future works.

---

10. *See, e.g.,* Joel Slemrod and Jon Bakija, *Taxing Ourselves: A Citizen's Guide to the Debate over Taxes* (4th ed., MIT, 2008), 72–74 (citing several polls to discuss Americans' perspectives regarding the fairness of progressivity in taxation. Note, however, that the authors identify numerous misconceptions where public perceptions do not match available data concerning actual progressivity in the tax burden distribution).

ENTITLEMENTS AND THE NATURAL ORDER

JOHN LOCKE

The Lockean description of the origin of mankind invokes individuals as free and equal persons,[11] living in a "state of nature" and lacking political authority to govern them.[12] This ideal state was short-lived, as some individuals inflicted harm on others, undermining the harmonic state of nature and pushing humanity into war.[13] According to Locke, abhorrence of war led humanity to join together to form civil society.[14] The idea of civil rights, especially those rights that concern private ownership of property, is central to the Lockean doctrine and its application to tax.[15] Locke posits that individuals are property holders in the state of nature, and he maintains that they continue to possess property under the regime of civil society.[16]

Locke's theory and conception of rights relies on the premise that in the state of nature, earth belonged to humanity as a whole.[17] According to this historical proposition, resources were initially owned in common by mankind.[18] Locke does not regard people in the initial state as having exclusive rights over resources.[19] In fact, anyone could have obtained shared resources for personal use by simply exerting the effort to do so.[20] This includes, for example, picking apples from a tree or gathering crops in a field.[21] Locke's basic tenet, which came to be known as the "labor-mixing principle,"[22] is that individuals are entitled to holdings that result from the application of their labor: "Whatsoever, then, he removes out of the state that Nature ha[s]

---

11. John Locke, *Concerning Civil Government, Second Essay* (1690), §21, *reprinted in* Mortimer J. Adler (Editor), *33 Great Books of the Western World* (6th printing., 1996), 25–84 ("The natural liberty of man is to be free from any superior power on earth").

12. *Id.* Locke explains that the meaning of freedom is that people are not subject to the will of others and that everyone possesses equal (but not necessarily the same) powers and jurisdiction over these powers. Thus, there is no hierarchy in the state of nature. Hierarchy, Locke claims, means slavery. *See also id.* at 25, ch. II, §4.

13. *Id.* at 28, ch. II–III, §§13, 16–21 (describing the state of war as a condition in which people lose their freedom to the impartial judgment of others).

14. *Id.* at 28, 44, 55, ch. II, VI, XI, §§13, 87–88, 134. In entering the Lockean type of civil society, people gave the right to govern themselves to the political authority. Locke presents this authority as a trustee, acting on behalf of the interests of its citizens. In this way, the political authority becomes almost a servant for the common good.

15. *See, e.g., id.* at 53, ch. IX, §124 ("The great and *chief* end, therefore, of men uniting into commonwealths, and putting themselves under government, *is the preservation of their property.*") (emphasis added).

16. *Id. at* 53, ch. IX, §§124-25.

17. *Id.* at 30, ch. V, §§24–25. Locke's interpretation of the beginning of time is that God gave power to "them" (i.e., mankind) not "him" (Adam). *Id.* at 30, ch. V, §24.

18. *Id.* at 30, ch. V, §§25–26; *see also* Justin Hughes, *The Philosophy of Intellectual Property*, 77 Geo. L.J. 287, 297 (1988).

19. Locke, *supra* note 11, at 31, ch. V, §§27–28.

20. *Id.* at 31, ch. V, §§28–31 ("Though the water running in the fountain be every one's, yet who can doubt but that the pitcher is his only who drew it out? His labour hath taken it out of the hands of Nature where it was common, and belonged equally to all her children, and hath thereby appropriated it to himself"). *Id.* at 28.

21. *Id.* at 30, ch. V, §27.

22. *See, e.g.*, Edward Feser, *There Is No Such Thing as an Unjust Initial Acquisition*, 22 Soc. Phil. & Pol'y 56, 61 (2005) (referencing Locke's "labor-mixing" principle).

provided and left it in, he ha[s] mixed his labour with it, and joined to it something that is his own, and thereby makes it his property."[23]

Locke's labor-mixing principle and conception of rights give rise to several key justifications in support of a system of private property. These justifications become imperative in the evaluation of tax issues, including, for example, the right to tax, the goals of taxation, and the tax rate structure. The first justification for a system of private property, and the one most commonly identified with the Lockean paradigm, addresses the individual and her right to autonomy; the other two, more modern justifications of the theory, concern labor and its value to society.

Locke's theory is grounded in fundamental respect for free will and the right to autonomy.[24] According to this view, the first justification for a system of private property rights holds that individuals have a right to self-ownership, to the labor they apply, and, thus, by extension, to the product of this labor.[25] Exercise of free will coupled with the assignment of labor is the means by which individuals expand their right of self-ownership over external resources and make these resources their own.[26]

Conversely, the second justification in support of a system of private property rights is that labor is virtuous in and of itself and, therefore, laborers deserve reward and encouragement.[27] This perspective draws from a theological belief that the exercise of labor is the manner by which individuals enjoy the goodness the world provides.[28] Since labor fulfills a godly design, it is virtuous on its own merit.[29] This idea corresponds with the conviction that labor is generally unappealing and requires remuneration to be performed.[30]

A third, more modern justification relies on utilitarian principles to suggest that labor deserves reward because it adds value that benefits society at large.[31] According to this line of thinking, the value one creates through labor ultimately trickles down to others and improves society's general well-being, or, in other words, enlarges the societal pie.[32] It is not enough merely to acknowledge the value of labor; rather, the right to private property must be established to motivate individuals to invest effort.[33] Over the long term, such a reward

---

23. Locke, *supra* note 11, at 30, ch. V, §26.

24. *Id.* at 30, ch. IV, §22 (holding that free will and the right to autonomy are virtues possessed by all individuals).

25. *Id.* at 30, ch. V, §27.

26. *Id.* at 30–31, ch. V, §§27–28.

27. Byrne, 1999, *supra* note 8, at 708–09 (citing Hughes, *supra* note 18, at 288).

28. *See, e.g.*, Locke, *supra* note 11, at 31–32, ch. V, §31.

29. *Id.* at 31, ch. V, §31 ("God, when He gave the world in common to all mankind, commanded man also to labour, and the penury of his condition required it of him"); *see also* Marjorie E. Kornhauser, *The Morality of Money: American Attitudes Toward Wealth and the Income Tax*, 70 IND. L.J. 119, 125 (1994) (suggesting that Americans' perspectives about wealth and money are partly drawn from the idea of serving God); Jeremy Waldron, Book Review, 102 ETHICS 401, 402 (1992) (reviewing Stephen Munzer, *A Theory of Property* (Cambridge University, 1990)).

30. Locke, *supra* note 11, at 35, ch. V, §48.

31. *Id.* at 34, ch. V, §§42–43.

32. *Id.* at 34, ch. V, §43; *see also id.* at 33, ch. V, §40 ("[C]onsider what the difference is between an acre of land planted . . . and an acre of the same land lying in common without any husbandry upon it, and he will find that the improvement of labour makes the far greater part of the value").

33. *Compare id.* at 34, ch. V, §44 (describing how the invention of property protects the products of labor: "[Man] . . . had . . . in himself the great foundation of property; and that which made up the great part of what he applied to the support of comfort of his being, when

system advances the exercise of effort and, consequently, the establishment of wealthier, more resilient nations.[34] One well-known example Locke offers for this "trickle-down" argument concerns uncultivated, nonproductive land. Locke explains that no matter how large and potentially prosperous uncultivated land might be, it is still worthless without human effort to cultivate it.[35] Further, labor is not only necessary to cultivate land, such as in sowing seeds or gathering crops, but it also creates more demand for the labor of others.[36] Accordingly, the benefits created by transforming uncultivated land to productive land eventually trickle down from the landowner to the broader society, including workers and consumers, through advantages such as additional job opportunities and greater productivity.

As the above discussion illustrates, the Lockean theory suggests that a system of private property rights acknowledges the innate bond between a person's free will, right to autonomy, and labor, or more accurately, the product of the person's labor. Private property rights also manifest society's gratitude for human effort and serve as a system of incentives to elicit productive outlays and the enlargement of the societal pie. Despite these important ends, Locke narrows the application of the labor-mixing principle and, accordingly, entitlement to private appropriation, with two restrictions known as the first and second "Lockean Provisos."[37]

According to the first Lockean Proviso, the accumulation of private property is permissible only to the extent that it can be maintained without spoilage.[38] Waste is undesirable under the Lockean model.[39] It follows that the first Proviso primarily allows personal appropriation when necessary for subsistence.[40] Thus, for example, a person cannot retain one hundred acorns and assert entitlement over them if she can only consume fifty acorns, leaving the other fifty to spoil. This person can rightfully appropriate only the fifty acorns she will use.

According to the second Lockean Proviso, appropriation of resources is permissible only "where there is enough, and as good left in common for

---

invention and arts had improved the convenience of life, was perfectly his own, and did not belong in common to others"), *with* Margaret Jane Radin, *The Liberal Conception of Property: Cross Currents in the Jurisprudence of Takings*, 88 COLUM. L. REV. 1667, 1683 (1988) ("In this [Hobbesian] model of human nature, limitless self-interest and the consequent urgent need for self-defense require the most expansive possible notion of private property").

34. Locke, *supra* note 11, at 33–34, ch. V, §§40–41.

35. *Id.* at 33–34, ch. V, §41 ("[S]everal nations of the Americans are of this, who are rich in land and poor in all the comforts of life . . . with the materials of plenty . . . yet, for *want of improving it by labour*, have not one hundredth part of the conveniences we enjoy") (emphasis added); *id.* at 34, ch. V, §43 ("It is labour, then, which *puts the greatest part of value upon land*, without which it would scarcely be *worth anything*") (emphasis added).

36. *Id.* at 34, ch. V, §43.

37. *Id.* at 30, ch. V, §26; *see also* Geoffrey P. Miller, Comment, *Economic Efficiency and the Lockean Proviso*, 10 HARV. J.L. & PUB. POL'Y 401, 401 (1987) (identifying the "Lockean Proviso" as stating that the "acquisition of unowned property is permissible 'at least where there is enough, and as good left in common for others.'").

38. Locke, *supra* note 11, at 33, ch. V, §37; *but see id.* at 34–35, ch. V, §§45–50 (explaining the development of storage and trade, which greatly undermines his first Proviso).

39. *Id.* at 31, ch. V, §30 ("Nothing was made by God for man to spoil or destroy."); *id.* at 35, ch. V, §46 ("[I]t was a foolish thing, as well as dishonest, to hoard up more than he could make use of").

40. *Id.* at 33, ch. V, §37 ("[M]en had a right to appropriate by their labour, each one to himself, as much of the things of Nature as he could use").

others."[41] Hence, if one hundred acorns constitute food supply of an entire village, one person cannot claim all one hundred acorns for herself, since this will not leave sufficient acorns for others. Locke, however, does not clarify how much of any resource should be left for others, making the application of the second Proviso rather ambiguous. Even more problematic are attempts to apply the Lockean Provisos to the conditions of modern economy.

Locke's doctrine envisions the world as populated with few people and sufficient resources for everyone.[42] Compared to this starting point, today's world is considerably more populous, with some goods becoming increasingly scarce.[43] Under these conditions, Locke's provisos are harder to sustain and justify.[44] Specifically, in a market economy, where resources are exchanged for money, individuals are able to appropriate resources beyond immediate needs and bargain any surpluses of perishable goods for monetary compensation, which never spoils.[45] Accordingly, appropriation beyond immediate needs, a practice forbidden under Lockean principles, is made possible by a market economy. Applying the labor-mixing principle to modern market conditions thereby results in "disproportionate and unequal possession of the earth," a state of affairs predicted by Locke centuries ago.[46]

Disparity in wealth and income, which causes much concern in modern civilizations, is acceptable and even encouraged under the Lockean paradigm.[47] In Locke's view, economic differences prod individuals to labor, which in turn advances the economy, improves human condition, and enlarges the societal pie.[48] It is not surprising, then, that in his theory of entitlement, Locke does not condemn inequality. Under the Lockean paradigm, it is industry and labor, not equality, which are virtuous.

---

41. *Id.* at 30, ch. V, §26. According to Locke, the "enough and as good" Proviso was not very limiting, as the Americas had access to what seemed at the time to be unlimited unclaimed resources. *See id.* at 33, ch. V, §41. Some interpret the "enough and as good" proviso as applying to the market as a whole; thus, making goods available for purchase becomes analogous with leaving "enough and as good." Byrne, 1999, *supra* note 8, at 711 (citing Arvid Pardo, *An Opportunity Lost*, in Bernard H. Oxman, David D. Caron, and Charles L. O. Buderl (Editors), *Law of the Sea: U.S. Policy Dilemma* (ICS, 1983), 23).

42. Locke, *supra* note 11, at 32–33, ch. V, §36.

43. Scarcity introduces conflicts over the allocation of resources. *See id.* at 32, ch. V, §33; Waldron, *supra* note 29, at 403 ("[T]alk of property makes little sense except against a background of scarcity").

44. According to Locke, money enables the unlimited accumulation of wealth because it permits an enhanced capacity of durable goods production. Locke, *supra* note 11, at 35, ch. V, §§46–48. This implies that money does not decrease social productivity but rather increases it. *See also infra* note 46.

45. Locke, *supra* note 11, at 35, ch. V, §47 ("And thus came in the use of money; some lasting thing that men might keep without spoiling, and that, by mutual consent, men would take in exchange for the truly useful but perishable supports of life").

46. *Id.* at 35, ch. V, §50; *see also id.* at 35, ch. V, §48 ("[A]s different degrees of industry were apt to give men possessions in different proportions, so this invention of money gave them the opportunity to continue and enlarge them"); *id.* at 35–36, ch. V, §§50–51 ("[I]t is plain that the consent of men have agreed to a disproportionate and *unequal possession of the earth* . . . they having, by consent, found out and agreed in a way how a man may, rightfully and without injury, possess more than he himself can make use of by receiving gold and silver. . . . For as a man had a right to all he could employ his labour upon") (emphasis added).

47. *Id.* at 33, ch. V, §48.

48. *Id.* ("Where there is not something both lasting and scarce, and so valuable to be hoarded up, there men will not be apt to *enlarge their possessions of land, were it never so rich, never so free for them to take*") (emphasis added).

Accumulation of money is fair, according to the Lockean doctrine precisely because money is a durable, nonperishable good that, Locke maintains, not only causes no harm when hoarded by individuals but benefits the entire society.[49] It is unclear, however, whether Locke would have been as forgiving of money accrual given what is known today about potential repercussions of large concentrations of accumulated wealth and income. Recent empirical work demonstrates that large concentrations of wealth and income provide wealthy individuals with disproportionate power and influence, stratifying society into classes of citizens and leading to sociopolitical unrest and slow economic growth.[50] In particular, there is a danger of perpetuating and magnifying these harms through the flow of poorly distributed fortune from one generation to the next.[51] In line with such evidence, it remains questionable at what point entitlement to private property becomes sufficiently unwarranted that it is no longer justifiable under the tenets of Locke's entitlement doctrine.[52] Additionally, in a market economy, money serves as a necessary means to attain subsistence needs. Once basic resources turn scarce, their dearth undermines the merit of unrestricted private appropriation, since "enough and as good" resources are not left for others.[53]

In view of Locke's basic stance that moral entitlement to holdings is the product of labor-mixing activities, society and its institutions must assume responsibility for protecting the resulting distribution of holdings and corresponding system of private property. To this end, individuals are required to share the financial burden of societal protection through payment of taxes.[54] Locke, however, does not discuss more extensive public responsibilities, such as construction of infrastructure, including highways and parks, nor does he consider utilizing the tax system to advance redistributive goals.[55] At first glance, then, the Lockean model of entitlement yields a relatively limited government and tax bill. Under a more probing examination, however, matters appear less clear-cut.

---

49. *Id.* at 35, ch. V, §50 (asserting that gold and silver "may continue long in a man's possession without decaying for the overplus"); *see also supra* notes 44–48.

50. Reuven S. Avi-Yonah, *Why Tax the Rich? Efficiency, Equity, and Progressive Taxation*, 111 Yale L.J. 1391, 1407-13 (2002) (reviewing Joel B. Slemrod (Editor), *Does Atlas Shrug?: The Economic Consequences of Taxing the Rich* (Harvard University, 2000)); James R. Repetti, *Democracy, Taxes, and Wealth*, 76 N.Y.U. L. Rev. 825, 832–36, 840–48 (2001); Roberto Perotti, *Political Equilibrium, Income Distribution, and Growth*, 60 Rev. Econ. Stud. 755, 755–57 (1993); Roberto Perotti, *Growth, Income Distribution, and Democracy: What the Data Say*, 1 J. Econ. Growth 149, 149–150 (1996).

51. Sagit Leviner, *From Deontology to Practical Application: The Vision of a Good Society and the Tax System*, 26 Va. Tax Rev. 405, 442-45 (2006) (discussing the harms of maldistributed intergenerationally transmitted wealth).

52. *Cf.* Locke, *supra* note 11, at 35, ch. V, §46 ("[I]f he would give his nuts for a piece of metal, pleased with its colour, or exchange his sheep for shells, or wool for a sparkling pebble or a diamond, and keep those by him all his life, he invaded not the right of others; he might heap up as much of these durable things as he pleased.").

53. *Cf.* John T. Sanders, *Justice and the Initial Acquisition of Property*, 10 Harv. J.L. & Pub. Pol'y 367, 372-73, 377-80 (1987) (discussing the "enough and as good" proviso).

54. *See, e.g.,* Richard A. Musgrave, *Public Finance and Distributive Justice*, in Richard A. Musgrave, *Public Finance in a Democratic Society* (Elgar, 2000), Vol. 3, 135, 136 [hereinafter Musgrave, *Public Finance and Distributive Justice*].

55. For an early discussion of public goods and their social role, *see* Adam Smith, *Wealth of Nations* (4th ed. 1850), 325; *see also* Robert Nozick, *Anarchy, State, and Utopia* (Basic Books, 1974), 230–31 (discussing the distributive role of society).

The three justifications for the Lockean paradigm defend entitlement to private property based on autonomy, desert, and productivity grounds. Convincing claims have been made, however, against the strength of any of these justifications to support entitlement to the *entire* share of market returns.[56] In real-world circumstances, it is generally impossible to draw a clear distinction between market returns resulting from one's effort and exercise of free will and those returns that derive from factors outside of the individual's control, such as luck, effort exerted by others, and societal infrastructures.[57] To the extent that wealth and income accruals result from factors other than personal effort and free will, claims to such accumulations may be morally questioned. For this reason, instead of embracing the prevailing market allocation unaltered, it may make more sense to consider possible infirmities in the existing distribution of holdings. Taking this view, taxation could be levied, not only because of its functions as a revenue-raising mechanism — necessary to secure the existing distribution of holdings — but also considering its potential to correct this distribution. That is, taxation may appropriate from individuals the share of market returns that is not rightfully theirs and redirect (i.e., redistribute) it toward a more entitled destination.

According to the productivity justification, allowing individuals to reap the rewards of their labor is meant to encourage future efforts. Taxation, however, does not necessarily depress productivity in the sense of removing, either wholly or partially, the incentive to engage in work and other productive endeavors.[58] Empirical research illustrates, for example, that monetary

---

56. *See, e.g.*, Murphy and Nagel, *supra* note 5, at 68–69 (discussing the various faults of resource distributions achieved by an unaltered free market economy); Michael J. Graetz, *To Praise the Estate Tax, Not to Bury It*, 93 Yale L.J. 259, 275–77 (1983) (making a case for market returns to depend on factors outside of any one individual's control, including forces of market supply and demand as well as societal conditions: "[M]ost production is based upon the *joint use* of different resources, typically provided by different people . . . some share of total market returns . . . [is also] attributable to societal conditions. . . . All receipts are *joint products*, both individual and societal. Because individual characteristics and social characteristics are both essential to their *joint outcome*, there is simply no means by which a percentage of individual and social 'dessert' can be calculated") (emphasis added); Edrey, *supra* note 8 (further developing the role society plays in the process of income production — coined and explored as the "joint venture").

57. For example, an athlete's accomplishments are the result of genetic and environmental factors over which she has no control. Similarly, talent, age, health, and social positions are greatly influenced by luck, a morally arbitrary factor. *See, e.g.*, Herbert Kiesling, *Taxation and Public Goods: A Welfare-Economic Critique of Tax Policy Analysis* (University of Michigan, 1992), 119–20 (discussing the issues of deservedness and reward as notions requiring an active action of the individual); Barbara H. Fried, *Fairness and the Consumption Tax*, 44 Stan. L. Rev. 961, 1007–09 n. 131 (1992). However, according to entitlement theorists, as long as initial entitlements were justly acquired and all subsequent transfers are freely entered into, inequality in resources, luck, and other people's effort may not make one less entitled to her holdings. *See, e.g.*, Nozick's theory of entitlement, *infra* notes 86–89 and accompanying text.

58. Slemrod and Bakija, *supra* note 10, at 121–22 (explaining that taxes have two countervailing effects. On the one hand, taxes reduce the marginal reward for productive activities and, by so doing, make these activities less attractive. This effect is known as the substitution or incentive effect. On the other hand, most taxes make individuals poorer so that they need to work more, rather than less, in order to maintain their living standard. This effect is known as the income effect).

rewards, including increases in after-tax wages, do not always correspond with the number of hours people work.[59] Such findings suggest the relationship between economic incentives and productive outlays depends on various factors, including the desire for power, satisfaction, and security.[60] That is, at least part of the reason people work is not driven by monetary considerations, and people may therefore respond to taxation in ways that are not entirely predictable.[61] In fact, recent studies suggest that the possibility of acquiring a *relatively* higher economic standing may be a more successful inducement to effort and productivity than simple economic rewards.[62] Thus, as long as after-tax market returns remain relatively high compared to returns of other, comparable taxpayers (however comparable taxpayers are conceived), an entitlement to the *entire* share of economic rewards may not be necessary.

Furthermore, evidence suggests that making some individuals better off does not inevitably lead to increased welfare for the entire society, as suggested by the trickle-down proposition. The presence of poverty, rising inequality, and social stratification, alongside considerable wealth and prosperity of the modern world,[63] undermines the argument that wealth trickles down the economic hierarchy.[64] Such conditions cast doubts over the workings of the market economy in general and unrestricted entitlement to private property

---

59. *See, e.g., id.* at 124–27 (reviewing literature and concluding that "[a]lthough, as with many economic questions, there is controversy, it is still fair to say that the consensus is that labor supply responsiveness [to taxation] is fairly low."). *Cf.* Joseph Bankman and Thomas Griffith, *Social Welfare and the Rate Structure: A New Look at Progressive Taxation*, 75 Calif. L. Rev. 1905, 1922–26 (1987) (finding that work contributes to social standing and self-esteem and showing that elasticity of labor is generally low, but higher for married women).

60. Carroll, for example, underscores the key role of nonmonetary motivations to work, including achieving professional gratification, power-lust, and philanthropic ambitions. Christopher D. Carroll, *Why Do the Rich Save So Much?*, in Joel B. Slemrod (Editor), *Does Atlas Shrug?: The Economic Consequences of Taxing the Rich* (Harvard University, 2000), 465, 477.

61. *Id.* at 480 (discussing aggregate effect of bequest taxes). For a good discussion on the complexity of factors to potentially influence individuals' inclination to work, *see* Byrne, 1999, *supra* note 8, at 725–26.

62. According to Frank, relative standing, in terms of income and wealth, is more significant than one's absolute standard of living. Thus, as long as greater effort results in an improvement in relative conditions, the imposition of tax does not create a disincentive for productive effort. Note, however, that taxation leads to at least some welfare loss, since taxpayers' optimal economic behavior may be affected by taxes even when there is no apparent change in the choices they make. This can happen when the income and substitution effects of taxation cancel each other. Robert H. Frank, *Progressive Taxation and the Incentive Problem*, in Joel B. Slemrod (Editor), *Does Atlas Shrug?: The Economic Consequences of Taxing the Rich* (Harvard University, 2000), 490, 499–505; *see also generally* Robert H. Frank, *Choosing the Right Pond: Human Behavior and the Quest for Status* (Oxford University, 1985); Robert H. Frank and Philip J. Cook, *The Winner-Take-All Society* (The Free Press, 1995).

63. *See, e.g.*, Congressional Budget Office, *Trends in the Distribution of Household Income Between 1979 and 2007* (2011) (finding after-tax income for the highest-income households grew more than it did for any other group. Between 1979 and 2007, income grew by 275% for the top 1% of households; 65% for the next 19%; 40% for the next 60%; and 18% for the bottom 20%). *Cf.* Yoram Margalioth, *Tax Competition, Foreign Direct Investments and Growth: Using the Tax System to Promote Developing Countries*, 23 Va. Tax Rev. 161, 162 & nn.1–2 (2003) (discussing deprived conditions of developing countries in particular).

64. For example, during the mid-1970s and late 1980s, many U.S. working families struggled to rise above the poverty line when faced with stagnated wages and crushing inequality, while other Americans enjoyed much better conditions. Gilbert argues that, overall, the working poor in the United States included about 15.6% of the population in 1996, compared to a lower rate of 13.9% in 1990. Neil Gilbert, *The Size and Influence of the Underclass: An Exaggerated View*, 37 Soc'y 43, 45 (1999). Many of the working poor occupy part-time or temporary jobs that pay little and provide

in particular. They challenge the legitimacy of inequality, including disparities created under the system of entitlement and, more profoundly, the soundness of the theory itself. At the very least, these conditions highlight the need for constraints on entitlement to private property in order to ease economic inequality and allow social, economic, and political benefits to reach citizens across the societal spectrum.[65]

It becomes evident that the levy of taxation not only may occur without violating the Lockean entitlement paradigm, but also may contribute to its integrity. Taxes need not reduce the incentive to engage in productive efforts, nor do they necessarily serve to eliminate its rewards or infringe upon one's right to free will and autonomy. On the contrary, taxes have the potential to ensure that effort is rightfully, but not excessively, compensated and that economic incentives remain at an efficient and effective level.

ROBERT NOZICK

Similar to Locke, Robert Nozick develops his theory from an initial "state of nature,"[66] a state of affairs lacking political authority where individuals live and obtain goods and services using whatever means they have in their possession.[67] Under these conditions, Nozick argues, individuals form a protective society.[68] Nozick's basic assumption is that this society naturally develops into a state very limited in powers and responsibilities, an undertone that precludes most forms of taxation, particularly those tax structures that are redistributive in nature.[69]

---

few opportunities to gain professional skills or develop careers, further decreasing their earning potential. James Midgley, *The United States: Welfare, Work and Development*, 10 INT'L J. Soc. WELFARE 284, 285–291 (2001).

65. This could be done, for example, by implementing redistributional measures within the tax system that aim at guaranteeing basic living conditions, such as shelter and education, for all. For the role of the tax system in advancing redistributive goals *see, for example*, Reuven S. Avi-Yonah, *The Three Goals of Taxation*, 60 TAX L. REV. 1, 11–22 (2006) (suggesting that personal income taxation, in particular, best serves to advance the goal of redistribution via the tax system); David A. Weisbach, *Should Legal Rules Be Used to Redistribute Income?*, 70 U. CHI. L. REV. 439, 439 (2003) ("[L]egal rules should not be used to redistribute to the poor . . . [because] the tax system is a better tool for redistribution"); Richard M. Bird and Eric M. Zolt, *Redistribution via Taxation: The Limited Role of the Personal Income Tax in Developing Countries*, 52 UCLA L. REV. 1627, 1682–83 (2005) ("Despite . . . many qualifications . . . the income tax, and particularly the personal income tax, is probably the only significantly progressive element found in most tax systems."). *Cf.* Walter J. Blum and Harry Kalven Jr., *The Uneasy Case for Progressive Taxation* (University of Chicago, 1953), 1 ("Progressive taxation is now regarded as one of the central ideas of modern democratic capitalism and is widely accepted as a secure policy commitment which does not require serious examination"). Notwithstanding the above references, the redistributive goal of taxation remains highly controversial and is often advocated to come with a hefty price on growth and efficiency. *See* Arthur M. Okun, *Equality and Efficiency: The Big Tradeoff* (Brookings Institution, 1975), 1 ("[P]ursuit of efficiency necessarily creates inequalities. And hence society faces a tradeoff between equality and efficiency."); Louis Kaplow and Steven Shavell, *Fairness Versus Welfare* (Harvard University, 2002), xvii; Louis Kaplow and Steven Shavell, *Fairness Versus Welfare*, 114 HARV. L. REV. 961, 966 (2001) (asserting that welfare is the only appropriate legal policy standard). For the view that fairness and equity considerations on one hand and efficiency constraints on the other may in fact enhance, rather than be in conflict with, each other, *see supra* note 50 and accompanying text.

66. NOZICK, *supra* note 55, at 10.

67. *Id.* at 10–12.

68. *Id.* at 12–17.

69. *Id.* at 12–17, 26–27, 113–118.

The meaning of entitlement under the Nozickean paradigm includes the Lockean right to own property justly acquired.[70] Nozick's conception of entitlement, however, expands beyond simple ownership to also emphasize the right to dispose of property.[71] These aspects of entitlement, Nozick prescribes, cannot be challenged without compelling justifications. In fact, according to Nozick, individuals' rights are so strong and extensive that they raise the question of what, if anything, the state can do without violating these rights.[72] Protecting individuals' rights is understood to require limiting state's powers to narrow functions, such as enforcement of contracts and protection against force, theft, and fraud.[73] In keeping with Nozick's view, "any more extensive state will violate persons' rights not to be forced to do certain things, and is unjustified."[74]

Nozick's assumption of a state limited in powers and responsibilities presupposes the merit of entitlements to existing property.[75] Nozick accordingly argues that just distribution of resources results from subsequent, freely entered exchanges.[76] Government meddling with private property through the levy of taxation becomes equivalent to forced labor because it requires individuals to undertake additional labor to compensate for taxes.[77] This, Nozick posits, violates basic rights and liberties, a far more devastating outcome than an insult to efficiency.[78] Government intervention by means of redistributive taxation — taking from one person to improve the lot of another — is perceived to be a greater rights and liberties violation, as it more aggressively interferes with individuals' possessions.[79] It is therefore clear that the Nozickean description of the state does not account for public

---

70. *See, e.g., id.* at 185 ("[E]ach individual deserves what he gets unaided by his own efforts; or rather, no one else can make a claim *of justice* against this holding").

71. *Id.* at 160 ("From each according to what he chooses to do, to each according to what he makes for himself . . . and what others choose to do for him and choose to give him of what they've been given previously (under this maxim) and haven't yet expended or transferred . . . *From each as they choose, to each as they are chosen*").

72. According to Nozick, individuals have rights, and there are things no one may do to anyone else without violating these rights. *Id.* at ix.

73. *Id.* at 26–27.

74. *Id.* at ix.

75. *Id.* at 224–26.

76. *Id.* at 186–87.

77. *Id.* at 172 ("Whether it is done through taxation on wages over a certain amount, or through seizure of profits, or through there being a big *social pot* so that it's not clear what's coming from where and what's going where . . . [such policies necessarily involve] appropriating the actions of other persons. Seizing the results of someone's labor is equivalent to seizing hours from him and directing him to carry on various activities . . . This process whereby they take this decision from you makes them a *part-owner* of you; it gives them a property right in you. Just as having such partial control and power of decision, by right, over an animal").

78. First and foremost, taxation is viewed as a violation of the right to self-ownership. *Id.* at 171–72. As Kymlicka notes, "If I own my self, then I own my talents. And if I own my talents, then I own whatever I produce with my self-owned talents." Will Kymlicka, *Contemporary Political Philosophy: An Introduction* (2d ed. Oxford University, 2002), 109.

79. Nozick, *supra* note 55, at 171–72. Progressive taxation does not aim to maintain the existing distribution of resources but rather to change it. A somewhat related argument is that progressive taxation constitutes "taking" under the Fifth Amendment. *See* Calvin R. Massey, *Takings and Progressive Rate Taxation*, 20 Harv. J.L. & Pub. Pol'y 85, 86, 105–06, 124 (1996) (arguing that the Takings Clause requires that federal taxation satisfy the benefit theory of taxation and be levied relative to benefits the taxpayer receives from the government. Because the benefit principle does not necessarily fit with progressive tax rates, progressive rates are understood to violate the Takings Clause).

education, childcare, or parks, as these outlays necessarily involve more elaborate forms of taxation than those required by a stripped-down societal model.

At the heart of the Nozickean doctrine are two rationales. The first rationale draws on the idea of free exercise of natural rights and entitlements and its prospect, over the long run, to improve everyone's well-being.[80] As Richard Posner, for example, claims, "The individual may be completely selfish but he cannot, in a well-regulated market economy, promote his self-interest without benefiting others as well as himself."[81] A second rationale interprets the theory as inherently drawing on the concept of self-ownership, derived from either the idea of equality (treating people as equals) or the notion of liberty (allowing individuals to live as they choose).[82] This line of thinking suggests that an entitlement to holdings is fundamental to the principle of treating individuals as equal beings who cannot be exploited as resources for others.[83] According to this logic, the theory of entitlement is the best paradigm by which to assess the nature and scope of any cost that can be legitimately incurred by one person for the benefit of another.[84] At the same time, treating people with respect, by respecting their individual rights, is to everyone's advantage, as this allows us "to choose our life and to realize our ends and our conception of ourselves . . . aided by the voluntary cooperation of other individuals possessing the *same* dignity."[85]

Similar to Locke, Nozick suggests that individuals' free exercise of labor is a method by which their right of self-ownership extends to external resources. Nozick acknowledges entitlement to holdings that result from any one of an individual's resources, including the fruits of her natural abilities, such as superior physical or intellectual attributes.[86] Nozick therefore assumes that individuals are morally entitled to what others, at times, consider the product of luck, social cooperation, or both.[87] Alternatively, it can be argued that under the Nozickean doctrine it is not luck or social cooperation, but rather effort expended in productive activity or productivity itself, that results in entitlement,[88] a more intuitively appealing system of

---

80. Nozick, *supra* note 55, at 157. Some argue, however, that Nozick does not provide any substantive support for his theory of entitlement. *See, e.g.*, Thomas Nagel, *Libertarianism Without Foundations*, 85 YALE L.J. 136, 137–38 (1975) (reviewing Robert Nozick, *Anarchy, State, and Utopia* (1974)); *cf.* Nozick, *supra* note 55, at 150 (stating the theory of entitlement as if it is self-evident).

81. Richard A. Posner, *Utilitarianism, Economics, and Legal Theory*, 8 J. LEGAL STUD. 103, 132 (1979); *cf.* Jeremy Bentham, C. K. Ogden (Editor), R. Hildreth (Translator), *The Theory of Legislation* (1864) (Humanities Press, Inc. 1931), 53 [hereinafter Bentham, *The Theory of Legislation*] ("Society is so constituted that, in labouring for our particular good, we labour also for the good of the whole. We cannot augment our own means of enjoyment without augmenting also the means of others").

82. Kymlicka, *supra* note 78, at 107–28.

83. *See, e.g.*, Nozick, *supra* note 55, at 30–31. Rights affirm individuals' "separate existences" and take seriously "the existence of distinct individuals who are not resources for others." *Id.* at 33.

84. Kymlicka, *supra* note 78, at 103–04. The theory of utilitarianism may be understood to undermine the existence of such limits. *Cf. infra* notes 141–52 and accompanying text.

85. Nozick, *supra* note 55, at 334 (emphasis added).

86. Nozick, *supra* note 55, at 225–26. *Cf.* Richard A. Posner, *The Ethical and Political Basis of the Efficiency Norm in Common Law Adjudication*, 8 HOFSTRA L. REV. 487, 499 (1980) (suggesting the value of individuals relies on their "capacity to produce for others").

87. *See, e.g.*, Nozick, *supra* note 55, at 226 ("Whether or not people's natural assets are arbitrary from a moral point of view, they are entitled to them, and to what flows from them").

88. *Id.* at 225.

rewards.[89] Notwithstanding either interpretation of entitlement, self-ownership and the corresponding notion of mutual gains represent a rather limited platform for treating people in the same manner while respecting their rights and liberties. It is not merely the actions of isolated individuals that affect society and its market economy. Civil rights and obligations, as well as background circumstances, luck, and institutional conditions, also play an important role in market production and the resulting distribution of entitlements.[90] Accordingly, if Nozick's principles are to truly convey notions of equality and liberty, they should lead to a more generous understanding of the state and taxation than what is generally envisioned under the Nozickean doctrine.[91]

When discussing the issue of background circumstances, Nozick initially appears responsive to the need to correct the distribution of entitlements generated under an unfettered market economy. Specifically, Nozick explores the possibility of compensating for inequality in circumstances caused by unlucky life events.[92] However, such compensation, according to Nozick, conflicts with his basic understanding of rights. In Nozick's words:

> The major objection to speaking of everyone's having a right *to* various things such as equality of opportunity, life, and so on, and enforcing this right, is that these "rights" require a substructure of things and materials and actions; and *other* people may have rights and entitlements over these. *No one has a right to something whose realization requires certain uses of things and activities that other people have rights and entitlements over.*[93]

Thus, without a mechanism to compensate effectively for diversity in assets, adjust for life circumstances, and affect the resulting distribution of possessions, Nozick's theory is highly susceptible to unequal patterns of distribution.[94]

---

89. *Cf. id.* at 224–25 (using a negative argument to support claim that people deserve that which comes from their natural assets); Marjorie E. Kornhauser, *Equality, Liberty, and a Fair Income Tax*, 23 FORDHAM URB. L.J. 607, 614 (1996) (defining the principle of desert as relying on personal traits such as ability, effort, and talent).

90. *See supra* note 57 and accompanying text.

91. Kymlicka, *supra* note 78, at 107–10 (discussing the notion of self-ownership). For an example of a theory based on the idea of self-ownership that leads to different conclusions than Nozick's theory does, *see* the discussion on Rawls's Theory of Justice, *infra* notes 188–237 and accompanying text. There are interesting similarities between Nozick's paradigm and Rawls's theory of justice. Nozick not only appeals to the principle of equality (broadly conceived), but he also makes a case against utilitarianism, which is an important part of Rawls's thesis. Rawls, for example, claims that utilitarianism fails to treat people as ends in themselves, since it allows some people to be sacrificed for the benefit of others. Accordingly, both Rawls and Nozick agree that treating people as equals requires placing limits on the manner they can be used for the benefit of others or society in general. People should have rights that are not subject to the utilitarian calculation. Rawls and Nozick disagree, however, on the question of which rights are most important to ensure that people are treated as ends in themselves. Generally speaking, Rawls sees the right to a given share of society's resources as one of the most important rights. Nozick, on the other hand, values most the right individuals have over themselves—the right to "self ownership." Kymlicka, *supra* note 78, at 107–10.

92. Nozick, *supra* note 55, at 235–38.

93. *Id.* at 238 (some emphasis added).

94. In Nozick's view, distributions that comply with his three principles are morally just regardless of the issue of inequality. *Id.* at 166 ("Rights do not determine a social ordering but instead set the constraints within which a social choice is to be made, by excluding certain alternatives, fixing others, and so on. . . . If entitlements to holdings are rights to dispose of them, then social choice must take place *within* the constraints of how people choose to exercise these rights").

The issue of inequality comes up again when Nozick lays out the three main tenets of his doctrine: (1) the principle of transfer — specifying that holdings justly acquired can be freely transferred;[95] (2) the principle of initial acquisition — offering an account of how people initially came to own their resources;[96] and (3) the principle of rectification — prescribing that entitlement to holdings unjustly acquired or transferred must be corrected.[97] According to Nozick, only those holdings that comply with these three tenets are rightfully possessed.[98] If all private possession is rightfully held, the entire distribution of resources is just and should not be disturbed.[99]

The first and second tenets of the Nozickean doctrine state that to justify the existing distribution of holdings, past acquisitions must be legitimate.[100] An illegitimate use of force or deception, for example, undermines the justness of entitlement to assets and, hence, the right to pass these assets to others.[101] Conversely, when past acquisitions and transfers are legitimate, there can be no justification for infringement upon privately held possessions. According to the third tenet, redistributive measures aimed at remedying injustice in past acquisitions or transfers of holdings, are morally justified.[102] Overall, then, when addressing incidents of unjust past acquisitions or transfers, Nozick's theory may allow for a more extensive state and tax schemes than Nozick initially posits.[103]

Unfortunately, it is difficult to conclusively and timely identify incidences of past injustice and, accordingly, the rightful owners of resources in such circumstances.[104] Nozick thus provides a rule of thumb for detecting victims and beneficiaries of unjust acts. He explains:

> (1) . . . victims of injustice generally do worse than they otherwise would and
> (2) . . . those from the least well-off group in the society have the highest probabilities of being the (descendants of) victims of the most serious injustice who are owed compensation by those who benefited from the injustices (assumed to be those better off, though sometimes the perpetrators will be others in the worst-off group).[105]

---

95. *Id.* at 150. According to Nozick, the topic of transfer involves "complicated truth," which he does not develop. He does mention, however, that this principle includes "descriptions of voluntary exchange, and gift and (on the other hand) fraud." *Id.*

96. *Id.* Unfortunately, much as with the underdevelopment of the principle of transfer, Nozick does not expand on the principle of acquisition. Nozick notes that the principle of acquisition raises several problems including figuring out which "unheld" things came to be held and how. *Id.*

97. *Id.* at 152–53.

98. *Id.* at 151.

99. *Id.* at 151–52. For example, according to the transfer principle, when a person owns a piece of land, he is free to engage in any transfer concerning that land as long as the initial acquisition of the land was freely made and not a result of unfair competition or fraud. If all land was justly acquired and transferred, then the entire distribution of land in a given society is fair as well.

100. *Id.* at 151.

101. *Id.* at 151–52.

102. *Id.* at 152–53. Nozick maintains that holdings acquired or transferred by means of, for example, stealing or fraud, are unjustified and ought to be returned to their rightful owners.

103. *Id.* at 230–31 ("Although to introduce socialism as the punishment for our sins would be to go too far, past injustices might be so great as to make necessary in the short run a more extensive state in order to rectify them.").

104. *Id.* at 231 (suggesting the lack of historical information).

105. *Id.*

Next, Nozick suggests that injustice in existing holdings could be rectified by a single, across-the-board measure of ex-post resource redistribution, tailored to appropriate from well-off members of society and bestow upon those at the bottom of the economic scale.[106] However, despite introducing this broad rule of thumb and the method of rectification, Nozick does not further clarify the conditions under which rectification takes place, nor does he address such issues as how to assess the effect of prior injustices or execute corresponding redistributive measures.[107] Coming short of sufficiently elaborating on the third tenet of rectification, Nozick leaves unanswered fundamental questions concerning the viability of this principle.[108] Accordingly, the extent to which rectification can truly be implemented by policymakers seeking to follow the Nozickean theory of entitlement remains to be seen.

A second, more blunt, indication of the elusiveness of the rectification principle is offered by Nozick himself. Generally, it can be assumed that provision of a minimum standard of living for all members of the society would benefit the most disadvantaged individuals and households at the expense of those more affluent citizens, who are better situated and possess the actual means to finance such outlays. In the spirit of the principle of rectification, it seems reasonable to presume Nozick would have endorsed such a provision. A guaranteed minimum standard of living has the potential to rectify past injustices by compensating those most likely to have suffered prior injustices at the hands of those expected to have gained from these acts. Nozick, however, is far from endorsing the provision of social minimums.[109] He stresses that arguments in favor of such provision do not address the question of whether the required redistribution compromises existing, rightfully held entitlements.[110] Notably, in emphasizing incidences where redistribution may cause injustice rather than examining the broader issue of whether the present distribution of holdings is just to begin with, Nozick practically abandons his principle of rectification.

Nozick's theory is further problematic when it comes to his description of the "state of nature" and the role this description plays in generating what Nozick offers as the foundation for a just societal order. Despite Nozick's attempts at portraying a starting point of free exercise of effort, talent, and transfers, alternative accounts of the beginning of time are often riddled with

---

106. *Id.* ("[T]hen a *rough* rule of thumb for rectifying injustices might seem to be the following: organize society so as to maximize the position of whatever group ends up least well-off in the society."). Note the similarity between this rule and the Rawlsian difference principle. *See infra* notes 213–15 and accompanying text.

107. Nozick, *supra* note 55, at 152–53; *but see* Byrne, 1995, *supra* note 8, at 785 (suggesting that while Nozick does not specify the circumstances that would constitute rectifiable injustice, he raises important questions about what to account for when the principle of rectification is to be developed).

108. Nozick, *supra* note 55, at 152–53.

109. *Id.* at 232–35 (discussing Bernard Williams, *The Idea of Equality, in* Peter Laslett & W. G. Runciman (Editors), *Philosophy, Politics, and Society* (Basil Blackwell, 1962), 110–31, reprinted in Joel Feinberg (Editor), *Moral Concepts* (Oxford University, 1969)).

110. *Id.* at 235.

images of violence and oppression.[111] Since the use of force and violence makes acquisitions and transfers illegitimate according to the Nozickean doctrine,[112] these descriptions call into question the justness of the present distribution of holdings. If one acknowledges that the present distribution of holdings is questionable, it is difficult to construe a valid argument in favor of Nozick's minimal state and against taxation and redistribution. Furthermore, the description of the initial state of the world as free of possession may also be brought into question. If, for example, an initial joint ownership paradigm is considered,[113] the inegalitarian implications of Nozick's theory are yet again debatable.[114]

In conclusion, Nozick's theory highlights several fundamentals in societal beliefs and mechanisms. Emphasizing the importance of privately held property rights, Nozick outlines a framework from which issues such as equality, political legitimacy, distributive justice, and taxation can be fleshed out and explored. Similar to Locke and contrary to egalitarian theorists, Nozick does not include equality among the principles necessary for normative assessment and generally criticizes other theorists who do.[115] Rather, Nozick is a proponent of allowing the market to function on its own terms. In Nozick's theory, the main reference to social solidarity, and, hence, the possible attainment of more than a minimal protective state, relates to the workings of the market economy. Nozick's third principle of rectification addresses infractions that occur in the course of market acquisitions and transfers. That the application of this principle is practically unattainable, however, has serious implications for the integrity of the Nozickean theory of entitlement. The only legitimate system of taxation under the Nozickean paradigm is generally understood to be that which is necessary to raise revenues for the maintenance of institutions needed to protect the system of private property and free market exchanges, such as the monetary and justice systems.[116] For this reason, placing a high value on an unrestricted market economy and generally assuming the merit of the prevailing distribution of resources, Nozick's theory often prescribes the administration of taxation in a manner that preserves, rather than disturbs, the societal status quo. In doing so, the theory avoids a candid consideration of plausible infringements in the initial distribution of resources and

---

111. *Id.* at xi ("I argue that a state would arise from anarchy . . . even though no one intended this or tried to bring it about, by a process which need not violate anyone's rights."); *cf.* Thomas Hobbes, *Leviathan* (1651; Oxford University, 1909), 94–98 (describing the beginning of time as a violent state of war of all against all).

112. Nozick, *supra* note 55, at 152–53; *see supra* notes 95–103 and accompanying text.

113. *Supra* notes 17–19 and accompanying text (discussing the Lockean description of the beginning of time).

114. Despite Locke's joint-ownership starting point, Locke's perspective on subsequent allocations of societal resources is similar to the description that Nozick provides. In addition, an "individually held" property rights approach is not uncommon. *See, e.g.,* Richard A. Epstein, *Takings: Private Property and the Power of Eminent Domain* (Harvard University, 1985), 5.

115. Nozick questions the starting point of equality. Nozick, *supra* note 55, at 215–16. He, moreover, claims that an argument that draws on equality cannot be used to justify greater equality and criticizes Rawls's original position for using such a circular proposition. *See id.* at 215 (citing Rawls, *supra* note 1, at 538–41); *id.* at 156–57 (challenging the idea of predetermined "patterned" distributions); *id.* at 198–202 (discussing competing incentives arising in the process of determining equal distribution).

116. *Id.* at 26–27 (discussing the practical implications of the minimal state).

the later chain of acquisitions and transfers and can accordingly be challenged on these grounds.[117]

UTILITARIANISM

BENTHAM AND THE PURSUIT OF HAPPINESS

Utilitarianism, a more contemporary doctrine than the theory of entitlement, is a normative platform essential to modern, particularly professional, tax analysis. The theory has its roots in the work of Jeremy Bentham.[118] It relies on two key fundamentals: the first concentrates on human welfare or "utility,"[119] while the second considers human welfare by appointing equal weight to each individual.[120] Utilitarianism is grounded in a vision of equality that prescribes that no one person is worth more than another.[121] In its most common formulation, the theory suggests that the right act or policy is that which produces the greatest utility for the greatest number of persons, calculated by adding up all utility units individuals enjoy.[122]

Bentham believed that individuals are governed by two main forces: pain and pleasure.[123] Seen in this light, human behavior is understood as the pursuit of utility, based on a reasoned calculation designed to maximize pleasure and minimize pain.[124] Human experience provides utility, for example, when it produces pleasure in the form of benefit, advantage, good, or happiness or when it prevents pain through avoiding unhappiness or mischief.[125] Happiness,

---

117. *See, e.g., id.* at 153 ("The general outlines of the theory of justice in holdings are that the holdings of a person are just if he is entitled to them by the principles of justice . . . To turn these general outlines into a specific theory we would have to specify the details of each of the three principles of justice in holdings . . . I shall not attempt that task here").

118. *See generally* Bentham, *The Theory of Legislation, supra* note 81.

119. *Id.* at 2 ("*Utility* is an abstract term. It expresses the property or tendency of a thing to prevent some evil or to procure some good. *Evil* is pain, or the cause of pain. *Good* is pleasure, or the cause of pleasure").

120. *Id.*

121. *Id.*

122. *Id.* ("That which is conformable to the utility, or the interest of an individual, is what tends to augment the total sum of his happiness. That which is conformable to the utility, or the interest of a community, is what tends to augment the total sum of the happiness of the individuals that compose it"); *see also infra* note 126 and accompanying text.

123. Bentham, *The Theory of Legislation, supra* note 81, at 2 ("Nature has placed man under the empire of *pleasure* and of *pain*. We owe to them all our ideas; we refer to them all our judgments, and all the determinations of our life." Bentham suggested that man's "only object is to seek pleasure and to shun pain. . . . These eternal and irresistible sentiments ought to be the great study of the moralist and the legislator. The *principle of utility* subjects everything to these two motives"); *see also* Jeremy Bentham, *The Psychology of Economic Man*, in W. Stark (Editor), *Jeremy Bentham's Economic Writings* (Allen & Unwyn, 1954), Vol. 3, 419, 433 [hereinafter *Bentham's Economic Writings*].

124. Bentham, *The Theory of Legislation, supra* note 81, at 18 ("Every one makes himself the judge of his own utility; such is the fact, and such it ought to be; otherwise man would not be a rational agent. He who is not a judge of what is agreeable to him, is less than a child; he is an idiot"); *see also Bentham's Economic Writings, supra* note 123, at 434 ("Men calculate, some with less exactness, indeed, some with more: but all men calculate").

125. *Bentham's Economic Writings, supra* note 123, at 437. For Bentham, utility is a multifaceted concept. It includes, for example, (1) intensity, (2) duration, (3) certainty or uncertainty, and (4) propinquity or remoteness. *Id.* at 435. Also important is the likelihood that the pleasure or

Bentham argued, is the most desirable form of pleasure and the goal of the utility calculus.[126] As each individual seeks to maximize her happiness, it is the role of society to bring about the greatest happiness to the greatest number.[127] In this view, each private act or policy decision is to be judged "according to the tendency which it appears to have to augment or diminish the happiness of the party whose interest is in question."[128] Utilitarianism is thus not concerned with moral issues per se, such as virtues, natural rights, or the social contract.[129] The theory suggests the government should abstain from such matters, since they are inappropriate considerations for policy formation.[130] Moreover, preoccupation with morality diverts the government from the true principle of policy-making: the pursuit of happiness, or utility.[131] In this view, while maximizing utility may overlap with moral aspirations, it ought to guide society even when distinct from morality.

Notwithstanding the budding divide between utilitarianism and morality, two main arguments exist in support of utilitarianism as a standard for moral worth.[132] According to the first argument, based on equality,[133] each individual possesses unique desires, characteristics, and interests and these should be given equal value because all individuals matter equally. The right act, which gives equal consideration to each individual, also maximizes total utility. The second argument places the focal point on the whole (i.e., society) rather than the individual.[134] According to this second, more commonly invoked rationale, maximizing the good is a primary, not secondary, goal of utilitarianism, and individuals are given equal consideration because it is in this way only that aggregate utility is maximized. Utilitarianism, in this light, is more

---

happiness will be followed by more of the same, and not by pain. *Id.* at 436. Bentham lists twenty-six categories of pleasure and pain that make up utility, including (but not limited to) sense, wealth, skill, amity, good name, power, benevolence, and association. *See* Bentham, *The Theory of Legislation, supra* note 81, at 21–27. Bentham also discusses how to measure the amount of pleasure and pain. *Id.* at 31–32.

126. *Bentham's Economic Writings, supra* note 123, at 421 ("My notion of man is, that, successfully or unsuccessfully, he aims at happiness, and so will continue to aim as long as he continues to be man, in every thing he does").

127. Jeremy Bentham, Bhikhu Parekh (Editor), *Bentham's Political Thought* (Croom Helm, 1973), 195 [hereinafter *Bentham's Political Thought*].

128. *Id.* at 67. Utilitarianism demands not only the value of individuals' acts or experiences be considered based on their prospect to maximize welfare but also the behavior of the government. Bentham, *The Theory of Legislation, supra* note 81, at 1–2; *see also id.* at 60 ("Morality in general is the art of directing the actions of men in such a way as to produce the greatest possible sum of good. Legislation ought to have precisely the same object").

129. *See, e.g.,* Bentham, *The Theory of Legislation, supra* note 81, at 3 (finding utility a calculation only of pleasure and pain).

130. *Id.* at 60–65.

131. *Id.* at 60; *see also id.* at 3 ("I am a partisan of the *principle of utility* when I measure my approbation or disapprobation of a public or private act by its tendency to produce pleasure or pain; when I employ the words *just, unjust, moral, immoral, good, bad,* simply as collective terms including the ideas of certain pains or pleasures. . . . He who adopts the *principle of utility,* esteems virtue to be a good only on account of the pleasures which result from it; he regards vice as an evil only because of the pains which it produces").

132. Some, however, claim the theory of utilitarianism rests on self-evident truths or draws on a set of axioms, not debatable rationales, and thus falls short of offering substantive normative merit. *Bentham's Economic Writings, supra* note 123, at 421 ("This position may, to some eyes, present itself in the character of an axiom: as such self-evident, and not standing in need of proof").

133. *See, e.g., infra* text accompanying note 154-56.

134. *See, e.g., infra* text accompanying notes 153.

concerned with the welfare of society as a whole than with the welfare of its individual members.[135]

Although Bentham sought to offer a theory that is compelling and simple to implement,[136] utilitarianism faces a number of practical challenges. Most of these challenges follow the paradigm from its inception and should be carefully considered in policy settings.[137] Importantly, the measurement and comparison of utility units of different individuals, key functions in utilitarianism, are highly difficult to apply because individuals are distinct in their preferences and welfare or utility functions.[138] Further, Bentham's initial apprehension of utilitarianism accounting for moral and social values only deepens with later developments of utilitarianism, triggering troubling normative dilemmas once the theory's method of analysis is taken into full view.

Specifically, in a vastly heterogeneous world, it is nearly impossible to accurately measure utility units obtained by different individuals and compare the utility gains and losses associated with different policy alternatives. If utility cannot be readily measured and compared, the utilitarian calculus provides little aid in policy settings.[139] Avoiding the need to address this challenge fully, Bentham argued the comparability of utility must be assumed as a matter of practicality. According to Bentham: "If we refuse to acknowledge the principle of utility, we fall into a complete circle of sophistry. . . . If you desire to reject the principle of utility . . . what is there to put in its place?"[140]

Even if one accepts Bentham's practical solution to the issue of measurement and comparability, utilitarianism remains in conflict with basic

---

135. The primary duty according to the second argument is not to treat people as equals, but to maximize total welfare. Treating individuals as equals emerges as a consequential effect of the utility calculation. *See infra* text accompanying notes 153–56.

136. Bentham, *The Theory of Legislation, supra* note 81, at 2–3 ("A *principle* is a first idea, which is made the beginning or basis of a system of reasonings. . . . Such a principle must be clearly evident. . . . Such are the axioms of mathematics").

137. *See, e.g., id.* at 45 ("The principle [of utility] is not denied, but its application is thought to be impossible").

138. *Id.* ("There are some specious objections which I do not wish to dissemble. 'How is it possible to take account of all the circumstances which influence the sensibility? How can we appreciate internal and secret dispositions, such as strength of mind, knowledge, inclinations, sympathies? How can we measure these different qualities?' . . . I allow that the greater part of these differences in sensibility cannot be appreciated; that it would be impossible to prove their existence in individual cases, or to measure their strength and degree").

139. Given that the pursuit of the greatest good for the greatest number often involves utility losses and gains for different individuals, without a workable standard of measurement and comparability, there is no certain way to assess whether the added value to those who gain offsets the losses to those who lose.

140. Bentham, *The Theory of Legislation, supra* note 81 at 18–19. Bentham prescribed that assuming the comparability of utility, and, hence, being able to use the theory for policymaking, is better than failing to take utility into account even when it is ill applied. *See id.* at 46; *see also* Hank Jenkins-Smith, *Continuing Controversies in Policy Analysis,* in David L. Weimer (Editor), *Policy Analysis and Economics: Developments, Tensions, Prospects* (Kluwer, 1991), 23, 25. The comparability of utility, however, has nonetheless remained a challenge for utilitarianism. *See, e.g.,* Lionel Robbins, *Interpersonal Comparisons of Utility: A Comment,* 48 Econ. J. 635, 636 (1938) ("I find it easy to understand the belief of Bentham and his followers that they had found the open sesame to problems of social policy. But, as time went on, things occurred which begun to shake my belief in the existence of so complete and continuity between political and economic analysis"). *But see id.* at 635 ("I am far from thinking that thorough-going utilitarianism *à la Bentham* is an ultimate solution . . . But I have always felt that, as a first approximation . . . the approach which counts each man as one, and, on that assumption, asks which way lies the greatest happiness, is less likely to lead one astray").

principles of moral worth.[141] Particularly, despite the aspiration of traditional utilitarianism to treat all individuals as possessing equal value, the theory may prescribe the degradation of some for the benefit of others when this practice increases aggregate utility.[142] Lying, inhumane punishment, and repressing minorities can be justified, and even encouraged, in the same vein. Put differently, traditional utilitarianism places all forms of happiness and pleasure on the same, one-dimensional metric of utility. In this way, each source of benefit is equally considered when it provides or subtracts similar units of value. Notwithstanding the benefits of such a straightforward method of calculation, it may be socially desirable to distinguish between different types of preferences based on their social desirability.[143] This distinction allows policymakers to take less desirable preferences out of the utility calculation or give them less utility weight,[144] while favoring other, more desirable, goals.[145]

The difficulty of utilitarianism to account for moral and social values is particularly troubling in the use of money as a proxy for utility.[146] When utilizing a tangible criterion such as money to capture utility, an individual's supply of monetary units represents access to, and enjoyment of, goods and services. These are ultimately translated to reflect gains and losses in utility. Using this method permits the comparison of a wide range of policies and greatly enhances the efficacy of utilitarianism.[147] However, when money substitutes for utility, utilitarianism is yet again challenged by troubling normative questions. Utilitarianism, as a paradigm, struggles to embody the

---

141. *Cf.* Rawls, *supra* note 1, at 13 (discussing Rawls's idea of justice and fairness in society).

142. *But see* Bentham, *The Theory of Legislation*, *supra* note 81, at 16 ("The only difference between politics and morals is, that one directs the operations of governments, and the other the actions of individuals; but their object is common; it is happiness. That which is politically good cannot be morally bad, unless we suppose that the rules of arithmetic, true for large numbers, are false for small ones. While we imagine that we follow the *principle of utility*, we may nevertheless do evil. . . . That which constitutes a bad man, is the habit of pleasures injurious to others; but this very habit supposes the absence of many kinds of pleasure. *One ought not to hold utility responsible for mistakes contrary to its nature, and which it alone is able to rectify. If a man calculates badly, it is not arithmetic which is in fault; it is himself*") (second emphasis added).

143. Nozick argued, for example, for the legitimacy of preferences in calculating utility. He theorized the existence of a neuropsychologist machine able to induce high levels of pleasure by injecting drugs into people. If pleasure is the greatest good, everyone would volunteer to use this machine. However, most people are unlikely to opt in favor of the machine, suggesting that happiness may not be all that people care about and that other qualities to life exist. *See* Nozick, *supra* note 55, at 42–45.

144. Such preferences could be those that undermine acceptable notions of moral behavior in society including, for example, preferences for slavery and other violent acts.

145. Those preferences could, for example, advance arts and poetry over plain pushpins even when both produce similar levels and duration of utility.

146. *Bentham's Economic Writings*, *supra* note 123, at 437–38; *Bentham's Political Thought*, *supra* note 127, at 119–24. *See also* Jenkins-Smith, *supra* note 140, at 25.

147. Utility calculation is accomplished, for example, through the determination of what individuals would pay to obtain a benefit or avoid a loss. Consider the Kaldor-Hicks proposition, where the policy option that maximizes aggregated dollars is elected, and those who lose are (ideally) compensated through lump-sum transfers. For a useful introduction to the Kaldor-Hicks proposition *see* Harvey S. Rosen, *Public Finance* (5th ed. McGraw-Hill, 1999), 241. *Cf. Bentham's Economic Writings*, *supra* note 123, at 438 ("In the way, and by means of compensation, there is no evil to which it may not happen to be, in the instance of the individual in question, reparable in the way of equivalent. Relation had to the individual in question, an evil is reparable, and exactly repaired, when, after having sustained the evil and received the compensation, it would be a matter of indifference whether to receive the like evil, coupled with the like compensation, or not").

complexity and, arguably, the supremacy of social and moral values. The principle of maximizing utility, as computed in monetary terms, offers a limited platform for policies that involve preferences for certain goods and services, such as the guarantee of a minimum level of nutrition or shelter for all,[148] when these may not be adequately expressed by, or compensated with, dollars.[149] However, as Bentham explains: "The *logic of utility* consists in setting out, in all the operations of the judgment, from the calculation or comparison of pains and pleasures, and in not allowing the interference of any *other* idea."[150] And so, introducing values other than utility or wealth maximization into utilitarianism might itself be a rejection of the theory. Accordingly, even though contemporary scholarship offers alternative explanations for safeguarding access to certain rights and liberties,[151] utilitarianism, as a normative platform, remains challenged when it comes to values.[152]

Practically, utilitarianism suggests that public policy should be based on the pursuit of happiness, the maximization of utility, and fundamental equality. Applying these principles to tax system design leads to two main tax policy alternatives. The first policy option recognizes that taxation lessens the amount of money, and thereby utility, enjoyed by individuals and demands the least sacrifice, in *collective* utility loss, while maintaining social welfare at a maximum level.[153] The second policy alternative prescribes that taxation levies an equal burden on each person, based on *individual* utility losses, while underscoring the idea of equal consideration.[154]

---

148. *See, e.g.*, Laurence H. Tribe, *Policy Science: Analysis or Ideology?*, 2 Phil. & Pub. Aff. 66, 87–88 (1972) (discussing the idea, for instance, that "individuals would not trade breathing rights for pollution rights (even *infinite* pollution rights) below a certain point").

149. *Id.* at 88. According to Tribe, a rich method of analysis that reflects the complexity and supremacy of social and moral preferences should evolve in the area of public policy. *See also id.* at 92–93 (discussing the issue of distribution for society as one that should reflect more than the gains or losses of individuals from goods and services).

150. Bentham, *The Theory of Legislation*, *supra* note 81, at 3 (second emphasis added).

151. *See, e.g.*, Rawls, *supra* note 1, at 118–23 (discussing Rawls's theory and design of the "veil of ignorance," which may safeguard rights and liberties).

152. *Id.* at 23; John C. Harsanyi, *Rule Utilitarianism, Equality, and Justice*, 2 Soc. Phil. & Pol'y, 115 (1985) (discussing the concepts of equity and justice from a utilitarian perspective). Consider critical tax scholars who often challenge the seemingly objective analysis of taxation as based on the underlying value judgments of those who occupy the dominant, well-off positions in society. Here, the issue of values is brought to the surface to underscore the subjectivity of contemporary — mostly utilitarianism-driven — tax analysis. *See, e.g.*, Dorothy A. Brown, *Race and Class Matters in Tax Policy*, 107 Colum. L. Rev. 790, 790–802 (2007) (exploring the debate over earned income tax credit, welfare programs, and the concepts of deserving and undeserving poor as racially based); Anthony C. Infanti, *Tax Equity* 55 Buff. L. Rev. 1191, 1249–50 (2008) ("The concept of tax equity is part of the 'entire system of values, attitudes, beliefs, morality, etc. that is in one way or another supportive of the established order. Cloaked in a mantle of positive connotations, tax equity is viewed as an indisputable good.'" Tax equity "seems nearly 'unchallengeable, [a] part of the natural order of things.") (quoting Carl Boggs, *Gramsci's Marxism* (Urizen, 1976), 7).

153. Musgrave, *Public Finance and Distributive Justice*, *supra* note 54, at 142.

154. Both types of policies attempt to safeguard the highest amount of aggregated utility either as a main or derivative goal. *See* Blum and Kalven, *supra* note 65, at 39–45 (discussing different formulations for equal sacrifice); Richard A. Musgrave, *The Theory of Public Finance: A Study in Public Economy* (McGraw-Hill, 1959), 77 (discussing allocation and distribution); Simons, *supra* note 4, at 6–10 (discussing satisfaction and sacrifice).

Early utilitarianism, by and large, advocated the second policy alternative.[155] Taxes were designed so that the loss in marginal utility of income—that is, the loss in utility from taking a dollar away from an individual—was the same for all persons.[156] It was Bentham who first suggested that the value of money decreases as the total amount of wealth possessed increases, a phenomenon later known as "the decreasing marginal utility of money."[157] In Bentham's words: "[T]he quantity of happiness [read 'utility'] produced by a particle of wealth (each particle being of the same magnitude) will be less and less at every [additional] particle."[158] And, so, taking a dollar away from a rich person inflicts less utility loss than taking a dollar away from a poor person. Therefore, if additional dollars increase utility but the incremental gain in utility decreases with increased wealth, aggregate utility rises with an equal (rather than unequal) distribution of fortune.[159] Based on this view, the principles of maximizing total utility and levying an equal tax burden on individuals both lead to the same approach: advancing a progressive tax structure.[160] Put differently, traditional utilitarianism complements a redistributive type of taxation where individuals with more financial means bear a gradually higher burden of taxation.

The application of utilitarianism to tax system design is not, however, entirely straightforward. The rate at which the value of money decreases is

---

155. *See, e.g.*, Mill, *supra* note 3, at 925–30 (conceptualizing the doctrine of equal sacrifice). Note that with respect to many other issues, Mill is far from endorsing utilitarianism as a basis for moral analysis.

156. Mill's doctrine of equal sacrifice ultimately aims for the extraction of the least total sacrifice from society. For a somewhat confused illustration of this idea, *see id.* at 927 ("As a government ought to make no distinction of persons or classes in the strength of their claims on it, whatever sacrifices it requires from them should be made to bear as nearly as possible with the same pressure upon all, which, it must be observed, is the mode by which least sacrifice is occasioned on the whole").

157. *Bentham's Economic Writings*, *supra* note 123, at 441–42; *see also* Jenkins-Smith, *supra* note 140, at 25. For a useful discussion on the decreasing value of money (or its "declining utility"), *see* Blum and Kalven, *supra* note 65, at 40–42 ("It seems likely that a dollar has less 'value' for a person with a million dollars of income than for a person with only a thousand dollars of income. To take the same number of dollars from each is not to require the same amount of sacrifice from them." Blum and Kalven conclude, "[i]nstead a fair tax would take more from the wealthier") *Id.* at 40.

158. Jeremy Bentham, *Pannomial Fragments*, in John Bowring (Editor), *The Works of Jeremy Bentham* (1838–43; Russell and Russell, 1962), Vol. 3, 211, 229. *Bentham's Economic Writings*, *supra* note 123, at 439, 441–42. Bentham applies this general rule not only to money but to all other sources and causes of pleasures. *See, e.g., id.* at 442 (finding that "[a]s it is with *money*, so is it with all other sources or causes of pleasure").

159. *Cf.* Jeremy Bentham, *Principles of the Civil Code*, in John Bowring (Editor), *The Works of Jeremy Bentham* (1838–43; Russell and Russell, 1962), Vol. 1, 297, 304–07 [hereinafter Bentham, *Principles of the Civil Code*]; *see also* Jeremy Bentham, *The Principles of Morals and Legislation* (1789; Hafner, 1948), 3.

160. Progressivity in taxation can be achieved through different mechanisms, including, for example, the rate and base structures. *See, e.g.*, Lawrence Zelenak, *The Myth of Pretax Income*, 101 Mich. L. Rev. 2261, 2264 (2003) (reviewing Murphy and Nagel, *supra* note 5, and exploring the policy implication that "[t]o some, justice requires an income tax base, while others insist that consumption is the only fair tax base. To some, progressive marginal tax rates are morally required; to others progressive rates are anathema"). Each approach to taxation can be adjusted to levy a heavier tax burden on the wealthy, including exemptions for basic goods and services in the context of consumption taxation and low (or zero) initial tax bracket in the income tax structure.

unknown, and questions as to who is equal and how to treat unequally situated taxpayers are also unresolved.[161] Although traditional utilitarianism generally fits with progressive tax structures, the exact details of the ideal system are far from obvious.[162] Moreover, utility derived from wealth is only one piece of the puzzle. The value of well-protected property rights is of no less importance and serves as a prerequisite for the creation of wealth and utility, weakening the case for progressivity.[163] The productivity of the economy depends, among other factors, on the effort invested by individuals. When the government takes a portion of the return on individuals' efforts, it might in turn reduce the overall exercise of effort and add costly distortions to the economy.[164] Further, raising taxes on high earners could disincentivize economic activity among highly productive members of society.[165] According to this view, progressive taxation bears the risk of reducing total revenue raised or otherwise leaving society worse off in terms of aggregate utility than it was prior to taxation.[166]

Considering the potentially adverse effects of taxation, especially progressive taxation, on economic productivity, modern utilitarianism requires that the loss in utility from taxation will be less than the gain in utility from revenue raised.[167] More precisely, contemporary utilitarianism suggests that for each individual or commodity taxed, the relation between the loss in utility from taxation and the gain in utility from revenue raised will be the same and that, viewed as a whole, there will be minimum loss of aggregate

---

161. *See, e.g.*, Edwin R. A. Seligman, *Progressive Taxation In Theory and Practice*, 9 Am. Econ. Ass'n Q. 7, 219–22 (2d ed. 1908); Musgrave, *supra* note 154, at 98–105, 109; Richard A. Musgrave, *The Role of the State in Fiscal Theory, in Public Finance in a Democratic Society* (Elgar, 2000), Vol. 3, 3, 8 [hereinafter Musgrave, *The Role of the State*]; Stanley W. Jevons, *The Theory of Political Economy* (MacMillan, 1871), 21; Robbins, *supra* note 140, at 635–41.

162. *See* sources cited in *supra* note 161. When addressing progressive tax rates, for example, it is unclear how progressive the rates should be and what should be the income ranges to correspond with these rates.

163. *Cf.* Bentham, *Principles of the Civil Code, supra* note 159, at 311 ("When security and equality are in opposition, there should be no hesitation: equality should give way").

164. However, *see supra* notes 58–62 and accompanying text for similar claims and some counter findings.

165. *See supra* notes 58–62.

166. *See, e.g.*, Richard A. Musgrave, *Social Science, Ethics, and the Role of the Public Sector, in Public Finance in a Democratic Society* (Elgar, 2000), Vol. 3, 104, 111–12 (explaining the manner in which the cost of redistribution can be taken into account — according to Musgrave, income decline and deadweight losses from progressive taxation must be weighed against the social gains from reducing inequality).

167. Bentham and Edgeworth argued for equal taxation based on the assumption of a fixed income base, but then qualified this conclusion when they allowed for the "detrimental effects" of taxation on the available base. Smith, on the other hand, called for taxes "to take out and to keep out of the pockets of the people as little as possible, over and above what it brings into the public treasury of the state." Smith, *supra* note 55, at 372. Beginning with Pigou, what was referred to as "announcement effects" took central stage in tax theory. Arthur C. Pigou, *A Study in Public Finance* (3d rev. ed., Macmillan, 1947), 55–75 (to achieve the goal of least total sacrifice, not only must there be an optimal distribution of the tax burden, but its level must be minimized. Announcement effects were measured in terms of the excess burden or the deadweight loss that results when taxes distort economic choices). The concept of announcement effects was later developed into the theory of optimal taxation. For more on this issue, *see* Peter A. Diamond and James A. Mirrlees, *Optimal Taxation and Public Production I: Production Efficiency*, 61 Am. Econ. Rev. 8 (1971); Musgrave, *The Role of the State, supra* note 161, at 3; Richard A. Musgrave, *Public Finance and Finanzwissenschaft Traditions Compared, in Public Finance in a Democratic Society* (Elgar, 2000), Vol. 3, 33.

utility and some gain in social welfare.[168] Consequently, once the effects of taxation and redistribution are understood and accounted for, a less progressive tax scheme than under traditional utilitarianism emerges. However, even this modern interpretation of utilitarianism, as it applies to taxation, raises critical normative dilemmas. For example, according to the theory's revised fundamentals, an individual who depends on this life-saving medicine should be taxed at the maximum tax rate on her treatment. The underlying assumption is that an individual who can afford this life-saving medicine and the taxes it entails is unlikely to reduce her consumption of the treatment even when taxed at the greatest extent. In other words, society's gain in utility from revenue raised in such circumstances will probably not be offset by a loss of utility from diminished medical use. From an intuitive, moral point of view, however, this option seems to constitute gross exploitation of one person's misfortune for the benefit of others.

From a broad societal perspective, the idea of diminishing aggregate utility may not necessarily be unappealing when other benefits are considered. Some scholars argue, for example, that in circumstances where a smaller societal pie allows for the provision of social minimums, it is a cost worth paying.[169] Additionally, like other theories explored in this chapter, utilitarianism rests on unstated assumptions about the status quo and pretax distribution of resources. In the quest for the greatest utility for the greatest number, utilitarianism relies on the existing distribution to serve as a baseline from which to assess the subtractions and gains in utility.[170] This approach naturally favors maintaining the status quo compared with alternative policy options that may, at least in the short run, reduce total welfare. More sound policymaking must first look into the existing pretax distribution of resources, including civil rights and liberties, and evaluate its merit. Only when the pretax distribution is found to be just and alternative allocations have been compared and excluded can the exercise of utility maximization be applied to the status quo and yield just results.[171]

---

168. Looking at income taxation, for example, some individuals may have a very elastic labor supply, meaning that when tax rates on labor income increase, these individuals significantly reduce their quantity of taxable labor. In this case, an increase in the tax rate is expected both to yield relatively little revenue and to cause a large loss of utility. Therefore, contemporary utilitarianism suggests that these individuals ought to bear a relatively light tax burden. In contrast, when people have an inelastic labor supply, taxes should be greater, since the gain in revenue will be greater than the loss of utility. Ramsey showed that, provided certain preliminary assumptions vis-à-vis commodity taxation, deadweight loss would be minimized with a rate structure that ensures proportional reduction of all product consumption. *See* Frank P. Ramsey, *A Contribution to the Theory of Taxation*, 37 Econ. J. 47, 54 (1927).

169. *See, e.g.*, Ronald M. Dworkin, *Is Wealth a Value?*, 9 J. Legal Stud. 191, 191–93 (1980). *Cf.* Ronald Dworkin, *Taking Rights Seriously* (Harvard University, 1977), ix–xi, 233, 238 [hereinafter Dworkin, *Taking Rights Seriously*]; Rawls, *supra* note 1, at 26–27, 186–87.

170. Daniel W. Bromley, *Institutional Change and Economic Efficiency*, 23 J. Econ. Issues 735, 736–38, 740–41, 757 (1989) (citing Daniel W. Bromley, *Economic Interests and Institutions: The Conceptual Foundations of Public Policy* (Basil Blackwell, 1989)).

171. Any other method mandates that the pretax distribution of resources be corrected prior to the pursuit of utility maximization. For an application of this perspective, *see* Mill, *supra* note 3, at 925–46 (claiming that the principle of equal sacrifice should be applied only after the pretax distribution is assured to be just). *Cf.* Knut Wicksell, *A New Principle of Just Taxation*, in Richard A. Musgrave and Alan T. Peacock (Editors), *Classics in the Theory of Public Finance* (Macmillan, 1958),

THE SOCIAL WELFARE FUNCTION

Over time the traditional utilitarian hypothesis prescribing that individuals have similar and comparable utility functions was rejected as scientifically unacceptable and immeasurable through empirical authentication.[172] Policy analysts who nonetheless embraced the premise of utilitarianism could have attempted to overlook the issue of distribution to focus exclusively on maximizing aggregate utility.[173] However, the paradigm was eventually expanded to explore new methods of comparing welfare or utility units in order to establish a system that more effectively addresses distributional as well as efficiency considerations.

Initially the economist Vilfredo Pareto introduced what is known today as the concept of "Pareto improvement."[174] The Pareto idea suggests that when comparing two economic distributions, one distribution is preferable to the other if at least one person is made better off and no one is made worse off (leading to a "Pareto efficient" allocation).[175] Although a powerful tool for ensuring the efficient distribution of resources, the Pareto platform does not provide a mechanism for ranking equally efficient allocations and, therefore, offers an incomplete tool for policymaking.[176] The "social-welfare function," an algebraic utility calculation designed to reflect normative judgments concerning the appropriate distribution of resources in society, emerged to fill the void.[177]

Unlike the entitlement premise, the social-welfare function relies on the assumption that the prevailing resource allocation in society might not be an

---

72, 72–75 (suggesting that for the benefit taxation to be equitable as well as efficient, the underlying distribution of income from which benefit taxes are drawn must also be just). *See generally* Murphy and Nagel, *supra* note 5, at 76–128; *but see* Zelenak, *supra* note 160, at 2262–63 (suggesting that the unquestionable embrace of the pretax income distribution was criticized already in the late 1960s by economist Carl Shoup).

172. Robbins, *supra* note 140, at 638–39.

173. Abram Burk, *A Reformulation of Certain Aspects of Welfare Economics*, 52 Q.J. Econ. 310, 326–27 (1938). One may question, however, the extent to which distributional issues are distinct from those of welfare or utility maximization. *See, e.g.,* Pierre Lemieux, *Social Welfare, State Intervention, and Value Judgments*, 11 Indep. Rev. 19, 19 (2006) ("The state can promote efficiency . . . in a second stage, it can . . . redistribute the supplementary output made possible by efficiency-enhancing interventions. Efficiency and distribution are two different issues . . . If redistribution obviously requires value judgments, wealth creation does not because having more goods is always desirable. . . . So thought many economists until the 1950s. By that time, however, the "new welfare economics" had all but destroyed these conclusions and shown that value judgments are also required for creating wealth—indeed, for even defining it").

174. Vilfredo Pareto, *Manual of Political Economy* (1906; Augustus M. Kelley, 1971), 451–52.

175. *Id.; see also* Manel Baucells & Steven A. Lippman, *Justice Delayed Is Justice Denied: A Cooperative Game Theoretic Analysis of Hold-Up in Co-Ownership*, 22 Cardozo L. Rev. 1191, 1196 n. 26 (2001) ("A Pareto improvement is a change that leaves some party to an economic exchange better off and no party worse off") (citing David M. Kreps, *A Course in Microeconomic Theory* (Princeton University, 1990), 153–56).

176. Richard A. Musgrave, *Equity and the Case for Progressive Taxation*, in Joseph J. Thorndike & Dennis J. Ventry Jr. (Editors), *Tax Justice: The Ongoing Debate* (Urban Institute, 2002), 9, 15.

177. *Id.* Total welfare originally meant the utility sum of individual members of society, giving an equal weight to each individual. Today, the empirically unattainable utility functions of different individuals are replaced with an artificial design of a welfare function of the entire society. In other words, individuals are treated as if they are comparable. Accordingly, the facts that marginal utility of income is downward-sloping and similar across individuals are simply assumed in the design of the function.

optimal one and that it is likely to require policy adjustments.[178] The utility calculation and, more fundamentally, policymaking itself become means in the advancement of normative judgments. The goal for policymakers, under the social-welfare paradigm, is to maximize societal well-being while focusing on the welfare of specific members of the society.[179] Now, the purpose of taxation includes not only revenue-raising functions but also redistributive aspects.[180] Analysts look at efficiency considerations while taking into account factors such as the distortions caused by taxation, the resources used to implement different tax structures, and administrative and compliance costs.[181] Pareto efficient tax systems, where no individual can be made better off without making someone else worse off, are then identified.[182] Next, applying a particular welfare function, a tax structure is chosen among plausible Pareto efficient tax systems.[183]

Although the social welfare function serves as an important development of utilitarianism, the theory still faces serious implementation difficulties. To begin with, there is little agreement on how to reveal the social, moral, and economic considerations needed to form the function.[184] The desirable distribution of resources and the manner in which society can determine this distribution are also unclear.[185] Further, it might be impossible to employ the function consistent with the basics of its design, because consistently applying any collective decision-making procedure is often considered an

---

178. *Cf. supra* text accompanying notes 69, 75, 93–94 (the Nozickean undertone regarding taxation and redistributive adjustments); Adolf Wagner, *Three Extracts on Public Finance*, in Richard A. Musgrave & Alan T. Peacock (Editors), *Classics in the Theory of Public Finance* (MacMillan, 1958), 1, 12–13 (claiming that proportional taxation is designed to maintain the relatively unequal positions of taxpayers).

179. Musgrave, *supra* note 166, at 112 (explaining that ultimately, the social-welfare function reflects the importance which society places on wealth and income for individuals of varying socioeconomic statuses, while leaving it to policymakers to construe the specific shape of the desirable distribution).

180. Wagner, *supra* note 178, at 14 (discussing the practical application of welfare economics to taxation). *See also* J. de V. Graaff, *Theoretical Welfare Economics* (Cambridge University, 1957), 26–27 (discussing distribution of outputs among final customers).

181. Peter A. Diamond & James A. Mirrlees, *Optimal Taxation and Public Production: II — Tax Rules*, 61 AM. ECON. REV. 261, 276–77 (1971).

182. Paul Anthony Samuelson, *Foundations of Economic Analysis* (10th prtg., Harvard University, 1975), 212.

183. Note, however, that both the advantages and disadvantages of the social welfare function stem from the theory's method of analysis. On its face, the theory separates efficiency considerations from value judgments while taking both into account. However, often no single alternative tax system dominates all other options. Thus, choosing among equally efficient tax structures must draw on value preferences.

184. *See, e.g.*, Giovanni Montemartini, *The Fundamental Principles of a Pure Theory of Public Finance*, in Richard A. Musgrave & Alan T. Peacock (Editors), *Classics in the Theory of Public Finance* (MacMillan, 1958), 137, 149–50 (questioning whether an organic, neutral body exists in society to decide collectively on social issues).

185. Policy outcomes may be ranked, for example, on the grounds that they reflect personal preferences or judgments (such as of analysts or politicians) regarding the community's preference for equality. *See, e.g.*, Erik Lindahl, *Some Controversial Questions in the Theory of Taxation*, in Richard A. Musgrave & Alan T. Peacock (Editors), *Classics in the Theory of Public Finance* (MacMillan, 1958), 214, 219 (suggesting determining the principles of the function based on the preferences of government officials; *cf.* Anthony B. Atkinson, Social Justice and Public Policy (MIT, 1983), 310 (asserting that "considerations of income inequality" must be "precisely formulated" if they are to provide tax guidance).

infeasible task.[186] The current paradigm also fails to clarify what constitutes welfare. The social welfare approach assumes that welfare can be captured and expressed in monetary terms. This makes the theory vulnerable to criticisms similar to those of traditional utilitarianism, particularly with respect to the difficulty of accounting for social and moral values.[187] One plausible way to work through these challenges is to go back to basics and openly contemplate the many underlying normative questions of taxation, including what constitutes welfare and what may be the optimal resource distribution for society. In this way, theories of political legitimacy, social justice, and economics remain vital to tax policy formation. It is possible that in the process of deliberation no one path will emerge as more correct or compelling than another. Questions over which idea to implement and what method of computation to follow in taxation are yet again debatable and call for a deliberate and honest discussion.

THE RAWLSIAN DESIGN: JUSTICE AS FAIRNESS

With his 1971 masterpiece *A Theory of Justice*, John Rawls centers the philosophical-political debate on the concept of fairness rather than on entitlement to holdings or the pursuit of happiness or utility.[188] Addressing the public sphere, Rawls works toward revealing the principles that ought to guide the political system.[189] Rawls begins his analysis by exploring how society can reach an agreement about its fundamental characteristics,[190] and he is especially concerned with defining aspects of social justice, including the division of the societal pie and the assignment of civil rights and liberties.[191] According to Rawls, one main reason the principles of justice that evolve from his theory are superior to other normative doctrines is that they develop from a plausible social contract.[192] That is, if people were truly positioned in a prestate

---

186. Kenneth J. Arrow, *Social Choice and Individual Values* (Wiley, 1951), 2–3 (demonstrating that it is impossible for any fair collective-choice process to resolve interpersonal differences consistently and appropriately while also satisfying certain axioms regarding the validity of the decision-making process).

187. *Supra* notes 146–52 and accompanying text.

188. Rawls, *supra* note 1, at 3.

189. *Id.* at 4, 7–8, 12.

190. *Id.* at 10, 15.

191. *Id.* at 4–5. Rawls recognizes that in a pluralistic society, individuals hold different religious, philosophical, and moral beliefs. *See* John Rawls, *Political Liberalism* (Columbia University, 1993), 29–32. Nevertheless, to coexist, it is necessary to find an "overlapping consensus" on what principles will be embraced and used to develop social institutions. *See, e.g.*, Rawls, *supra* note 1, at 340.

192. *Id.* at 10–11. Different thinkers, including Hobbes, Locke, Kant, and Rousseau, endorse the social contract approach but arrive at very different results. They are all, however, subject to the same criticism: that they rely on a state of nature or a contract that never existed, and thus citizens and governments cannot be bound by it. As Dworkin says: "A hypothetical contract is not simply a pale form of an actual contract; it is no contract at all." Dworkin, *Taking Rights Seriously*, *supra* note 169, at 151. However, as Dworkin notes, it is possible to view the social contract not primarily as an agreement, actual or hypothetical, but as an intellectual exercise for arriving at certain moral fundamentals. *Id.* at 169. Accordingly, the idea of a state of nature is invoked to model the moral views of individuals rather than to describe a historical precondition. Rawls, *supra* note 1, at 11 ("[T]he original position of equality corresponds to the state of nature in the traditional

condition and had to decide which principles should govern their society, they would have reasonably chosen his principles.[193]

Rawls arrives at his principles of justice based on his interpretation of the "original position."[194] The Rawlsian original position is a hypothetical—as opposed to a historical—event, in which individual representatives of society (the "deliberators" or "negotiators") decide on the principles that will guide the political order of the future, emerging state.[195] The deliberators are free, equal, and rational individuals who represent all segments of society, but lack knowledge of their own abilities or status in it.[196] They are acquainted with basic theories of human psychology, economics, and social structure, to the exclusion of their own particular views or psychological characteristics.[197] Thus, according to the Rawlsian original position, the deliberators are situated in a nonbiased, yet educated, sphere. They are, as Rawls puts it, behind a "veil of ignorance."[198]

According to Rawls, people are committed to the idea of a good life, which may be advanced through the pursuit of whatever life plans they have.[199] Rawls posits that the resources most needed to carry out this commitment are called "primary goods."[200] Only social primary goods can be distributed by social institutions. These goods are the result of social cooperation and include, among other things, income, wealth, opportunity, power, rights, and liberties.[201] In choosing the principles of justice, the deliberators seek to maximize their access to social primary goods.[202] The deliberators understand that mutual cooperation increases the possibility of pursuing their individual goals, encouraging them to establish social alliances.[203] Positioned behind a

---

theory of the social contract. This original position is not, of course, thought of as an actual historical state of affairs, much less as a primitive condition of culture. It is understood as a purely hypothetical situation characterized so as to *lead* to a certain conception of justice") (emphasis added). The Rawlsian hypothetical contract is therefore a way of understanding a certain conception of fairness, and a way of realizing the consequences of that conception for the social order.

193. Rawls, *supra* note 1, at 12; *see also id.* at 123–30.

194. *Id.* at 11, 15–19.

195. *Id.* at 10; *see also id.* at 11 ("This original position is not, of course, thought of as an actual historical state of affairs, much less as a primitive condition of culture. It is understood as a purely hypothetical situation").

196. *Id.* at 11 ("Among the essential features of this situation is that no one knows his place in society, his class position or social status, nor does any one know his fortune in the distribution of natural assets and abilities, his intelligence, strength, and the like. I shall even assume that the parties do not know their conceptions of the good or their special psychological propensities"). Rawls asserts that in choosing principles of justice, the deliberators' natural fortune and social circumstances should not enter into the process. Thus, he characterizes the original position as "the appropriate initial status quo." *See id.* at 10–12.

197. *Id.* at 119; *see also id.* at 74.

198. *Id.* at 118; *see also id.* at 11.

199. *Id.* at 10–11, 54, 131–32.

200. *Id.* at 54. There are two kinds of primary goods: social and natural. The second kind of goods, "natural primary goods," includes health, intelligence, vigor, imagination, and natural talents. Natural primary goods are affected by social institutions, but are not directly distributed by them. *Id.*

201. *Id.* at 54–55.

202. *Id.*

203. *Id.* at 4. In the process of optimizing the access to social primary goods, conflicts over the allocation of goods are expected to occur. *Id.*

veil of ignorance, each deliberator remains oblivious to her place in society and is expected to be sympathetic to a wide spectrum of interests.[204]

It becomes clear, therefore, that to maximize social benefits, the deliberators must seek long-term societal stability.[205] The deliberators are accordingly interested in eliciting the willing cooperation of all members of the society,[206] making the coming together of mutual interests inherent to the Rawlsian design.[207] According to Rawls, assuming a veil of ignorance and rational self-interested deliberators "achieves much the same purpose as benevolence" because the deliberators must identify with other individuals and consider their interests as their own.[208] In this manner, agreements made in the original position put individuals on a level playing field so that the original position naturally yields an egalitarian starting point for the political order under consideration.[209]

Rawls reasons that because the deliberators are morally equal, unaware of their status in the society to emerge and their personal talents and other characteristics, each deliberator will agree to an equal access to social primary goods.[210] Rawls assumes risk-averse behavior, prescribing that each deliberator be unwilling to gamble on ending up disadvantaged.[211] However, the deliberators can enlarge the societal pie if some individuals are provided better access to social primary goods than others.[212] For this reason, a self-interested pursuit of the best possible life prospect gives rise to the deliberators accepting

---

204. *Id.* at 120–21.

205. *Id.* at 6.

206. *Id.* at 13–14. The desire to elicit the willing cooperation of all members of the society is central to the Rawlsian analysis even when the allocation of goods that one receives according to the resulting order will be less than he would have originally desired. *Id.* at 13.

207. *Id.* at 12–13. Rawls admits to modifying the original position in order to make sure that it yields principles that match common intuitions of fairness. While Rawls at times claims that the construction of the original position has no necessary bearing on his resulting principles of justice, in other places he acknowledges that the two are interdependent. *Id.* at 18 ("[W]e have a choice. We can either modify the account of the initial situation or we can revise our existing judgments, for even the judgments we take provisionally as fixed points are liable to revision. By going back and forth, sometimes altering the conditions of the contractual circumstances, at other[] [times] withdrawing our judgments and conforming them to principle, I assume that eventually we shall find a description of the initial situation that both expresses reasonable conditions and yields principles which match our considered judgments duly pruned and adjusted").

208. *Id.* at 128; *see also id.* at 12–13, 153–56 (prescribing that the life plans of each individual are important in and of themselves, so that no representative will be willing to agree to a principle that allows anyone to be used and sacrificed to achieve someone else's goals).

209. *Id.* at 55, 65–66, 86–93, 130.

210. *Id.* at 118, 130 (explaining it would be rational for each individual interested in furthering his life plans to accept a greater than an equal share, but irrational to accept anything less).

211. *Id.* at 144. Some economists explored social interactions in similar terms of gambling. *See, e.g.,* John C. Harsanyi, *Cardinal Utility in Welfare Economics and in the Theory of Risk-Taking,* 61 J. Pol. Econ. 434, 434–35 (1953); Abba P. Lerner, *The Economics of Control: Principles of Welfare Economics* (MacMillan, 1944), xiii; William Vickrey, *Measuring Marginal Utility by Reactions to Risk,* 13 Econometrica 319, 324-28 (1945); John C. Harsanyi, *Cardinal Welfare, Individualistic Ethics, and Interpersonal Comparisons of Utility,* 63 J. Pol. Econ. 309, 316 (1955). However, the introduction of risk aversion may weaken the moral merit of Rawls's theory to the extent that the resulting distribution stems from a utility maximization calculation rather than from the premise of equal worth.

212. Rawls, *supra* note 1, at 130–31. For example, when additional incentives are provided for those accomplishing a socially desirable task, more of that task might be pursued, making everyone better off.

some discrepancies in the access to social primary goods, leading to a societal order more complex than a strictly egalitarian one.

Rawls hypothesizes that the deliberators select what he calls "the difference principle."[213] According to the difference principle, "[a]ll social values — liberty and opportunity, income and wealth, and the social bases of self-respect — are to be distributed equally unless an unequal distribution of any, or all, of these values is to everyone's advantage."[214] Any difference — that is, any inequality in the access to social primary goods — is just only if it serves to improve the lot of the worst-off members of society. Stated another way, in the original position the deliberators agree to some disparity in the access to social primary goods on the condition that the most disadvantaged individuals are made better off under an unequal, rather than equal, distribution.[215] The difference principle is hence set to ensure that the deliberators optimize their access to social primary goods in case they end up at the bottom of the social ladder,[216] while allowing them to also optimize this access under alternative scenarios (the maximin strategy).[217]

Notwithstanding the general supremacy of Rawls's difference principle, inequality in what Rawls calls "natural primary goods" — including health, intelligence, and other inherited traits — is not subject to the difference principle.[218] Rawls, for example, argues for the justness of equality in economic opportunity. This includes, particularly, "equal chances of education and culture for persons similarly endowed and motivated."[219] Accordingly,

---

213. *Id.* at 65–70, 131.

214. *Id.* at 54.

215. *Id.* at 65, 68. More specifically, Rawls's general rule comprises three components arranged according to a principle of "lexical order." *Id.* at 37–38. This order prescribes that some social goods are more important than others and cannot be sacrificed to improve their distribution. For that matter, equal access to liberty takes precedence over equal access to opportunity, which is more important than equal access to resources. *Id.* at 38. Within each category, inequality is allowed only when it benefits the least well off. *See id.* at 65.

216. *See, e.g.,* Musgrave, *supra* note 176, at 16–17 (explaining that under the veil of ignorance, the problem of distributive justice becomes one of choice under uncertainty and depends on individuals' levels of risk aversion. Assuming extreme risk aversion, maximin distribution, which maximizes the welfare of the least advantaged members of society, will be chosen. A utilitarian view of distribution as a matter of rational choice is thus retained under Rawls's design, but only after incorporating the veil of ignorance paradigm).

217. Rawls, *supra* note 1, at 72–73 (although rejecting the equalization of the difference principle with the "maximin criterion" as the latter may imply extreme attitudes toward risk); *see also id.* at 133. Imagine the following distributive scheme in a three-person world: (1) 9: 6: 0; (2) 10: 3: 2; (3) 5: 5: 5. Rawls's principles make a case for option (3) if the likelihood to be in the best or the worst position in society is unknown. Under the third option, ending up in the worst position still gives those at the bottom more than they would receive occupying the bottom of options (1) or (2). It is difficult, however, to assess the rationality of gambling without knowing something about the probability of ending up with each choice, or about people's inclination to risk. Such doubts come back to the claim that Rawls arrives at the difference principle only because he designs the veil of ignorance so as to yield it. *See supra* note 207. *Cf.* Lawrence G. Sager, *Pareto Superiority, Consent, and Justice,* 8 Hofstra L. Rev. 913, 921–22 (1980) (arguing that the worst off should prefer inequality if there is a chance for a better position but no chance for a worse one). On the one hand, Rawls is opposed to large accumulations of wealth, and this presumably extends to unequal distributions of wealth even when the poor are not made worse off. On the other hand, it is possible to argue that the Rawlsian paradigm is not sufficiently egalitarian in that it may allow significant wealth and income disparities as long as the position of the worse off is improved to some, even if minor, extent.

218. Rawls, *supra* note 1, at 54; *see also id.* at 69.

219. *Id.* at 243.

individuals not similarly endowed and motivated may be unable to enjoy the same opportunities as others. When the underlying distribution is just, inequality in the allocation of resources that results from voluntary exchanges under the conditions of fair competition is also allowed.[220] However, in a free market economy, inequality in natural characteristics generally leads to other forms of disparity. If a naturally gifted pianist and an ungifted person are each given an equal opportunity to play in an orchestra, for example, the former would outperform the latter. In a market economy, the naturally endowed individual—the person who is healthier, more intelligent, and more imaginative —is more likely to receive a higher-paying job and be in a better position to provide a good life for her family and other loved ones. Not oblivious to this predisposition, Rawls states that too much inequality is inherently offensive as it undermines social institutions, including individuals' right to equality of opportunity.[221]

Equal opportunity puts individuals on a level footing so that their lives are shaped based on the choices they make rather than on arbitrary circumstances.[222] In Rawls's view, natural talents and social circumstances are a matter of luck that yields no moral entitlement. In Rawls's words: "No one deserves his greater natural capacity nor merits a more favorable starting place in society."[223] Moreover, social institutions are "put in jeopardy when inequalities of wealth exceed a certain limit; and political liberty likewise tends to lose its value, and representative government to become such in appearance only."[224] Rawls relies on either transfer payments or a negative income tax structure to prevent too much inequality.[225] He, nonetheless, avoids clarifying how much inequality is too much. Rather, at one point Rawls suggests that the limits of inequality are "a matter of political judgment guided by theory, good sense, and plain hunch."[226]

To conclude, Rawls reasons that from behind a veil of ignorance, people would agree on principles of general equality with the goal of maximizing the

---

220. *Id.* at 57–58, 131; Nagel, *supra* note 4, at 2016 ("Rawls always emphasizes that the main target of evaluation for his principles of justice is the basic structure of society, which determines the ex ante allocation of opportunities and expectations at birth. If the basic structure is fair, then inequalities arising through the free exercise of their autonomy by individuals living out their lives inside that structure are not objectionable from the standpoint of justice").

221. Rawls, *supra* note 1, at 245–46. Unfortunately, Rawls leaves the idea of equality of opportunity fairly undeveloped, allowing major controversies in its interpretation. Kymlicka, *supra* note 78, at 56 (finding that although people generally accept the principle of equality of opportunity, they differ on the issue of its implementation. "Some people believe that [enforcing] non-discrimination in education and employment is sufficient [to comply with such a requirement]. Others argue that affirmative action programmes are required for economically and culturally disadvantaged groups, if their members are to have a genuinely equal opportunity to acquire the qualifications necessary for economic success").

222. RAWLS, *supra* note 1, at 16.

223. *Id.* at 87. Rawls states that the conditions that characterize the original position should not be misunderstood. The idea is to clarify the restrictions most reasonable to impose on principles of justice. "Thus it seems reasonable and generally acceptable that no one should be advantaged or disadvantaged by natural fortune or social circumstances." *Id.* at 16.

224. *Id.* at 246.

225. *Id.*

226. *Id.* (in the context of limiting inherited wealth). *Cf.* Neil H. Buchanan, *What Do We Owe Future Generations?*, 77 GEO. WASH. L. REV. 1237, 1279 (2009) ("The concerns that motivated Rawls . . . were not simply a matter of looking at who had the smallest incomes and trying to help those individuals by transferring resources to them from those with more to give. He was not,

welfare of the worst-off members of society. This egalitarian undercurrent requires political intervention in the workings of the market economy.[227] Read in this light, the Rawlsian theory of justice provides a standard against which the fairness of both the pre- and posttax distributions of resources is to be evaluated. In a society structured in accordance with the Rawlsian rules of justice, the purpose of taxation is "to preserve an approximate justice in distributive shares" and "raise the revenues that justice requires."[228] In a society not structured in accordance with the Rawlsian rules of justice, the tax system takes on an additional role of redistribution intended to ensure that the after-tax allocation of resources complies with the fundamentals of the theory.[229]

Because the free market economy and competitive prices do not take human needs into account, raising revenue becomes a means to level the playing field and provide for certain societal basics, including freedom of political thought and equality of opportunity in education.[230] Therefore, a society structured in accordance with the Rawlsian doctrine applies constant adjustments.[231] Such adjustments bear the risk of reducing the size of the societal pie. This, however, does not necessarily undermine Rawls's theory of justice given that the main goal of the Rawlsian society and its institutions is to aid in the establishment of justice more than to maximize total welfare.[232]

In a system that evolves from a just distribution, Rawls appears to prefer a proportional consumption tax to raise revenue.[233] Rawls argues that such a structure treats all individuals equally and taxes what is taken out of the common pool rather than what is productively added to it.[234] Rawls nonetheless admits that progressive tax rates may be necessary to prevent harmful accumulations of resources and protect equality.[235] It is unclear, however, whether strong arguments for a progressive tax structure emerge from Rawls's

---

in other words, advocating some mechanical and arbitrary narrowing of living standards for its own sake. He was instead concerned that the least fortunate were excluded from full participation in society").

227. RAWLS, *supra* note 1, at 62–63 (stressing the importance of fairness considerations more than efficiency constraints).

228. *Id.* at 245–46.

229. *Id.* at 245. For instance, if the pretax distribution of income, a Rawlsian social primary good, fails to satisfy the difference principle, the tax system can then be the mechanism utilized to ensure that the after-tax allocation of income is just. This could be achieved through collecting revenues from well-off taxpayers and transferring these funds to the least advantaged.

230. *Id.* at 244 (asserting that ensuring social minimum is necessary because "[a] competitive price system gives no consideration to needs and therefore it cannot be the sole device of distribution").

231. *Id.*

232. *Id.* at 64–65.

233. *See, e.g., id.* at 246 ("Leaving aside many complications, it is worth noting that a proportional expenditure tax may be part of the best tax scheme").

234. *Id.* The justness of taxing consumption goes all the way back to the work of Thomas Hobbes. Hobbes, *supra* note 111, at 179. Several authors have more recently advocated in favor of consumption taxation. *See generally* Joseph Bankman and David A. Weisbach, *The Superiority of an Ideal Consumption Tax over an Ideal Income Tax*, 58 STAN. L. REV. 1413 (2006); Joseph Bankman and David Weisbach, *Consumption Taxation Is Still Superior to Income Taxation*, 60 STAN. L. REV. 789 (2007); Daniel Shaviro, *Beyond the Pro-Consumption Tax Consensus*, 60 STAN. L. REV. 745 (2007); Edward J. McCaffery and James R. Hines Jr., *The Last Best Hope for Progressivity in Tax*, 83 S. CAL. L. REV. 1031 (2009).

235. Rawls, *supra* note 1, at 246.

framework.[236] In fact, the theory might be too general to favor any one particular form of taxation over another.[237]

SUMMARY AND CONCLUSIONS

This chapter explores three theories of normative analysis and the manner in which these theories may inform tax policymaking in a modern society. Regardless of their specific differences, the normative perspectives presented here crystallize the idea that what individuals can expect to receive in fair return for their labor and capital depends on the merit of the pre- and post-tax distributions of resources in society. This merit is evaluated differently by each of the normative doctrines. All three theories, however, raise questions and employ analytic tools essential to public and, particularly, fiscal policymaking.

According to the theory of entitlement, the principles of natural or divine law entitle each person to the benefits gained from the exercise of free will and effort. Followers of this paradigm usually embrace unaltered the pretax distribution of resources and any proceeding rewards obtained through voluntary exchanges. To some, the justness of private entitlement and, accordingly, the existing distribution of resources, is self-evident. Others find justification by asserting the moral deservedness of reward for effort or the importance of incentives created under a system of entitlement. Still others emphasize individuals' rights and liberties and, more generally, the prospect of mutual advantage. Regardless of one's perspective on either the Lockean or more modern Nozickean interpretation, those who adhere to the entitlement paradigm believe that safeguarding the right to private property and, thereby, the existing distribution of holdings, is a necessary step in determining the role of the government in civil society. Entitlement theorists, then, offer a framework from which to analyze government authority, particularly to intervene in the private affairs of individuals, including through the levy of taxes.

The entitlement theory does not prescribe that people's possessions should be equally distributed, nor does it follow other predetermined distributional ends. Rather, the theory prescribes that the pretax distribution of resources is just if it represents the product of an unfettered market economy. This includes, for example, distributions that are the result of unequal bargaining relationships, such as those involving natural monopolies and cartels. According to certain interpretations of entitlement, taxation deprives individuals of their right to autonomy. Even without extending the entitlement concept to

---

236. An insightful analysis that involves the application of the Rawlsian doctrine to the tax system is offered by Musgrave. *See* Musgrave, *supra* note 176, at 16–17 (applying the maximin analysis while taking into account the announcement effects of taxation).

237. *See, e.g.*, Byrne, 1995, *supra* note 8, at 777; *cf.* Rawls, *supra* note 1, at 246–47; *but see* Sugin, *supra* note 8, at 1993–94 (suggesting that "[r]ather than searching in theories of justice for required precepts of taxation, we might more fruitfully ask what constraints, if any, a particular theory of justice imposes on the tax system. Application of such an approach to Rawls's theory of justice may explain his apparent preference for a flat consumption-based tax. . . . If Rawls's discussion of economic justice is treated as offering limitations rather than mandates for taxation, then a variety of tax systems may be part of a just Rawlsian society").

this degree, entitlement theorists discourage most forms of taxation and especially those tax schemes aimed at redistribution, because the imposition of taxes is expected to violate (at least some) rightfully held property rights. However, the entitlement doctrine does not disqualify all forms of taxation and redistribution.

Entitlement theorists advocate for strong civil, especially property, rights and for the value of the political order in protecting its citizens and enabling the workings of a market economy. To this end, taxation is required as a means, at the very least, of raising the revenue needed to fund society and its institutions. Additionally, the doctrine fails to account persuasively for the justness of entitlement to the entire share of returns on labor and capital and may, therefore, allow for some portion of market returns to be redistributed. It can be argued that a portion of these returns is the product of luck, societal conditions, or infringements in the workings of the free market economy, such as holdings tainted by force or deception. This portion, the argument goes, ought to be redistributed to a more just destination than that which is created under the status quo. Advocates of the Lockean paradigm may endorse redistribution as long as it ensures that effort invested is rightfully, but not excessively, rewarded and economic incentives remain at an efficient and effective level. Likewise, for the Nozickean doctrine to maintain integrity, its proponents ought to accept some redistribution, even if reluctantly, when this allows the rectification of past injustices in the acquisition or transfer of holdings. For these reasons, although the entitlement doctrine precludes very progressive tax structures, it may allow for other, less aggressive, schemes.

In developing a different line of thinking, Bentham and his followers depart from the entitlement premise. Instead of reaching out to a natural or divine order, utilitarianism turns to reason, simplicity, and the pursuit of happiness and utility. The underlying principle of utilitarianism is that all individuals and society as a whole are dominated by two forces: pleasure and pain. The first is good and should be pursued, while the second is bad and must be avoided. The key goal for people and governments becomes the pursuit of the greatest good for the greatest number while placing pleasure and pain on the same metric of utility. Because marginal utility declines as income rises, traditional utilitarianism suggests that aggregate utility is maximized by an equal — as opposed to unequal — distribution of resources. On a public policy scale, this objective leads to the demand for an equalization of resources among members of the society. The tax system that develops under this premise prescribes a redistributive (i.e., progressive) tax structure so that whatever the pretax distribution of resources may be, the after-tax allocation aims at maximum equality. However, a more profound examination of the theory and its repercussions reveals that absolute equality might be an undesirable goal for society.

Inequality, at least to some extent, provides an important incentive for economic productivity, making absolute equalization an unwise societal aspiration. Moreover, the assumption of a fixed amount of resources, which can be equally divided among members of society, was also refuted. Modern utilitarianism clarifies that taxation can negatively affect market production by reducing the gain from productive effort. This effect, and its distribution across households and individuals, is difficult to estimate. For this reason, taxation might not only distort economic activity and reduce the societal pie and total revenue raised but could also treat similarly situated taxpayers differently. According to a more modern interpretation of utilitarianism, as it applies to taxation, the after-tax loss in utility from taxation and the after-tax gain in utility from revenue raised must be comparable with a minimal loss in aggregate utility and, overall, net gain in social welfare. Unfortunately, although this interpretation of utilitarianism solves a number of issues concerning the cost associated with taxation and redistribution, serious doubts remain concerning the merit of the theory. Specifically, by focusing on aggregate utility, utilitarianism might allow the subordination of moral and social considerations to efficiency constraints, resulting in tax systems that put individuals in a position where they are used as means for others, rather than as equal beings and ends in themselves.

More recently, attempts have been made to rationalize the implementation of what is known as the social welfare function. The social welfare function is reached by artificially constructing a collective function based on value judgments about the desirable distribution of resources in society. It aspires to weigh fairness considerations independently from efficiency constraints, while taking both into account. The feasibility of disjointedly analyzing these issues is, nevertheless, questionable. Even more troubling is that there is little agreement on how the social, political and economic considerations, which ought to guide the construction of the social welfare function, are to be revealed and implemented with consistency and integrity.

Finally, the Rawlsian doctrine suggests that the principles to guide the political system should be decided from behind a veil of ignorance. In contrast with entitlement theorists, Rawls offers a hypothetical — rather than historical — starting point where representative men and women gather to lay down the principles of justice to govern the society expected to emerge. The representatives are rational, mutually disinterested, risk-averse individuals, seeking to further their own life plans and unaware of their particular characteristics or status in the emerging society. Drawing on the risk-averse assumption, a maximin solution is derived. In other words, according to Rawls the general principle that will be unanimously decided from behind the veil of ignorance is the equal distribution of chances to acquire social primary goods, including income, wealth, power, and opportunity, coupled with the difference principle. Rawls's difference principle prescribes that inequality in the distribution of chances to acquire primary social goods may be tolerated only to the extent that it improves the lot of the least advantaged members of society. Further, while Rawls allows for some disparity, he argues against "too much inequality" and calls for using the tax system to constantly correct the market distribution of resources in addition to its revenue-raising function.

To conclude, under all three normative theories explored in this chapter, a person living in civil society can reasonably expect to receive only a net reward for his effort and capital: the gross amount of returns less taxes raised for the maintenance of the existing societal order and its institutions. If the pretax distribution of resources is without merit, however merit is conceived by each of the theories, individuals should expect the levy of additional taxes as a redistributive measure. Accordingly, the one conclusion consistent with all three normative theories is that a key role for taxation is to intervene in the free market economy, at the very least, for the purpose of raising revenue.

Whether it is based on rewarding effort but not luck or societal conditions, rectifying past injustice, maximizing utility, or fairness considerations, some form of redistribution of resources can also be justified. The degree of government intervention and the level of redistribution ultimately depend on society's views on social and, especially, distributive justice and the efficiency cost of policy implementations. Accordingly, the extent to which the present tax discourse avoids incorporating a well-defined normative framework concerning the meaning and attainment of justice, alongside efficiency-based analyses, is both puzzling and disturbing. While this chapter does not claim that normative perspectives can be agreed upon or proven, it suggests that a candid and comprehensive elaboration of normative beliefs and values and how they shed light on taxation would lead to a better understanding of society and an improved tax system. This, in the long run, may bring society closer to the realization of tax policies that are normatively worthy and socially, politically, and economically within reach.

In a modern democracy that is diverse and constantly changing, policy issues are likely to raise a mix of normative perspectives. Moreover, a tax structure that fits certain societal conditions might be unworkable in others. By embracing the coexistence of normative beliefs — rather than searching for one ideal theory — various tax structures can evolve. Fairness considerations drawn from the Rawlsian doctrine could, for instance, support adjustments to the pretax resource distribution, either through tax expenditures or the finance of spending programs directed toward the less fortunate. At the same time, entitlement theory can justify shying away from extreme levels of taxation. Utilitarianism may add depth to both perspectives by emphasizing the value of redistribution in increasing societal welfare on the one hand while underscoring the efficiency cost of going too far with equalization on the other. In the process of generating a viable tax discourse, fundamental disagreements about normative perspectives are likely to arise. These issues tend not to be the focus of tax analysis and debate. However, as this chapter illustrates, if tax policy is to evolve in a clear and effective manner, these underlying beliefs and assumptions should be made the subject of serious discourse — sooner rather than later.

III

STATE AND
LOCAL TAXATION

CHAPTER 3

SOME REFLECTIONS ON THE MERITS OF THE PROPERTY TAX

James Charles Smith, University of Georgia School of Law

Although the property tax has an ancient pedigree, the levy continues to generate steady streams of criticisms and reform proposals. Consider three examples from 2008. In Georgia, House speaker Glenn Richardson announced a plan to eliminate most school property taxes,[1] replacing lost revenues with a broader sales tax, to apply to services as well as goods. Richardson's proposal would have ended the preferential treatment of groceries under the Georgia sales tax. His bill was hotly debated during the 2008 legislative session. Amendments substantially trimmed the scope of the bill, substituting a cap on local government property tax revenues for outright repeal but calling for a repeal of the property tax on automobiles. The Georgia House voted in favor of the revised bill, 110-62, but this was ten votes short of the 120 needed to pass a constitutional amendment. "Republican leaders vowed to use the vote as a campaign issue this fall."[2]

In Florida, a proposed constitutional amendment denominated "Amendment 5" calls for the elimination of all property taxes earmarked for schools. Revenues for schools would be kept intact, with funds provided by a combination of a one-cent increase in the state's six-cent sales tax, other budget cuts, and a menu of undetermined other taxes. Florida property owners would receive a tax cut of about 25 to 40 percent, depending on where they live. Backers of the measure include the Florida Association of Realtors, which has pledged $1 million to help promote the amendment. A number of groups have formed to oppose the plan, and the courts are also involved. A coalition of teachers, school boards, businesses, and farm groups has filed a lawsuit challenging Amendment 5.[3]

---

1. James Salzer, *Critics: School Tax Cut Flawed*, Atlanta Journal-Constitution, Dec. 29, 2007, at A1.
2. Mike Billips, *House Rejects Proposed Property Tax Plan*, Macon Telegraph, March 6, 2008.
3. Mary Ellen Klas & Nirvi Shah, *Florida Tax Debate: Swap One Tax for Another? 2 Sides Making Their Cases*, Miami Herald, July 23, 2008.

In Colorado, a statute passed in 2007 called for a freeze in property tax rates. At first blush, a "tax freeze" sounds like good news to property owners, but the actual purpose was to increase revenues for local school districts due to the impact of rising property values throughout Colorado. Normally, Colorado local governments would have reduced mill levies (the tax rate) to account for the rising property values, to hold tax revenues constant. The freeze was estimated to result in increased local taxes of $117 million in 2008 and nearly $3.8 billion over 10 years. The state government planned to reduce its funding for schools and divert the savings to fund other programs. After a group of taxpayers filed suit, in May 2008 the trial court struck down the statute as unconstitutional under the state Taxpayer's Bill of Rights, which requires statewide voter approval for tax increases. Governor Bill Ritter is appealing the decision to the state supreme court.[4]

The controversies surrounding property tax reforms in Georgia, Florida, and Colorado are not exceptional. Rather, the opposite holds true. Such proposals reflect business as usual, and similar stories about property tax battles regularly appear in most of the other forty-seven states. This feature is characteristic of the history of the property tax in the United States. States constantly tinker with their property taxation systems, usually in small, incremental ways, occasionally devising larger changes.

Modern battles over property taxation often focus on the connections between how taxes are raised and what the government spends tax dollars for. Certain taxes fund certain programs. In most systems, a significant portion of ad valorem taxes is used to fund public schools. It does not have to be this way; state income taxes, sales taxes, or other taxes could fund public schools, and property taxes could fund the operations of state governmental agencies.[5] Does this make a difference theoretically? This takes us back to a consideration of the philosophical justifications for taxation. Is there a need to justify the property tax by reference to the government's use of the property tax revenues? To state the point another way, should the characteristics of the property tax system depend, to some extent, on the use of tax proceeds? Conventional analysis divorces evaluation of the tax from the government's spending of tax revenues, treating them as separate spheres of inquiry,[6] but in the field of property taxation, the predominance of local taxing matched to local spending invites mutual consideration.[7]

---

4. John Ingold, *Court Chills Mill-Levy Freeze: State Promises Quick Appeal*, Denver Post, June 1, 2008.

5. Indeed, at the beginning of the twentieth century, property taxes were the source of more than half of state tax revenues; a century later they constituted less than 2 percent of state tax revenues. *See* Jerome R. Hellerstein and Walter Hellerstein, *State and Local Taxation: Cases and Materials* (8th ed., Thompson West, 2005) 6 (Table 3). Property taxes remain the mainstay of local government revenues, contributing nearly three-quarters of such revenues, although they once were the source of substantially all local tax revenue. *Id.* at 8-9 (Table 4).

6. One exception is the work of Charles McLure, who has written about the "tax assignment" problem — namely, figuring out what type of tax is most appropriate for what level of government in a federal system. *See, e.g.*, Charles E. McLure Jr., *The Tax Assignment Problem: Ruminations on How Theory and Practice Depend on History*, Nat'l Tax J. 54 (2001).

7. The benefit theory of property taxation, discussed *infra* at notes 26-30 and accompanying text, is one consequence of attempting to rationalize the tax by reference to the services it funds.

THE NORM OF FAIR MARKET VALUE

The underpinning of modern American property tax systems is the concept of fair market value. An owner owes a tax that is proportional to the "fair market value"[8] of the taxable property, which fluctuates over time. Most tax systems provide, in principle if not always in practice, for annual assessments based on the property's value. This fundamental feature is why property taxation is often called *ad valorem* taxation—that is, according to value. Although the concept of taxation based on fair market value is simply stated, ambiguities and practical difficulties arise frequently, whenever the property in question is not of a type frequently sold on markets in transactions that yield ascertainable prices. Countless tax disputes concern the assessment of real property, with numerous administrative tribunals and courts forced to make decisions that are often hard.[9] In addition, political pressures on assessing authorities can lead to variations from the fair market value standard for particular classes of property (e.g., residential).

The fair market value paradigm is so deeply engrained in U.S. practice that we tend to take it for granted, almost as a "natural law" of property taxation. Historically, however, property taxation did not necessarily include the concept of value. British and colonial taxes were often levied on specified classes of property, on what may be called a "unit basis." A person paid a property tax according to the number of livestock owned, or there was a set tax per house.[10] The value concept developed in the New England colonies for land shortly before the American Revolution, but at the time of the Revolution the middle and southern colonies generally taxed land at a set amount per acre.[11] Taxation on an ad valorem basis did not become entrenched until the nineteenth century. It is easy to see, intuitively, the appeal of this fundamental concept. If one accepts the premise that a tax burden ought to have some correlation with the taxpayer's ability to pay, why should the same tax be levied on every acre of land within a jurisdiction; or on every house; or on every automobile? Everyone knows such assets have widely disparate values, and an owner of the more valuable asset should be expected to shoulder a larger tax burden. Although the norm of taxation according to ability to pay is deeply engrained,[12] and justifiably so, implementation by means of value assessment has proven to be difficult to attain in practice. The remainder of this essay examines the degree to which the fundamental concept of value-based taxation properly serves as a cornerstone for the tax system.

---

8. As a technical matter, the owner owes a tax based on the assessed value of the property, but the assessed value is ordinarily pegged (at least in principle) to fair market value.

9. *See generally* Hellerstein, *supra* note 5, at 124-191.

10. *See* Robert A. Becker, *Revolution, Reform, and the Politics of American Taxation, 1763-1783* (Louisiana State University, 1980), 7 (practice followed in many colonies of taxing land equally by the acre worked to the advantage of large, wealthy landowners); Glenn W. Fisher, *The Worst Tax? A History of the Property Tax in America* (University Press of Kansas, 1996) 23-24.

11. Glenn Fisher, *supra* note 10, at 22-24.

12. Becker claims that "by 1763 [this norm] had become so self-evident a truth in New England that few public men dared deny it, but as with most self-evident truths, they had some difficulty determining what it meant in a practical way." Becker, *supra* note 10, at 8.

SEVERAL CRITICISMS OF THE PROPERTY TAX SYSTEM

THE CORRELATION BETWEEN THE PROPERTY TAX AND ABILITY TO PAY IS WEAK

Does ability to pay rationalize the property tax? Conventional wisdom makes this claim.[13] The principal justification for tethering property taxation to property value is said to be fidelity to the concept of taxing based on ability to pay. Nevertheless, the actual fit between ability to pay and property taxation as practiced in the United States is poor. The fit is tenuous for two reasons. First, real property is taxed the same, based on value, whether or not the owner is using the property to generate income. Thus, there is no match between revenue generated by a property and the tax that is due. Consider, for example, Property *A* and Property *B*, both of which have a present fair market value of $1 million. Property *A* is rented to a tenant, and generates an annual net rent of $60,000. Property *B* is undeveloped rural land, which presently generates no income. Standard property taxation imposes the same tax on the owners of both properties, notwithstanding the fact that the owner of Property *A* is able to pay a tax out of the net income generated by the property, and the owner of Property *B* has no such ability whatsoever.[14] In a loose sense, the capital value of property may be a proxy for a property's income, but it is a highly imperfect proxy. The property tax does not take account of the income, if any, that the taxpayer has from which he can pay the tax: neither the income generated from the property nor the taxpayer's income, more generally, from all sources.

Second and more importantly, the fit between tax and ability to pay is weak because the property tax is assessed regardless of how much equity the owner has in the property. Consider two identical houses, each with a market value of $200,000. One is owned free and clear; the other is subject to a mortgage loan for 95 percent of value — that is, $190,000. The mortgage, of course, requires substantial monthly payments to amortize the debt. The owner of the unencumbered real property has a far greater ability to pay a property tax, yet the two owners pay the same tax. Because the property tax does not take account of mortgage debt on the property, there is very little, if any, correlation between the owner's ability to pay and property tax assessments. In principle, fidelity to the tax performance criterion of ability to pay means that all property owners should pay based on their net equity in property, not based on the gross value of property. In other words, if ability to pay is the governing norm, the property tax as we know it should be transformed into a tax on net wealth.[15]

---

13. Glenn Fisher, *supra* note 10, at 349-57 (theory that property tax is levied on value of capital).

14. *See* Hellerstein, *supra* note 5, at 97 ("a tax on nonliquid assets presents special difficulties" because it "requires payment even from owners who have experienced no increase in net wealth, either through property appreciation or income").

15. Historically, the failure to adopt property equity as the tax base was justified by the fiction that the property tax is "not a personal tax" levied on the landowner but a tax imposed on the land. Edwin R. A. Seligman, *Progressive Taxation in Theory and Practice* (2d ed., Princeton University, 1908), 306.

There is a counterargument for the house example that is worth considering. Perhaps the owner of the mortgaged house, who pays the "full tax" despite that fact that his property value is only $10,000, is in effect paying a property tax based on the mortgagee's property interest. Real property tax systems could impose a tax upon holders of secured debt, but in the United States they have rarely done so.[16] Arguably, the owner of the mortgaged house is no better off if he is taxed only on his equity *and* the mortgagee is taxed on its ownership interest, because the mortgagee will bargain for passing on its tax to the borrower. Even if that is true, it is no justification for taxing gross property value, rather than net property value. What it demonstrates is not the fairness of taxing the full value of mortgaged property to the equity owner as a proxy for taking the mortgagee, but that all interests in real property, including mortgages, should be taxable, if any interests are taxable.

Consider, for example, the owner of a $200,000 parcel of real property, which is (i) subject to a judgment lien for $190,000, or (ii) subject to a conservation easement, which reduces the appraised property value to $120,000. In the first case, the owner is in the identical position, concerning value, as the owner of the house with a $190,000 mortgage. Observe that the owner of the judgment lien, if taxed on its interest, will not be able to "pass on" the tax to the owner. In the second case, our existing property tax system gives the owner a tax break, imposing the tax only on the net value of $120,000. Property taxation could treat the mortgage scenario and the conservation easement scenario the same way. There may be a good policy reason for the distinction (i.e., a desire to subsidize conservation easements); my point is that there the differential treatment cannot be supported based upon comparative ability to pay.

Comparison to the federal income tax system is instructive. A person engaged in business or another profit-seeking activity pays a tax based upon the net amount of income, not upon the gross receipts. Costs and expenses are deducted from receipts to arrive at net income. If we hypothesize an "income tax" system that allows no deductions for business costs and expenses, we have a very different system, which few people (if any) would find defensible, at least as an "income tax" based on "ability to pay."[17] Yet a property tax system that looks to gross property value, rather than net value, is in principle no different from an "income tax" system that allows no deductions for costs and expenses,

---

16. More than a century ago, some states did tax mortgage holders, evidently on an annual basis. *See* Seligman, *supra* note 15, at 306 (tax systems "generally tax the landowner on the full value of the land, and very frequently tax the mortgagee in addition on the amount of the mortgage"). Under the practice described by Seligman, if neither the landowner nor the mortgagee is given a credit on account of the property right owned by the other, in effect double taxation results.

17. Such a system might well be defended as a sensible means of raising revenue, although others would disagree. Witness the debate over Ohio's recent substitution of a Commercial Activities Tax—essentially a tax on gross receipts—for its corporate net income tax. *See, e.g.,* Alana Shockey, *Trade-Offs and the Waiting Game: Ohio's Commercial Activity Tax*, State Tax Notes, June 30, 2008, at 1035.

assuming that one would still describe such a tax as an "income tax," rather than a gross receipts tax.[18]

THE PROPERTY TAX BASE IS TOO SMALL

The tax base is too small in several respects. First, in most states, little or no personal property (other than personal property attached to land as fixtures and, in a number of states, automobiles) is subject to property tax. Real property wealth represents a diminishing fraction of societal wealth, and that decline began as long ago as the Industrial Revolution in the nineteenth century. In preindustrial communities, land represented a large fraction of total wealth. Personal property consisted chiefly of goods, which for most people were not highly valuable. Intangible personal property, such as stocks, bonds, and other types of investment property, were not a significant part of agrarian-centered economies. In modern economic systems, a major tax system, such as the property tax, that ignores most of the potential tax base is anachronistic and inequitable.

Years ago, prior to widespread use of the income tax, advocates for a property tax limited largely to real property justified their position by observing that personal property taxation was harder to administer than real property taxation. Tangible personal property was portable and often hard for government employees to locate and verify, and intangible personal property was even harder to detect and assess. Owners of personal property, it was thought, would engage in massive underreporting of their assets.[19] Although today there would still be significant hurdles to administer a comprehensive personal property taxation system, the hurdles are no different in kind from those faced and managed by the income tax system.[20] To pay a tax on income, taxpayers must in principle report financial details with respect to their transactions involving financial assets, and the Internal Revenue Service (IRS) takes steps to enforce the tax laws by measures such as requiring financial institutions and other market participants to report to the government details of transactions undertaken by asset owners. Historically, many states in principle sought to tax all property, including intangible personal property, but such efforts failed

---

18. As a technical matter, one might describe such a tax as a "gross income" tax. It would be described as a gross receipts tax only if in addition to denying deductions for the "expenses" of generating income, it also denied a deduction for "costs of goods sold." *See* Treas. Reg. §1.61-3 ("'gross income' means the total sales, less cost of goods sold").

19. *See* Seligman, *supra* note 15, at 305:
Our attempt to tax intangible personalty leads to a heavier burden on those who are the same time honest and fairly well-to-do than on those who happen to be dishonest and wealthy. Since the temptations to evade the tax are likely to grow with its size, it may be assumed that fraud will increase in proportion to wealth . . . . Progressive taxation of personalty under actual conditions would be an utter delusion.

20. In light of the well-publicized problems the Internal Revenue Service has encountered with taxing foreign-source income earned by U.S. taxpayers—particularly in connection with income from intangibles sourced in tax haven jurisdictions—some would argue that the income tax system is not "managing" this issue effectively. *See, e.g.*, Adam H. Rosenzweig, *Why Are There Tax Havens?*, 52 Wm. & Mary L. Rev. 923 (2010).

because of the unwillingness or inability of local administrators to assess and tax property other than real estate.[21]

The second shortcoming with respect to the tax base size is that in all states the property tax base does not even succeed at capturing all wealth consisting of real property. A large variety of exemptions remove much real property that could be taxed. Not only is most publicly owned property exempt from property tax,[22] but exemptions also extend to different types of privately owned real property, most of which are thought to serve charitable purposes. Churches, for example, are generally exempt from tax, and in some states veterans' organizations are exempt.[23]

In many states, as a result of the efforts of special interests that lobby the state legislature, commercially valuable real estate is exempted or given significant tax breaks. For example, timber and other properties with natural resources often are exempt from paying annual taxes, with the tax deferred, being calculated and payable only upon severance of the resource.

To attract or retain industry, states often extend tax abatements to firms that build major new facilities, such as automobile manufacturing facilities and sports stadiums, or rehabilitate existing facilities. Those abatements can be worth millions of dollars and often extend for as long as fifteen or twenty years. Tax abatement reduces property tax for firms that build new facilities or rehabilitate existing ones. The mechanics of how the tax abatement works can vary. New improvements may be exempt from taxation; or the overall tax on the developed property may be frozen at a specified dollar amount; or the tax may be set at a reduced percentage of the normal tax on an asset of that class; all for a specified term of years.

By failing to tax most personal and real property, the states are compelled to apply a much higher tax rate on nonexempt real property than would apply if the states reached a robust tax base. This outcome makes the property tax more susceptible to public criticism, and it raises equity concerns because property owners who own little or no real property avoid the tax. Substantial homestead exemptions in many states exacerbate the equity problem.

PROPERTY TAX ASSESSMENT RATIOS AND RATES VARY ACCORDING TO PROPERTY TYPE

The tax assessment ratio and rate are often not uniform, despite a state constitutional base that in most states historically required uniform

---

21. *See* Ajay K. Mehrotra, *Forging Fiscal Reform: Constitutional Change, Public Policy, and the Creation of Administrative Capacity in Wisconsin, 1881-1920,* 20 J. of Policy History 94, 97-98 (2008).

22. One exception is public housing, which, being publicly owned, is not taxed directly. Public housing authorities are obligated to make payments in lieu of taxes (PILOT) payments to the local governments where their dwellings are located. The purpose is to reimburse the government for services it provides to the public housing communities, such as police and fire protection.

23. E.g., Ga. Code §48-5-41(14)(A) ("Property which is owned by and used exclusively as the headquarters, post home, or similar facility of a veterans organization"). A 2006 amendment, approved by referendum, extended the veterans' exemption to property used exclusively "for the purpose of refurbishing and operating historic military aircraft acquired from the federal government and other sources, making such aircraft airworthy, and putting such aircraft on display to the public for educational purposes." *Id.* §48-5-41(14)(B).

taxation.[24] The traditional principle of uniformity of taxation of all property is honored more in the breach than in the observance. Modern state systems usually divide property into a number of classifications, such as residential, industrial, commercial, agricultural, or timberland, and apply different rates to the various classes. For example, all states have some method to limit property taxes on agricultural land. The traditional approach, used in twenty-seven states, limits the value to its current use (this can be determined by capitalizing the profits generated by farming activities on the land). A variation, now used by thirty-one states, taxes agricultural land according to its current use but imposes a deferred tax on the full market value for a fixed number of years if the property is converted to a nonfarm use.[25]

From the standpoint of tax efficiency, a small tax base and differential tax rates are troublesome. An efficient tax system is one that achieves neutrality by avoiding inducements that cause people to alter their behavior solely on account of the tax consequences of their actions. In terms of neutrality, the ideal property tax system does two things: tax all property, and apply the same tax rate to all property. This is considered to have the virtue of allowing economic resources to be allocated to those most valuable uses. For reasons of administration, such an ideal is perhaps not possible to achieve; but the point, if one cares about economic neutrality, is to minimize rather than maximize departures from the ideal, which induce economic distortions.

In all U.S. states, departures from the ideal of taxing *all property* at the *same rate* are monumental, not modest. Personal property is seldom taxed, and the real property tax system usually consists of a complex hodgepodge of rules for various types of real property. This affects behavior, as people consider what types of property to acquire and whether to improve existing property that they own. With respect to real property, the capacious exemption of personal property causes underinvestment in real property and overinvestment in personal property. Similarly, there is overinvestment in exempt or preferred real property, compared to other real property. This results in an allocation of resources that is inefficient, meaning that societal wealth is diminished as a consequence of the property tax system.

THE PROPERTY TAX SYSTEM PROBABLY IS REGRESSIVE

It appears to me that modern property tax systems are regressive in nature. There is an enormous literature analyzing whether particular taxes are regressive or progressive,[26] and there is no one agreed-upon definition or measure of regressivity or progressivity. The general idea is that a regressive tax is one that falls more heavily upon poorer people, and a progressive tax is one that falls more heavily upon richer people.[27] The most common definition uses income

---

24. In some states (e.g., South Carolina), property tax classification (i.e., assessment of different property at different percentages of fair market value) is embodied in the state constitution. S.C. Const. art. X, §1.

25. Ronald C. Fisher, *State & Local Public Finance* (3d ed. Thomson/South-Western, 2007), 344.

26. For a short discussion and several references, *see* Hellerstein, *supra* note 5, at 98-102.

27. *Id.* at 99 (a regressive tax takes "a larger percentage" of the income of low-income taxpayers "than it takes from those with higher earnings").

as the metric for comparison, asking whether the tax burden on individuals rises or falls as their income rises.[28]

Presently there is no strong consensus among economists as to whether the property tax is generally regressive, proportional, or progressive. For the majority of the twentieth century, most economists contended that "the property tax is on balance somewhat regressive when compared to current money income."[29]

The Consumption Theory

The conclusion that the property tax is regressive followed from what is known as the consumption theory of property taxation. This theory embraced the proposition "that property taxes operated as excise taxes on commodities and increased the price of the taxed goods."[30] Under this view, the property tax affects housing markets by increasing the cost of housing consumed. For non-housing, the tax increases the cost of goods or services produced using the property that is taxed. In other words, the property tax is a tax on consumption of the property itself.

The Capital Value Theory

The consumption theory came under attack in the 1970s, with economists led by Henry Aaron asserting that the property tax was a type of "capital value" tax.[31] Gradually this view became mainstream dogma, reaching the point where "it is now the predominant new conventional wisdom about the property tax among many economists."[32] The capital value tax theory challenged the view that the burden of the property tax attached to consumption, claiming instead that it reduces income from capital ownership, thereby reducing capital value. When the property in question is land, with or without improvements, the tax reduces the fair market value of the land. Real property tax rates vary considerably in the United States, as they are set by state and local governments acting individually, and capital value tax proponents have attempted to explain the economic effects stemming from differences in tax rates. They have concluded that

> If capital is perfectly mobile, while workers and consumers are perfectly immobile, the tax-rate differential causes lower wages and land values and higher prices for locally produced consumer goods (housing) in the higher-tax jurisdictions as compared to the lower-tax ones. If workers, consumers, and capital are perfectly mobile, any tax-rate differential lowers the value of land in the higher-tax jurisdictions as compared to the lower-tax rate jurisdictions.[33]

---

28. Ronald Fisher, *supra* note 25, at 297.
29. E.g., Dick Netzer, *Economics of the Property Tax* (Brookings Institution, 1966), 40.
30. Ronald Fisher, *supra* note 25, at 358.
31. Henry J. Aaron, *Who Pays the Property Tax? A New View* (Brookings Institution, 1975).
32. *See* Hellerstein, *supra* note 5, at 100-101; Ronald Fisher, *supra* note 25, at 358.
33. *Id.* at 370.

The Benefit Theory

A rival theory, the benefit view of the property tax, emerged to challenge both the consumption tax theory and the capital value theory. The benefit theory considers only the real property ad valorem tax and does not purport to speak to taxes on other forms of property. It focuses on the property tax's role as the prime source of revenue for local governments, and like the capital value theory considers as important the diversity in local tax rates. Under the benefit theory, property owners contract with their local governments to provide services, such as schools, police protection, roads, public parks, and running trails.[34] The benefit theory assumes that residents (taxpayers) are mobile and that their decisions on where to live are influenced (if not determined) by the amount of the property tax and the services that the tax "buys."[35] Thus, the benefit approach sees the property tax as a market exchange, in which taxpayers bargain to acquire local services, and not really as a "tax" at all.

Weaknesses of the Three Theories

Neither the capital value theory nor the benefits theory adequately explains why the property tax is not regressive. For residential rental housing, the capital value theory implies that the property tax reduces landlords' profits and therefore does not result in an increase in rents paid by tenants. This is theoretically possible, but it is hard to believe that none of the cost is passed on. An issue with some parallels concerns the effect on rents of vigorous governmental enforcement of housing codes, either through administrative enforcement or by courts. Economists here are split, with many recent scholars, including Judge Posner, concluding that code enforcement often leads to either rent increases or disinvestment by owners in their housing stock, including abandonment.[36] Proponents of the capital value theory have not attempted to explain how the property tax affects owner-occupiers. Most Americans own their own homes, and a homeowner is both a producer of housing (an owner of capital) and a consumer of housing. Thus, the capital value theory is able to shed no light whatsoever as to whether the property tax applied to homeowners is regressive, proportional, or progressive.

Proponents of the benefits theory tout their approach as demonstrating that the property tax is not regressive,[37] apparently because it is in exchange for services and is paid voluntarily to the local government of the taxpayer's choice. Yet the basic insight of the theory — that the tax is paid in exchange for local services

---

34. *See* Hellerstein, *supra* note 5, at 101.

35. *See* George R. Zodrow, *Reflections on the New View and the Benefit View of the Property Tax,* in Wallace E. Oates (Editor), *Property Taxation and Local Government Finance* (Lincoln Institute of Land Policy,. 2001), 79, 85 ("the combination of interjurisdictional competition . . . and perfectly mobile consumers 'voting with their feet' ensures that local communities are homogeneous with respect to individual demands for local public services").

36. Richard Posner, *Economic Analysis of Law* (6th ed. Aspen, 2003), 482-85. For a contrary view, *see* Bruce Ackerman, *Regulating Slum Housing Markets on Behalf of the Poor: Of Housing Codes, Housing Subsidies, and Income Distribution Policy,* 80 Yale L.J. 1093 (1971).

37. *See* Hellerstein, *supra* note 5, at 101 ("The benefit view alters the entire context for regressivity studies. If the property tax is the price for a bundle of local services, the net burden of the tax can only be determined by comparing what is paid with what is received."); Zodrow, *supra* note 35, at 105 ("the benefit view argues that the tax involves no redistribution").

that the taxpayer presumably values more than the amount of the tax — seems beside the point. Every tax can be said to be a payment to a government in exchange for government-provided services, including the federal income tax; and that perspective logically says nothing about the income or wealth characteristics of the people who end up paying the tax. Moreover, calling the property tax "voluntary" also has nothing to do with whether it is progressive or regressive. Intuitively, we tend to view some taxes as "voluntary" and other taxes as "involuntary" or compulsory. To the extent that this feature is relevant, a more precise analysis would place taxes on a spectrum from "voluntary" to "involuntary." One can avoid a tax on alcoholic beverages, cigarettes, lottery tickets, or luxury automobiles by not buying the goods. Although we tend to view an income tax as involuntary, a person can stop earning income by quitting work and putting a stop to other activities that generate income. Death taxes are much harder to avoid, except, of course, by the decedent! Such classifications, however, have nothing to do with the determination of the wealth or income characteristics of the payors of a particular tax. Some people may consider a tax that is regressive and voluntary (e.g., the cigarette tax, regressive because lower-income people tend to smoke more than higher-income people and devote more of their income to the tax; but it is questionable how voluntary the tax is for those addicted to nicotine) to be fairer than a tax that is regressive and involuntary (e.g., a poll tax[38]); but again, a voluntary tax with a certain regressivity index is just as "regressive" as an involuntary tax with the same regressivity index.

All three theories — the consumption theory, the capital value theory, and the benefit theory — are theoretical propositions about economic effects and the behavior of affected participants. In principle, empirical research could shed light on their comparative merits in describing real-world tax effects; however, no definitive empirical studies exist, and it is uncertain whether it is possible to design such studies in a fashion that would make them sufficiently reliable.[39] The extant empirical work on property taxes yields no firm conclusions as to incidence of the tax or regressiveness/progressiveness. For example, a 2003 study conducted in Dallas County, Texas, concluded that total residential "property taxes combined are approximately proportional" to the owners' income, but that school taxes were proportional or slightly progressive, and city taxes were regressive (i.e., lower-income cities tended to have higher property tax rates).[40]

In the absence of solid empirical work, one must evaluate the property tax by focusing on what we do know about the features of the tax system and the wealth characteristics of those who pay the tax (the taxpayers).

For two reasons, modern U.S. property tax systems appear to me to be regressive. First, the tax rate is a flat percentage of assessed value, and the percentage does not increase as property value increases, in contrast to the federal income tax and most state income taxes. This amounts to a proportional tax, if taxable

---

38. A poll tax is an equal tax imposed on natural persons, such as $100 per adult.

39. The literature focuses on the economic effects of differential real property tax rates and seeks correlations between the overall rate of tax (high or low) and the income levels of residents. A persuasive empirical study would compare local governments with no property taxes, but which are the same in all other respects, with local governments with property taxes. No such pairs of local governments exist in the United States.

40. Elizabeth Plummer, *Evidence on the Incidence of Residential Property Taxes Across Households*, 56 Nat'l Tax J. 739 (2003).

real property is viewed in isolation. But if we seek to determine whether the tax is progressive, proportional, or regressive by looking at the property owner's entire income (not just income produced from real property), the property tax is likely to be regressive from the standpoint of many individuals. Lower-income and middle-income people often hold a large fraction of their wealth as equity in personal residences. Higher-income people do tend to own more expensive residences, but they have a greater share of their wealth in other personal property assets, which generate (or may generate) income.

Second, almost all states (forty-six plus the District of Columbia) have homestead exemptions or credits, which are available only to homeowners.[41] In some states, the exemption is a fixed dollar amount that functions to forgive the tax from a specified dollar amount of property valuation, with the excess taxable at the normal rate applicable to residential real estate.[42] In over half the states the homeowner is entitled to the homestead exemption regardless of income level or age.[43] In some states, the homestead exemption is not a specified dollar amount but a set percentage of fair market value. Instead of a homestead exemption, some states offer a credit. If the credit applies to the property tax itself, it operates much like an exemption; the difference is that the credit is a fixed dollar amount of tax benefit, but the value of the exemption varies according to the tax rate (millage rate) for each year. In some states, the homestead credit is funded by the state government as a credit against the state income tax. Thirty-three states have "circuit-breaker" homestead provisions, giving relief to lower-income owners or to disabled owners,[44] either as their only type of homestead tax relief or as a supplement to a homestead provision available to all homeowners. With a circuit breaker, the taxpayer is entitled to a tax benefit when the property tax exceeds some specified percentage of the taxpayer's income. Usually the benefit is a rebate or a refundable credit applied to the state income tax.[45]

Homestead exemptions discriminate against renters, who as a group are less wealthy than homeowners. A handful of states have alleviated the discriminatory effect of homestead exemptions by enacting tax relief for residential tenants,[46] but such measures are not widespread.[47]

---

41. Ronald Fisher, *supra* note 25, at 339.

42. In Georgia, for example, the standard homestead exemption is $2,000. Because properties are assessed at 40 percent of fair market value, the exemption has an actual value of $5,000. Some Georgia counties have set a higher exemption by local legislation, and additional exemptions are available for elderly homeowners, disabled veterans, and survivors of owners who served in the military or as law enforcement officers or firefighters.

43. Ronald Fisher, *supra* note 25, at 339 (27 states "allow the exemption broadly for taxpayers of all ages").

44. *Id.* at 340-41.

45. *See* Glenn Fisher, *supra* note 10, at 193-94.

46. A few states confer tax benefits on residential tenants to compensate for the unavailability of a property tax deduction. Indiana, for example, allows a renter's deduction equal to the lesser of the actual amount of rent paid or $3,000. Indiana Dep't of Revenue, Information Bulletin #38 (May 2008), available at http://www.in.gov/dor. Legislation raised the maximum deduction from $2,500 to $3,000 beginning in 2008. The tenant must use the dwelling unit as his principal residence and the dwelling must be subject to Indiana property tax. *Id.*

47. Long ago, the noted economist Edwin R.A. Seligman persuasively demonstrated that it is not practically possible to devise a progressive method of general property taxation without making drastic changes to the fundamental tenets of property taxation. Seligman, *supra* note 15, at 305-9.

Even if I am correct that the U.S. property tax is generally regressive, that characteristic does not necessarily condemn the tax. For more than a century, scholars have debated the merits of progressive taxation, as compared to proportional or regressive taxation; and among those who in general support progressive taxation, there is no consensus as to *how* progressive a particular tax ought to be (i.e., only slightly progressive, moderately progressive). In listing the regressive nature of the property tax in this essay as a criticism, I have disclosed my position that progressive taxation is generally good public policy[48] and that regressive taxes are often socially undesirable; but I acknowledge that others disagree.[49]

MERITS OF THE PROPERTY TAX SYSTEM

Are there any merits in the present property tax system, as practiced in most states? Four possible virtues are worthy of consideration.

THE PROPERTY TAX SYSTEM FACILITATES LOCAL GOVERNMENTAL AUTONOMY

The property tax constitutes, by far, the major source of revenue for local government: in 2004, 73.2 percent of the tax revenues of local governments came from the property tax.[50] Heavy reliance upon the property tax by local governments is not new. Early in the nineteenth century, most states assigned the bulk of governmental responsibilities to their local governments, reflecting the Jeffersonian ideal that control of taxing and spending by local citizenries would make government responsive to the people.[51] In thirty-four states, the state government also levies a tax on real property,[52] but it is generally much smaller than the local property taxes. The other sixteen states have no statewide property tax on real property.[53]

Not only is the property tax the primary source of local government revenues; it is subject to local control. Payments are made directly to the local government, and the tax is administered by local government. This confers upon local governments a degree of autonomy in their decision making. Today there is less autonomy in most states than there was in the past, due to state laws, statutory and constitutional, that circumscribe local discretion in what

---

48. The economic policy debates go back at least as far as the nineteenth century. Prior to the adoption of the U.S. income tax, Seligman campaigned for progressive taxation. See his classic work *Progressive Taxation in Theory and Practice* (1894; 2d ed., Princeton University, 1908).

49. *See* Hellerstein, *supra* note 5, at 98 (not stating a position, but noting that revenue sources such as cigarette taxes, general sales taxes, and lotteries "may be very regressive," but they are often politically popular and considered by many to be fair).

50. U.S. Census Bureau, The 2008 Statistical Abstract, Table 441, Local Governments— Revenue by State: 2004, available at http://www.census.gov/compendia/statab/cats/state_local_govt_finances_employment.html.

51. *See* Glenn Fisher, *supra* note 10, at 206.

52. Michael F. Lorelli, *Special Report: State and Local Property Taxes* (August 2001, No. 106). Washington, D.C.: Tax Foundation.

53. Since 1982, the Texas Constitution has prohibited statewide ad valorem taxes. Tex. Const. Art. 8, §1-e: "No State ad valorem taxes shall be levied upon any property within this State."

property to tax and how much to tax it. For example, many local governments are subject to state-mandated ceilings in millage rates and are forced to follow statewide exemptions for certain types of properties and for certain property owners. For example, local governments generally lack the freedom to decide whether to give a homeowner a homestead exemption and, if so, how much.

Despite such restrictions on local taxing autonomy, local governments still set the property tax and collect it directly. If local governments lost their "power of the purse strings," their budgets could remain intact if state governments replaced their property tax revenues with equivalent funds. The state, of course, could choose to allow local governments a great deal of freedom with the money it supplies — as much as they now enjoy with respect to property tax revenues — but that is unlikely for political reasons. There is something innately attractive about exercising control over money when you voluntarily pass it on to another entity or person. Federal funds provided to state and local governments are earmarked for specific projects. The experiment with federal revenue sharing died in 1987, as Congress succumbed to the desire to specify the use of the funds it appropriated.[54] Part of the reason was a desire of congressmen to take credit, with their constituents, for their assistance in building certain projects or infrastructure or in funding certain initiatives.

If local governments had to depend directly upon state governments for most or all of their revenues, it is highly unlikely that local governments would have the same degree of autonomy. It would prove almost irresistible for state elected officials, legislators, and executives to impose their own judgments on local governments as to how *state funds* should be spent.

One difficulty with justifying property taxation by reference to the promotion of autonomy for local governments is that it assumes the goodness of such autonomy. Whether, or under what conditions, local governmental autonomy is a virtue is a debatable proposition.[55]

THE IMMOVABILITY OF LAND MAKES THE PROPERTY TAX RELATIVELY EASY TO ADMINISTER

Local governments are able to tax property effectively and comprehensively, when they confine their efforts to real property, because land is immovable. Every local government, by definition, governs a geographical area that is relatively small. The real property tax base cannot exit the jurisdiction. From the government's perspective, it is a captive asset.[56] It is true that

---

54. United States government revenue sharing began in 1972, with Congress furnishing an annual amount of federal tax revenues to the states and their subdivisions. The Reagan Administration ended the program, replacing revenue sharing with block grants.

55. Arguably, local governments are more subject to capture by partisan politicians, who abuse their power, than larger governments are. The perception that local governments unfairly assessed and administered property taxes led to Wisconsin's adoption of a state income tax. Several of the leading advocates of the new income tax proposed that it completely replace property taxation, but instead the State retained both. The new income tax was rationalized as a replacement of taxing personal property. *See* Mehrotra, *supra* note 21, at 95, 103-5.

56. The immobility of land also results in two significant additional administrative advantages. The problem of multiple jurisdictions asserting the authority to tax the same asset is avoided, and the local government is able to collateralize the owner's obligation to pay the tax by invoking a tax lien. *See* Hellerstein, *supra* note 5, at 97.

owners of real property can affect the tax base by choosing to invest, or disinvest, in improvements to real property, but they cannot take their land elsewhere.[57] Other potential sources of tax revenue have the characteristic of mobility (i.e., the ability to exit the taxing jurisdiction) to some degree. Sales tax revenues may decline if retailers shift their operations to other nearby jurisdictions or if many local residents choose to shop elsewhere, substituting out-of-town or Internet purchases for local purchases. If a local government imposes a local income tax, its employment base may stagnate or decline for a number of reasons, including decisions of residents to move elsewhere, even if they do not alter their source of income. Likewise, personal property taxation may be compromised by the flight of personal property, whether tangible or intangible, out of the reach of the local jurisdiction. Thus, compared to the other principal tax alterative, the real property tax is especially suitable for the local generation of tax revenues because land and improvements are immobile.

THE PROPERTY TAX IS A PROXY FOR EXTENSION OF THE INCOME TAX TO REACH IMPUTED INCOME

The property tax system serves as an antidote to an income tax loophole: the problem of imputed income. Homeowners who occupy their residences are not required to report income based upon the value of possessing their property. A property tax levied on a homeowner, in economic effect, is a tax on the imputed income attributable to that property.

IN STATES WITHOUT AN INCOME TAX, THE PROPERTY TAX IN EFFECT TAXES INCOME GENERATED BY PROPERTY

Forty-one states have a broad-based income tax; seven states have no income tax, and two (New Hampshire and Tennessee) tax only limited types of income.[58] In these states, the property tax serves as a proxy for an income tax. The proposition may not be obvious, but it follows from a consideration of what it means, economically, to levy a tax that is a percentage of property value. A property has value because it has the capability to produce rents. Rents, therefore, are a function of property value, and a tax on value is no different from a tax on rents, provided we adopt a sufficiently broad definition of rents.

---

57. It is well acknowledged that taxing improvements as well as land creates an incentive for landowners to refrain from adding improvements, or to "underimprove" their land (i.e., add less valuable improvements than they would but for the tax on improvements). This insight underlay Henry George's famous call for the land tax, which would impose zero tax on structures and a high rate on land (sufficient to raise the desired revenues). Because the supply of land is fixed (perfectly inelastic), arguably a higher land tax does not affect landowners' behavior. Some states have adopted a weak version of George's proposal by taxing land at a higher rate than structures.

58. The states without an income tax are Alaska, Florida, Nevada, South Dakota, Texas, Washington, and Wyoming. Hellerstein, *supra* note 5, at 929.

CONCLUSION

An evaluation of the merits of the property tax, as presently administered in the United States, is a task necessarily comparative in nature. If one accepts the inevitability of government, then taxes are a necessity. As Benjamin Franklin observed, "In this world nothing can be said to be certain, except death and taxes."[59] Thus, it makes little sense to ask, in the abstract, whether the weaknesses of the property tax outweigh its strengths. Instead, the relevant question is whether other existing tax mechanisms, such as the income tax and the sales tax, are comparatively better. My conclusion is that both competitors are substantially better, despite their own flaws.

In terms of the costs of administration, the sales tax appears the least expensive to administer. The typical transaction is a merchant's sale to a buyer, with a price paid in dollars, resulting in an easy calculation of the proper tax; and the merchant is charged with remitting the tax to the appropriate governmental unit. Income taxation presents significantly greater administrative challenges. Taxpayers self-report their income, and other facts, such as family characteristics and deductible expenses, bear on calculation of the proper tax. Yet for individual taxation in the United States, a large percentage of income is reflected in payments of fixed amount of dollars, usually withheld and reported by the payor to the IRS, making it easy for the government to check taxpayer returns to verify the reporting of such income. The property tax system has to overcome a unique administrative hurdle, not shared by the sale tax or the income tax. The property tax depends upon the value of the real property, and it is not determined by examining the particulars of a transaction engaged in by the taxpayer during the tax year. Ideally, fair market value should be redetermined by the taxing authority, at least annually.[60] It takes sophisticated tax assessors, with access to current and reliable market date, to assess all of a jurisdiction's parcels of real property. That assessment, along with the millage rate, produces an amount of tax presumptively owed by the taxpayer. That step is not conclusive for all taxpayers, however, because a taxpayer has the right to challenge the assessed value. Many owners do challenge assessments, often succeeding in convincing an official or an administrative body that a lower assessment is justified. Undoubtedly, many times when taxpayers succeed in lowering their assessments, they have produced evidence that objectively justified the reduction, but there is a perception that in many counties taxpayers prevail not because the initial assessment was "wrong" but because of favoritism shown to a politically influential taxpayer or for some other reason. Similar challenges to the amount of a sales tax or an income

---

59. Letter to Jean-Baptiste Leroy, 1789, reprinted in *The Works of Benjamin Franklin* (1817).

60. An ideal property tax system (which would be impossible to administer) would redetermine property value continuously. In other words, in lieu of picking one calendar date (such as January 1 or July 1) for assessing value, the government would measure the value of a parcel of land for each of the 365 calendar days in a year and average those values. One may assert that in practice, such fine-tuning would not significantly change actual tax outcomes. Real estate values, however, can fluctuate markedly, although they are more stable than oil futures and stock prices. They also fluctuate dramatically due to the construction and destruction of improvements, whose value is not accounted for properly in jurisdictions that tax based on a single annual assessment date.

tax do not arise, because there is an objective yardstick for measurement in the vast majority of transactions that give rise to a tax.

With respect to equity, the property tax is deficient compared to the income tax, because it is more likely to be regressive in nature. An income tax is not necessarily progressive; its progressivity depends upon the tax's characteristics, including tax rates, types of deductions allowed, and credits. In general, however, the federal income tax and most state income taxes are more progressive than the property tax, because they commonly use graduated tax rates (i.e., taxpayers with higher incomes pay a higher percentage of their income to the government than taxpayers with lower incomes do).

There do not appear to be significant differences between the property tax and the sales tax with respect to progressivity and regressivity. Both are generally flat rate taxes, applied to determined values. Generally, richer people will buy more expensive goods and pay more sales tax, and buy more expensive real property and pay more property tax, than the less well-off. Both types of tax systems can include measures that make them more progressive. A sales tax system can reduce the rate, or exempt the tax, on "necessities" such as groceries and drugs, and it can impose higher taxes on luxury goods. Similarly, homestead exemptions can be crafted to give significant tax relief to homeowners who have relatively inexpensive homes, while retaining hefty taxes on expensive residences.

The political value of the promotion of local governmental autonomy is hard to quantify. In principle, local governments could replace property tax revenues with local sales taxes, local income taxes, or both, provided states amended their laws to allow such measures. This is an experiment that might work, or might fail, but it is worth noting that in our long history, it apparently has not been tried anywhere in the United States. Perhaps the reason is that despite recurrent criticisms of the property tax and occasional reforms spurred by so-called tax revolts, most Americans accept the property tax. We have had it with us since the founding of our nation, and people find it tolerable though not pleasurable. To eliminate the property tax means either a drastic cut in government services or a replacement by other taxes, such as increases in sales or income taxes of the development of a new tax of some sort. Many people, if asked whether they would like the property tax repealed, would be all for it, but if they were told they'd have to pay the same amount in higher sales or income taxes, they would be less keen on repeal. If they were risk-averse, they might also consider the possibility that repeal would produce both gainers and losers, and they might be among the latter, who would pay a higher replacement tax than their property tax savings. Although the property tax appears to be inferior to its alternatives, viewed from the perspectives of policy and administrative cost, it has persisted due to tradition and political acceptance.

IV
NONPROFIT
ORGANIZATIONS

CHAPTER 4

A NORMATIVE RATIONALE FOR THE CHARITABLE INCOME TAX EXEMPTION

David A. Brennen, University of Kentucky
College of Law

What is the normative rationale for the federal income tax exemption for nonprofit charitable corporations? Even though the exemption dates back to 1894, Congress has failed to rationalize it fully.[1] Though scholars and courts have attempted over the years to come up with a coherent rationale for the charitable tax exemption, their attempts are focused almost exclusively on economic efficiency. Thus, the charitable tax exemption is typically framed by noted tax scholars such as Boris Bittker and Henry Hansmann as an economically efficient means of providing certain goods and services to the public.[2] Hansmann's theory of exemption is particularly noteworthy because he positions his theory as an explicitly economic rationalization for the charitable tax exemption that accounts for the bulk of so-called "public goods" provided by charities. However, even Hansmann's broadly accepted economic theory of the charitable tax exemption has been challenged, principally on non-economic grounds.[3]

No matter how appealing economic efficiency might seem, it is axiomatic that law, and more particularly tax law, is about much more than economic efficiency. Tax law is about broader conceptions of justice, fairness, and other aspects of a democratic society that extend beyond economic principles. For example, even though the federal estate tax burden is borne almost exclusively by wealthy taxpayers, its temporary repeal has been promoted politically as, alternatively, an end to the death tax and an end to a tax on small family farms. The references to "death" and "family" are presumably intended to evoke

---

1. *See* Revenue Act of 1894, ch. 349, §32, 28 Stat. 509, 556; *see also* Revenue Act of 1909, ch. 6, §38, 36 Stat. 11, 112; Revenue Act of 1913, ch. 16, §2(G), 38 Stat. 114, 172.

2. *See, e.g.,* Boris Bittker and George Rahdert, *The Exemption of Nonprofit Organizations from Federal Income Tax*, 85 Yale L. J. 299 (1976); Henry Hansmann, *The Rationale for Exempting Nonprofit Organizations from Corporate Income Taxation*, 91 Yale L. J. 54 (1981).

3. *See, e.g.,* Rob Atkinson, *Altruism in Nonprofit Organizations*, 31 B.C. L. Rev. 501 (1990); Rob Atkinson, *Theories of the Federal Income Tax Exemption for Charities: Thesis, Antithesis, and Synthesis*, 27 Stetson L. Rev. 395 (1997); Nina J. Crimm, *An Explanation of the Federal Income Tax Exemption for Charitable Organizations: A Theory of Risk Compensation*, 50 Fla. L. Rev. 419 (1998); Evelyn Brody, *Of Sovereignty and Subsidy: Conceptualizing the Charity Tax Exemption*, 23 J. Corp. L. 585 (1998).

emotionally (as opposed to efficiency) based opposition to a tax imposed during a distraught time such as death or a tax imposed on hard-working farm "families." Likewise, the tax exemption for charities is about much more than money, economics, or optimal/efficient profit. Instead, the charitable tax exemption is principally about accomplishing a values-based mission. That mission may at times be at odds with the notion of a pure profit motive that dominates the private market narrative.

While efficiency analysis may be relevant to some aspects of conceptualizing a charitable mission, there are many other non-economic aspects of such a mission that may not be based on economic principles. Traditional economic analysis may, for example, aid in understanding the exemption's economic impact. However, efficiency alone simply does not fully explain the varied and rich non-economic aspects of the charitable tax exemption. In emphasizing the distinctive characteristics of nonprofits, including tax-exempt charities, from for-profit organizations, Professor Robin Paul Malloy has explained

> [N]on-profits generally seek to promote values that are difficult to measure in economic terms. The non-profit framework, therefore, raises some important cultural-interpretive issues. The focus on values, and the rejection of a pure profit motive, are two very important points of divergence from the conventionalized norms expressed in our private market narratives.[4]

Accordingly, this chapter offers a framing of the tax exemption that serves as an alternative to the long-standing economic theories of many tax scholars. The chapter demonstrates that a principal normative justification for the exemption, in addition to economic efficiency, is what this chapter calls "contextual diversity." Though "diversity" is often used to denote a goal or aim of the charitable tax exemption (i.e., to diversify the marketplace), "contextual diversity" is intended to focus attention on a principled type of diversity that considers social context (such as impact of achieving diversity through affirmative action as opposed to color blindness).

This chapter first founds a normative explanation for the exemption on Malloy's law and market economy theory (LMT). LMT addresses the relationship among law, markets, and culture. As an illustration of the difference between traditional law and economics and LMT, this chapter addresses the way in which LMT is compatible with critical race theory (CRT, a mode of examining the law for hidden biases or unexplained assumptions along race, class, or gender lines) in discerning normative rationales for law. These normative rationales enable richer reflections of justice, fairness, and equality, values that are not necessarily reflected in positive economics or efficiency.

Second, this chapter presents a theory of the charitable tax exemption that is in line with LMT and based on the value of diversity. "Contextual diversity" references alternative understandings of LMT to build on insights of traditional economic analysis and to present an alternative rationale for the charitable tax exemption. Using contextual diversity as a principal value-based rationalization for the charitable tax exemption not only captures the essence

---

4. Robin Paul Malloy, *Law in a Market Context: An Introduction to Market Concepts in Legal Reasoning* (Cambridge University, 2004), 214.

of the exemption but also provides direction for potentially reforming and reinventing this area of the law.

Finally, this chapter demonstrates that predominant traditional theories of charitable tax exemption do not capture the full essence of the normative aspects of the exemption. It briefly identifies some of the implications of contextual diversity theory on the structure of tax-exempt charity law.

INTERSECTIONS OF ECONOMIC AND CRITICAL THEORIES OF LAW

LMT, including its interplay with CRT, is just one example of how different theoretical approaches to law can come together to partially expose important elements of a substantive area of law. LMT is a theory of law that is based on economic principles, but that extends beyond traditional economic analysis to incorporate other humanistic values into an understanding of law and social interaction. It posits that law is more fully understood when economic analysis is combined with other analytical approaches to demonstrate the dynamic and ever-changing aspects of human interaction. This section demonstrates how traditional understandings about economic analysis of law could be diversified by accommodating other approaches to law, such as CRT. Such accommodation could lead to better, more diverse understandings of the structure of tax-exempt charity law and potentially improve future development of this area of law.

LAW AND MARKET THEORY

Traditional economic analysis of law is premised on the idea that efficiency leads to wealth maximization. Yet, economic analysis affords an incomplete means for making decisions about the proper structure of law. Indeed, law is about social interaction. Thus, law is necessarily about justice, fairness, equality, and other aspects of social existence. While economic analysis has a definite role to play, that role must account for the many other aspects of human existence aside from those that are amenable to precise scientific understanding.

One of the major failings of traditional economic analysis is the inability to theorize decision making that is not "rational" in an economic sense but yet is fully justifiable on other grounds. People often act for purely nonselfish reasons, such as out of concern for the well-being of others, out of habit, in response to tradition, or as a result of the subordinating power of others. These various reasons for human action require reference to more than economics to be properly understood. Thus, to structure laws that do not question the assumption of people as self-interested actors would not necessarily respond to real societal dynamics. Charities operate, not out of private self-interest, but instead to promote public benefit or to serve a mission. This is distinct from for-profit corporations, which operate to maximize economic profits. Therefore, attempts to articulate a rationale for the charitable tax exemption by resorting to economic analysis alone necessarily miss this important distinguishing aspect of charitable operations.

In his LMT theory, Malloy explains that efficiency and wealth maximization are inadequate measures for assessing social well-being.[5] In this regard, Malloy challenges areas of tension in law and economics' account of the primary means of wealth formation in the market and the nature of market choice. First, Malloy explains that the primary tension in LMT is between the concepts of efficiency and creativity, not between efficiency and social responsibility. There is no need to understand the counterpart of social responsibility as efficiency, because a properly functioning market incorporates an ethic of social responsibility. According to Malloy, efficiency, in law and economics terms, is grounded in the static notions of habit, convention, and continuity. Efficiency is reactive and is grounded in making the most of current understandings of the market. Creativity, on the other hand, is much more dynamic. According to Malloy, creativity is grounded in notions of potentiality, discontinuity, and indeterminacy. Thus, creativity is necessarily proactive and ever-evolving.

Second, drawing on the tension between efficiency and creativity, Malloy argues that creativity in the market is the primary means of wealth formation, not efficiency. Efficiency just cannot account for the process of creativity. Efficiency requires ideal environments based on habit-informed conventions and pre-established relational choices. Creativity, on the other hand, relies on habit-deforming and transforming exchange relationships that permit the discovery of something new and different. Creativity is by nature indeterminate, habit-breaking, and convention-challenging. Since it cannot be observed directly, creativity can be examined only by looking at the contextual communities that foster it. As Malloy explains, "One must identify the types of communities which, by ethics and social values, tend to foster diversity, experimentation, and unconventional networks and patterns of exchange."[6] These are communities that embrace inclusion and diversity and that think about the market process in terms that are broader than economic efficiency.

Third, Malloy explains that market choice involves a process of interpretation — it is not a rational or objective fact that can be determined scientifically by cost and benefits analysis, unimpacted by social influences. Rather, market choice is the result of one's interpretation of market incentives and disincentives as informed by personal experiences rather than by abstract notions of objectivity and rationality. A person's cultural biases (whether relating to race, sex, or sexual orientation, for example) have a decided impact on how she defines, interprets, and weighs the costs and benefits of a particular action. This distinction between rational choice and interpretation is a key aspect of Malloy's divergence from traditional law and economics. As Malloy explains:

> This distinction is important because the process of interpretation is community based, and because it indicates that even though exchange takes place as a

5. *See* Robin Paul Malloy, *Law and Market Economy: Reinterpreting the Values of Law and Economics* (Cambridge University, 2000), 106–35.
6. *Id.* at 3 (emphasis added).

continuous part of a dynamic system, our understanding of the exchange process is shaped by the interpretive "lens" or "screen" through which we view it. Furthermore, this lens or screen, as an indexical reference in semiotics, is grounded in a system of values informed by experience rather than by purely objective and rational choice.[7]

In essence, the reliance in law and economics on methodological individualism is flawed because it extracts the individual from the cultural interpretive community in which she is embedded. At the same time, it disconnects the individual from history and context, thus ignoring the interplay between an individual's experiences and her cultural-interpretive framework for understanding.

CRITICAL RACE THEORY

Instead of simply relying on economic principles to articulate a coherent rationale for the charitable tax exemption, traditional law and economic analysis should (and could) be combined with other analytical approaches to law in order to add a screen or lens through which to rationalize charitable tax exemption law.[8] CRT is an approach that provides this novel perspective. CRT developed in the latter part of the twentieth century as a response by progressive scholars of color to critical legal studies, which in turn was a response to legal realism.[9] Legal realists criticized the rule of law as overly formalistic, promoting, under the guise of neutrality and objectivity, a system of laws actually driven by policy, economics, and politics. Critical legal scholars took the realists' agenda a step further by describing it as not only political, but also ideological and hegemonic. As time passed, some scholars of color became disenchanted with critical legal studies because of its failure to acknowledge white supremacy and otherwise meaningfully critique racial power and racial hegemony. These scholars developed their own race-conscious approach to legal analysis, seeking to expose the legal and social construction of race itself with the goal of eradicating racial subordination.

CRT is characterized primarily by its opposition to three mainstream beliefs about racism: (1) that colorblindness will eliminate racism; (2) that racism is an individual act, not a systemic problem; and (3) that problems of racism can be addressed without dealing with other forms of societal injustice such as sexism, homophobia, or economic exploitation.[10] One of the central concepts in CRT is that race is a social construct, an idea. In other words, the concept of race occurs not naturally, but by invention in society.

---

7. *Id.* at 4.

8. Similarly, Professors Beverly Moran and Dorothy Brown have broken ground in the tax law arena by examining the federal income tax through a "colored" lens. *See, e.g.,* Beverly I. Moran, et al., *A Black Critique of the Internal Revenue Code*, 1996 Wis. L. Rev. 751; Dorothy A. Brown, *Racial Equality in the Twenty-First Century: What's Tax Policy Got to Do With It?*, 21 U. Ark. Little Rock L. Rev. 759 (1999); Dorothy A. Brown, *The Marriage Bonus/Penalty in Black and White*, 65 U. Cin. L. Rev. 787 (1996).

9. Emily M.S. Houh, *Critical Intervention: Toward an Expansive Equality Approach to the Doctrine of Good Faith in Contract Law*, 88 Cornell L. Rev. 1025, 1051, 1054–58 (2003).

10. Devon W. Carbado and Mitu Gulati, *The Law and Economics of Critical Race Theory*, 112 Yale L. J. 1757, 1766–67 (2003) (reviewing Francisco Valdez et al., *Crossroads, Directions, and a New Critical Race Theory* (Temple University, 2002)).

Understanding race as a social construct helps to explain both racial existence and racial hierarchy. Another important concept in CRT is its rejection of racial essentialism: the assumption that a particular race has a certain essence. CRT rejects this essentialist approach to race. Instead, for CRT, race is contextual. According to Kimberle Crenshaw, CRT is committed to the idea that racial identities are intersectional and that racial minorities' vulnerability to discrimination is a function of specific intersectional identities.[11]

CONNECTING LAW AND MARKET ECONOMY THEORY AND CRITICAL RACE THEORY

Malloy's LMT parallels CRT in its challenges to traditional law and economic analysis.[12] Both theories reject the primacy of efficiency as espoused in traditional economic analysis. LMT challenges efficiency from a market perspective, while CRT challenges efficiency from an equality perspective. For LMT, creativity, not efficiency, is the primary means of wealth creation in the market. Similarly, for CRT, racism is not just a problem of individual choice but instead is the result of systematic racial subordination. Thus, both theories reject the notion that law should be constructed on the calculus of individual choice. Instead, the focus should be on the diversity of societal structures that create the circumstances leading to the choice.

In addition to challenging traditional law and economics as too focused on efficiency, LMT and CRT both acknowledge the overt political nature of market actors, affirmatively acknowledging the societal/contextual influences on lawmakers, judges, and those subject to law. Traditional law and economic theory attempts to conceal many of these contextual influences by projecting an air of neutrality or objectivity through use of the science of economics. However, Malloy unmasks this charade by explaining how law and economics scholars misunderstand both the impact of racial subordination on market exchange processes and the indeterminate nature of the market exchange process.

Because CRT offers a view of social context that is just as legitimate as that offered by traditional law and economics, it seems reasonable to examine the charitable tax exemption through the dual lenses of CRT and traditional law and economic analysis. Though tax laws by nature appear readily amenable to economic analysis, this conclusion fails to take account of the uniqueness of the laws concerning charities. Unlike many laws that deal with raising government revenue, tax laws imposed on charities do not have this overt revenue-raising goal. Instead, the goal of tax laws imposed on charities is to enhance the mission of charities. In fact, it is only when a charity diverts from its mission that its tax exemption is jeopardized.[13] As one examines the

---

11. *See id.* at 1774–75.
12. *See* Houh, *supra* note 9, at 1063–66.
13. *See, e.g., Branch Ministries v. Rossotti,* 211 F.3d 137 (D.C. Cir. 2000) (litigation involving Branch Ministries' tax-exempt status instigated by Branch Ministries' ad in a national newspaper against Bill Clinton); Kelly Brewington, *NAACP Retains Tax Exemption Despite Bond's Speech, IRS Says,* Balt. Sun, Sept. 1, 2006, at A1 (discussing the IRS's challenge to the National Association for the Advancement of Colored People (NAACP)'s tax-exempt status because of its leader's speech against President Bush); Benjamin Weiser, *An Empire on Exemptions?: Televangelist Pat Robertson*

complex nature of the charitable tax exemption, one must ask: "Why are charitable corporations not required to pay income taxes?" The exemption has traditionally been rationalized on efficiency grounds. However, efficiency cannot be used to rationalize all aspects of the charitable tax exemption. What about the other conceptions of justice and fairness that are not reflected in the calculus of economic efficiency? Thus, LMT offers an analytical approach to the charitable tax exemption that helps us to better rationalize it.

In support of this proposition—that LMT permits a better rationalization of the charitable tax exemption than traditional law and economics—this chapter will do three things. First, it outlines a theory of the charitable tax exemption—contextual diversity theory—premised on LMT concepts.[14] Second, it compares and contrasts contextual diversity theory with many of the pre-1990 theories of the charitable tax exemption that are based almost exclusively on principles of traditional economic efficiency. Finally, it briefly identifies some of the implications of contextual diversity theory on the structure of tax-exempt charity law.

A DIVERSITY THEORY OF CHARITABLE TAX EXEMPTION

DIVERSITY AS A VALUE

Diversity is the driving force behind the charitable tax exemption. The diversity made possible by the exemption breeds creativity, ingenuity, and other things that stimulate society and, in turn, market growth and development. The charitable tax exemption contributes to diversity by offering alternative means of accomplishing societal objectives in a market context. Thus, charities offer alternatives to for-profit corporations and to government.

Charities are just one of the many types of corporate entities that operate in the United States. A key distinction between nonprofit charitable corporations and for-profit corporations is the lack of shareholders in the former. This means that while for-profit corporations are generally presumed to be profit-motivated institutions, nonprofit charities are mission-driven and are legally prohibited by the nondistribution constraint from extracting profits from the corporation for private or personal gain. Thus, nonprofit charities provide a viable alternative to the for-profit way of running a corporation, resulting in more diverse outputs. For example, for-profit corporations perform research concerning potentially very profitable drugs for treatment of HIV and AIDS, while nonprofit charitable corporations search for a far less profitable and less

---

Gained Fortune, and Critics, in Sale of His Cable Network, Wash. Post, Feb. 13, 1994, at H1 (discussing controversy over appropriateness of revoking CBN's tax exempt status given its commercially successful broadcast network).

    14. *See generally*, David A. Brennen, *A Diversity Theory of Charitable Tax Exemption—Beyond Efficiency, Through Critical Race Theory, Toward Diversity*, 4 Pitt. Tax Rev. 1 (2006).

costly vaccine for the same disease.[15] Imposing a tax on income incidentally earned from these mission-driven activities would only serve to slow accomplishment of the benefit.[16]

In addition to providing an alternative form of organization, charities also offer an alternative to government. Like nonprofit charities, government does not have shareholders and is mission-driven. One key difference between government and corporations is government's ability to impose a tax as a means of financing the production of its goods and services. However, unless the public is willing to support the acquisition of particular goods or services with direct outlay of tax monies, those goods or services will not be acquired by government and, hence, will not be supplied to the public by government. Accordingly, to the extent that provision of a particular good or service has support among citizens, yet lacks sufficient political support for government backing, it will be up to nonprofit charities to supply the good or service—financing that supply with tax-exempt profits or tax-deductible donations.

DIVERSITY IN CONTEXT

Diversity as a value should be considered in context. "Context" refers to that aspect of law that requires consideration of multiple points of interest.[17] For example, diversity as a value does not mean that charities should be able to advance any conceivable private purpose. Thus, tax-exempt charities, because of the public policy doctrine, cannot engage in invidious racial discrimination against black people. Simply recognizing that racial preferences promote diversity is not enough. LMT teaches us that law must also account for racial preferences in various contexts and from various perspectives. Law must contextually mediate public and private societal interests regarding racial preferences. For instance, a critical race perspective of law would indicate that there is a meaningful difference between socially beneficial race-based affirmative action (equalizing opportunities) and the societal harm advanced by racial discrimination (continued racial subordination). Thus, contextual diversity suggests that even though racial preference in the context of racial subordination is not permissible in tax-exempt charity law,[18] racial preference in the context of affirmative action might be permissible.

"Context" also explains other aspects of exemption law that limit private profit taking and private benefit, lobbying and political campaigning, competitive business functions, and private endowments. Granted, each of these limitations imposed on charities appears to impinge on what a charity may do and, thus, seems to hamper certain types of diversity. One must bear in mind that the aim of the charitable tax exemption is to allow for activities that benefit public interests, not private ones. The purpose of these limitations is

---

15. *See Jerry Avorn Discusses This Year's Flu Vaccine Shortage*, All Things Considered (NPR radio broadcast Oct. 6, 2004) (describing nonprofit efforts to develop an AIDS vaccine as compared to for-profit efforts to seek potentially more financially profitable drugs for treatment of AIDS).

16. An income tax on charity income would "cut retained earnings . . . and hence would further cripple a group of organizations already capital-constrained." Hansmann, *supra* note 2, at 74.

17. *See* Malloy, *supra* note 5, at 115.

18. *See Bob Jones Univ. v. United States*, 461 U.S. 574 (1983).

to mediate between the private individual tendency for authoritative control and the public interests advanced by the charitable entity. Thus, the diversity value advocated in this chapter is not unbridled diversity; rather it is "contextual diversity" in the sense that the scope of permissible charitable activity is not without limits.

Contextual diversity theory may not provide a rationale for every aspect of the charitable tax exemption. However, its application may explain many facets of the charitable tax exemption not captured by traditional economic theories. Contextual diversity offers a normative rationalization of the charitable tax exemption that can assist, in conjunction with economic analysis, in better outlining appropriate contours of charitable exemption law. Consider the example of tax-exempt law's public policy requirement that charitable activity be consistent with established public policy. Established public policy is often conceived of in application as federal government policy or majoritarian compliance.[19] Contextual diversity would suggest that adoption of the public policy doctrine was inappropriate as a judicial response to the harm at issue in *Bob Jones University v. United States* in the sense that it was overkill. Indeed, "established public policy" does not define the bounds of charity. Instead, LMT suggests that the scope of "charitable" is varied, diverse, dynamic, and transformative. What is "charitable" activity may be consistent with, have nothing to do with, or be completely contrary to "established public policy" as presently conceived.

The meaning of the term "charitable" has variance across cultural-interpretive communities. The designation of an activity as "charitable" can be understood as an interpretation or representation of particular underlying values. In some contexts, "charitable" stands as a representation of fulfilling a public purpose with respect to others who are truly in need, with no pejorative connotation. In other contexts, "charitable" denotes action taken in support of subordinated people and functions as a sign of one's nobility in dealing with inferior beings. As a sign of public policy, "charitable" may take on multiple advanced meanings and may function, depending upon the context, as an interpretation of underlying sociolegal values supporting invidious racial discrimination. We cannot determine the appropriate contextual meaning of "charitable" by reference only to positive economics and its emphasis on efficiency analysis. We need a more textured and nuanced approach to exchange relationships in a market context.

For example, understanding the problems of permissible and impermissible racial preferences requires consideration of the contextual positioning of the parties involved. Markets are not fully objective, neutral avenues of exchange; they are the product of human practice and culturally informed values. Thus, when faced with the issue of the permissibility of invidious racial discrimination by charities, a careful consideration of the context of this type of racial preference reveals that mere racial preference was not the problem in *Bob Jones University*. The problem, as CRT teaches us, was the continued racial subordination of blacks long after the end of legalized slavery. Accordingly,

---

19. *See* Johnny Rex Buckles, *Reforming the Public Policy Doctrine*, 53 Kan. L. Rev. 397 (2005); *see Bob Jones University*, 461 U.S. 574, 606–12 (1983) (Powell, J., concurring).

prohibiting racial subordination (the underlying problem), instead of prohibiting acts that are contrary to "established public policy," would better advance the goals of contextual diversity. In recommending the abolition of the public policy limitation in favor of an explicit rule prohibiting invidious racial discrimination by charities, this chapter draws on the teachings of CRT regarding legal rules that are "originally" prompted by racial discord but that avoid explicitly mentioning race in the formally adopted rule. As the late Professor Jerome Culp explained: "This liberal view of the Constitution and race, that race is better left unexplored, prevailed in much of the constitutional drafting."[20]

EFFICIENCY THEORIES OF CHARITABLE EXEMPTION

Traditional theories of the charitable tax exemption — at least those promulgated prior to 1990 — are principally based on concepts of economic efficiency. These efficiency-based theories explain the charitable tax exemption as either a subsidy by government for public goods, a necessary result of using net income to define tax liability, or a means of compensating charities for capital constraints. Other efficiency-based theories contend that the exemption is either a payment for an entity's ability to garner donative support or a means of compensating charities for the risk they assume in providing public goods. In terms of explaining the economics for why charities are tax-exempt, these traditional theories do a pretty good job. However, these traditional theories lack significant non-economic components that, ultimately, make them incomplete. These economic theories for the exemption do not explain the existence of the many non-economic aspects of the exemption and, thus, cannot fully guide us in sculpting the contours of the law.

PUBLIC BENEFIT SUBSIDY THEORY

The first of the efficiency-based theories of charitable tax exemption is the public benefit subsidy theory. This theory posits that the charitable tax exemption is a means by which government encourages organizations engaged in providing public goods to continue to do so. The most notable proponent of this theory has been the government itself. In *Bob Jones University*, the Supreme Court notes:

> Charitable exemptions are justified on the basis that the exempt entity confers a public benefit — a benefit which the society or the community may not itself choose or be able to provide, or which supplements and advances the work of public institutions already supported by tax revenues. History buttresses logic to make clear that, to warrant exemption under §501(c)(3), an institution must fall within a category specified in that section and must demonstrably serve and be in harmony with the public interest. The institution's purpose must not

---

20. *See, e.g.*, Jerome McCristal Culp Jr., *Toward a Black Legal Scholarship: Race and Original Understanding*, 1991 Duke L. J. 39, 67–77.

be so at odds with the common community conscience as to undermine any public benefit that might otherwise be conferred.[21]

In addition to the government, scholars have advocated this public benefit subsidy theory for exemption. An essential aspect of the theory is that government subsidizes certain "goods" or services that government either cannot or will not supply on its own—perhaps due to constitutional or political constraints. Thus, the point of the charitable tax exemption is to permit government to essentially "pay" private entities that supply these public goods and services.

An implicit assumption underlying the public benefit subsidy theory is the idea that government, under neutral principles, can determine what constitutes a public good or service.[22] Hence, elements of the rational market participant pervade this theory. Also of economic dimension is the idea implicit in the public benefit subsidy theory that the government is somehow "paying" charities for what they produce. Given these economic dimensions, the traditional public benefit subsidy theory partially rationalizes many aspects of the charitable tax exemption. Nevertheless, there is much about the exemption that this theory does not address.

The public benefit subsidy theory does not address why this government financial support for charities must take the form of a tax exemption. Why not have the government make direct grants to nonprofits that provide goods and services that benefit the public? The public benefit subsidy theory also does not articulate a coherent rationale for how the decision is made as to what goods and services benefit the public, indicating that neutral market principles might drive the process of deciding what benefits the public. However, this is not necessarily so. In *Bob Jones University*, the private university provided what was identified in the statute as a public benefit—education—yet the Court held that the education in that case was not entitled to exemption due to the presence of invidious racial discrimination. Efficiency analysis alone, arguably, does not provide a rationalization for this aspect of charitable tax exemption. Hence, the public benefit subsidy theory's reliance on "neutral" efficiency principles simply does not provide a basis for understanding how a public benefit is determined.

BASE-DEFINING THEORY

Recognizing deficiencies in the public benefit subsidy theory, Boris Bittker and George Rahdert developed a theory of charitable tax exemption that focused explicitly on the economic aspects of the exemption. Bittker and Rahdert's base-defining theory posits that charities (and many other nonprofits) are exempt from the federal income tax because they are not suitable targets of the income tax.[23] Bittker and Rahdert state that charities "should be wholly exempted from income taxation, because [(1)] they do not realize income in the ordinary sense of that term and because [(2)] even if they did, there is no

---

21. *Bob Jones University*, 461 U.S. at 591–92.
22. *See* Atkinson, *Altruism, supra* note 3, at 606.
23. *See* Bittker and Rahdert, *supra* note 2, at 304.

satisfactory way to fit the tax rate to the ability of the beneficiaries to pay."[24] According to Bittker and Rahdert, charities are exempt from the income tax by necessity.

In support of their theory, Bittker and Rahdert explain that measuring the income of a charity is a conceptually difficult, if not impossible, task. To begin with, measuring an entity's income requires a determination of the entity's gross income in excess of expenses incurred in acquiring the income. Gross income is any economic enrichment that is not excluded from income by Congress. One common congressional exclusion from income is "gifts." In looking at what a charity's typical revenues might be (interest on endowment funds, membership dues, gifts/donations), Bittker and Rahdert conclude that, with the exception of interest on endowment funds, charities simply do not produce revenues that represent the types of enrichment that constitute taxable income. They explain this conclusion from two perspectives. On the one hand, membership dues, gifts, and donations to the charity would likely be viewed as excludable gifts from members/donors to the charitable entity. Even if not viewed as gifts to the institution, these charitable revenues might be viewed as excludable gifts to the charity's beneficiaries — the charitable entity itself acting as a mere conduit for passing the revenues to the beneficiaries.

In addressing the expense side of the net income equation, Bittker and Rahdert explain that even if one were to conclude properly that charitable revenues constituted gross income, a separate difficulty involves determining what to count as deductible expenses incurred in acquiring the income. Bittker and Rahdert identified charitable expenditures as potentially including items such as staff salaries and medical welfare programs for indigents. One way of deducting an expense is by positioning it as an "ordinary and necessary expense incurred in carrying on a trade or business" activity.[25] Bittker and Rahdert explain, however, that treating charitable activity as a "trade or business" is self-contradictory because, unlike for-profit enterprises, charities are mission-focused, not profit-focused. Additionally, even if the definition of "business" were expanded to include the business of providing charitable benefits, a charity would essentially end up having no tax liability because, as a result of the nondistribution constraint, all revenues must be devoted to mission purposes and no revenues may go as profits to insiders. Thus, net income would always equal zero, resulting in no tax liability. Another way of deducting expenses is by positioning the expense as eligible for the charitable contribution deduction. However, Bittker and Rahdert explain that, as with the business expense scenario described above, either structural impediments in the statute authorizing the charitable deduction, or the necessary zeroing out of income that would result from allowing the deduction, indicate that charities should not be permitted to take a charitable contribution deduction for charitable expenses.

In addition to the income measurement problems associated with imposing an income tax on charities, Bittker and Rahdert raise concerns

---

24. *Id.* at 305.
25. I.R.C. §162(a).

about the appropriate tax rate to apply to charities — further supporting their base-defining rationale for the charitable tax exemption. Under their theory, tax rates are important because they implicate conceptions of efficiency related to either the "benefit" or "ability to pay" theories of taxation. The idea here is that tax law generally attempts to match tax burden with the taxpayer's circumstances. Bittker and Rahdert argue that a charity's income should be imputed to its beneficiaries for rate determination purposes, since it is most likely the beneficiary who would bear the burden of any tax on the charity's income. They explain that the problem is that the beneficiaries are usually unknown at the time the income is received and, thus, it is nearly impossible to determine an appropriate income tax rate. Even if the entity were taxed as a surrogate for the beneficiaries, Bittker and Rahdert explain that not knowing who the beneficiaries are would necessarily mean that a tax on income would be inefficient — potentially overtaxing some beneficiaries and undertaxing others. They further explain that, aside from the identification-of-beneficiary aspect of the rate issue, these beneficiaries, were they to receive these charitable benefits directly, would be able to exclude them from income as gifts. Thus, however the matter is approached, Bittker and Rahdert conclude that there is simply no way of coming up with a proper tax rate if charities were to be subject to the income tax.

As an economic explanation of the charitable tax exemption, Bittker and Rahdert's base-defining theory does a good job of demonstrating that for the most part, imposing an income tax on charities would likely not yield much in the way of income tax revenues. However, their theory fails to fully explain the many non-economic aspects of the charitable tax exemption, such as the difference between a zero or near-zero tax liability and tax exemption, political activities and lobbying, the definition of "charitable," and private foundation rules.

Throughout their base-defining theory, Bittker and Rahdert explain that even if the federal income tax were to apply to a charity's income, it is quite likely that no tax revenue would result. This view of the charitable tax exemption as nothing more than elimination of a financial obligation completely overlooks the many other non-economic aspects of the charitable tax exemption. As Evelyn Brody explains quite well in her sovereignty theory of the charitable tax exemption:

> While most observers have described tax exemption as a subsidy, a zero rate of tax differs qualitatively, not just quantitatively, from a one-percent rate of tax. Tax exemption maintains an independent distance between charities and the state. Similarly, exemption differs in an important political way from an equivalent system of direct grants.[26]

Thus, in Brody's words, there is a "qualitative" dimension to the charitable tax exemption that is not captured by a pure dollars and cents analysis. This qualitative difference is what lies at the heart of the normative justification for the exemption.

---

26. Brody, *supra* note 3, at 592–93.

Central to the charitable tax exemption is defining the term "charitable." Though Bittker and Rahdert address this issue, they fail to fully develop the non-economic aspects of their theory. For instance, when addressing the relevance of racial discrimination to the concept of "charitable," Bittker and Rahdert explicitly minimize the importance of this connection by referring to the race issue as a "minor problem[] of interpretation."[27] While they drafted their base-defining theory in 1976, well before the 1983 *Bob Jones University* case, the predominant view even in 1976 was that racial discrimination rendered some purposes noncharitable because of racial discrimination's inconsistency with federal public policy.[28] The other "minor" issue identified by Bittker and Rahdert also involved an issue of paramount importance to people of color: whether charities have an obligation to provide free or reduced-cost services to those who are unable to pay in a variety of contexts. Could a critical race perspective add to our understanding of this aspect of the charitable tax exemption?

Bittker and Rahdert's base-defining theory fails to explain this and other non-economic aspects of the term "charitable." Instead of recognizing this as a limitation of their base-defining theory, they chose to minimize the non-economic issues as "minor." Importantly, it is not only in the context of race, or even with regard to defining "charitable," that Bittker and Rahdert must account for various aspects of the charitable tax exemption in some non-economic way. For example, with regard to private foundations, their base-defining theory could not rationalize why the various private foundation excise taxes exist. Thus, the architects of the base-defining theory resort to a type of contextual diversity, as a means of rationalizing these special penalty taxes. In rationalizing the private foundation excise tax rules, Bittker and Rahdert state that "[p]rivate organizations displaying independence, flexibility, and originality are bound to tread on toes, and when the toes belong to public officials, an adverse legislative reaction should not come as a surprise."[29] Rationalizing the private foundation excise taxes as a type of penalty imposed for contravening government "territory" or "authority" seems consistent with this chapter's notion of contextual diversity. That is, LMT states that market participants are constantly seeking to gain authoritative control in the marketplace.

Bittker and Rahdert's base-defining theory uses a similar type of non-base-defining (non-economic) analysis to fully account for the educational exemption for museums, colleges, and orchestras. Because their beneficiaries are not necessarily poor, as is the case with many other types of charities, the improper rate aspect of the base-defining theory does not account for these particular types of "educational" institutions. So, instead of relying exclusively on base-defining/economic concepts to explain these upper-echelon charities, Bittker and Rahdert again resort to a type of contextual diversity analysis. Accordingly, Bittker and Rahdert rationalize that the benefits of "educational" institutions extend beyond the immediate beneficiaries to "an indefinably wide audience

---

27. Bittker and Rahdert, *supra* note 2, at 331.
28. *See E. Ky. Welfare Rights Org. v. Simon*, 426 U.S. 26, 30 (1976); *Green v. Connally*, 330 F. Supp. 1160 (D.D.C. 1971); Rev. Rul. 71-447, 1971-2 C.B. 230; Rev. Rul. 75-231, 1975-1 C.B. 158.
29. Bittker and Rahdert, *supra* note 2, at 334–35.

over the entire income spectrum."[30] Additionally, they explain that "it is precisely in the area of education, including the arts, that private institutions are especially well suited to serve as independent centers of power and influence in our society, fostering innovation and diversity with a dedication that government agencies can seldom muster or sustain. This separate rationale for tax exemption applies particularly to educational institutions."[31] Thus, when economics fail to explain some important and varied aspect of the charitable tax exemption, Bittker and Rahdert resort to notions of "diversity" and "context" to fill in the theoretical gaps.

CAPITAL FORMATION SUBSIDY THEORY

Five years after the publication of Bittker and Rahdert's base-defining theory, Professor Henry Hansmann published his own theory applicable to the charitable tax exemption, which responds, in explicit economic terms, to Bittker and Rahdert's approach.[32] In his capital formation subsidy theory of tax exemption, Hansmann explains that the rationale for the charitable tax exemption concerns the access of charities to capital markets. For him, the tax exemption compensates charities for the lack of access to capital markets. Further, this so-called "capital subsidy" promotes "efficiency when employed in those industries in which nonprofit firms serve consumers better than their for-profit counterparts."

Central to Hansmann's capital subsidy theory is the notion of contract failure. Contract failure is a type of market failure that "derives from the inability of some or most consumers to make accurate judgments concerning the quality, quantity, or price of services provided by alternative producers."[33] Contract failure is most prevalent with donative nonprofits (nonprofits that receive revenues mostly through donations) as opposed to commercial nonprofits (nonprofits that receive revenues mostly through sales activities). Hansmann's classic example of a donative nonprofit that typifies contract failure is the American Red Cross. A person making a contribution to the Red Cross is buying disaster relief services from the Red Cross for some unknown third party. This is a circumstance of contract failure because the consumer/donor must blindly rely on the Red Cross to determine who gets disaster relief, how much they get, and under what terms they get it. Consumers are not as concerned with nonprofit firms as they would be with for-profit firms about donations being diverted to shareholders because nonprofit firms do not have shareholders. Thus, according to Hansmann, because of the nondistribution constraint, donative nonprofits are more efficient than for-profit firms in circumstances of contract failure.

In addition to contract failure, Hansmann points to constraints on the ability of nonprofits to obtain capital as another important component explaining the income tax exemption. The three major sources of funding for nonprofits are debt, donations, and retained earnings. Nonprofits do not

---

30. *Id.* at 334.
31. *Id.* at 335.
32. Hansmann, *supra* note 2, at 54–57.
33. *Id.* at 67–68.

have the same access to equity capital that for-profit firms enjoy, because nonprofits cannot issue shares. Professor Hansmann explains that debt capital is difficult for nonprofits to obtain because of the risk involved in lending to nonprofits. Donations are also problematic because donations are uncertain and inadequate. Thus, nonprofits must rely almost exclusively on retained earnings in order to finance growth. While restraint on access to capital markets does not by itself justify the tax exemption, Hansmann argues that coupling this restraint with the fact that many nonprofits operate under circumstances of contract failure means that the exemption is needed. If we want markets to operate at optimal efficiency, and if we accept that nonprofits are the most efficient producers of contract failure goods/services, then it makes sense that we subsidize nonprofits in order to increase the rate at which nonprofits can expand.

Although Hansmann's capital formation subsidy theory articulates a clear rationale for why the charitable tax exemption is efficient, it does not articulate a clear basis for understanding aspects of the exemption that have no necessary connection to economic efficiency. His theory's deficiency is most apparent in the conclusion that the tax exemption should be denied to many commercial nonprofits that produce simple standardized services, as opposed to complex services. Typical of Hansmann's view is the statement that "[t]here would obviously be little point . . . in granting the exemption to a nonprofit hardware store."[34] What he misses here is that even a hardware store might provide the type of benefit, under certain circumstances, that society wants, needs, or otherwise values. For example, what if the hardware store employed only people who are handicapped or blind? What if the hardware store provided an employment opportunity to racial minority groups or others who would not otherwise have employment? If for-profit firms choose not to open a hardware store that employs these populations, these people might be jobless or dependents of government. Thus, even though the hardware store might not operate under conditions of classic contract failure, and even though it might not be economically efficient to operate a hardware store by employing these populations, it is still of real value to society that this hardware store operate. To the extent that granting tax exemption allows this to happen, then society is all the better for it.

Hansmann's theory fails to account for non-efficiency-based justifications for the exemption when he argues that nonprofit hospitals should not be eligible for tax exemption. This is based on the lack of contract failure or need for capital evident in the hospital industry. Hansmann's efficiency-based justification for a hospital exemption misses other important considerations. To illustrate, consider Professor Jill Horwitz's empirical research concerning hospitals, which concludes that — despite the myriad calls for ending tax exemption for hospitals that do not serve the poor — empirical research shows that tax-exempt nonprofit hospitals provide societal benefits that for-profit hospitals simply do not provide.[35] The special benefits of nonprofit, as

34. *Id.* at 87.
35. Jill R. Horwitz, *Why We Need the Independent Sector: The Behavior, Law, and Ethics of Not-for-Profit Hospitals*, 50 UCLA L. Rev. 1345, 1347 (2003).

compared to for-profit and government, hospitals include the provision of "more profitable services than government hospitals and more unprofitable services than for-profit hospitals."[36] Importantly, Horwitz, consistent with this chapter's theory of contextual diversity, suggests that "[t]he near exclusive focus on charity care as an acceptable justification for tax exemption is too narrow. Tax policy should reflect the other important public benefits disproportionately provided by not-for-profit hospitals."[37] There is no evidence that tax exemption plays no role in allowing hospitals to provide these additional benefits.

POTENTIAL IMPLICATIONS FOR THE STRUCTURE OF TAX-EXEMPT CHARITY LAW

This analysis has several very important implications for the structure of tax-exempt charity law. The primary insight is that justifications for the exemption depart from the traditional templates constructed by efficiency analysts. While we can continuously re-evaluate what does and does not provide benefits to society, and hence is entitled to tax-exempt charitable status, we must be careful when proscribing particular functions as beyond the realm of charity. This is because we simply never know when new and different value may be produced by current or future activities.

This chapter suggests that efficiency should not be the only guide for how tax-exempt charity law is crafted. Instead, we should draw on lessons from LMT that it takes many perspectives in order to obtain a clearer picture of the meaning ascribed to particular interpretations of the relationship among law, markets and culture. Thus, to the extent that we can draw on other than positive economic visions of law to make decisions about tax-exempt charity law, we do so to our benefit. Accordingly, we should identify worthy and appropriate values for law and then think about the best way to approach and implement these values in a market context.

CONCLUSION

Law involves a process of interpretation, which is subjective. Tax law is no different. Although tax law is often represented by quantitative analysis in terms of its impact, this should not obscure the nonquantitative and interpretive aspects of tax law. Tax-exempt charity law and its allegiance to "mission" as opposed to "profit" is a perfect vehicle for exploring the non-efficiency-based aspects of tax law. This chapter takes part in such analysis by articulating what is termed a "contextual diversity" theory of charitable tax exemption. Contextual diversity requires that various aspects of the charitable tax exemption be examined, not only with the aim of maximizing efficiency, but also

---

36. *Id.* at 1364.
37. *Id.* at 1349.

with the broader aim of advancing conceptions of justice that go beyond positive economic analysis to include fairness and other ideas important to a democratic society. Thus, in addition to using economic analysis to examine tax-exempt charity law, scholars and others could possibly discover more diverse and different meanings in tax-exempt charity law by drawing on appropriate non-economic legal approaches to law, such as CRT or others. This intellectual collaboration could not only broaden the discourse about the charitable tax exemption; it could potentially lead to discoveries about this area of law that we never knew existed. Thus, instead of thinking of the charitable tax exemption as simply an efficient means of providing certain goods and services to the public, our horizons might be broadened by thinking of the exemption in a different way. That is, we could think of the charitable tax exemption as a means of diversifying the market and thus allowing for more creative and wealth-producing opportunities. However, the charitable tax exemption is also subject to contextual constraints that act to limit the scope of charitable activity. In the end, the objective should be justice, as well as efficiency.

THE CONTROVERSY OF THE TAX EXPENDITURE: HEALTH CARE AND HOUSING

CHAPTER 5

CREATING HEALTH POLICY THROUGH THE TAX CODE

Lucinda E. Jesson, Commissioner of the Minnesota Department of Human Services (on leave from Hamline University School of Law)

Today's health care system is based on employer-provided health insurance. The term "employer-based health insurance," however, masks the fact that this insurance is subsidized through the United States federal tax code. Employers can deduct the cost of providing health coverage from taxable income as a business expense. They do not pay payroll taxes on compensation that is provided as insurance. More significantly, the amount employers contribute toward health coverage is generally excluded, without limit, from employees' taxable income. The net result is that the U.S. Treasury is funding a significant amount of our private health care system.

The tax code, however, subsidizes U.S. health care in a manner that is anything but efficient.[1] The tax exclusion contributes to rising health care costs. As an open-ended benefit, which encourages excess costs, the tax exemption serves to increase both the value of health insurance benefits and overall health care costs. Moreover, it provides "upside-down" subsidies, which disproportionately benefit high-income families. Finally, the tax benefits are often unavailable for non-employer-based health insurance, leaving both the unemployed and the self-employed at a disadvantage. As a result of its design, the exclusion for employer-provided health insurance is the largest individual "tax expenditure" item.

Liberals and conservatives alike use the tax system to promote social change agendas. The recent reform legislation, which builds upon the employer-based system to increase access, is just the most recent example of Democrats' efforts to intertwine taxes and health care. But one need only look back a decade ago to the creation of health savings accounts to witness Republican measures to advance their health polices through the tax code. For both parties, tax subsidies are a politically sensitive way to promote change. One can appear to reduce the government's role in health care while subsidizing a goal by providing a tax subsidy rather than creating a new government department.

---

1. Here and throughout this chapter, I consider whether using the current tax code as the backbone of our health care system is "efficient." I understand that this is a different inquiry from one of tax efficiency, as defined in terms of tax neutrality.

Moreover, by financing health care through the tax system, the expenditure becomes virtually automatic. Unlike appropriations for the Health and Human Services budget and Veterans Administration health care, this tax exemption is not subject to annual appropriation from Congress.

How did we get here? This chapter will first review the history of how the United States' health care system was shaped, in large part, by tax policy definitions of what to "exclude" from our income. We then move to examine how health and tax policy are intertwined as legislators decide what to "tax," both with regard to institutions such as hospitals and with regard to items such as snack food and sodas. Finally, the chapter considers recent health reform initiatives and the tax and policy implications of the 2010 health reform bill, the Patient Protection and Affordable Care Act.

HOW TAX EXCLUSIONS CREATED THE PREDOMINANT HEALTH CARE FINANCE PROGRAM IN THE UNITED STATES

Recent data tell us that today approximately 59% of Americans obtain health insurance through employment. This rate of employer coverage marks another step in a long-term decline in coverage. In 2000, for example, employer coverage accounted for about 64% of coverage for Americans.[2] The descent is particularly noticeable for small employers. Large employers benefit from both increased bargaining power and broader, more stable risk pooling. This means smaller employers are at a price disadvantage when it comes to purchasing health insurance. As a result, small employers are far less likely than larger employers to offer health insurance as a part of employee benefits packages.

The decline in coverage can also be explained by a trend in a very different direction: the premium trend. The annual employer benefits survey conducted by the Henry J. Kaiser Family Foundation reflects that premiums for employer-based health care coverage increased 114% from 1999 to 2007, far outstripping employee's earnings increases. This premium trend also explains why health insurance is the United States' number one tax expenditure. In 2007, the Congressional Budget Office (CBO) calculated an estimated $246 billion in forgone revenue from both personal income taxes and payroll taxes to support this employment-based coverage.[3] To put this number in context, consider the fact that the amount is more than half of the estimated federal spending on Medicare for that same year. This amount includes money employers are not taxed for employee health insurance (they can deduct these funds from business taxable income) and the money employers save in Social Security and Medicare taxes. The amount also includes the savings for employees on the unpaid income tax on health care benefits paid by employers. Finally, the coverage exclusion includes certain money set aside by employees to pay for

---

2. Elise Gould, *Employer-Sponsored Health Insurance Erosion Continues, Will Likely Accelerate Through 2009* (Economic Policy Institute Sept. 10, 2009).

3. Joint Committee on Taxation, *Tax Expenditures for Health Care* (July 30, 2008).

health expenditures. These different accounts (known as health savings accounts, flexible spending accounts, or cafeteria plans) allow employers to set up plans into which an employee can place and spend funds on a pretax basis.

If, as Table 5-1 illustrates, the exclusion of Medicare benefits and other pretax treatments are included, the value of the tax expenditure for health climbs even higher.[4]

Table 5-1. Calendar Year Tax Expenditures for Health 2007

Value of Tax Expenditures	Billions of Dollars
Exclusion of employer sponsored health care	246.1
Income	145.3
FICA	100.7
Exclusion of Medicare benefits from income	39.3
Hospital Insurance (Part A)	20.2
Supplementary Medical Insurance (Part B)	13.3
Prescription Drug Insurance (Part D)	4.8
Exclusion of subsidies to employers who maintain prescription drug plans	1.0
Deduction for medical expenses above 7.5% of adjusted gross income	8.7
Self-employed health insurance deduction	4.8
Exclusion of medical care and TRICARE insurance for military dependents and retirees not enrolled in Medicare	2.1
Exclusion of health insurance benefits for military retirees enrolled in Medicare	1.0
Health savings accounts	0.3
Health coverage tax credit	0.1

EVOLUTION OF THE EMPLOYER-BASED INSURANCE MODEL

Congress first entered the intersection between tax and health policy when it enacted the charitable tax exemption in 1894, exempting organizations organized and conducted solely for charitable, religious, or educational purposes from the corporate income tax. At the time, hospitals operated primarily for the poor and mentally ill. As Paul Starr wrote:

> We now think of hospitals as the most visible embodiment of medical care in its technically most sophisticated form, but before the last hundred years,

---

4. *Id.*

hospitals and medical practice had relatively little to do with each other. From their earliest origins in preindustrial societies, hospitals had been primarily religious and charitable institutions for tending the sick, rather than medical institutions for their cure.[5]

Beginning in the early twentieth century, hospitals became the loci of medical care. This change in status resulted not only from the advance of science but from the creation of private health insurance. Before the 1930s, health insurance in America was largely unknown. Experts believed that adverse selection was an insurmountable hurdle to broad coverage, so a purchase of health insurance then was akin to a purchase of flood insurance today — you spent the money only when very likely to be sick. Despite this mindset, in 1929, Baylor University Hospital took an extraordinary step and agreed to provide hospital care to a group of teachers for six dollars a year. The arrangement spread to other groups of enrollees and then to additional hospitals. While these first ventures were competing efforts by single hospitals, the concept evolved from single-hospital plans into the formation of BlueCross.

The American Hospital Association established the BlueCross system during the Great Depression, largely to guarantee more patients (and a more consistent revenue stream) during this time of economic hardship. Under the BlueCross insurance plan, an insured individual chose from any participating hospital. BlueShield plans, begun by physician groups to cover nonhospital medical expenses, followed shortly thereafter.

During the 1930s, individuals accounted for the majority of plan subscribers. Less than 3 percent of the population had employer-provided coverage. The advent of group enrollment came in the next decade, not as a result of health planning, but both as a result of the gains in the labor movement and in reaction to the wage controls enacted during World War II. Firms competing for workers (and unions engaged in collective bargaining) quickly turned to a wider benefit package, including hospital insurance, to meet their goals. By 1942, 20% of the population had hospital insurance but no coverage for other medical expenses.

The growth of health insurance drove the need for regulatory clarity. The Stabilization Act of 1942, which expressly exempted insurance and pension benefits from strict limits on wage increases, provided clarity with regard to wartime wage controls. Tax consequences for employees receiving benefits, however, remained murky. The lack of clarity stemmed from twenty-year-old regulations. First, a 1919 Treasury regulation deemed an employer's payment of premiums on health insurance taxable income to the employee. In 1921, the provision was revised to state that, at least in the case of group insurance, the payments were not taxable income.[6]

In 1943, the IRS issued a clarifying ruling that indicated amounts paid by employers for insurance were not income to employees, essentially permitting employers to deduct premiums as ordinary and necessary business expenses and allowing employees to accept the benefit without tax ramifications.

---

5. Paul Starr, *The Social Transformation of American Medicine* (Basic Books, 1982), 145.
6. Jay A. Soled, *Taxation of Employer-Provided Health Coverage: Inclusion, Timing, and Policy Issues*, 15 Va. Tax Rev. 447, 450–51 (1996).

The net result: a substantial incentive to route health insurance through employers. However, the ruling left open the issue of tax treatment for self-insured plans and employer-provided individual insurance.

In 1954, Congress provided clarity when it adopted a provision that explicitly allowed an exclusion from income for coverage under employer-provided accident and health insurance. Section 106, which later became Section 106(a), reads as follows: "General rule—Except as otherwise provided in this section, gross income of an employee does not include employer-provided coverage under an accident or health plan." This exclusion applies to commercial and self-insured plans. Across time, the phrase "accident or health plan" was defined to include not only health insurance but also short-term and long-term disability coverage and reimbursement arrangements such as flexible spending accounts and health reimbursement accounts. Significantly, self-employed individuals do not have the protection of section 106(a) since they are not considered "employees" under the Code.[7]

ADVANTAGES AND DISADVANTAGES OF THE EMPLOYER-BASED MODEL

Problems with an Employment-Based System

The two primary criticisms of the current model are that the tax subsidy is "upside-down," in that it favors high-income families, and that it leads to higher demand and, as a result, higher health care costs. Let us examine both criticisms.

The U.S. federal income tax system is progressive. Under it, the percentage of income that is taxed increases for each portion of income that exceeds set thresholds. For example, a family with $120,000 in taxable income would pay 15 percent on the first $50,000 of taxable income, 25 percent on income between $50,001 and $100,000 of taxable income, and 35 percent on the remaining income between $100,001 and $120,000. In contrast, a family with $70,000 in taxable income pays 15 percent on their first $50,000 taxable and 25 percent on the remaining taxable income between $50,001 and $70,000. Furthermore, a family with $50,000 in taxable income pays only 15 percent on the entire $50,000. While this example simplifies sometimes complex calculations, it demonstrates that in our progressive system, the value of the tax exclusion grows as the family income increases. It is worth more, in short, to the families with higher incomes.

Let us consider Curt's family. Curt's employer, All Happy Cleaners, provides health insurance worth $10,000 a year. If Curt's income puts him in the 10 percent tax bracket, Curt's taxes will go down by $1,000 due to the health insurance exclusion. But when All Happy provides the same insurance to Julie, a highly compensated executive with an income that places her in the 35 percent tax bracket, Julie's taxes go down by $3,500 as a result of the tax

---

7. Self-employed individuals (including sole proprietors, general partners in a partnership, limited partners who receive guaranteed payments, and individuals who receive wages from S-corporations in which they are more than 2% shareholders), can obtain tax savings from an above-the-line deduction authorized under section 162(1).

exclusion for health insurance. In effect, the government is underwriting health coverage by providing a larger discount to high-income households.

This approach is criticized not only because of its regressive nature (which is a fairness issue to many) but because of its economic inefficiency. If the goal of the tax exclusion is to maximize health insurance coverage, this approach does so in an inefficient manner. It provides large subsidies to high-income individuals, many of whom would obtain insurance with a much smaller subsidy. At the same time, it offers an inadequate subsidy to low-income individuals, a group needing a greater incentive to spend what little money they make to obtain health insurance. The combination of a disproportionately high tax on those spending less, while taxing a smaller percentage from those spending more, contributes to an inefficient tax system. Moreover, the current tax treatment favoring those in higher tax brackets may lead to employer choices to select the most comprehensive coverage.[8]

The fact that the purchaser of health insurance (the employer) is not the user (the employee) also leads to systemic problems. One problem may simply be that because the purchase is being made on behalf of a group, the needs and desires of individual employees may not be met. For example, an older employee with chronic conditions may value benefits differently than a younger female employee concerned about maternity care.

The more fundamental disconnect is that employees become less sensitive to costs when they are shielded by employer-purchased insurance from the true costs. In short, enrollees may use more medical care than necessary. In insurance terms, this is referred to as "moral hazard." In lay terms, people are more careful spending money when it is their own. If they engage in a cost benefit analysis in a third-party payment system, it may be based only upon their out-of-pocket expenses rather than the true cost of care.

Certainly, the purchase of insurance with low cost-sharing leads to greater utilization, which in turn makes health care more expensive. Although the recent history of higher deductibles and co-pays has blunted this effect, it has not disappeared. Consider that 80% of health care costs are incurred by 20% of the population. One night at a hospital typically "spends" the amount of most deductibles and may even reach the yearly out-of-pocket maximum. For this 20% of our population, many of whom suffer from chronic conditions that fuel health care costs, any financial incentive to minimize costs disappears, at least for the rest of the benefit year.

Finally, linking coverage to jobs, in an economy where many employers do not offer health care coverage at a reasonable cost, leads to "job lock": another example of inefficiency built into our intertwined tax and health systems. Purchasing insurance on the individual market, from which 14.6 million nonelderly Americans currently have coverage,[9] is an uncertain gamble,

---

8. Paul Ginsburg, *Employment-Based Health Benefits Under Universal Coverage*, 27 Health Affairs 3, 675–677 (2008).

9. U.S. Gov't Accountability Office, GAO-12-439, *Private Health Insurance: Estimates of Individuals with Pre-Existing Conditions Range from 36 Million to 122 Million* (March 2012), 1, available at http://www.gao.gov/assets/590/589618.pdf. Some of the problems in the insurance market (pre-existing condition exclusion, higher costs that vary depending upon health factors) should dissipate as the insurance reforms in the Patient Protection and Affordable Care Act take effect in 2014.

particularly for one with either a history of health problems or a pre-existing condition. Employees are less likely to leave a job with health insurance to work for a small employer with an uneven track record of employee benefits or start their own business, even if the alternative work is more attractive.

Advantages of an Employment-Based System

Employer-provided insurance keeps intact the large risk pools essential to insurance. Employers might not be willing to play this role without the substantial tax subsidy they currently enjoy, and without employer-provided insurance, many employees, particularly the healthy ones, might opt out of insurance altogether, leading to adverse selection. Adverse selection is when, all things being equal, people with poorer-than-average health expectations tend to enroll in health insurance while healthier people, and those people with fewer resources, are more likely to be "free-riders." Free riding is easier in our society, where the uninsured are rarely turned down for medical emergencies. To capture the costs, however, hospitals and physicians shift many uncompensated care costs to those who are insured. If employers can be induced to provide insurance through the provision of tax subsidies, although this may not be done in the most efficient manner given the regressive nature of the benefits, it may be more efficient than if the government ran the health care system directly.

Moreover, whether the tax subsidy is regressive is a matter of definition. A recent issue brief by the Commonwealth Fund notes that while the average tax subsidy for health benefits in absolute dollars is larger for workers higher on the income scale, the subsidy amounts to nearly 10 percent of after-tax income for very low-wage workers and only 1 percent of after-tax income for those with high incomes. As the authors state:

> Employers typically pay the same premium for health insurance for all eligible workers, irrespective of income level, although payments vary based on whether the plan is for single or family coverage. Over the past decade, premiums have generally increased far faster than wages. As a result, employer payments for health insurance premiums represent a substantial share of total compensation for low-and middle-income employees and a much lower share for upper-income employees and corporate executives. Thus, the federal tax exemption for employer-paid premiums is of particular value to low-wage and middle-income workers and their families.[10]

Following this logic, the employer health insurance tax subsidy may mean more to Curt's family after all.

Additional advantages the tax subsidy creates are the administrative efficiencies of employer purchasing. Employers can bargain more aggressively than individual employees. Overhead costs such as marketing are lower, which is reflected in overall lower costs.

Finally, given their long track record as purchasers, many medium and large employers have developed the expertise and relationships necessary to

---

10. Cathy Schoen et al., *Progressive or Regressive? A Second Look at the Tax Exemption for Employer-Sponsored Health Insurance Premiums*, The Commonwealth Fund Issue Brief (2009), 53.

bargain effectively. Some have led reforms not only in payment but in quality as well. The Leapfrog Group's focus on medical errors and the University of Michigan's employer "value-based purchasing" initiatives predated and led the way for many of the efforts we see reflected in today's health reform debate.

FLEXIBLE SPENDING BENEFITS, MEDICAL DEDUCTIONS, AND HEALTH SAVINGS ACCOUNTS

While the largest health-related tax expenditure relates to employer-provided insurance, three additional significant benefits are available to individuals: the itemized deduction for medical expenses that exceed 7.5 percent of annual income; flexible spending accounts (FSAs), which are employee salary reduction arrangements providing exclusion from gross income for amounts used to reimburse employees for medical expenses; and health savings accounts (HSAs), which are used in conjunction with a high-deductible health insurance plan.[11] In the following paragraphs we briefly describe the itemized deduction and flexible spending accounts, which are more long-standing in the tax code, and then move to the relatively recent creation of HSAs.

Congress first provided an income tax deductible for medical expenses in 1942. Today, to the extent an individual spends more than 7.5 percent of adjusted gross income on unreimbursed medical expenses, that taxpayer may claim an *itemized deduction*. Claiming an itemized deduction assumes that the taxpayer has sufficient personal deductions to claim an itemized deduction (i.e., allowable itemized deductions exceed the standard deduction) and that the medical expenses qualify for the deduction. The definition of medical expenses for these purposes is narrower than that of those that qualify for FSAs and HSAs; it does not include nonprescription medications, for example. It may include the cost of health insurance premiums to the extent they are not excluded from taxable income already.

A recent dispute over deductibility of hormone therapy, sex reassignment surgery, and breast augmentation surgery for a transgender individual highlights the intersection between health policy and this portion of the tax code. Many insurance policies exclude coverage for what is commonly referred to as a "sex-change operation." That certainly was the case for the petitioner in *O'Donnabhain v. Commissioner*,[12] a 2010 Tax Court decision. Petitioner sought to deduct as a medical care expense the amounts paid related to reassignment surgery. Born a genetic male, petitioner was diagnosed with gender identity disorder (GID) in 1997. After several years of taking prescribed feminizing hormones and undergoing plastic surgery, petitioner underwent the reassignment surgery in 2001 and later claimed deductions for the related expenses.

The Internal Revenue Service (IRS) disallowed the deductions, claiming that the treatments did not treat a "disease" but, rather, were nondeductible

---

11. Another large tax expenditure is the deduction for health insurance premiums of self-employed individuals. This deduction does not "even the playing field" between the self insured and enrollees of group health plans, for a variety of reasons that are beyond the scope of this chapter.

12. 134 T.C. No. 4, 2010 WL 364206 (U.S. Tax Ct. 2010).

"cosmetic surgery or other similar procedures."[13] In a lengthy opinion, the Tax Court disagreed, finding that petitioner suffered from severe GID, that GID is a well-recognized and serious mental disorder, and that petitioner's hormone therapy and sex reassignment surgery "treated" the disease. As the Court stated, "[r]espondent's contention that petitioner undertook the surgery and hormone treatments to improve appearance is at best a superficial character-ization of the circumstances that is thoroughly rebutted by the medical evidence."[14]

Most medical deduction deductions are less contentious. In 2008, 10.8 million tax returns, accounting for approximately 6% of all returns, claimed the deduction.[15] For those who are insured, the claimed expenses primarily consist of payments for expensive medical items not covered by insurance. The most frequently listed expenses are mental health care, dental treatments, and long-term care. This list reflects the lack of coverage in many plans for these items. Dental insurance often will not cover expensive root canal surgeries. Moreover, because Medicare covers only up to 100 days of nursing home care, long-term care is an expensive item for seniors who do not (at least yet) qualify for Medicaid. But while these expenses are uncovered by many plans and the AGI threshold of 7.5 percent applies to all, it is only the taxpayer who has sufficient personal deductions in general who can claim this itemized deduction.

Flexible spending accounts (FSAs) are funded on a salary reduction basis under a cafeteria plan so that employees can reduce their compensation by a set amount, which is then available to them to spend on certain medical expenses on a pretax basis. Cafeteria plans include a requirement that monies remaining in an FSA at the end of a plan year must be forfeited. This "use it or lose it" rules leads some to criticize FSAs as a government-subsidized program that contributes to excess consumption. While this criticism can be directed at all the employer-based tax subsidies, it is a particular issue for the FSA. These accounts are most often offered by employers that provide insurance and, as a result, are frequently used for items that have a strong personal consumption component, such as eyeglasses.

FSAs were created by the Revenue Act of 1978. As of 2009, there were no legal limits on contributions to a health FSA, although employers often set a cap. Nonprescription drugs are covered as "medical expenses" that can be reimbursed under an FSA, further contributing to the "excess consumption" concern. FSAs can cover neither the amounts paid for health insurance pre-miums nor the amounts paid for long-term care coverage. In 2006, 73 percent of large employers (more than 200 workers) and 20 percent of smaller busi-nesses offered health FSAs.[16]

---

13. Section 213(d)(9) provides that the statutory definition "medical care" for purposes of the insurance tax deduction for medical expenses does not include cosmetic surgery or similar proce-dures unless they are necessary to ameliorate a deformity related to a congenital abnormality, a personal injury, or disfiguring disease.

14. *O'Donnabhain*, 134 T.C. at 25.

15. Joint Commission on Taxation, *Background Materials for Senate Committee on Finance Roundtable on Health Care Financing*, JAX-27-09 (2009).

16. *A Primer on Tax Subsidies for Heath Care*, presented by Larry Lovitt for the Kaiser Family Foundation (April 2009), available at http://www.kaiseredu.org/tutorials/taxsubsidies/player.html.

Health savings accounts (HSAs) are relatively new arrangements that provide the opportunity to pay for out-of-pocket medical expenses on a tax-favored basis. Contributions to an HSA are deductible, and distributions from an HSA for qualified medical expenses are excludable from gross income.

As with individual retirement accounts (IRAs), an individual makes the decision to create and fund an HSA. Unlike an IRA, an HSA can be funded only by an individual with a high-deductible health plan (HDHP) purchased either through an employer or on the individual market. An HDHP is defined, using 2008 dollars, as a plan that has an annual deductible of at least $1,100 for individual, or $2,200 for family, coverage. In contrast to the FSA, an individual is not required to provide substantiation to the custodian of an HSA that a distribution is for a qualified expense. Nor do HSAs share the "use it or lose it" rule governing FSAs. Rather, earnings on amounts in an HSA accumulate on a tax-free basis. As a result, for those individuals with an HDHP, HSAs provide the opportunity not only to pay for current medical expenses on a tax-favored basis but also to save for future medical and (in a manner similar to an IRA) certain nonmedical expenses on a tax-favored basis as well. Finally, HSAs can be rolled over to a new employer, much like IRAs.

HSAs were adopted in 2003, when the Medicare Prescription Drug, Improvement and Modernization Act added section 223 to the Internal Revenue Code (IRC) as part of a push toward consumer-driven health plans (CDHPs). As discussed earlier, one of the disadvantages of employer-based health insurance is that employees are insulated from the true cost of care. As a result, for those with generous coverage, there is little incentive to seek out medical care that provides good outcomes at a lower cost. The goal of CDHP was to move from a system with few incentives for individuals to spend health care dollars wisely to a system where consumers had "skin in the game." Ideally, individuals sensitized to the cost of health care (but shielded from catastrophic medical costs) would spend their dollars more carefully and contribute to an overall effort to control spiraling health care costs. They would do so by spending their HSA dollars as their own. In essence, HSAs embodied the same cost control goals as managed care did in the 1990s. The difference, advocates opined, is that with consumers in control of decision making, HSAs would not meet the same backlash faced by health maintenance organizations (HMOs).

Not everyone favored HSAs. Critics argued that they would disproportionately attract the relatively young and healthy, leaving other insurance products with a less healthy risk pool through adverse selection. This is a particular concern where an HSA/HDHP is offered alongside traditional health insurance plans. In this scenario, critics were concerned that healthy employees would chose the HDHP, which would lead to adverse selection and increase costs of traditional plans offered as an alternative to HSAs. Moreover, many questioned the adequacy of available information that would permit consumers to make informed choices. As an example, I once asked my son's pediatrician the costs of the two alternatives to treat a broken wrist. I did not have an HSA but was trying to be a cost-conscious consumer.

The pediatrician had no idea of the cost difference between a full cast and a splint.

Even where costs are transparent, medical decision making is often complex, leading to somewhat paternalistic concerns that those with HSAs would make poorly informed decisions when faced with financial concerns as well as poor health. More fundamentally, critics argued that CDHPs such as HSAs would motivate patients to avoid or delay health care because of the costs, particularly preventive visits. This, they argued, would only increase overall costs in the long term. Finally, critics noted that not only would patients need cost information to make cost-benefit decisions, but they would also need comparative data on provider and hospital performance as well as information that would allow them to assess their own health risks. When I considered the alternatives to treat my son's wrist, for example, I wanted not only the costs but the risks and benefits of alternative treatments. To our pediatrician's credit, she certainly provided the risk/benefit information.

Finally, critics question whether patients (even when equipped with cost and quality information) are in the best position to make health care decisions related to provider and treatment options. Often, the costliest decisions face patients when they are ill and most dependent on a physician's recommendations.

Because HSAs are relatively new, it is not yet clear who is correct: HSA proponents or their critics. Studies of early usage of CDHPs found that enrollees in high-deductible plans were more likely than those in traditional preferred provider organizations (PPOs) to delay seeking care because of costs.[17] Of greater concern is the finding that enrollees in CDHPs were much more likely than those in other plans to discontinue their chronic-illness medicines.[18] When health expenditures are measured by disease, we learn that 80 percent of health care dollars are attributable to treating chronic conditions such as hypertension, arthritis, heart disease, asthma, mental conditions, and diabetes.[19] If HSA enrollees are more likely to skip prescriptions to treat chronic conditions, the creation of this tax-favored entity may be more likely to increase, rather than limit, health care costs in the long term.

CDHPs have certainly increased over the past decade, but not as dramatically as predicted. The U.S. Treasury Department predicted that 25 to 30 million people would be covered by an HSA-eligible plan and have an account by 2010. As of 2009, 5 million adults (4 percent of the population) were enrolled in an HDHP plus an HSA. HDHPs covered not only these 5 million but 11 million more. Of the total 16.2 million people in HDHPs, over 6 million were eligible for an HSA but had not opened the accounts.[20] The characteristics

---

17. Anna Dixon et al., *Do Consumer-Directed Health Plans Drive Change in Enrollees' Health Care Behavior?*, 27 Health Affairs 4 (July/August 2008).

18. Jessica Greene et al., *The Impact of Consumer-Directed Health Plans on Prescription Drug Use*, 27 Health Affairs 4 (July/August 2008).

19. Gerard F. Anderson, *Physician, Public, and Policymaker Perspectives on Chronic Conditions*, 163 Archives Internal Med. 437 (2003).

20. Paul Fronstin, *Findings from the 2009 EBRI/MGA Consumer-Driven Health Care Survey*, Employee Benefit Research Institute Issue Brief 337 (Dec. 2009).

of HSA enrollees provide fodder for both proponents and critics of consumer-driven health care. Those enrolled in HSAs are, indeed, more engaged in wellness programs and cost-conscious behaviors. They also are healthier, more educated, and wealthier, reflecting the adverse selection concerns voiced by critics.[21]

But HSAs are still new. More importantly, their design is flexible, so that preventive visits and even drugs for chronic conditions may be paid for on a first-dollar basis, thereby mitigating some concerns raised by critics and enrollees. As employers and health plans promoting HSAs continue to massage their design, some of the unintended consequences of consumer-driven health care may be addressed.

HEALTH POLICY DEVELOPS THROUGH TAXATION CHOICES

The face of our health care system is painted not only by congressional choices regarding deductions from income, but by what is taxed in the first place. For, although our society gravitates toward what is subsidized (employer health insurance, FSAs, HSAs), that leaves the option that it will avoid what is taxed. There are numerous health care examples that influence behavior through taxation. Many states, for example, choose not to impose sales taxes on prescription drugs. They choose, however, to impose alcohol and cigarette taxes, as does the federal government. Nonprofit nursing homes, hospices, and health plans, on the other hand, benefit from preferential tax treatment. In the following paragraphs we explore two very different tax choices: "sin" taxes on certain foods and drinks, and the treatment of many hospitals as tax-exempt charities.

DECISION ON WHETHER TO TAX: SIN TAXES ON FOOD AND DRINK

Obesity has increased dramatically in the United States over the past thirty years. Today, two-thirds of Americans are either overweight or obese.[22] As our collective weight increases, so do related health conditions such as type-II diabetes, heightened levels of cholesterol, and increased presence of heart disease. The costs for treating these conditions have increased accordingly. As costs increase, so do the calls for sin taxes on unhealthy food and drinks. The intent behind these taxes is to "reduce consumption of [these] product[s], raise revenue, and improve public health."[23]

---

21. *See* Dixon et al., *supra* note 17; Greene et al., *supra* note 18.
22. Centers for Disease Control and Prevention. Behavioral Risk Factor Surveillance System. *Prevalence and Trends Data Nationwide (States and DC) (2007) Overweight and Obesity (BMI)*. http://apps.nccd.cdc.gov/brfss/list.asp?cat=OB&yr=2010&qkey=4409&state=All (last visited July 27, 2012).
23. Jason M. Fletcher et al., *Can Soft Drink Taxes Reduce Population Weight?*, Contemp. Econ. Pol'y, 2 (2009), available at http://www.med.yale.edu/eph/faculty/labs/fletcher/fft.pdf.

Two rationales are set forth by proponents of sin taxes. One rationale views obesity as driven by individual choice, thus blaming individuals for making poor and irrational diet decisions. Proponents following this rationale urge "fat taxes" in order to curb individual behavior by making unhealthy choices more expensive than healthy alternatives.

A second rationale views obesity as a nationwide epidemic caused by environmental factors such as an oversaturation of fast food restaurants and junk food with manipulative advertising campaigns. From this rationale, proponents of fat taxes urge reformation of advertising tax deductions and the imposition of fat taxes in order to raise revenue to fund health education programming.

Simple calculation of expending more calories than one consumes lends itself to the personal responsibility argument; that obese individuals exercise less self-control in overeating and not enough motivation to exercise. But it is far from that simple. Genetics and other physiological causes contribute to one's ability to gain or lose weight. Furthermore, societal contributors, such as increased calories in food, larger portion sizes, and less physically demanding jobs, contribute to the increased levels of obesity. In short, there are a myriad of factors that contribute to obesity. When reviewing the three types of taxes that public health proponents advocate, not in the name of tax efficiency, but in the name of public health, consider whether they will actually achieve the public health goal of reducing obesity.

"Junk" Food Taxes

As of 2000, seventeen states and two major cities imposed taxes on unhealthy foods and beverages such as soft drinks, candy, chewing gum, and snack foods (potato chips, pretzels, etc.).[24] Although some health experts suggest that fat taxes be levied according to the food's saturated or *trans* fat content rather than the whole "snack food" category, legislative bodies have been more receptive to the practical approach of taxing well-recognized categories of food that are commonly regarded as unhealthy.

Some states simply impose on "junk food" the general sales tax applicable to all other nonfood purchases rather than a selective excise tax. Traditionally these taxes are rationalized as a revenue-raising endeavor rather than as a control on individual behavior. For example, since 1992 "[p]roducts ... commonly packaged and sold as candy, including health and diet food products, [have been] subject[ed] to sales tax whether sold over the counter or in a vending machine" in the State of Minnesota.[25] Table 5-2 sets forth examples of the soft drink and snack food state taxes in effect in 2000:

---

24. Jeff Stranad, *Conceptualizing the "Fat Tax": The Role of Food Tax in Developed Economies*, 78 S. Cal. Rev. 1221, 1224 (2005) (citing Kelly D. Brownell and Thomas R. Frieden, *Ounces of Prevention—The Public Policy Case for Taxes on Sugared Beverages*, 360 New Eng. J. Med. 1805 (Apr. 30, 2009))

25. Minn. Rev. Notice No. 92-09, *Sales and Use Tax—Application to Candy and Soft Drinks* (Feb. 18, 1992), available at http://www.revenue.state.mn.us/law_policy/revenue_notices/ RN_92-09.pdf.

Table 5-2. State Taxes on Soft Drinks and Snack Foods as of 2000

State	Year enacted	Tax applied
California	1933	Sales tax (7.25%)on soft drinks
Maine	1991	Sales tax (5.5%) on snack foods, soft drinks, carbonated water, ice cream, toaster pastries
New Jersey	1966	Sales tax (6%) on candy, carbonated soft drinks
Texas	1961	Sales tax (6.25) on carbonated and noncarbonated packaged soft drink beverages, diluted juices, candy
Washington	1989	$1 per gal of syrup

Sugar-Sweetened Beverages.

While early taxes on candy and other junk foods were nominal (or at least in line with taxes on nonfood items), recent tax initiatives made in the name of public health go much further. Most recently, New York Governor David Paterson's 2010–2011 budget proposals included a severe tax on sugary beverages in order to discourage individuals, especially children and adolescents, from excessive consumption of these beverages.[26] The 2009–2010 year's proposal, which would have imposed an additional 18 percent tax on nondiet soft drinks, sodas, and beverages, as well as fruit drinks that contain less than 70% natural fruit juice, did not make it through budget enactment. However, this tax made its way back to the budget the following year.

While Governor Patterson's eye-catching initiative failed, other states have imposed specific excise taxes (albeit less extreme ones) on sugar-sweetened beverages specifically. A September 2009 article in the *New England Journal of Medicine* examined trends in the consumption of sugar-sweetened beverages, evidence linking such beverages to adverse health outcomes, and several "approaches to designing a tax system that could promote good nutrition and help the nation recover health care costs associated with the consumption of sugar-sweetened beverages."[27] The authors proposed a tax on "sugar-sweetened" (including high-fructose corn syrup) drinks (not diet beverages) that they state would "raise much needed dollars while likely reducing obesity prevalence, which is a major drive of health care costs . . . Ultimately the government needs to raise more money to cover the deficit, and in terms of raising that revenue, a tax on sugar sweetened beverages is really a no brainer."[28]

---

26. Robert L. Megna, *State of New York 2010-2011 Executive Budget Briefing Book*, available at http://www.budget.ny.gov/pubs/archive/fy1011archive/eBudget1011/fy1011littlebook/HealthierNY.html.

27. Kelly D. Brownell et al., *The Public Health and Economic Benefits of Taxing Sugar-Sweetened Beverages*, 361 New Eng. J. Med. 1599 (Sept. 16, 2009), available at http://content.nejm.org/cgi/content/full/NEJMhpr0905723.

28. *Id.*

Not surprisingly, the American Beverage Association opposes any such taxes. In response to the article quoted above, Susan Neely, President and CEO for the American Beverage Association, issued the following statement (in part):

> While the authors suggest a 1-cent per ounce tax for any beverage with caloric sweeteners, there is no science to support that this would have a measurable impact on our nation's waist line. Importantly, taxes will not teach our children how to live a healthy lifestyle. In fact, excise taxes on soft drinks simply do not reduce obesity rates. West Virginia and Arkansas are two prime examples — both have excise taxes on soft drinks, yet rank fifth and sixth highest in the nation for obesity rates. Furthermore, a study out of George Mason University's Mercatus Center shows that even a 15-cent per can tax would result in only a .02 change in body mass index. This amount isn't even measurable on a bathroom scale. And, importantly, our industry has reduced calories per ounce produced by more than 24 percent since 1998, yet obesity rates continued to climb during that same time period.[29]

The American Beverage Association may be onto something; the tax levels currently in place are too low to effectuate a change. But taxes on sugary beverages may become part of the agenda. A Kaiser Family Foundation poll in 2009 found that 52 percent of respondents favored an increased tax on soda and sugary drinks as a way of financing health care reform.[30] But whether these Americans would support the steep tax necessary to affect the public health outcome in reducing obesity epidemic is an open question.

Tax on Advertising.

Section 162(a) of the IRC allows the deduction of "all the ordinary and necessary expenses paid or incurred during the taxable year in carrying on any trade or business." By regulation the IRS interprets this provision to allow "advertising and other selling expenses" to be deducted as an ordinary business expense in the year that they were incurred.[31] Thus, sin tax proponents assert that manufacturers have an incentive to advertise foods of low nutritional value because "[t]his provision permits the food industry to spend a great deal of money on developing and using marketing practices directed toward children, and then allows advertisers to deduct the advertising expenses incurred during the year."[32]

The IRC draws an important distinction between "expenses," which confer an immediate benefit and are deductible in the tax year they are incurred, and "capital expenditures," which confer a benefit beyond the current tax year and must be amortized over the life of the benefit. Rather than allowing an immediate deduction, sin tax proponents have urged Congress to amend the IRC to require amortization of the advertising costs of low-nutrition food over the

---

29. American Beverage Association, *Industry Critics Continue to Push Ineffective Approaches to Combating Obesity with Latest Paper* (Press Release, Sept. 16, 2009), available at http://www .ameribev.org/news–media/news-releases–statements/more/171/.

30. The Henry J. Kaiser Family Foundation, *Kaiser Health Tracking Poll: Public Opinion on Health Care Issues* (June 2009), available at http://www.kff.org/kaiserpolls/upload/7925.pdf.

31. Treas. Reg. §1.162-1(a).

32. Valerie Byrd Fulwider, *Future Benefits? Tax Policy, Advertising, and the Epidemic of Obesity in Children*, 20 J. Contemp. Health L. & Pol'y 217 (Winter 2003).

period of the benefit. In support of their argument, commentators point to the United State Supreme Court's ruling in *INDOPCO, Inc. v. Commissioner of Internal Revenue (INDOPCO)*, which required a corporation to capitalize its legal and investment banking expenses related to a merger with another corporation because there was a *long-term* benefit of the merger to the corporate taxpayer.[33] However, Revenue Ruling 92-80 specifically states that the *INCOPCO* decision will not affect a trade or business's ability to deduct advertising costs under §162(a).[34]

Congressional action, advocates point out, could overrule the revenue ruling and reduce what is effectively a government subsidy (through permitting the deduction of advertising costs) of junk food promotion. In response to such arguments, the food and beverage industries turned to legislators to voice their opposition to advertising cost reform. The pressure appears to be working. A recent report from the Joint Hearing before the Committee on Labor, Health and Human Services Agency stated that "the media and food industries have demonstrated their commitment to fighting childhood obesity. Now, the government must step in to address the main causes of childhood obesity, including the lack of recess and physical education in schools and proper nutrition in school lunches."[35]

Ongoing Debate Regarding the Effectiveness of New Sin Taxes

Proponents of sin taxes urge the adoption of new and increased taxes both to raise revenue and protect the public health. Even small taxes on widely consumed foods can raise substantial revenue. The state of Arkansas imposed a two-cent tax per twelve-ounce can of soda and $40 million was raised per year. Even more striking, the imposition of a 7.25 percent sales tax on soft drinks in California generates an estimated $218 million in revenues annually.[36]

Beyond revenue generation, it is unclear whether these small taxes have a significant effect on sales and consumption. A recent article by the *Milbank Quarterly* predicts that "[s]mall taxes or subsidies [for calorie-dense, unhealthy foods] are not likely to produce significant changes in BMI . . . but that nontrivial pricing interventions may have some measurable effects on Americans' weight outcomes, particularly for children and adolescents, low-SES [socioeconomic status] populations, and those most at risk for overweight."[37] Imposition of a selective excise tax on cigarettes has demonstrated that for every 5 percent tax increase, there is likely to be a 2 percent decline in sales.[38] Perhaps the same would be true for soda and nonnutritional snacks.

However, not all excise taxes have the intended consequence, a lesson we could have learned early in American history. Consider the first whiskey tax.

---

33. *INDOPCO, Inc. v. Comm'r*, 530 U.S. 79 (1992).
34. Rev. Rul. 92-80, 1992-2 C.B. 57.
35. *Watch What You Eat: Food Marketing to Kids: Hearing Before the S. Comm. on Appropriations, Subcomm. on Labor, Health and Human Services Agencies*, 110th Cong. 2 (Sept. 23, 2008).
36. Michael F. Jacobson and Kelly D. Brownell, *Small Taxes on Soft Drinks and Snack Foods to Promote Health*, 90 Am. J. Pub. Health, Vol. 6 (June 2000).
37. Lisa M. Powell and Frank J. Chaloupka, *Food Prices and Obesity: Evidence and Policy Implications for Taxes and Subsidies*, 87 Milbank Quarterly 1 (2009).
38. Jacobson and Brownell, *supra* note 36.

In 1790, Treasury Secretary Alexander Hamilton proposed a tax on whiskey to help repay the new nation's war debts. A tax of six cents per gallon on large producers and nine cents per gallon on small producers was levied, but whiskey consumption continued unabated. The demand for alcohol appeared inelastic, a fact that enticed Congress to continue to impose excise taxes on alcohol across the centuries. As Democrats noted after Franklin Delano Roosevelt proposed to repeal Prohibition and impose alcohol taxes in its place, "if only given a chance, Americans might drink themselves into a balanced budget."[39] Another popular Depression-time slogan argued that "sellers of such morally suspect products should give some of their profits back" for the common good.[40] As one can gather from the current debate over junk food and soda taxes, it turns out that Patrick Henry's "give me liberty or give me death" was not the only early American phrase that resonates throughout our history. So does the rhetoric on sin taxes.

Despite the ambiguous data about the effectiveness of the use of sales taxes to achieve public health outcomes, lifestyle tax proposals continue to proliferate. One prominent example is the white paper from Senators Max Baucus and Charles Grassley, ranking members of the influential Senate Finance Committee, setting forth policy options for health reform in May 2009. Their options included both a tax increase on alcoholic beverages and an excise tax on sugar-sweetened beverages. With regard to the sugar-sweetened beverages, the senators noted that they contributed to obesity, "which drives up health care costs within the system." They then set forth the option of imposing a new federal tax on beverages sweetened with sugar, high-fructose corn syrup, or similar sweeteners. The tax would not apply to artificially sweetened beverages.[41]

DECISION NOT TO TAX: NONPROFIT HOSPITALS

The 1950s were known in the health care and tax worlds for clarifying the exclusion from income for coverage under employer-provided health insurance, thus propelling employer-provided insurance to its current status. That decade was also known for standard setting for nonprofit hospitals. In their "earliest origins . . . hospitals were primarily religious and charitable institutions for tending to the sick, rather than medical institutions existing for their cure."[42] Prior to the twentieth century, most Americans lived in rural areas and never had the occasion to visit a hospital. Individuals suffered illnesses and even underwent surgical procedures at home. Additionally, women gave birth at home. Hospitals in the United States emerged from institutions,

---

39. Brenda Yelvington, *Excise Taxes in Historical Perspective*, in William F. Shughart, II ed., *Taxing Choice: The Predatory Politics of Fiscal Discrimination* (Transaction Publishers, 1997), 31, 40.

40. Jendi B. Reitner, *Citizens or Sinners? The Economic and Political Inequity of "Sin Taxes" on Tobacco and Alcohol Products*, 29 Colum. J.L. & Soc. Probs. 443, 444 (1996).

41. Statement by Sens. Baucus and Grassley, Senate Finance Committee Chairman and Ranking Member, *Policy Options for Financing Comprehensive Health Care Reform* (May 18, 2009) http://finance.senate.gov/newsroom/chairman/release/?id=c86aadcd-5f2b-42e8-a4d2-c38bf43a9e3e (last visited July 27, 2012).

42. Starr, *supra* note 5; Helena G. Rubinstein, *Nonprofit Hospitals and the Federal Tax Exemption: A Fresh Prescription*, 7 Health Matrix 381 (1997).

such as almshouses, that primarily provided care to the sick and the poor who were unable to pay for physician home visits or did not even have shelter. Thus, hospitals were rooted in a tradition of charity.

As the twentieth century progressed, hospitals began to offer medical cures, rather than just a place for the sick and the poor to receive care. World War II brought profound changes in hospital care as advances in military surgery introduced safe blood transfusions, penicillin, and trauma-trained surgeons.[43] The 1970s brought the greatest changes in the role of hospitals because of the expansion of the pharmaceutical industry. Advancements in pharmaceuticals meant the transformation of the management of diseases and conditions, including many cancers. Hospitals were transformed from shelter for the sick and the poor to a "modern complex in which seriously ill patients are treated at a high speed with highly technical equipment and by skilled specialist staff."[44]

While the role of hospitals and their charitable activities changed throughout the past century, policymakers struggled to determine exactly what qualifies a hospital for tax-exempt status. A 1956 Revenue Ruling set forth clear expectations. It required a tax-exempt hospital to be operated "to the extent of its financial ability for those not able to pay for the services rendered." Shortly thereafter, the Tax Court upheld denial of exempt status where a hospital devoted between 2 percent and 5 percent of its revenue to charity care. But after the passage of Medicare and Medicaid, when many of the poor and elderly served by nonprofit hospitals became eligible for these government programs, the IRS shifted away from a charity care focus to a broader "community benefit" standard. In Revenue Ruling 69-545, the IRS suggested that the existence of a community board, an open emergency room treating indigent patients free of charge, an open medical staff, and treatment of government-insured patients would provide adequate evidence that the hospital was serving charitable purposes meriting exempt status. This ruling made "promotion of health" for the general benefit of the community a "charitable purpose" even when many members of the community (the poor, the uninsured) would not benefit. It was reinforced by IRS Revenue Ruling 83-157, which eliminated the requirement that a tax-exempt hospital operate an emergency room. As a result, today federal tax status for hospitals is not directly tied to the provision of charity care.

This largely untethered tax saving provided to nonprofit hospitals is substantial. According to a 2003 comprehensive study of nonprofit hospitals by the Government Accountability Office (GAO), of the roughly 3,900 non-federal, short-term acute-care general hospitals in the United States, the majority—about 62 percent—were nonprofit. Today that number is even higher, with just under 3,000 nonprofit hospitals.[45] A report issued by the

---

43. Martin McKee & Judith Healy, *The Role of the Hospital in a Changing Environment*, 78 Bulletin of the World Health Organization, 803, 804 (2000).

44. *Id.*

45. *Nonprofit, For-Profit, and Government Hospitals: Uncompensated Care and Other Community Benefits Before the H. Comm. on Ways and Means*, 109th Cong. (2005) (statement of David M. Walker, Comptroller General of the United States), available at http://www.gao.gov/new.items/d05743t.pdf.

CBO in 2006 stated that in 2002, hospital tax exemptions were worth an estimated $12.6 billion nationwide, approximately half from the federal exemption.[46]

While the value of the tax expenditure is clear, the value of the community benefits provided by nonprofit hospitals has been difficult to define, quantify, and standardize. This has led to calls for clearer standards and the disclosures at both the federal and state legislatures. The same CBO study that examined the value of the hospital tax expenditure also found that despite their tax favored status, nonprofit hospitals overall provided only slightly more charity care than for-profit hospitals. This finding provided further fuel for the Senate Finance Committee (and Senator Grassley in particular) to repeat concerns about the amount of charity care and community benefits provided by nonprofit hospitals, as well as past conversions of nonprofit assets for use by for-profits.[47] However, despite hearings drawing attention to the issue by the House Ways and Means Committee in 2005 and the Senate Finance Committee in 2006, neither Congress nor the IRS mandated a specific level of charity care. Indeed, the Revenue Rulings since 1969 can be read to state that hospitals need not provide *any* charity care in order to be granted tax exempt status.[48]

The seismic shift in approach between the 1956 and 1969 Revenue Rulings was controversial. The shift was not uniformly adopted by states, many of which had existing statutes or case law that reflected a charity care–based standard. State and local officials from New Hampshire to Utah stepped up enforcement challenges of hospital behavior and tax-exempt status.

Then came Illinois. In 2004, the Illinois Department of Revenue, in a rare instance of a taxing authority revoking tax-exempt status based on a hospital's failure to provide charity care, denied exemption for Provena Covenant Hospital in 2002.[49] The issue in *Provena Covenant* was essentially how much charity care a hospital had to provide in order to be "charitable" and qualify for a property tax exemption for its real estate.

In 2002, Provena Covenant reported charitable activities totaling 0.7% of that year's total revenue. While the hospital had a sliding-scale payment system, patients typically were not notified they were eligible for charity care, and their bills were sent, instead, to collection agencies. As the court noted, while the hospital's charitable activities totaled $831,724, the value of the property tax exemption was $1.1 million. The final administrative decision found that neither the medical center nor the hospital dispensed charity to all who needed it and, in fact, placed obstacles in the way of those needing the medical services and hospitalization. The Illinois Circuit Court, however, reversed the

---

46. Heather Devlin, *Non-Profit Hospitals, Tax-Exemption and Community Benefits*, Geo. H. Pol. Center Issue Br. (Jan. 2009), available at http://ays.issuelab.org/research/listing/non_profit_hospitals_tax_exemption_and_community_benefits.

47. *Nonprofit Hospitals and the Provision of Community Benefits*, CBO Paper (Dec. 2006), available at http://www.cbo.gov/ftpdocs/76xx/doc7695/12-06-Nonprofit.pdf

48. *See* Rev. Rul. 83-157; *see generally* Daniel M. Fox and Daniel C. Schaffer, *Tax Administration as Health Policy: Hospital, The Internal Revenue Service and the Courts*, 16 J. Health Pol., Pol'y & L. 251 (1991).

49. *See* Provena Covenant Med. Ctr., No. 04-PT-0014 (Ill. Dep't. of Revenue, Sept. 29, 2006) (final admin. decision), available at http://www.revenue.state.il.us/legalinformation/hearings/pt/pt06-26.pdf.

administrative decision; then the Illinois Appellate Court reversed the Circuit Court's decision.[50]

The Appellate Court found that Provena Covenant met only one of six "distinctive characteristics of a charitable institution," noting that it spent less than 1% of its revenues on charity and that few of its funds derived from donations. Furthermore, the court found that, given its lack of promotion of its sliding-scale charity care policy, its charity was "illusory." In addition, the court noted that its bad debt and lost revenue from Medicare and Medicaid could not be counted toward a "charitable purpose." Finally, the court declined to recognize "off-site charity," which would contribute under a federal community benefit analysis. In March 2010, the Illinois Supreme Court affirmed the Appellate Court's decision.[51]

The initial *Provena Covenant* decision was followed by increased challenges not only to hospitals, but to nonprofit medical clinics as well, particularly in Ohio and Michigan. Legislative battles followed these high-profile court cases in several states. In Illinois, legislation would have required hospitals to spend at least 8% of their annual operating costs on free care.[52] While this legislation failed, other states sought similar legislative changes. New York restricted nonprofit billing and collection activities, as did California. Texas tied charity care to property tax exemptions, with mandatory reporting, and Rhode Island imposed charity care conditions on licensure.[53] In Minnesota, similar obligations were imposed through agreements between nonprofit hospitals and the Minnesota Attorney General's office.

Of course, a debate over how much (if any) charity care should be required by a tax-exempt hospital would not be complete without a fight over how to define charity care. The American Hospital Association adopted a more inclusive (from the hospital perspective) definition: uncompensated care (the total of charity care and bad debt expense) *and* Medicaid and Medicare shortfalls all constitute charity care. The Catholic Health Association (CHA)'s charity care definition is narrower. It excludes bad debt and Medicare shortfalls from its definition.[54]

Not surprisingly, the IRS entered the controversy. In December 2007, it issued the new Form 990 (the tax form filed by tax-exempt organizations each year) to address board size and structures, director independence, audit committee practice, and written conflict of interest and governance practices. This new focus on expanded disclosure of executive pay and perks (such as first-class travel and housing allowances provided to officers and directors) and detailed compensation breakdowns for highly paid employees reflects growing

50. *Provena Covenant Medical Center v. Dep't of Revenue*, 894 N.E.2d 452 (Ill. App. Ct. 2008).
51. *Provena Covenant Medical Center v. Dep't of Revenue*, 2010 WL 966858 (Ill. 2010).
52. H.R. 5000, 94th Gen. Assem., Reg. Sess. (Ill. 2006). *See* Press Release, Ill. Att'y Gen. Lisa Madigan (proposing legislation that would require hospitals to spend 8 percent on free care), available at http://www.ag.state.il.us/pressroom/2006_01/20060123.html.
53. Nicole Bellows et al., *Endangered Species? Not-for-Profit Hospitals Face Tax-Exemption Challenge*, Healthcare Financial Management (Sept. 1, 2004) (explaining the Rhode Island charity care), available at http://www.hfma.org/Templates/Print.aspx?id=170.
54. Fred Joseph Hellinger, *Tax-Exempt Hospitals and Community Benefits; A Review of State Reporting Requirements*, 34 J. Health Pol. Pol'y L. 37, 39 (2009).

skepticism among state and federal regulators over the level of compensation paid by tax exempt entities. But the IRS did not stop there. In Schedule H of the new Form 990, tax-exempt hospitals are subject to expanded reporting of subsidized care and services provided to justify their tax breaks. Beginning in tax year 2009, hospitals must report their community benefit in a fashion that largely follows the CHA definition. Schedule H requires a report of the number of persons receiving charity care and the proportion of operating expense attributable to that care. It also requests information on debt collection practices, Medicaid shortfalls, and other community health programs. When these new reporting obligations go fully into effect in with the tax returns filed in 2010, Congress and an increasingly skeptical media will be able to assess more readily the compensation and charity care/community benefit practices of nonprofit hospitals, and then ask again: Is change called for?

USING THE TAX CODE TO DEVELOP AND ENFORCE HEALTH POLICY: THE RECENT DEBATE

OVERVIEW OF RECENT REFORM OPTIONS

While a health reform platform is one of the constants in recent political campaigns, the issue was at the forefront of the 2008 presidential election. Each of the three leading Democratic candidates heralded a health reform plan. Republican front runner and nominee Senator John McCain also established a plan, which built upon an earlier proposal by President George W. Bush to change the tax subsidy for employer-provided insurance. The following sections present a summary of the tax-related reform proposals that surfaced during the Bush Administration, leading up to the 2008 presidential election. The first three proposals would impose a fundamental shift in our current system, while the fourth reflects the central thrust of Democratic plans proposed during the 2008 campaign. The later proposals represent minor modifications to the code.

Republican Proposals

Replace Deduction for Employer-Based Health Insurance with a Flat Deduction.

President George W. Bush proposed to eliminate the current exclusion and replace it with a tax deduction for individuals who purchase health insurance—whether on their own or through an employer. In his proposal, a fixed amount would be deducted from taxable income, regardless of whether the taxpayer received health care from his employer or through the individual market. The deductions were $7,500 for an individual plan or $15,000 for a family plan. These deductions did not change if one spent $3,000 on an individual plan or $9,000 on an individual plan.

Replace Deduction for Employer-Based Health Insurance with a Flat Credit.

Senator John McCain popularized an approach that would also eliminate the current exclusion but replace it with a tax credit if the family purchased health insurance either through their employer or otherwise. He proposed a $2,500 credit for single coverage and $5,000 credit for family coverage. The flat credit would focus resources at the low end of the income distribution in a way a deduction would not, because many lower-income families do not have income to take advantage of a deduction.

Replace Deduction for Employer-Based Health Insurance with a Credit That Is More Generous for Low-Income Families.

This proposal is essentially the McCain approach but with higher credits for low-income families. It is driven by the concern that the amounts of the proposed credit — even if the credit is refundable so that you get it even if you do not have tax liability — still do not cover the majority of the insurance cost, leaving many Americans without a realistic health care choice.

Democratic Proposals

Mandate Health Insurance Following the Massachusetts Model.

Democratic candidates John Edwards, Hillary Clinton, and Barack Obama each proposed health plans that combined individual and employer mandates with sliding-scale subsidies, expanded Medicaid eligibility, and insurance reforms. Their model was the Massachusetts Plan.

In April 2006, Massachusetts moved the national health reform debate by enacting a plan that aimed to expand health care coverage to nearly all of the uninsured by requiring all residents to purchase health insurance by July 2007. It also created a state-subsidized health insurance program for residents with incomes up to 300 percent of the federal poverty level.[55]

Under the plan, a new "Commonwealth Health Insurance Connector" certifies and offers insurance products and connects individuals and small business with appropriate matches. Individuals who can afford insurance but do not purchase it are penalized on their state income taxes. Companies with ten or more employees that do not provide coverage face an assessment of up to $295 per worker per year. Meanwhile, the state provides public sliding-scale subsidies to families with incomes up to 300 percent of the poverty level to purchase private insurance plans through the Connector,[56] and Medicaid coverage expands for children with family incomes up to 300 percent of the

---

55. Act Providing Access to Affordable, Quality, Accountable Health Care of 2006, Mass. Acts, ch. 58, §12 (codified as Mass. Gen. Laws ch. 111M, §2 (West Supp. 2010)); *Massachusetts: Major Coverage Expansion Legislation*, States in Action: A Quarterly Look at Innovations in Health Policy (The Commonwealth Fund), Apr. 17, 2006, available at http://www.commonwealthfund.org/Content/Newsletters/States-in-Action/2006/Mar/March-2006/States-to-Watch/Massachusetts–Major-Coverage-Expansion-Legislation.aspx.

56. 2006 Mass. Acts, ch. 58 §45 (codified as Mass. Gen. Laws ch. 118H, §3 (2008)). The "connector" is defined as "the commonwealth health insurance connector, established by subsection (a) of section 2 of chapter 176Q" of the General Laws of Massachusetts. *Id.* (codified as Mass. Gen. Laws ch. 118H, §1 (2008)).

federal poverty level.[57] By the end of 2009, Massachusetts had achieved near-universal coverage — and costs were soaring.

Miscellaneous Health-Related Tax Proposals

Modify Health Savings Accounts.

One proposal restricted HSA contributions to the lesser of the individual's deductible or a statutory limit. Another looks to increase the penalty for withdrawals for nonmedical expenses from 10 percent to 20 percent and/or to require certification from either an employer or independent third party that HSA withdrawals were made for medical expenses.

Eliminate or Change Flexible Spending Accounts.

This proposal sought to limit the amount that can be contributed to an FSA or eliminate FSAs altogether. It was made to address the concern that the "use it or lose it" nature of FSAs leads to unnecessary health care consumption at the end of benefit years.

Standardize the Definition of Qualified Medical Expenses.

Currently, no standard definition exists for what qualifies as a medical expense for HSAs, FSAs, or itemized medical expense tax deductions. This proposal sought to apply a standard definition of "medical expense" and apply that definition to all deductions.

Modify the Itemized Deduction for Medical Expenses.

This proposal would either raise the 7.5 percent floor for claiming deductions or eliminate that deduction altogether.

Require Minimal Level of Charitable Activity from Nonprofit Hospitals

Advocates for this proposal would require nonprofit hospitals to maintain a minimal level of charitable activity; limit charges to uninsured, indigent patients; and limit aggressive collection actions. Hospitals violating these standards would be subject to an excise tax. This proposal was fleshed out in a postelection white paper released by Senators Baucus and Grassley on May 18, 2009.

Health Reform and Tax Policy in the Obama Administration

Not surprisingly, given the outcome of the 2008 presidential election, the health reform bills that passed in the House and Senate in late 2009 followed the broad approach of the Democratic presidential candidates.[58] Both bills included an individual mandate requiring most Americans to have basic health insurance. To address those who struggle to afford insurance, the bills provided for a Medicaid expansion and premium subsidies for individuals with incomes up to 400 percent of the federal poverty level. To ensure access

---

57. *Health Care Access and Affordability Conference Committee Report* (2006), available at http://www.allhealth.org/briefingmaterials/ConferenceReportpowerpoint-253.pdf.

58. S. 3590, 111th Cong. (2010); H.R. 3962, 111th Cong. (2009).

and address problems such as pre-existing condition exclusions, the bills created health insurance exchanges with strict restrictions on underwriting and pricing where individuals and small businesses could buy insurance.

To pay for this significant access expansion (projected to cover more than 30 million additional Americans each year), the bills imposed a number of taxes and penalties. Both the Senate and House looked to excise taxes on sectors (such as the medical device industry) that would benefit from increased coverage. Both sought to squeeze costs and overpayments from Medicare providers and insurance. But a payment gap remained. To address this gap, the House bill sought $460 billion in tax surcharges on high-income taxpayers, while the Senate bill imposed an excise tax on insurers of employer-sponsored health plans with aggregate values that exceed $8,500 for individual coverage and $23,000 for family coverage. This Senate tax (dubbed the "Cadillac tax") would be equal to 40 percent of the value of the plan that exceeds the threshold amounts and would be imposed on the issuer of the policy.

The fight over the Cadillac tax loomed large in January 2010. Health policy experts largely hailed the tax, predicting that it would reduce the incentives for employers to provide excessive insurance and, as a result, lead to more careful use of health care. In short, by ending the subsidy for excessively generous insurance, we would lower spending. Moreover, the tax change would be progressive in nature—removing a tax subsidy for those with generous insurance to fund health coverage for the poor and working poor. Finally, experts asserted that the reduction in insurance costs for companies would ultimately result in wage increases for workers.

"Not so fast!" countered insurance companies, unions, and some health policy experts. Limiting the current exemption could adversely affect those at high risk of losing their health coverage. It would disproportionately affect older workers, those in high-cost geographic areas, and wage-earners in high-risk industries, such as construction. Insurance plans with high-risk members would be unfairly burdened. Finally, unions argued that across the years they had traded wage increases for more generous health insurance in the collective bargaining process. To impose an excise tax on the insurance plans would unfairly penalize union members.

The Cadillac tax was not the only tax-related provision in the House and Senate bills. Both bills included an increase in the tax on distributions from HSAs and limits on contributions to flexible spending accounts. The Senate bill also included an increase in the threshold for the itemized deduction for unreimbursed medical expenses to 10 percent of adjusted gross income. Both bills projected saving in Medicare and Medicaid spending due to payment system changes.

Certainly, there were differences between the House and Senate bills beyond the tax provisions. The House bill included a proposal to create a government-run health insurer to compete with private plans. The Senate did not. The House included an employer mandate for all but the smallest employers. The Senate did not. With regard to the junk food/soda tax proposals discussed earlier in this chapter, neither bill took the steps outlined in Senators Baucus and Grassley's white paper to tax sugar-sweetened beverages.

In an attempt to bridge differences between the two bills, on February 22, 2010, President Obama provided his reform proposal in anticipation of a White House Health Care Summit with Democratic and Republican leaders.[59] The proposal adopted the framework of the Senate bill. It included neither a public plan nor an employer mandate. It enhanced premium subsidies and Medicaid expansion, while also closing the prescription drug "donut hole" for seniors. Significantly for our purposes, it delayed the implementation of the high-cost health plan tax for everyone until 2018. In essence, the President outlined changes to the Senate bill designed both to placate some House liberals and, arguably, to pass under Senate reconciliation rules, which permit passage of a bill that will reduce the budget with only 51 votes.

The plan came to fruition on March 23, 2010, when President Obama signed comprehensive health reform legislation, the Patient Protection and Affordable Care Act (now commonly abbreviated as the "ACA" and referred to as "Obamacare").[60] The ACA requires most U.S. citizens and legal residents to have health insurance. It creates state-based insurance exchanges through which individuals and small businesses can purchase coverage, with premium and cost-sharing credits available to lower income families. It requires employers to pay penalties for employees who receive tax credits for health insurance through an exchange, with exceptions for the smallest employers. It imposes new requirements on health plans in the exchanges, including guaranteed issue, premium rating, and prohibitions on pre-existing condition exclusions in the individual market. Finally, the ACA expands Medicaid coverage to include all individuals who earn up to 133 percent of the federal poverty level. The Medicaid expansion, insurance reforms, and mandates are all phased in over the next several years.

But while Democrats and Republicans alike describe the comprehensive reform bill as a dramatic game-changer (they disagree on the value of the change), the new law does not change the underlying premise of this chapter: health policy in America appears destined to remain intertwined with taxation. It does not move to a single-payer system, with the government as payer, as liberals advocated. The ACA does not move to a voucher system, as Republicans had proposed in the mid-1990s. Rather, it builds upon the employer-based health care system. It creates incentives for employers to provide health care, particularly for low-income employees who might otherwise receive premium assistance through the exchanges. The ACA creates Medicaid expansions that call upon states to provide premium assistance to any Medicaid beneficiary with access to employer-sponsored insurance if doing so is cost-effective for the state. It leaves untouched (at least until 2018) the open-ended tax subsidies, which serve to increase both the value of health insurance benefits and overall health care costs.

---

59. The White House, *Putting Americans in Control of Their Health Care*, http://www.whitehouse .gov/health-care-meeting (last visited July 27, 2012).

60. Patient Protection and Affordable Care Act, Pub. L. No. 111-148. On March 30, 2010, President Obama signed the Health Care and Education Reconciliation Act of 2010, which amends certain aspects of the ACA. Health Care and Education Reconciliation Act of 2010, Pub. L. No. 111-152.

Moreover, the IRS emerges as the chief enforcer of the backbone of reform: the individual mandate. Those without coverage pay a phased-in tax penalty of the greater of $695 per year up to a maximum of three times that amount per family or 2.5% of household income.

While the reform legislation creates a new role for the IRS, it does not directly impose charity care requirements on nonprofit hospitals, as discussed earlier in this chapter. The bill does, however, require nonprofit hospitals to conduct community needs assessments and adopt an implementation strategy to meet the identified needs; adopt and widely publicize a financial assistance policy, limit charges to patients who qualify for financial assistance to the amount generally billed to insured patients, and impose some limits on extraordinary collection actions. Failure to meet the requirements will result in a tax of $50,000 per year. Moreover, while soda and junk food avoided additional taxes in the reform law, tanning salons were not so lucky. Based upon public health concerns that indoor tanning before age 35 increases the risk of developing the most deadly form of skin cancer, tanning salons now are subject to a new 10 percent excise tax on indoor tanning.

While the final reform bill allows for less flexibility in FSAs (an individual can no longer be reimbursed for over-the-counter medications unless they are prescribed, and starting in 2013 the total annual contribution will be limited to $2500), the fact that HSAs emerged unscathed surprised many observers. During the 2008 presidential campaign, policy advisors to then-candidate Obama had raised the specter of HSA elimination. After all, weren't these accounts essentially tax breaks for the healthy, educated, and affluent consumers? It was not to happen. Congress balked, and at the end of the day, the president declared his support for making HSAs available to individuals through the exchanges.

CONCLUSION

On the same day that President Obama signed the ACA into law, 13 state attorneys general filed a lawsuit challenging the constitutionality of the law, in particular the Medicaid expansion and individual mandate provisions. Chief among the arguments was that the law violates the Tenth Amendment to the U.S. Constitution because it exceeds the powers delegated to the federal government by the constitution. Chief among the responses was that the bill is grounded in Congress's ability to lay and collect taxes. It is grounded in the tax code.

The Supreme Court agreed, upholding the individual mandate as a valid exercise of Congress's taxing authority.[61] Although the bill refers to the "shared responsibility payment" for those who choose to forgo health insurance as a "penalty" and not a tax, the Court looked beyond Congress's terminology to discern the function of the payment. By "disregarding the designation of the exaction, and viewing its substance and application,"[62]

---

61. *National Federation of Independent Business v. Sebelius*, 132 S.Ct. 2566 (2012).
62. *Id.* at 2595.

the Court determined that the shared responsibility payment was a tax and not a penalty for four reasons. First, the tax is not so high that there is no choice but to buy health insurance. In fact, the tax is less than the cost of health insurance. Second, the tax is not limited to willful violations. There is no scienter requirement. Third, the tax is collected solely by the IRS through the normal means of taxation, but the IRS may not use punitive methods, such as criminal prosecution, to collect it. Finally, there are no other legal consequences for failing to purchase insurance. It is expected that four million people will choose to pay the tax instead of buying health insurance; "[t]hat Congress apparently regards such extensive failure to comply with the mandate as tolerable suggests that Congress did not think it was creating four million outlaws."[63] Rather, it suggests that the shared responsibility payment is an option that citizens may lawfully choose as an alternative to purchasing health insurance.

Although the individual mandate is enforced through taxation, and the subsidies that undergird reform are, indeed, refundable tax credits, the bill is not a tax reform bill—it is health reform. The major goals of the bill are not horizontal and vertical equity, which presumes that taxes should be "fair" and "progressive," although the cap on FSAs and the increase in the floor for the itemized medical expense deduction to 10 percent represent movement in that direction.[64] Nor did the goals of the ACA appear in line with Adam Smith's canons of taxation in *The Wealth of Nations* that include accepted criteria of efficiency: equity (similar treatment of economically similar taxpayers); neutrality (nondistortion of the market); certainty of incidence and liability; administrative efficiency; and net revenue-restraining effect. Rather, the oft-stated goals of the health reform bill were to ensure access to affordable health coverage for all Americans; reduce long-term growth of health care costs; and improve the quality of care.

That health reform was enacted through a taxation vehicle reflects not only the history of health insurance in the United States but a reality about our tax policy: the tax system does not just raise revenues. It administers social policy and programs. The 2010 Health Reform bill is the latest—and perhaps grandest—example of this fact.

But while fairness in terms of tax policy did not drive health reform, the 2010 health reform legislation begins, ever so slightly, to move toward a health care system that is both more efficient and fairer. The progress is slight because the changes build upon an employer-based system that, prompted by tax subsidies, is far from efficient. As discussed earlier in this chapter, tax incentives are given to high-income families who already can afford insurance. Tax incentives favor those in higher tax brackets, which may lead to employer choices to select the most comprehensive coverage. The current system not only results in a system that is regressive in nature, but it also encourages overconsumption by those with insurance. Finally, it disproportionately benefits employees who

---

63. *Id.* at 2597.

64. Horizontal equity requires that all similarly situated taxpayers be treated equally in order that the system be "fair" whereas vertical equity is said to require that those with greater income be taxed at higher marginal tax rates so that the system promotes justice. *See* Sheldon D. Pollack, *The Failure of U.S. Tax Policy* (Penn State University, 1997), 232–33.

work for the large and medium-sized employers, which, because of the benefits of risk-sharing, are far more likely to provide health insurance.

Congress could have turned from the employer-based system to the single-payer system promoted by liberals. The much-heralded and derided "public option" would have been a strong step in this direction. Or it could have embraced the earlier Republican proposal to eliminate the current exclusion and replace it with a tax deduction or credit to be used to purchase health insurance. Congress chose, instead, to build upon the current system. Having made this choice, Congress could have taken a large step to address the tax inequities within the employer-based system by adopting the Senate proposal to withhold the tax advantage for a small number of "Cadillac Plans." Health economists generally agreed that this 40 percent excise tax on high-cost plans would help control costs without affecting the insurance of most Americans. But while the Cadillac tax remains in the bill, it does not go into effect until 2018. The United States will have held two presidential elections before its implementation.

Nor does the health reform bill address the current HSA dilemma. Instead, it continues to support HSAs, which—at least in practice to date—disproportionally benefit high-income individuals. People struggling to pay premiums find it hard to set aside extra money in an HSA. A 2008 GAO report concluded that the average adjusted gross household income for taxpayers from the ages of 19 to 64 who reported activity in an HSA was about $139,000, as opposed to $57,000 for other tax filers. That should not be a surprise, given that more than 40% of enrollees in HSA-eligible plans had not opened an account.[65]

The 2010 health reform moves toward a system that is fairer and more efficient, but it does so slowly. Many of the uninsured will find that new insurance options do not take effect until 2014. But in 2014, insurers will have to take all applicants regardless of pre-existing conditions. Everyone earning less than 133 percent of the poverty line will be eligible for Medicaid. Americans who do not receive employer-based insurance whose income falls between 133 percent and 400 percent of the poverty line will be offered premium assistance through tax credits to purchase insurance through exchanges. Whether these benefits outweigh the pain that may come through increased insurance premiums and Medicare payment changes remains to be seen. But if the exchanges do serve to create a viable individual market, they may serve as a pathway from an employer-based insurance system to a defined-contribution system similar to the 401(k) contribution, which funds retirement for many Americans. In short, it may be a pathway to health insurance driven more by individuals and less by their employers.

While we wait to see the outcome of the latest great American Experiment, we continue with our employer-based health care system. Created by historic accident, it endures because of both politics and values. Politics fuels its continuation because incremental change frequently is the more palatable option. It is easy to envision a superior system if one erases the past sixty years. It is

---

65. John E. Dicken, *Health Savings Accounts: Participation Increased and Was More Common among Individuals with Higher Incomes* (United States Government Accountability Office 2008), 6.

difficult to envision the enormity of the transition costs of wholesale change, even if the change could pass Congress.

Values fuel its continuation because it combines a market-based approach with the provision of health care to the most vulnerable. These are values that require emergency rooms to treat those in dire medical conditions;[66] values that use tax policy to promote increased access to medical services through treatment of nonprofit hospitals; values that provide tax subsidies to encourage the purchase of health insurance; values that derive from those twin American pillars: respect for private enterprise and care for the vulnerable.

Yet as we move forward, we should pay heed to how our historic and ongoing use of tax subsidies to undergird an employer-based health system fueled the often toxic 2010 health reform debate. Much was made about a "government takeover" of health care. Little public discourse addressed the fact that when the current cost of tax expenditure for employer-based insurance is included, government *already* pays for over 60% of health care in the United States.[67] Such is the result of using the tax system to promote social welfare. We obfuscate reality. While this has immediate practical benefits within Congress, it detracts from our political dialogue.

Much remains to be accomplished if health reform is to achieve its goals. Implementation will be complicated and expensive. Much of the legislation is left to interpretation by the Secretary of Health and Human Services and to implementation by state officials, many of whom oppose the reform they are tasked to deliver. Moreover, the delayed implementation of reform will lead to intense political tests as Americans look for progress today from a bill that largely takes four years to implement. Some parts of the reform effort will not work as expected. For example, will we have the necessary primary care providers participating in public programs? In short, patience and continued change are called for, a certainty that leads us back to the need for enlightened public dialogue. And any enlightened dialogue will acknowledge the intertwined nature of our tax and health care systems.

---

66. Emergency Medical Treatment and Active Labor Act (EMTALA), 42 U.S.C. §1395dd (2008).

67. Steffie Woolhandler & David U. Himmelstein, *Paying for National Health Insurance — And Not Getting It*, 21 Health Affairs 4, 88 (July/Aug. 2008) (citing 59.8 percent as the calculated percentage of the United States' current tax-financed health care system).

CHAPTER 6

THE COMPLEX RELATIONSHIP BETWEEN TAXES AND HEALTH INSURANCE

Amy B. Monahan, University of Minnesota Law School

The United States has a truly unique regulatory scheme for health insurance. Not only are most non-elderly Americans covered by privately financed health insurance, but that insurance is primarily provided through an employer rather than the open market. This regulatory scheme is driven almost entirely by the federal income tax code, which provides unique tax advantages to employer-provided health coverage. These tax advantages stem not from a well-thought-out and well-developed tax or health policy but from what most would characterize as historical accident. During World War II, when strict wage controls were imposed and marginal tax rates were very high, the war board ruled that the value of employer-provided health insurance would not be included in an employee's wages. The IRS similarly ruled in 1943 that such coverage would not be included in an employee's taxable income.[1] The result was that many employers began offering such coverage in an attempt to compete for employees in a tight wartime labor market. Since that time, the prevalence of employer-provided coverage has grown significantly. In 2009, approximately 65% of nonelderly Americans were covered by employer-provided health insurance coverage.[2]

While the tax treatment of employer-provided health care coverage is now firmly entrenched, few are happy with it as a matter of policy. It is easy to criticize on economic efficiency grounds because it distorts the market for health insurance and medical goods in many ways. It is also easy to criticize on fairness grounds, because it makes health insurance more affordable only for those who are employed by an employer who has chosen to offer coverage to employees, and for the self-employed. In addition, risk of bad health is not

---

1. For a brief overview of the history of the tax exclusion for employer-provided health benefits, *see* David A. Hyman & Mark Hall, *Two Cheers for Employment-Based Health Insurance*, 2 Yale J. Health Pol'y L. & Ethics 23, 25 (2001).

2. U.S. Census Bureau, *Health Insurance Coverage Status and Type of Coverage by Selected Characteristics: 2009*, http://www.census.gov/hhes/www/cpstables/032010/health/h01_001.htm.

pooled in a manner that reflects social solidarity; rather, our system stratifies risk and allows "good" risks to pay substantially less than "bad" risks for the same coverage. And there are also concerns about outcomes; the United States spends more for health care than any other country, both on a per capita basis and as a percentage of GDP, and yet our health outcomes lag behind other nations and many individuals remain uninsured. The tax subsidies that we currently provide to employer-sponsored health insurance cost over $100 billion per year. Given that the tax preference is perceived as economically inefficient, as unfair, and as part of a system that leads to poor health outcomes, it is not surprising that when fundamental health care reform was being debated in 2009 and 2010, the tax treatment of health insurance and medical expenses was very much part of the debate.

The passage of the Patient Protection and Affordable Care Act, as amended (PPACA), did indeed include tax changes, but perhaps not the type that were anticipated. In large measure, PPACA leaves in place the existing tax treatment of employer-provided health insurance and simply adds new tax incentives and penalties. Most prominently, PPACA provides significant tax credits to subsidize the purchase of health insurance, imposes tax penalties on individuals who fail to obtain health insurance coverage and employers who fail to offer coverage, and also imposes an excise tax on high-cost employer health plans. Although PPACA was passed in March 2010, most of its tax provisions and many of its insurance provisions will not become effective until 2014. Once PPACA's provisions become fully effective, we may very well see improvements in both efficiency and broader policy goals, but, as with everything, much depends on the details.

This chapter will first provide an overview of the current tax treatment of health insurance and medical expenses. Not only are these provisions currently effective, but they will, with only minor changes, continue in effect even once PPACA is fully implemented in the coming years. The second section will examine the tax treatment of health insurance and medical expenses from an efficiency perspective, which has been the source of many critiques of this area of tax policy. From there, the chapter will take a broader perspective to examine a more complete array of policy issues and examine how PPACA, once fully implemented, will affect both efficiency and broader policy concerns, paying special attention to the special role that the tax code will continue to play in this important area.

THE EXISTING TAX TREATMENT OF HEALTH INSURANCE AND MEDICAL EXPENSES

The existing tax code provisions concerning health insurance and medical expenses can be fairly characterized as incoherent. Health insurance premiums can sometimes be paid with pretax dollars or deducted from taxable income, depending on the employment status of the taxpayer and the choices her employer has made. Unreimbursed out-of-pocket medical expenses can sometimes be paid with pretax dollars or deducted from taxable income, again depending on factors such as employment status, which benefits the taxpayer's employer has chosen to make available to employees, and how much money an individual has spent on medical care in a given year. Other benefits, such as tax credits for health insurance purchase, have been made available on limited and temporary bases. The following subsections provide a brief overview of this tangled web of health care tax provisions.

HEALTH INSURANCE PREMIUMS[3]

The exclusion or deductibility of health insurance premiums varies based on an individual's employment status and whether her employer has chosen to offer group health insurance coverage. Individuals who receive employer-provided health insurance coverage may exclude from their taxable income any amounts that their employer contributes to such coverage. In addition, if the employer has set up a cafeteria plan under section 125 of the Internal Revenue Code of 1986 (IRC, or the Code), employees may pay any required employee contribution for coverage on a pretax basis. The result is that, for such individuals, the entire cost of health insurance premiums is excluded from taxable income. Such amounts are also exempt from payroll taxes.[4] This favorable tax treatment is available not just for the employee's coverage but also any coverage the employer makes available for the employee's spouse or dependents. It does not, however, extend to unmarried partners or children who do not meet the tax code definition of a dependent.[5]

Individuals who are self-employed may deduct the amount of any health insurance premiums for the individual and his or her spouse and dependents, but payroll taxes must be paid on such amounts.[6] Individuals who are not self-employed and either are not offered or do not accept employer-provided health coverage must pay for any desired health insurance with after-tax dollars.[7]

Individuals who are employed by an employer that offers group health care coverage therefore enjoy a distinct financial advantage with respect to health insurance purchasing — even putting aside other financial advantages such as group underwriting and lower administrative costs.[8] The tax benefit for such

---

3. This subpart addresses only the tax treatment of health insurance premiums, rather than the tax treatment of payments received from health insurance plans. The tax treatment of benefits received from health insurance plans is remarkably consistent and in most cases simple. Payments made through a health insurance plan to reimburse an individual for medical expenses are excluded from income pursuant to sections 104 and 105 of the Code, regardless of whether the health insurance is purchased through an employer or in the individual market.

4. *See* I.R.C. §§3121(a)(2) and 3306(b)(2).

5. If an employee's nonspouse partner is covered by an employer plan, the employee is taxed on the fair market value of the coverage provided to the partner.

6. I.R.C. §162(l). The deduction is an above-the-line deduction and is therefore available in full to all eligible taxpayers, even those who do not itemize their deductions.

7. In Massachusetts, state law essentially requires employers to establish cafeteria plans under section 125 of the tax code in order to allow employees to purchase individual health insurance coverage on a pretax basis through the state-based insurance exchange. *See* Mark A. Hall et al., *Using Payroll Deductions to Shelter Individual Health Insurance from Income Tax*, 46 Health Services Res., 2011.

8. Group health plans enjoy significantly lower administrative expenses, referred to as "loading" charges, than individual plans do. Estimates suggest that group plans spend 5–10% of premiums on administrative costs, while such costs are equal to 30–40% of premiums in the individual

coverage provides a significant subsidy for most taxpayers. For example, assume that Taxpayer A and Taxpayer B desire the same insurance coverage, an individual policy that costs $3,750. Taxpayer A is offered her desired coverage through her employer, while Taxpayer B is not. Both taxpayers are in the 25% marginal rate bracket. Taxpayer A needs to earn only $3,750 in wages to purchase such coverage. Taxpayer B, however, must earn $5,000 in wages to have sufficient after-tax funds available for his purchase. If we take into account payroll taxes of 7.65%[9] and an assumed state income tax rate of 5%, the amount of wages necessary to pay for a $3,750 policy rises to $5,162. Under these assumptions, Taxpayer A receives an effective subsidy of $1,412 to purchase her health insurance coverage, solely because her employer makes such coverage available to her, and regardless of whether her employer makes any contribution toward such coverage.

OUT-OF-POCKET EXPENSES

There are several different tax code provisions that grant favorable tax treatment to medical expenses incurred by a taxpayer that are not reimbursed by insurance or other sources. Two of these arrangements, flexible spending accounts and health reimbursement arrangements, are available only through an employer. The remaining two, health savings accounts and the deduction for expenses that exceed 7.5% of adjusted gross income, are available to all taxpayers. Each will be briefly discussed in turn.

In order to qualify for favorable tax treatment under any of these provisions, the unreimbursed expenses in most cases must meet the definition of expenditures for "medical care" contained in section 213 of the Code, which provides that "medical care means amounts paid . . . for the diagnosis, cure, mitigation, treatment, or prevention of disease, or for the purpose of affecting any structure or function of the body."[10] The term also includes transportation costs associated with medical care, qualified long-term care services, and health insurance premiums, but it does not include cosmetic surgery unless related to a congenital abnormality, personal injury resulting from accident or trauma, or disfiguring disease.[11]

Expenses That Exceed 7.5% of Adjusted Gross Income

Any medical expenses that are not reimbursed by insurance or through one of the tax-advantaged mechanisms described next are deductible by an

---

market. Mark V. Pauly and Len M. Nichols, *The Nongroup Health Insurance Market: Short on Facts, Long on Opinions and Policy Disputes*, Health Aff. W325, W326 (Oct. 23, 2002). Additionally, group underwriting and federal nondiscrimination requirements result in all individuals in the group paying the same premium amount, regardless of health status. *See* 29 U.S.C. §1182. This provides a significant financial advantage to the less healthy members of a group.

9. This includes only the employee portion of payroll taxes. Employers pay an equal amount, and economists generally agree that while the employer portion is technically paid by the employer, it effectively reduces employee wages.

10. I.R.C. §213(d)(1).

11. I.R.C. §§213(d)(1) and (9).

individual to the extent such expenses in a given taxable year exceed 7.5% of the individual's adjusted gross income.[12]

Flexible Spending Accounts

A health care flexible spending account may be offered by an employer through a cafeteria plan established under section 125 of the Code. These accounts, which are currently unlimited in amount,[13] allow an individual to set aside money for unreimbursed medical expenses on a pretax basis, and any reimbursements from such accounts are excluded from the individual's taxable income. As a result, a health care flexible spending account allows the first dollars an individual spends on unreimbursed medical care to be tax-advantaged (in stark contrast to the 7.5% deductibility floor that is generally applicable). However, this benefit is available only if an employer elects to sponsor such an arrangement, and it also requires both the employer and the employee to be willing to make a gamble.

Under current rules, the amount an employee elects to contribute to a flexible spending account each year must be used during the year for which the election is made. This is based on the requirement that cafeteria plans must offer only current benefits and may not allow deferred compensation. Thus, amounts set aside in a flexible spending account may not roll over to future years. If an employee incurs fewer unreimbursed medical expenses than anticipated, she loses the unused funds.[14] In addition, under current regulations the entire amount an employee elects to contribute to a flexible spending account must be available during the entire year. For example, if the employee elects to contribute $1,000 to the account, she must be eligible for reimbursement of the entire $1,000 on her first day of eligibility. If the employee terminates employment after seeking reimbursement for $1,000 but after only contributing $500, the employer must bear the loss. The idea is that the flexible spending account must function as insurance; there must be a risk of loss involved.[15] So while a flexible spending account is much more advantageous from a tax perspective than the deduction allowed under section 213, it comes at a price to both the employer and employee.

Health Savings Accounts

Individuals who participate in a health savings account also have the ability to pay unreimbursed medical expenses in a tax-advantaged manner.

---

12. I.R.C. §213. The threshold for deducting such expenses will increase to 10 percent in 2013 as part of PPACA's reforms.

13. In practice, many employers set annual dollar amount limits on such accounts. As part of PPACA's reforms, there will be a new, statutory limit of $2,500 per year per employee on such accounts beginning in 2013.

14. Forfeited amounts can revert to the employer or can be used to offset administrative expenses of the plan. Such amounts can also be returned to employees on a "reasonable and uniform" basis or credited to the following year's accounts on a "reasonable and uniform" basis. Prop. Treas. Reg. §1.125-5(o)(1).

15. Flexible spending accounts, available only under a cafeteria plan, must offer a "qualified benefit" under section 106 of the Code. As a result, the flexible spending account must be a "health and accident plan" and must entail a risk of loss commonly seen in insurance arrangements.

Health savings accounts allow eligible individuals to contribute money on a pretax basis (up to specified dollar amounts each year) and use the money that accumulates in such accounts to pay for qualifying medical expenses without such amounts being included in taxable income.[16] Unlike flexible spending accounts, health savings account balances are not forfeited at year-end and can be established by a taxpayer without employer involvement. However, in order to be eligible to participate in a health savings account, an individual must be covered by a qualifying high-deductible health plan, and only a qualifying high-deductible health plan.[17] While health savings accounts are not dependent on employment status or employer choices, the taxpayer would need to secure coverage under a high-deductible health plan in order to be eligible to establish a health savings account. If an individual desires a health savings account and her employer does not offer a qualifying high-deductible health plan, she would need to secure such coverage in the individual market. If the high-deductible health plan is purchased on the individual market, the premiums are not deductible unless the individual is self-employed. Health savings account funds cannot be used to pay the premiums for the high-deductible health plan. As a result, even if an individual desires a health savings account with a high-deductible health plan, if her employer does not offer such an arrangement, she is unlikely to purchase one on the individual market, because the high-deductible plan cannot be purchased with tax-advantaged funds.

Health Reimbursement Arrangements

Health reimbursement arrangements offer tax advantages similar to those provided by flexible spending accounts and health savings accounts.[18] A health reimbursement arrangement is funded solely by an employer and can be used to reimburse employees (and their spouses and dependents) for medical care expenses. Reimbursements made under a health reimbursement arrangement are exempt from federal income tax. Amounts contributed to such an arrangement by an employer to an employee's account can be carried forward to future years and are not forfeited at year-end. Despite this ability to roll over amounts from year to year, an employee cannot receive a cash payment of the account balance upon termination of employment. For this reason, HRAs are not portable. Like flexible spending accounts, the availability of this tax benefit is contingent upon an employer deciding to sponsor such an arrangement. Unlike flexible spending accounts, the employer not only has to choose to sponsor the arrangement, but also to fund it.

---

16. An individual may spend the amount in her health savings account however she chooses. If the money is spent for any purpose other than qualifying medical expenses, the amount is subject to ordinary federal income tax and a 10% excise tax. I.R.C. §223(f). The excise tax increased to 20% in 2011 as part of PPACA's reforms.

17. A qualifying high deductible health plan must require the policyholder to satisfy a minimum deductible. For 2011, the minimum deductible is $1,200 for individual coverage and $2,400 for family coverage. Only preventive care may be covered without regard to the deductible.

18. *See* IRS Notice 2002-45, 2002-2 CB 93.

CREDITS

There are very limited tax credits available to make health insurance purchase more affordable. Effective in 2002, individuals who receive certain "trade adjustment assistance payments"[19] or who are over age 55 and receive pension benefits from the Pension Benefit Guarantee Corporation qualify for the refundable "health coverage tax credit."[20] The credit is currently equal to 72.5 percent of the cost of qualified health insurance.[21] Available data show that very few eligible individuals took advantage of the health coverage tax credit.[22] Other health insurance credits have also been made available, but with limited scopes and durations.[23]

THE INEFFICIENCIES OF THE EXISTING TAX TREATMENT

Efficiency is considered one of the fundamental norms of tax policy, but the term is often used in different ways, or imprecisely. It can be used to refer to allocative efficiency within society as a whole, to how well-targeted tax benefits are (e.g., the extent to which the intended benefits go to the intended beneficiaries versus amounts captured by unintended beneficiaries), or to how efficiently tax revenues are collected. To further confuse matters, the tax norm of "neutrality" is often used to refer to what economists would call efficiency.[24] This chapter (and this book) are concerned with the tax norm of neutrality and the concept of economic efficiency. A tax system is considered neutral, or economically efficient, where it does not interfere with the free market by preferencing certain activities or economic decisions over others. We are concerned, then, with allocative efficiency, which is achieved when "resources are produced and allocated so as to produce the 'optimal' level of each output and

---

19. These are payments authorized by the Trade Adjustment Assistance Act to employees who were laid off or had hours reduced because their employer was adversely affected by increased imports from other countries.

20. I.R.C. §35.

21. The amount of the credit had been 65 percent prior to May 2009, rose to 80% in May, 2009, and was reduced to 72.5 percent beginning in March, 2011.

22. The U.S. Government Accountability Office (GAO) found that fewer than 30,000 of the hundreds of thousands of potentially eligible individuals each year took advantage of the credit. *See* Letter from the United States Government Accountability Office to Senator Max Baucus et al., April 30, 2010, available at http://www.gao.gov/new.items/d10521r.pdf.

23. For example, in 2009, Congress amended section 3001 of the Code to provide a subsidy for the cost of Consolidated Omnibus Budget Reconciliation Act (COBRA) continuation coverage for certain workers. Pursuant to that program, a worker who was involuntarily terminated between September 1, 2008, and February 28, 2010, was eligible for an IRS-provided subsidy of 65 percent of the cost of COBRA continuation coverage. Designed to help laid-off workers afford coverage, the provision has been criticized by employers who must initially pay the 65 percent subsidy for eligible workers and then seek reimbursement from the IRS through payroll tax refunds. It is unknown at present time what effect, if any, it had on COBRA coverage rates. One large COBRA administrator estimated that only half of the eligible individuals have taken advantage of the subsidy. Ianthe Jeanne Dugan, *Despite Subsidy, COBRA's Bite Still Stings for Many*, Wall St. J., December 29, 2009, at A14.

24. *See, e.g.*, Joel Slemrod and Jon Bakija, *Taxing Ourselves: A Citizen's Guide to the Debate over Taxes* (3rd ed., MIT, 2004), 131.

to distribute the outputs in line with the value consumers place on them."[25] A critique based on the allocative efficiency of our taxation of health insurance premiums and medical expenses follows.

BACKGROUND

Under an efficiency analysis, market intervention is unjustified in the absence of market failure. Economists, after all, start from the premise that individuals, in the absence of market failure, will make rational, preference-maximizing decisions. Even if health insurance coverage rates were only 50 percent among workers and the self-employed, the decisions of the 50 percent without health insurance coverage would not be problematic in a fully functioning market with rational purchasers who direct their resources in a manner consistent with their preferences. The assumption of rational purchasers is problematic in the health care area, because there is evidence to suggest that individuals do not always act rationally when purchasing such insurance or when making medical consumption decisions.[26] Nevertheless, we shall at this point adopt the economists' assumption that individuals are rational decision-makers. So our first inquiry under an efficiency analysis is whether some type of market failure affects the purchasing decisions of workers and the self-employed that justifies market intervention in the form of a tax subsidy for health insurance purchase and in the form of a tax preference for the consumption of medical goods over other goods. After all, it is clear that the tax code provisions dealing with health insurance and medical expenses distort market decision making by preferencing the purchase of health insurance and medical services over other consumer goods.

There are two primary types of market failure that have been identified with respect to health insurance: adverse selection and moral hazard. Adverse selection affects purchasing behavior, and it occurs when individuals use private information that is not easily discovered by the insurance company to determine whether or not to buy insurance as well as how much insurance to buy. At average prices, an individual with reason to believe that he or she has relatively high risk of health problems is more likely to buy insurance than an individual with reason to believe that he or she has a relatively low risk of health problems. Similarly, the individual with perceived high health risks is likely to buy more insurance than an individual with perceived low health risks. This behavior is perfectly rational at the individual level, but it results in a market where those who end up purchasing insurance have a risk level that is greater than the community average. This greater-than-average risk level in turn causes insurers to raise their prices, a phenomenon referred to as "lemons pricing" because the insurers are pricing their product on the assumption that there are more lemons (i.e., bad risks) within the purchasing population than

---

25. Jeremiah Hurley, *An Overview of the Normative Economics of the Health Sector*, in Anthony J. Culyer and Joseph P. Newhouse, eds., *Handbook of Health Economics* (Elsevier, 2000), 55, 60.

26. *See, e.g.* Jeffrey Liebman and Richard Zeckhauser, *Simple Humans, Complex Insurance, Subtle Subsidies*, in Henry J. Aaron and Leonard E. Burman, eds., *Using Taxes to Reform Health Insurance: Pitfalls and Promises* (Brookings Institution, 2008), 230; Richard G. Frank, *Behavioral Economics and Health Economics*, NBER Working Paper 10881 (2004).

within the general population. Unfortunately, lemons pricing leads the risk pool to become even worse, as only those with higher levels of risk find the increased prices palatable. This cycle of increasing premiums and increasing risk levels among the insured population can result in what is known as a "death spiral," where the insurance market collapses when no one is willing to pay the premiums that a plan is charging. Adverse selection is not always so extreme. Mild adverse selection can simply result in high-risk individuals paying a high premium for generous coverage and low-risk individuals paying a low premium for less-than-desired coverage.[27]

In addition to adjusting their prices to reflect greater-than-average risk levels, insurers also respond to the problem of adverse selection by undertaking various measures to try to sort good risks from bad. For example, insurers will engage in medical underwriting, to the extent allowed by state law, in order to evaluate an individual's health risks better. In many states, insurers have the ability to deny coverage altogether if they determine that they do not want to accept the risk that covering the individual would entail. Even where insurers are limited in their ability to deny coverage or engage in medical underwriting, insurers often design and market their products in ways calculated to appeal to certain risk segments.

The inefficiencies caused by adverse selection are therefore twofold. First, because of the higher-than-average prices, low-risk individuals are more likely to find that the price of health insurance exceeds its perceived benefits, and they will therefore go without insurance even if they would otherwise desire to purchase insurance. In addition, insurer efforts to sort good risks from bad, whether through medical underwriting or product design, add to an insurer's overhead costs, again making it less likely that individuals who are weighing the costs and perceived benefits of insurance will find insurance purchase attractive. Both types of adverse selection are thought to have a much larger impact on individual and small-group markets than on large-group markets.[28]

Evidence suggests that health insurance markets are significantly affected by adverse selection, although there is some disagreement about the exact extent of its impact.[29] One method of overcoming adverse selection, and by many accounts the preferred method of combating it, is to provide

27. *See* Wynand P.M.M. Van de Ven and Randall P. Ellis, *Risk Adjustment in Competitive Health Plan Markets*, in Anthony J. Culyer and Joseph P. Newhouse, eds., *Handbook of Health Economics* (Elsevier, 2000), 755,774–75. This is caused by low-risk individuals being forced to choose ungenerous plans in an effort to signal to insurers that they are low-risk. The low-risk individuals then benefit from low premiums but are stuck with coverage that is less comprehensive than desired. Other effects are also possible. For example, either low-risk or high-risk individuals may be prevented from obtaining as much coverage as they wish because of adverse selection. *See id.*

28. Large groups have much lower administrative overhead costs and do not need to engage in any individual risk-sorting. In addition, the tax preference that is available to large-group coverage offered by an employer, along with any direct employer contribution to coverage, helps lower the effective cost of coverage, thereby encouraging more low-risk individuals to elect coverage. Large groups may, however, be subject to significant adverse selection among the various plans they offer to employees. *See, e.g.*, David M. Cutler and Sarah J. Reber, *Paying for Health Insurance: The Trade-off between Competition and Adverse Selection*, 113 Quarterly J. Econ. 433 (1998).

29. *See* David M. Cutler and Richard J. Zeckhauser, *The Anatomy of Health Insurance*, in Anthony J. Culyer and Joseph P. Newhouse, eds., *Handbook of Health Economics* (Elsevier, 2000), 563, 616–23 for an overview of the literature.

risk-adjustment payments to plans or to risk-adjust premiums.[30] This is an incredibly difficult and detailed process, but suffice it to say that the basic idea is to subsidize plans to which high-risk individuals are attracted while taxing plans to which low-risk individuals are attracted so that risks are cross-subsidized and individuals are able to choose the coverage level that they desire regardless of their risk profile. If done well, such risk-adjustment payments significantly eliminate the need to try to distinguish between good and bad risks, therefore lowering overhead costs of insurance companies. In order for a risk-adjustment scheme to work, either insurance purchase needs to be compulsory or subsidies for insurance purchase must be available, otherwise low-risk individuals will choose not to participate.[31] Cross-subsidization is only possible, after all, if there are low-risk individuals in the pool.

The second type of market failure that has been identified with respect to health insurance is moral hazard. Whereas adverse selection affects purchasing decisions, the moral hazard we are primarily concerned with affects the behavior of insureds after they have purchased insurance. Put simply, moral hazard is the phenomenon in which insurance coverage itself makes covered individuals more likely to suffer a loss covered by the policy than if they did not have insurance. In the health insurance context, this means that individuals with health insurance are more likely to consume medical services than they would be if they did not have such coverage. Moral hazard is not necessarily a bad thing if it leads to individuals getting necessary medical care that they would not otherwise be able to afford. But if individuals are receiving unnecessary medical care simply because they have insurance and do not bear the true cost of such care, much inefficiency results.

Efforts to combat moral hazard typically include efforts to increase the out-of-pocket costs associated with medical treatment by implementing deductibles, copayment, and coinsurance requirements. While evidence shows that increasing out-of-pocket costs reduces the utilization of medical services, it also shows that reductions occur not only for treatments with poor effectiveness but also for treatments considered very highly effective.[32]

THE TAX PREFERENCE FOR EMPLOYER-PROVIDED HEALTH INSURANCE COVERAGE

Does the tax preference for employer-provided health insurance coverage help to address any of the inefficiencies just discussed? Interestingly, the tax preference appears to help ameliorate the inefficiencies caused by adverse selection but exacerbate the problem of moral hazard. The efficiency-based goal of combating adverse selection is to allow individuals to buy desired insurance coverage without the burden of lemons pricing or increased

---

30. The basic idea behind risk-adjustment is to subsidize generous plans that disproportionately attract higher-risk participants and tax plans that disproportionately attract lower-risk participants. *See id.* at 624–25.

31. *Id.,* at 625.

32. *See, e.g.,* Kathleen N. Lohr et al., *Use of Medical Care in the RAND Health Insurance Experiment,* 24 Med. Care S1, S31–38 (1986) (finding that cost sharing was generally just as likely to lower use when care was thought to be highly effective as when it was thought to be only rarely effective).

overhead costs that make insurance purchase unattractive. First and foremost, the tax preference for employer-provided coverage encourages individuals to purchase group coverage through their employer. In terms of combating adverse selection, this is helpful in that group coverage enjoys much lower administrative costs than individual coverage does.[33] This should lead to fewer individuals being priced out of insurance based on high overhead costs (often referred to as "loading charges" in the insurance context) and will decrease the problem of lemons pricing. In addition, the tax preference encourages employers not only to offer coverage, but also to contribute to its cost. Employer contributions toward health insurance are, in fact, more valuable than cash compensation to an employee (assuming, of course, that the employee values health insurance). Unlike cash compensation, employer contributions toward health insurance are both deductible to the employer and excluded from the employee's taxable income. The result is that not only do most employers contribute to the cost of coverage, they contribute generously.[34] This further lessens the problems of adverse selection by lowering the effective price of coverage, which in turn lessens the problem of lemons pricing. From an efficiency standpoint, the exclusion for employer-provided insurance may be justified. It certainly is not perfect, but it does appear to address adverse selection concerns reasonably well.

One problem created by the tax preference is that by creating an incentive for individuals to elect employer-offered coverage, individual preferences are likely to be distorted. An individual who is offered health insurance by her employer may find that the insurance does not match her preferences for coverage. She may prefer a different network of physicians, a different deductible or copay level, or a different plan structure. Nevertheless, the tax subsidy available for the purchase of employer-provided coverage in most cases will compel the purchase of the employer's policy. Assume that the employer policy[35] costs $6,000 per year and that the policy available on the individual market that matches the employee's preferences costs $5,000.[36] If that employee is in the 25 percent marginal tax bracket, she will have to earn over $6,600 in wages in order to pay for the individual coverage with after-tax dollars and will therefore purchase the less-desired employer policy so long as the benefits of the individual policy are not worth an additional $1,600 to her. Of course, one would assume that an employer would act as an effective agent for its employees and select health coverage that satisfies the preferences of employees. However, even if the employer is acting as a competent agent for

---

33. Pauly and Nichols, *supra* note 8, at 326 (noting that overhead costs in the individual market can be as high as 30–40 percent of premium cost, compared to 5–10 percent in the large group market).

34. On average, in 2010, employers who offered coverage paid 81 percent of the cost of single coverage and 70 percent of the cost of family coverage. Kaiser Family Foundation and Health Research and Educational Trust, *Employer Health Benefits 2010 Annual Survey* (2010), 70, available at http://ehbs.kff.org/pdf/2010/8085.pdf.

35. In 2009, 86 percent of firms offering health benefits offered employees only one plan option. *See id.* at 56. The likelihood of a firm offering multiple health plan options to employees is positively correlated with firm size. Among firms with 200 or more employees, 45 percent offer more than one health plan. *Id.*

36. This, of course, assumes an ideal world with a fully functioning individual health insurance market. Insurance markets in most states fall well short of this ideal.

the employees, they must aggregate employee preferences. This will lead to some employees being dissatisfied. In addition, there is some reason to be cautious when characterizing employers as effective agents for employees in this context.[37] In the end, it is likely that the tax preference for employer-provided coverage distorts individual preferences.[38]

The primary problem with such preference distortion is that it creates an incentive for individuals to buy more coverage than they would otherwise value, leading to an increase in moral hazard. Because the tax preference makes employer-provided health insurance more valuable than an equivalent amount of cash compensation, individuals may become "overinsured." Over-insurance leads to the rational overconsumption of medical care (particularly when out-of-pocket costs are typically paid with after-tax money, which drives health insurance plans to be structured with high premiums and low out-of-pocket costs). After all, once health insurance premiums have been paid, there is relatively little marginal cost to consuming medical care, and doing so is sometimes thought of as getting a return on health insurance premium payments. As individuals overconsume medical care, health insurance companies adjust premiums to reflect this increased level of utilization, making health insurance less affordable. As health insurance becomes less affordable, our tax subsidy provided by the exclusion for premiums becomes even less effective at achieving our policy goals. From an efficiency standpoint, eliminating the tax preference for health insurance should lead to optimal levels of health insurance purchase,[39] lower levels of medical care utilization, and decreased health insurance and health care costs.[40] Our current tax treatment moves in the opposite direction. In the end, when we combine the relatively positive aspects of a reduction in adverse selection with an increase in the likelihood for moral hazard, the tax preference for employer-provided health insurance gets a very mixed efficiency rating.

THE DEDUCTION FOR HEALTH INSURANCE PREMIUMS OF THE SELF-EMPLOYED

The efficiency analysis of the deduction for self-employed individuals is more complicated. Just as before, adverse selection is the primary form of market failure with which we are concerned, and, as with the employer preference, the function of the deduction for self-employed individuals is to subsidize insurance purchase. However, the critical difference is that this

---

37. *See* Amy B. Monahan, *Value-Based Mandated Health Benefits*, 80 U. Colo. L. Rev. 127, 145–48 (2009).

38. However, if the alternative to employer-provided coverage is no coverage (either because of affordability or a poorly functioning individual market), concerns about preference distortion would be significantly lessened.

39. Administrative, or loading, costs will likely prevent truly optimal insurance purchasing decisions. These loading costs cover administrative, marketing, underwriting, management, and claims processing expenses and can make up a significant portion of health insurance premiums. *See supra* note 8.

40. Eliminating the tax preference would, however, leave the problem of adverse selection to be addressed through other means.

subsidy does not support the formation of employer risk pools. Rather, the subsidy goes to individual market purchases. And nothing about this subsidy is going to ameliorate the effects of adverse selection in the open market. The exact effects will vary based on the state-level regulation at issue, but insurance companies will likely price coverage based on worse-than-average risk levels, engage in significant medical underwriting or coverage denials, or use various product design and marketing mechanisms to sort the good and bad risks. The deduction for self-employed individuals does help to offset the increased premium prices that result from this behavior, but it does not actually eliminate inefficiencies in the market.

That said, the deduction for health insurance premiums for the self-employed may very well address a different type of market inefficiency, one that would otherwise be present in the labor market. If only employer-provided health insurance premiums were granted a tax preference, and self-employed individuals were not eligible for a similar preference, the labor market would be distorted. Individuals who were contemplating self-employment might choose to be an employee instead, based on the economic value of the exclusion for employer-provided health insurance. Allowing a deduction for health insurance premiums of the self-employed helps level the playing field and should eliminate this particular labor market distortion. Perhaps this labor market benefit justifies the less-than-efficient health insurance market adjustment described in the preceding paragraph.

THE TAX TREATMENT OF OUT-OF-POCKET MEDICAL EXPENSES

Not only do most of the tax preferences for out-of-pocket medical expenses fail to address the existing inefficiencies in the health insurance and medical care markets, but many in fact add inefficiency to the system. Each of the tax preferences available for such expenses will be examined in turn.

Deductions for Medical Expenses That Exceed 7.5 Percent of AGI

The itemized deduction that is available for unreimbursed medical expenses that exceed 7.5 percent of a taxpayer's adjusted gross income does not address the problem of adverse selection and may, in fact, contribute to the problem of overconsumption of medical care. Once the threshold amount is met or is near, an individual would be wise to move any future medical expenses to the current year in order to gain the most benefit from the tax deduction, or even to purchase medical services that would not be purchased at all absent the tax benefit. This could potentially lead to inefficient consumption because of the distortion caused by the tax deduction. That said, at the point where an individual has spent more than 7.5 percent of her income on unreimbursed medical care, her demand for medical services may very well be inelastic because of a significant illness, and she may not in fact have additional discretionary dollars to spend in order to take advantage of the tax break given to additional expenditures. In any event, very few Americans claim the deduction for medical expenses in a given year.[41]

Flexible Spending Accounts

Like the deduction for medical expenses, the tax preference for flexible spending accounts does not address either adverse selection or moral hazard, and in fact, it creates an inefficient preference for medical consumption over the consumption of other goods. The "use it or lose it" rule for flexible spending accounts simply compounds the general inefficiencies of these accounts. The rule distorts medical decision making. For some individuals it may promote underconsumption of medical services. Imagine an individual who has an unexpected medical expense that he did not budget for in making his flexible spending account election for the year. When the expense occurs, he does not have tax-advantaged funds available from which to be reimbursed. The result may be that he postpones such medical care until a future year when he can have such funds available. Similarly, imagine an individual who has mistakenly elected to defer too much money to her flexible spending account. Come year-end, when faced with the possibility of forfeiting her remaining flexible spending account dollars, she may rationally choose to consume medical services of very little utility in order to prevent such forfeiture.[42]

Health Savings Accounts

Health savings accounts are quite purposefully structured in order to reduce moral hazard. Because individuals are faced with a large deductible before insurance begins covering expenses, and because they own the amounts in their savings accounts, they should be less likely to consume medical services that do not provide them benefit equal to their cost (at least until the deductible is met). Research suggests that individuals covered by a health savings account and high-deductible health plan consume fewer medical services than those with other types of insurance coverage.[43] Unfortunately, the evidence also suggests that individuals enrolled in such plans engage in "risky" cost-savings behavior (such as not going to the doctor when they believe they should, or taking a lower-than-recommended dose of a prescription drug) more often than those enrolled in plans with lower deductibles.[44]

Health savings accounts raise an additional concern regarding adverse selection. In any type of multiple-plan environment, all other things being equal, you would expect the relatively healthy to prefer health savings accounts over other types of health plans, because the healthy get to reap

---

41. Approximately 7 percent of federal income tax returns filed claim the medical expense deduction. *See* Justin Bryan, *Individual Income Tax Returns, 2007* (IRS, 2009), available at http://www.irs.gov/pub/irs-soi/09fallbulincomeret.pdf.

42. Employers may ameliorate the effects of the use-it-or-lose-it rule somewhat by adding a two-and-a-half-month grace period to their flexible spending account plan, which provides participants with an additional amount of time to incur reimbursable expenses without forfeiture. *See* Prop. Reg. §1.125-1(e).

43. *See, e.g.,* Anna Dixon et al., *Do Consumer-Directed Health Plans Drive Change in Enrollees' Health Care Behavior?*, 27 Health Aff. 1120 (2008).

44. *See id.*

the financial rewards of low medical consumption under a health savings account plan. Empirical data regarding adverse selection in this context tend to show favorable selection of health savings account plans by the healthy and also the well-educated and wealthy. On balance, health savings accounts show moderate promise in combating moral hazard, but also a moderate adverse selection problem when they are offered within multi-plan environments.

Health Reimbursement Arrangements

Health reimbursement arrangements do not appear to help combat either adverse selection or moral hazard. They are simply a means of tax-favored financing of medical consumption. They do not entail any type of group-level risk pooling, nor do they have any mechanism to address any moral hazard that might result from insurance coverage that is purchased through a health reimbursement arrangement. Indeed, such an arrangement might actually exacerbate moral hazard because employees cannot take any balance with them when they leave employment, thereby encouraging them to consume medical services rather than leave money on the table.

Credits for Health Insurance Purchase

It is somewhat difficult to analyze the current, limited tax credits for health insurance in terms of their efficiency. Tax credits clearly can be an efficient means to address different forms of market failure, for example, by addressing externalities.[45] However, there is no publicly available evidence that individuals who are receiving trade adjustment payments or are over age 55 and receiving a pension from the Pension Benefit Guarantee Corporation make suboptimal health insurance purchasing decisions caused by market failure. Given the lack of evidence, it is impossible to determine whether current tax credits are efficient.

LOOKING BEYOND EFFICIENCY CONCERNS

Overall, analysis of the tax preference for health insurance premiums for the employed and self-employed, along with the preference granted to health savings accounts, furnishes superficial, but relatively weak justification on efficiency grounds. None of the myriad preferences for out-of-pocket expenses can be justified on such grounds. With that in mind, we turn now to look at what other policy concerns should be considered in debating and critiquing the tax treatment of health insurance and out-of-pocket medical expenses.

Focusing solely on the economic efficiency of the health insurance market potentially ignores other fundamental policy issues that affect health insurance and medical care in this country. Whether the result of rational decision making or not, many Americans find both health insurance and medical care to be

---

45. For a discussion of the efficiency of tax credits as a policy tool, *see* Lily L. Batchelder et al., *Efficiency and Tax Incentives: The Case for Refundable Tax Credits*, 59 Stan. L. Rev. 23 (2006).

unaffordable. Many Americans receive less-than-optimal care or find accessing needed medical services difficult. Even among those able to afford coverage, selecting coverage has very high decision-making costs, and many individuals are likely to take various decision-making shortcuts in arriving at such decisions. Difficult decision making also affects medical treatment decisions. It is also hard to be satisfied with the fairness of our current system, where affordability of health care coverage is often determined by irrelevant factors such as the individual's employment status and her employer's decisions regarding coverage. There is the additional concern that those who go without coverage are not doing their fair share and are placing additional burdens on those who must finance care for those without insurance. In general, our current health care system lacks a strong element of social solidarity regarding the sharing of health risks. Last but not least, medical costs continue to rise at a pace that exceeds inflation and appears unsustainable.

Tax reforms that are aimed at increasing economic efficiency would sometimes help to address the other policy issues raised above, but at other times they would actually work against those goals. For example, amending the tax code to impose a financial penalty for failing to purchase health insurance coverage could help address adverse selection concerns, while at the same time improving the perceived fairness of, and increasing the social solidarity of, our health insurance system.[46] On the other hand, if one were to address the moral hazard concern by repealing or limiting the exclusion of employer-provided health insurance coverage, affordability concerns would likely be exacerbated. Similarly, a tax subsidy to address affordability more broadly might create new inefficiencies in the system by increasing moral hazard and potentially providing a windfall to those who would have purchased coverage in the absence of a subsidy. Health care appears, therefore, to be one of the areas of tax law where focusing solely on economic efficiency potentially undercuts significant policy goals. The following section explores how federal health care reform balanced both efficiency and broader policy concerns, with a particular focus on how the law used the tax code to implement the law's goals.

FUNDAMENTAL HEALTH CARE REFORM AND TAXES

In March 2010, President Obama signed into law the Patient Protection and Affordable Care Act, along with the amending Health Care and Education Affordability Reconciliation Act of 2010 (both acts are collectively referred to as PPACA). PPACA, once its provisions become fully effective in future years, will fundamentally change how health insurance is offered, priced, and paid for in this country and represents the first significant effort to address some of the policy issues discussed above. This section will provide a brief overview of PPACA's major provisions before examining PPACA's likely effects

---

46. For an overview of the various justifications for an individual health insurance mandate, *see* Allison K. Hoffman, *Oil and Water: Mixing Individual Mandates, Fragmented Markets, and Health Reform*, 36 Am. J. L. & Med. 7 (2010).

on both efficiency and broader reform goals, concluding with a look at the continued role that tax policy will play in health policy as PPACA's provisions become effective.

Background

PPACA enacts fundamental, multi-faceted health care reform that is primarily aimed at increasing health insurance coverage rates. PPACA's reforms fundamentally change insurance markets, provide significant subsidies to help low- and moderate-income individuals afford insurance and medical care, require most employers to offer health care coverage to employees, require most individuals to purchase health insurance coverage, offer limited tax credits to small employers to offer health insurance coverage, and put in place a significant excise tax on high-cost employer-provided health coverage. The details of these changes are discussed briefly in the following paragraphs.

Insurance Market Reforms

Once PPACA's insurance reforms become fully effective in 2014, health insurers will be required to offer coverage to every applicant and will be able to vary premiums only based on four factors: age, family size, geographic area, and tobacco use. This represents a dramatic shift from the status quo, where premium pricing and coverage rules are left to the individual states, the majority of which allow insurers both to deny coverage and vary rates significantly based on medical underwriting. Additionally, PPACA prohibits insurers from excluding coverage for pre-existing medical conditions and from rescinding an insurance contract once issued, sets maximum deductibles that a policy may impose, and prevents insurers from selling policies with lifetime maximums. As with the pricing and issuance reforms, these changes also represent a dramatic shift from the status quo.

PPACA also requires states to set up insurance exchanges for the individual and small-group markets in order to streamline insurance purchasing. These exchanges play a critical role in administering the tax credits discussed in the following paragraphs, and they also impose additional requirements on health insurance policies sold through them.[47]

Subsidies

To address affordability concerns, PPACA includes significant subsidies for both insurance purchase and out-of-pocket medical expenses. PPACA offers refundable, advanceable[48] tax credits to subsidize health insurance premiums for individuals with incomes between 100 and 400 percent of the federal

---

47. For example, policies purchased through an exchange must contain "essential health benefits" as defined by the Secretary of Health and Human Services.

48. "Advanceable" refers to the ability of taxpayers to receive the benefit of the credit prior to filing their income tax return for the year at issue. In general, tax credits are not refundable, and an individual must wait until filing to receive the economic benefit. Because individuals who cannot otherwise afford health insurance would have a cash flow problem if they had to pay premiums and wait many months to receive a tax credit, the credit was made advanceable.

poverty limit. These credits vary in amount based on the percentage of income that an individual is required to spend on health insurance. For example, take an individual whose income is 200 percent of the federal poverty limit. Under PPACA, that individual is required to spend a maximum of 6.3 percent of his household income on health insurance. If the benchmark health insurance policy[49] costs more than that amount, the tax credit is equal to the difference between the cost of the benchmark policy and the individual's required contribution. If we assume the individual makes $21,780, or 200 percent of the federal poverty limit per year, that would create an expectation that the individual would contribute $1,372 per year (6.3 percent of income) toward health insurance coverage. If the applicable premium for the benchmark plan is $7,000 per year, the individual would be entitled to a tax credit of $7,000 – $1,372, or $5,628. That amount can then be used to purchase any coverage available on the exchange; the individual is not limited to the benchmark plan. If the taxpayer's tax liability for the year is less than the credit amount, the difference is refunded to the taxpayer. In order to be eligible for the tax credit, the individual must purchase his insurance coverage through a state-based exchange. The exchange may request the Treasury to make an advance determination of an individual's eligibility for a premium tax credit during the annual open enrollment period. For individuals who qualify, Treasury pays the insurer directly, and the individual's subsequent amount due is reduced. In addition to the premium tax credit, PPACA also requires insurance companies to lower the cost-sharing requirements on policies issued to individuals with income between 100 and 400 percent of the federal poverty limit, provided the individual enrolls in silver-level coverage within the exchange.[50]

Employer Requirements

Effective in 2014, PPACA imposes a monetary penalty on employers with 50 or more full-time employees that do not offer health insurance coverage, or that do offer coverage but at least one of whose employees receives a tax credit or cost-sharing reduction. Employers that do not offer coverage and have at least one full-time employee who receives a premium tax credit face a fee of $2,000 per full-time employee, excluding the first 30 employees from the assessment. For example, if the employer has 70 full-time employees, its penalty would be calculated by subtracting 30 from 70, and multiplying the resulting 40 by $2,000, for a total of $80,000 per year. Employers with 50 or more employees that offer coverage, but have at least one full-time employee receiving a premium tax credit, will pay the lesser of $3,000 for each employee receiving a premium credit or $2,000 for each full-time employee, excluding

---

49. The benchmark health insurance policy is the second-lowest-cost "silver" plan available to the taxpayer. If, however, the premiums for the plan actually selected by the taxpayer are less than the difference between the premiums for the second-lowest-cost silver plan and the applicable income percentage the taxpayer is required to pay for coverage, the tax credit will be equal to the premium amount of the plan actually selected. PPACA §1401(a).

50. In general, PPACA requires insurers to reduce the out-of-pocket maximum for individuals with income between 100 and 200 percent of the federal poverty limit by two-thirds, for individuals with income between 201 and 300 percent of the federal poverty limit by one-half, and for individuals with income between 301 and 400 percent of the federal poverty limit by one-third. PPACA §1402.

the first 30 employees from the assessment. For example, if an employer with 60 employees offers coverage, but five employees are eligible for and receive a premium tax credit through the exchange, the employer would face a fee of $15,000: the lesser of (1) the number of employees receiving the credit multiplied by $3,000 and (2) the number of employees minus 30, multiplied by $2,000. An employee who is offered coverage by her employer is eligible for a premium tax credit only if she otherwise satisfies the eligibility criteria and if her required contribution for employer coverage exceeds 9.5 percent of her annual household income, or if the plan fails to provide "minimum value."[51] For example, if an employee earns $21,780 per year (currently 200 percent of the federal poverty level), but is eligible for employer-provided coverage, she could receive a premium tax credit only if the required contribution for her employer coverage exceeds $2,069 per year (9.5 percent of her income). Employers with fewer than 50 full-time employees are completely exempt from any of the above penalties.

Individual Requirements

Under PPACA, many individuals will face a monetary penalty if they fail to purchase health insurance. Beginning in 2014, an individual generally must have "minimum essential coverage" for herself and her dependents or face a monetary penalty equal to the greater of (1) $695 per individual, up to a maximum of $2,085 per year, or (2) 2.5 percent of household income.[52] Minimum essential coverage includes various forms of government-provided insurance (Medicare, Medicaid, Tricare, veteran's coverage, etc.), coverage under an eligible employer-sponsored plan, and any plan offered in the individual market within a state. The penalty does not apply to individuals who cannot afford coverage. Generally speaking, coverage is unaffordable if its cost exceeds 8 percent of the individual's household income.[53]

Tax on High-Cost Plans

One of the more controversial provisions of PPACA is the excise tax that will be imposed on high-cost employer health coverage beginning in 2018. Section 9001 of PPACA will impose an excise tax of 40 percent on the cost of employer-provided health plans that exceed a specified threshold. In 2018, the relevant threshold for single coverage is $10,200 and $27,500 for family coverage. The amounts are higher for older individuals and those employed in high-risk professions. Current research suggests that 12 percent of insured workers would be affected by the excise tax in 2019, prior to any changes by employers to make plans less generous in response to the tax. The percentage of affected workers is expected to "increase rapidly thereafter" because the

---

51. A plan fails to provide minimum value if the plan's share of the total allowed costs of benefits provided under the plan is less than 60 percent of such costs. PPACA §1401(a).
52. These amounts phase in during 2014 and 2015. The fees in the first two years are lower than those listed.
53. There are also provisions in PPACA for waiving the penalty where the individual has "suffered a hardship with respect to the capability to obtain coverage under a qualified health plan." PPACA §1501.

method of indexing the threshold amount is not predicted to keep pace with the rate of health insurance premium increases.[54]

Small Business Premium Tax Credits

Small employers are not subject to PPACA's penalties for failing to provide health care coverage to employees. Instead, PPACA provides such employers with a limited incentive to provide such coverage. Beginning in 2010, employers with fewer than 25 full-time equivalent employees and average wages of less than $50,000 may be eligible for a tax credit. In order to qualify, the employer must provide health insurance to employees and pay at least 50 percent of the cost of such coverage.[55] Initially, the maximum credit available is 35 percent of the employer-paid portion of the premiums. Beginning in 2014, the maximum amount will increase to 50 percent of the employer-paid premiums but will be available for only two consecutive years. The net result is that the maximum number of years an employer may receive the credit is six years (four years from 2010 through 2013, and two years beginning in 2014 or thereafter). It is unclear how many employers will be eligible for the credit and how many of those are likely to take advantage of it.[56]

Does PPACA Enhance Efficiency?

It is unclear whether PPACA will be efficiency-enhancing. It leaves in place the current tax preference for employer-provided coverage, which will retain the efficiencies previously discussed. Recall, however, that while the exclusion for employer-provided coverage reduces some of the problems caused by adverse selection, it also increases the potential for moral hazard. On first glance, PPACA also appears to put in place certain efficiency-enhancing law changes. It appears to strengthen the employer-based system by, for the first time, taking steps to penalize employers that do not offer health coverage to employees.[57] From an efficiency perspective, this could very well be justified on the grounds that the improvement in adverse selection effects is sufficient to outweigh any resulting moral hazard concerns. Additionally, the imposition of the excise tax on high-cost health plans should significantly lessen any moral hazard concerns by creating what is likely to be extremely effective downward pressure on the generosity of employer plans.

---

54. Richard S. Foster, *Estimated Financial Effects of the "Patient Protection and Affordable Care Act," as Amended, 2010*, at 13, available at https://www.cms.gov/ActuarialStudies/Downloads/PPACA_2010-04-22.pdf.

55. In order to receive the maximum credit, the employer must have ten or fewer full-time equivalent employees who are paid average annual compensation of $25,000 or less per full-time employee.

56. *See* posting of Tim Jost to *Health Affairs Blog*, http://healthaffairs.org/blog/2010/05/18/implementing-health-reform-the-small-employer-tax-credit/ (May 18, 2010) (citing IRS estimates of 4 million eligible small businesses, trade group estimates of 1.8 million eligible businesses, and Congressional Budget Office estimates of a $3–4 billion annual expenditure).

57. It is far from clear whether PPACA's so-called employer mandate will have the desired effect. *See, e.g.,* Amy Monahan and Daniel Schwarcz, *Will Employers Undermine Health Care Reform by Dumping Sick Employees?*, 97 Va. L. Rev. 125 (2011).

When these efficiency-enhancing provisions are examined more closely, it becomes less clear that the changes will actually achieve their desired effects. For example, while PPACA for the first time penalizes employers who fail to provide health coverage to their employees, it exempts the smallest employers from its penalty provisions. Because small employers are the least likely to offer employees group coverage, it is unclear whether the mandate will actually result in significantly more employers offering coverage. And while PPACA offers such small employers an incentive, in the form of a tax credit, to begin offering group coverage, the credit's limited scope and duration make its incentive effects appear relatively weak.

Employers of all size are, however, subject to the excise tax on high-cost employer plans, which has the potential to be efficiency-enhancing as a counterpressure against moral hazard. Recall that moral hazard is likely to be a problem when individuals are insulated from medical care costs. And the higher the cost of health coverage, the more likely it is to cover a wide variety of services with low out-of-pocket costs. While the excise tax is couched in terms of a revenue provision, its real impact will be significant downward pressure on health insurance premiums. Faced with an excise tax of 40 percent, most employers will restructure their plans so that the cost is below the applicable threshold. There are two primary methods to decrease health insurance premiums: increase cost sharing or decrease the benefits provided. Doing either should help to lessen the problem of moral hazard and therefore be efficiency-enhancing provided that the changes themselves are efficient. For example, it would be efficiency-enhancing to increase cost sharing for services that are clinically less effective or to decrease coverage for such services. Across-the-board cuts run the risk of reducing utilization of highly efficient medical treatments in addition to less efficient treatments.[58] So while the tax on high-cost plans might be efficiency-enhancing, much depends on how firms respond to such changes.

Outside of employer-provided coverage, PPACA also makes changes that at first glance appear likely to enhance efficiency. First and foremost, the individual mandate has the potential to significantly address adverse selection concerns by including nearly everyone in the risk pool and therefore lessening the problem of lemons pricing. However, its ability to effectively counter adverse selection is dependent in large part on the mandate having as few exceptions as possible and getting the broadest population possible into the risk pool. The problem, of course, is that there must be some affordability threshold, or you would risk forcing individuals into bankruptcy. PPACA sets the affordability threshold at 8 percent of household income. In other words, if the cost of health insurance available[59] to you exceeds 8 percent of your household income, you do not face the penalty for non-coverage. While those who earn between 100 and 400 percent of the federal

---

58. *See, e.g.*, Lohr et al., *supra* note 32. These risks can be addressed through the use of value-based insurance design, which attempts to increase utilization of highly effective services while reducing utilization of less-efficient treatments. *See, e.g.*, Michael E. Chernew et al., *Evidence That Value-Based Insurance Can Be Effective*, 29 Health Aff. 530 (2010).

59. For this purpose, the lowest-cost "bronze" plan available in the individual's state exchange is considered the lowest-cost plan available.

poverty limit will be eligible for tax credits that may make coverage affordable for purposes of the mandate, current estimates suggest that many individuals with income above 400 percent of the federal poverty limit will in fact be exempt from the mandate on affordability grounds.[60] According to CMS estimates, 16 percent of the nonelderly population will in fact be exempt.[61]

Even among those who are subject to the penalty, it is unclear whether the penalty imposed is sufficient to force insurance purchase. After all, those who are subject to the penalty for noncoverage will weigh the cost of the penalty against the cost and benefit associated with health coverage. The penalty for failing to purchase coverage is a maximum of $2,085 per year or 2.5 percent of household income, whichever is greater. Take a healthy family that has $180,000 in household income, enough to be subject to the individual mandate penalty if they fail to purchase coverage. In making their coverage decision, they will weigh a $4,500[62] penalty against an assumed $13,000 in premiums. Depending on the value to them of the health insurance provided, they may choose to simply pay the penalty, particularly since they know that if they develop health problems during the year, they can purchase insurance[63] without worrying about coverage denials, pre-existing condition limitations, or medical underwriting. So while the individual mandate has the potential to be efficiency-enhancing, its affordability threshold and relatively small penalty size may result in very little effect on coverage rates and therefore very little impact on adverse selection.

On the positive side, the large overhead costs, which contribute to adverse selection particularly in the individual market, may be significantly lessened once PPACA's insurance market reforms take full effect in 2014. Beginning in 2014, each state must establish an insurance exchange for the individual and small-group market that will streamline insurance purchasing. All plans offered through the exchange will have to offer the same package of benefits, but different plan designs and levels of cost sharing will be available. Insurance companies will not be permitted to enforce pre-existing condition limitations, and the only health factor on which premiums can vary is tobacco use. These reforms should reduce the costs that insurance companies currently bear in trying to sort good risks from bad, and also in their marketing expenses. Insurance companies must take all comers and are significantly limited in how they can price coverage for individuals. Because of the individual mandate, the group of insureds may come closer to reflecting community average risk than is the case under our current system. However, as noted above, the individual mandate as currently written will not necessarily result in coverage levels sufficient to get enough low-risk individuals into the insurance pool to avoid lemons pricing. And even though insurance companies might still have an incentive to use alternative sorting mechanisms such as plan design and

---

60. *See* Amy B. Monahan, *On Subsidies and Mandates: A Regulatory Critique of ACA*, 36 J. Corp. L. (2011).

61. Foster, *supra* note 54, at 7.

62. This amount is the greater of $2,085 and 2.5 percent of their annual household income.

63. The state-based exchanges will have annual open enrollment periods, so exchange-based coverage may not be available for such individuals for up to one year. Non-exchange-based plans do not have these enrollment restrictions but may be priced accordingly.

marketing to attract better-than-average risk, PPACA contains risk-adjustment mechanisms that diminish if not eliminate the gain that might result from a better-than-average risk level. This risk-adjustment mechanism may be sufficient to decrease overhead costs, which should help lessen, if not eliminate, adverse selection problems caused by high overhead costs. In the end, PPACA appears likely to make relatively modest improvements to health insurance market efficiency through both tax and insurance market changes.

PPACA's Broader Reforms

PPACA was not, of course, solely aimed at enhancing economic efficiency. Instead, PPACA also makes significant improvements in insurance and medical affordability for low- and moderate-income individuals, puts in place a new approach to social solidarity that emphasizes the sharing of medical risks instead of actuarial fairness, and improves fairness and equity across certain dimensions. It is interesting to note that in achieving these reforms, PPACA did not break the tie between health insurance and the tax code. Rather, it expanded the relationship to be even broader than before.

The tax code is the primary means through which PPACA enhances the affordability of health insurance, through a complex system of premium tax credits. These credits, along with related limits on cost-sharing requirements, will help make health insurance and medical care more affordable for individuals earning less than 400 percent of the federal poverty limit. They are not, of course, a perfect solution. There will be some individuals who continue to find health insurance and medical care unaffordable. And there will be some individuals who receive federal subsidies who do not need them. Nevertheless, these subsidies are expected to have significant impact on the number of Americans with health insurance coverage.

The tax code is also the primary means through which the government will encourage individuals to purchase coverage, by imposing a monetary penalty on those who elect not to purchase affordable coverage that is available to them. While the individual mandate has certain efficiency gains associated with it, it also helps to enforce a vision of social solidarity, in which medical losses are shared within a community, and also a vision of fairness in which each individual is expected to contribute to the system rather than free-ride. Of course, how well the individual mandate contributes to each of these relevant goals will depend on the details. Does the individual mandate really force the majority of individuals into the insurance pool? As noted above, my intuition is that it will not.[64] If the individual mandate lacks teeth, not only will inefficiencies be worsened, but broader reform goals will be unmet.

The employer mandate is also administered through the tax code and potentially helps to promote fairness by lessening the disparity in health insurance caused by employer choices. If the employer mandate is effective, most employed individuals should have access to employer-provided coverage

---

64. The CMS report estimates that 16 million, most of whom are currently uninsured, will receive coverage through an exchange, and most of those will receive tax credits. Currently there are 56.9 million uninsured. Foster, *supra* note 54, at 3–4.

and all of its resulting advantages. However, the fact that the mandate does not apply to employers with less than 50 full-time employees carves out a significant group from the reach of the mandate. Small employers are precisely those who are least likely to offer health insurance to employees, and leaving them out of the equation is a significant shortcoming. Of course, PPACA does offer tax credits to these employers, but the eligibility criteria are strict, the cost is high to the employer, and the credits are only temporary. On the whole, PPACA tends to leave small employers out of the equation and therefore preserves a significant source of health insurance disparity. However, the more robust individual market should help to lessen the practical impact of this employer disparity because those individuals employed by small employers should have good access to coverage on the individual market regardless of their health history. Nevertheless, the new employer tax provisions appear to add complexity to the Code without producing significant results.

While the individual mandate and insurance market reforms address certain forms of perceived unfairness in the current system, they leave in place other forms of unfairness and even create some new ones. They leave in place the preference for employer-provided coverage, which creates inequity between individuals based on their employment status and the choices of their employers. The effect of this inequity is somewhat lessened by the individual insurance market reforms, but critical elements remain. Individuals who are not offered coverage by an employer must still purchase that coverage with after-tax dollars and face the higher administrative fees associated with individual coverage. In addition, the tax on high-cost health plans creates some new inequities. The cost of medical care in the United States varies significantly by region, and health insurance premiums vary accordingly. The result could be that individuals living in high-cost states will receive much less generous coverage than their counterparts in relatively low-cost states because of the pressure of the excise tax. This might not be a bad thing, if the excise tax forces those high-cost states to evaluate the drivers of high costs and eliminate those that are inefficient. However, if the high cost of living or the costs associated with graduate medical education are disproportionately borne by residents of certain states, they will bear an extra burden because of the excise tax.

THE ROLE FOR TAX

In our current system, the federal income taxation of health insurance premiums and out-of-pocket medical expenses significantly impacts how individuals buy and pay for coverage. Despite widespread criticism of the existing tax treatment of health insurance premiums and medical expenses, PPACA retains the interrelationship between the provision of health insurance and taxes, but it also takes the relationship in new directions. Retained tax preferences for employer-provided coverage will mean that most nonelderly Americans will continue to receive coverage through an employer. This may even be somewhat strengthened by penalties employers will face for failing to offer coverage to employees. In addition, the tax code will be the primary means of enhancing insurance affordability, through the provision of advanceable, refundable tax credits available to certain Americans to subsidize the cost of individual insurance purchased through a state-based exchange. And finally, the tax code will play a primary role in exerting pressure against moral hazard, by imposing a significant excise tax on insurance coverage that is "too generous."

CONCLUSION

As in many areas of tax policy, this brief case study of the interrelationship between taxes and health insurance and medical care illustrates that it is unwise to focus solely on economic efficiency in determining tax policy. Clearly, everyone has an interest in economic efficiency, but, particularly in areas with such significant social impacts, broader concerns must also be on the table. The recent health care reform legislation is happily an example of taking both efficiency and broader policy concerns into account and, while this chapter has suggested that there are shortcomings in the law, it will nevertheless be a fascinating experiment to monitor.

7

WHY (OR WHETHER) THE TAX SYSTEM SHOULD ENCOURAGE HOMEOWNERSHIP AND HOW A TAX BENEFIT FOR HOUSING SHOULD BE STRUCTURED

Roberta Mann, University of Oregon School of Law

The deduction for qualified residence interest (QRI) is the second largest individual tax expenditure, after the exclusion for employer-provided health insurance. While homeownership has long been viewed as a social good, the QRI deduction has faced criticism. Commentators have argued that it is not consistent with the structure of the income tax system; it is economically inefficient, skewing investment towards private residences; it is inequitable, discriminating against low-income people (a group that may disproportionately include people of color) and certain religious minorities; and it is environmentally unsound, encouraging sprawl, excessive energy use, and inefficient transportation choices. In late 2008, the entire world reeled from a global economic crisis that started with a housing bubble inflated by excessive debt facilitated by subprime mortgages and spread around the economy by mortgage-backed securities.

Assuming that homeownership provides useful societal benefits, this chapter will explore how the tax system could create incentives for homeownership while avoiding the problems of the QRI deduction. The chapter will examine options including adding a homeownership benefit to the standard deduction, creating a refundable housing credit, providing a deduction for contributions to a housing savings account, and including a shelter credit available for renters and homeowners alike. The chapter will also address whether the housing benefit should be linked to debt financing. The ideal benefit would be equitably distributed, would not unduly influence housing prices, would not encourage excessive debt, and would respect environmental as well as social goals.

ASSUMPTION THAT HOMEOWNERSHIP IS A SOCIAL GOOD

Part of being a secure America is to encourage homeownership. So somebody can say, this is my home, welcome to my home. Now, we've got a problem here in America that we have to address. Too many American families, too many minorities do not own a home. There is a home ownership gap in America. The difference between Anglo America and African American and Hispanic home ownership is too big. And we've got to focus the attention on this nation to address this. And it starts with setting a goal. And so by the year 2010, we must increase minority homeowners by at least 5.5 million. In order to close the homeownership gap, we've got to set a big goal for America, and focus our attention and resources on that goal.[1]

Homeownership has been credited with building wealth, increasing happiness, and improving educational outcomes for children of homeowners.[2] Most significantly, homeownership is said to benefit the entire community. Homeowners are more likely to vote in local elections and work to solve local problems.[3] If homeowners are better citizens than renters, wider homeownership should create economic and political stability. Recent studies have shed doubt on the assumption that homeownership is an unalloyed blessing. Homeownership may have been mistakenly credited as the cause of the positive outcomes that resulted from "unobserved household characteristics."[4] Several researchers have found a negative correlation between homeownership and happiness. Andrew Oswald noted that homeownership reduces labor mobility.[5] Richard Florida noted the same phenomenon, further commenting on its negative effect on the economy overall, stating:

As homeownership rates have risen, our society has become less nimble: in the 1950s and 1960s, Americans were nearly twice as likely to move in a given year as they are today. Last year fewer Americans moved, as a percentage of the population, than in any year since the Census Bureau started tracking address changes, in the late 1940s. This sort of creeping rigidity in the labor market is a

---

1. President George W. Bush, *President Calls for Expanding Opportunities to Home Ownership*, Remarks by the President on Homeownership, St. Paul AME Church, Atlanta, GA, June 17, 2002, available at http://georgewbush-whitehouse.archives.gov/news/releases/2002/06/20020617-2.html, last visited June 12, 2012.

2. Kristopher S. Gerardi and Paul S. Willen, *Subprime Mortgages, Foreclosures, and Urban Neighborhoods*, Fed. Res. Bank of Boston Public Policy Paper 08-6 (Dec. 22, 2008), 6, available at http://www.bos.frb.org/economic/ppdp/index.htm, last visited June 12, 2012.

3. Dennis DePasquale and Edward L. Glaeser, *Incentives and Social Capital: Are Homeowners Better Citizens*, 45 J. Urb. Econ. 354, 354 (1999).

4. Gerardi and Willen, *supra* note 2, at 5.

5. *See* Andrew J. Oswald, *The Housing Market and Unemployment: A Non-Technical Paper* (May 1999) ("By making it expensive to change location, high levels of home-ownership foster a spatial mis-match between workers' skills and the available jobs." *Id.* at 2). *See also*, Andrew J. Oswald, *A Conjecture on the Explanation for High Unemployment in the Industrialized Nations: Part I* (1996) ("[M]uch anecdotal evidence suggests that joblessness is a large source of unhappiness in society." *Id.* at 1). Daniel N. Shaviro, *The 2008 Financial Crisis: Implications for Income Tax Reform*, http://ssrn.com/abstract=1442089 (Jan. 31, 2011), 22 ("the higher transaction costs of moving when one is a homeowner, rather than a renter, may slow economic adjustment when jobs disappear in some regions and arise in others.").

bad sign for the economy, particularly in a time when businesses, industries, and regions are rising and falling quickly.[6]

Daniel Shaviro also linked high homeownership rates to a stagnant economy, noting that "the higher transaction costs of moving when one is a homeowner, rather than a renter, may slow economic adjustment when jobs disappear in some regions and arise in others."[7] Grace Bucchianeri found that the average homeowner derived more pain than joy from her home.[8] Homeowners seem to be fatter, more tired, and more stressed than renters.[9] In an international life satisfaction survey, the United States was ranked 14th.[10] Of the top five ranked countries, only one, Norway, had a homeownership rate higher than the United States.[11] Life satisfaction does not appear to be directly correlated with homeownership (see Table 7-1).

Table 7-1. Happiness and Homeownership[12]

Country	Satisfaction Ranking	Percentage Homeownership
Denmark	1	46
Finland	2	66
Norway	3	76
Sweden	4	38
Netherlands	4	58
United States	14	66

---

6. Richard Florida, *How the Crash Will Reshape America*, Atlantic (March 2009) available at http://www.theatlantic.com/magazine/archive/2009/03/how-the-crash-will-reshape-america/7293/6/, last visited June 13, 2012.

7. Shaviro, *supra* note 5, at 22.

8. Grace W. Bucchianeri, *The American Dream or the American Delusion: The Private and External Benefits of Homeownership for Women* (2011), 22, available at http://real.wharton.upenn.edu/%7Ewongg/research/American%20Dream%20or%20American%20Delusion%202011-04-22.pdf, last visited June 12, 2012.

9. *Id.* at 16.

10. *See* Francesca Levy, *Table: World's Happiest Countries*, Forbes (July 14, 2010) (reporting on a Gallup Survey), available at http://www.forbes.com/2010/07/14/world-happiest-countries-life style-realestate-gallup-table.html?partner=popstories, last visited June 12, 2012. In an earlier survey, the United States was ranked 11th. OECD (2009), *Society at a Glance 2009—OECD Social Indicators* 254–55 (table available at http://www.oecd.org/document/40/0,3746,en_2649_37419_47507368_1_1_1_37419,00.html, last visited June 12, 2012).

11. Kees Dol and Marietta Haffner, eds., *Housing Statistics in the European Union 2010* (The Netherlands, 2010) 64, Table 3.5, Occupied Housing Stock by Tenure 1980–2008, available at http://www.bmwfj.gv.at/Wirtschaftspolitik/Wohnungspolitik/Documents/housing_statistics_in_the_european_union_2010.pdf, last visited April 23, 2013. For U.S. housing statistics, *see* Robert R. Callis & Melissa Kresin, *Residential Vacancies and Homeownership in the Second Quarter 2011*, U.S. Census Bureau News (July 29, 2011), available at http://www.census.gov/hhes/www/housing/hvs/qtr211/files/q211press.pdf, last visited June 12, 2012. For Norwegian housing statistics, *see* Statistics Norway, *Housing: My Home Is My Castle* (2008), 18, http://www.ssb.no/norge_en/bolig_en.pdf, last visited June 12, 2012.

12. *See* Callis and Kresin, *supra* note 11, at 2.

The housing market in the United States has had quite a reality check. Encouraged by housing prices that continued to rise from 1997 until 2006,[13] Americans believed that housing prices would never decline because "there is a limited supply of land and a growing number of households."[14] Because of the meltdown of the housing market in 2008 and resulting financial liquidity concerns, Fannie Mae (Federal National Mortgage Association, FNMA), a government-sponsored enterprise tasked with maintaining liquidity in the mortgage markets, was taken into government conservatorship on September 6, 2008.[15] In contrast to the rosy statements made in earlier years about encouraging the American dream and increasing homeownership, in September 2009, Fannie Mae's chief executive officer sounded a more realistic note, saying that one of the issues faced by the organization is determining "what is the sustainable rate of homeownership?"[16]

He further stated, "I doubt we can sustain the homeownership rate we saw in recent years. That's not necessarily bad news, because people are reducing their debt and saving money." Nonetheless, a majority of renters seek to be homeowners,[17] and the federal government wants to help them. The United States government has long been committed to providing "a decent home and suitable living environment" for all its citizens, as exemplified by the Housing Act of 1949.[18] Eighty-four percent of respondents to Fannie Mae's 2003 National Housing Survey stated that a major reason to buy a home is because "it is a good-long term investment."[19] Forty-six percent of respondents cited the tax benefits of homeownership.[20]

---

13. Martin Hutchinson, *Five Years from U.S. Housing Peak, Still No Bottom*, Reuters Breakingviews (Apr. 16, 2011), available at http://blogs.reuters.com/columns/2011/04/15/five-years-from-u-s-housing-peak-still-no-bottom/, last visited June 12, 2012.

14. *Special Report: The Global Housing Boom*, Economist (June 15, 2005), available at http://www.economist.com/node/4079027, last visited June 12, 2012.

15. Testimony of Herbert M. Allison Jr., President and Chief Executive Officer, Fannie Mae, Hearing before the House Committee on Financial Services, Washington, D.C., Thursday, Sept. 25, 2008, available at http://archives.financialservices.house.gov/hearing110/allison092508.pdf, last visited June 12, 2012.

16. Remarks by Michael J. Williams, President and CEO, Fannie Mae, at the Exchequer Club, Washington, DC, Sept. 9, 2009, available at http://www.fanniemae.com/portal/about-us/media/speeches/2009/speech-williams-exchequer-club.html, last visited June 12, 2012.

17. *See* Fannie Mae Foundation, *Fannie Mae National Housing Survey 1998: Baby Boomers, Generation Xers and Home Ownership* 2 (FNMA, 1998), available at http://www.fanniemae.com/global/pdf/media/survey/survey1998.pdf, last visited June 12, 2012 (60% of renters rated buying a home as a very important priority).

18. The Housing Act of 1949, ch. 338, 63 Stat. 413 (1949) (codified as amended at 42 U.S.C. §1441 (1949)).

19. 2003 Fannie Mae National Housing Survey, *Understanding America's Homeownership Gaps* (2004), 5, available at http://www.fanniemae.com/global/pdf/media/survey/survey2003.pdf, last visited June 12, 2012.

20. *Id.*

GOVERNMENT SUPPORT FOR HOUSING

DISPROPORTIONATE EFFECTS

The federal government provides a majority of its housing assistance through the tax code.[21] For 2010, the federal government provided a total of $36 billion in direct assistance for public housing (including Indian and Native Hawaiian housing) and rental assistance payments.[22] The QRI provides the highest level of tax subsidy to homeowners, estimated by the Joint Committee on Taxation to reduce tax revenues by $91 billion in 2010.[23] Tax subsidies for homeowners continue to expand in different ways. Homeowners can deduct mortgage insurance premiums.[24] Homeowners can deduct their property taxes, totaling $15 billion in forgone tax revenue in 2010.[25] Since 1997, home sellers have been able to exclude up to $500,000 of gain on the sale of their principal residences, representing another $15 billion of forgone tax receipts in 2010.[26] Nobel laureate economist Vernon L. Smith credits the 1997 provision excluding up to $500,000 of gain on the sale of a principal residence with "fueling the mother of all housing bubbles."[27] For a limited time, from April 8, 2008, until April 30, 2010, first time homebuyers received help from the tax system at an estimated cost of $13.6 billion[28] in forgone tax receipts.[29] Also for a limited time, from January 1, 2007, until January 1, 2013, homeowners facing foreclosure could avoid tax on the income resulting from debt cancellation.[30] The tax system also subsidizes housing by excluding the imputed income from home ownership from taxation. Imputed income consists of the untaxed rental value of an owner-occupied home. Indeed, some

---

21. U.S. Dept. of Hous. & Urb. Dev., *FY 2010 Budget: Road Map for Transformation* (hereinafter HUD FY 2010), 39, available at http://www.hud.gov/budgetsummary2010/fy10budget.pdf, last visited June 12, 2012, and Joint Committee on Taxation, *Estimates of Federal Tax Expenditures for Fiscal Years 2010–2014* 39, JCS-3-10 (Dec. 15, 2010) (hereinafter JCS-3-10).

22. *See* HUD FY 2010, *supra* note 21, at 37.

23. I.R.C. §163(h)(3) and JCS-3-10, *supra* note 21, at 39.

24. I.R.C. §163(h)(3)(E).

25. I.R.C. §164; JCS-3-10, *supra* note 21. In 2008 and 2009, even homeowners who did not itemize deductions could deduct real property taxes, by means of special add-on to the standard deduction. I.R.C. §§63(c)(1)(C) and (c)(7), added by P.L. 110-289, Sec. 3012.

26. I.R.C. §121; JCS-3-10, *supra* note 21.

27. Vikas Bajaj & David Leonhardt, *Tax Break May Have Helped Cause Housing Bubble*, NY Times A1 (Dec. 19, 2008).

28. The Joint Committee on Taxation estimated forgone revenue of $0.3 billion for 2008 and $8.7 billion for both 2009 and 2010, and the JCT further estimated returns of $7.3 billion between 2011 and 2014 from credit repayments and forfeitures. JCS-3-10, *supra* note 21, at 39.

29. I.R.C. §36. The credit evolved over time. First, the Housing and Economic Recovery Act of 2008 established a $7,500 credit that must be repaid in equal installments over 15 years. Second, the American Recovery and Reinvestment Act of 2009 established an $8,000 credit with no requirement of repayment unless the house was no longer the taxpayer's principal residence within the next three years. The Worker, Homeownership and Business Assistance Act of 2009 continued the $8,000 credit through 2010. The buyer need not be a true "first-time" homeowner. Rather, the buyer must not have owned a home within the three-year period before the purchase. I.R.C. §36(c). This provision was added by P.L. 110-289, Div C, Title I, Subtitle B, §3011(a), 122 Stat. 2888, and amended by P.L. 111-5, Div B, Title I, Subtitle A, Part I, §§1006(a)–(c), (d)(2), (e), 123 Stat. 316, 317.

30. I.R.C. §108(a)(1)(E) and §108(h), added in 2007 by P.L. 110-142, Sec. 2.

commentators view the exclusion of imputed income from owner-occupied housing as the most significant tax subsidy for homeownership.[31]

Income and Racial Effects

The disparity between tax benefits for housing and direct assistance has both a racial and an income component, although the two components are interrelated.[32] The Department of Housing and Urban Development (HUD) did a comprehensive study of the racial composition of public housing residents in 1994.[33] Over 60 percent of the families living in public housing were either African American or Hispanic, compared to just over 30 percent of the overall population in the census tract where the housing was located.[34] Since 1997, over 70 percent of white households have lived in owner-occupied housing.[35] Over the same time period, although the homeownership rates of African Americans and Hispanics increased, they remained below 50 percent for African Americans and barely above 50 percent for Hispanics.[36]

The income distribution of recipients of direct assistance and the income distribution of tax subsidies are strikingly different. Rental assistance vouchers go to over two million households with extremely low incomes.[37] Forty percent of families receiving rental assistance vouchers have incomes lower than half of the poverty line.[38] Over 90 percent of recipients of public housing are extremely low-income.[39] In contrast, in 2009, 63 percent of the total benefit of the home mortgage interest deduction accrued to households with incomes over $100,000.[40] The federal poverty line for 2011 for a family of four was $22,350.[41] Less than 1 percent of the total benefit of the home mortgage interest deduction accrued to households with incomes under $30,000.[42] Calvin Johnson calculates that the tax benefit of the housing tax subsidy is distributed as follows: bottom quarter, 2 percent; second to bottom quarter, 3 percent; second to top quarter, 10 percent; 75–89.9th percentile, 19 percent; top 10 percent, 66 percent.[43] African Americans and Hispanics derive less benefit from the QRI because they tend to have lower income

---

31. *See* Calvin Johnson, *The Taxation of the Really Big House*, 122 Tax Notes 915 (2009); Thomas Chancellor, *Imputed Income and the Ideal Income Tax*, 67 Or. L. Rev. 561, 601-09 (1988).

32. Although the components are interrelated, they are not perfectly correlated. *See* Dorothy A. Brown, *Shades of the American Dream*, 87 Wash. U. L. Rev. 329, 352 (2009) ("Homeownership disparities by race and ethnicity are not solely attributable to difference in income. Even at high income levels, a smaller percentage of blacks and Latinos are homeowners than whites").

33. John Goering et al., *The Location and Racial Composition of Public Housing in the United States*, U.S. Dep't. HUD, Office of Policy Development and Research (Dec. 1994).

34. Goering et al., *supra* note 33, at 18.

35. U.S. Census Bureau, *Table 991, Occupied Housing Units—Tenure, by Race of Householder: 1991–2009*, available at http://www.census.gov/compendia/statab/2012/tables/12s0991.pdf, last visited June 12, 2012.

36. *Id.*

37. HUD FY 2010 Budget, *supra* note 21, at 9.

38. *Id.*

39. *Id.* at 10.

40. JCS-3-10, *supra* note 21, at 60.

41. Federal Register, Vol. 76, No. 13, January 20, 2011, pp. 3637–38.

42. JCS-3-10, *supra* note 21, at 60.

43. Johnson, *supra* note 31, at 918.

than whites. Professor Dorothy Brown notes that "for the majority of blacks, homeownership is a poor financial investment."[44]

For minorities, the home represents a greater percentage of their wealth.[45] Eric Belsky found that "the median ratio of home equity to net worth for minorities is roughly two-thirds, compared to less than half for whites. For homeowners in the bottom income quartile, the median ratio is 82.8 percent, compared to just 31.4 percent for top-quartile owners."[46] On the assumption that homeownership is a social good, and to promote the "ownership" society, the government encouraged loose lending standards—e.g., subprime mortgages.[47] Subprime mortgages were disproportionately granted to minority groups.[48] The subprime mortgage meltdown disproportionately affected minority homeowners.[49] Minority groups are disproportionately affected by foreclosures, which certainly cause misery.[50]

Like any deduction, the QRI deduction is an upside-down subsidy.[51] The home mortgage interest deduction allows a deduction for interest paid on acquisition debt on a principal residence (and one other residence) on a total loan amount of up to $1 million.[52] It produces greater benefit to higher-rate-bracket taxpayers.[53] If a taxpayer in the 15 percent rate bracket has a $10,000 mortgage payment, her tax liability will decrease by $1,500. If a taxpayer in the 35 percent rate bracket has a $10,000 mortgage payment, his tax liability will decrease by $3,500. It is also likely that the higher-bracket (wealthier) taxpayer will have a larger mortgage payment than the lower-bracket (poorer) taxpayer. Thus, if the 35 percent rate bracket taxpayer pays $30,000 of mortgage interest, he will get a reduction in tax liability of $10,500. The wealthier taxpayer will have a higher payment because he purchased a more expensive house. The increased benefit is caused by the relationship between tax deductions and tax liability. A tax deduction reduces taxable income. Taxable income times tax rate equals tax liability. Thus, the higher the tax bracket, the greater the benefit from a deduction. In contrast, a tax

---

44. Brown, *supra* note 32, at 332. Brown also notes that the minority disparity in homeownership also applies, to a lesser degree, at higher income levels. *Id.* at 352.

45. *See* Melvin L. Oliver & Thomas M. Shapiro, *Black Wealth/White Wealth: A New Perspective on Racial Inequality* (Routledge, 1995), 106 (stating that housing constitutes a significantly greater percentage of black wealth (62.5%) than of white wealth (43.3%).

46. Eric S. Belsky, *Housing Wealth Effects and the Course of the U.S. Economy: Theory, Evidence and Policy Implications*, 4 Harv. Jt. Center for Housing Studies 5 (Nov. 2008).

47. President Bush's "housing policies and hands-off approach to regulation encouraged lax lending standards." Jo Becker et al., *White House Philosophy Stoked Mortgage Bonfire*, NY Times A1 (Dec. 21, 2008).

48. Gerardi and Willen, *supra* note 2, at 3.

49. *Id.*

50. *Id.* at 7 ("Non-monetary costs [of foreclosures] include the psychological hardship that goes along with losing one's home, which can often lead to adverse effects on family life, such as divorce or health problems").

51. Stanley S. Surrey and Paul R. McDaniel, *Tax Expenditures* (Harvard University, 1985), 77.

52. I.R.C. §163(h)(3)(B); (h)(4) (definition of qualified residence). There is also an interest deduction for home equity debt up to $100,000. *See* I.R.C. §163(h)(3)(C).

53. For further illustrations on how the QRI deduction favors the wealthy, *see* Roberta F. Mann, *The (Not So) Little House on the Prairie: The Hidden Costs of the Home Mortgage Interest Deduction*, 32 Ariz. St. L. J. 1347, 1358–64 (2000) (hereinafter Mann, *Prairie*).

credit produces the same reduction in tax liability irrespective of the rate bracket of the taxpayer.[54] A tax credit directly reduces tax liability.

Arguably, the government has an interest in assisting its citizens in obtaining decent housing. The problem may be the design of the subsidy. It would be difficult to subsidize low-income housing through a tax provision, as extremely low-income Americans rarely pay taxes. However, a refundable credit could be used to subsidize homeownership by nontaxpayers, as in the earned income tax credit.[55] Moreover, as the QRI deduction is an itemized deduction, it provides no benefit to the 62 percent of taxpayers who take the standard deduction.[56]

Sexual Orientation Impact

Even at similar income levels, the QRI deduction lacks horizontal equity. Several scholars have analyzed the effect of the Internal Revenue Code (IRC) on gay and lesbian couples.[57] The tax treatment of homeownership might be viewed as an area in which unmarried couples might get the better of the IRC.[58] The QRI deduction is limited to interest on a principal amount of $1 million. The statute states: "The aggregate amount treated as acquisition indebtedness for any period shall not exceed $1 million ($500,000 in the case of a married individual filing a separate return)."[59]

It is not clear from the language of the statute whether this $1 million limit applies per residence or per taxpayer, although the first paragraph of the pertinent Code section refers to "in the case of a taxpayer," which could be read as applying the provision on a per-taxpayer basis.[60] Married taxpayers are limited to a total of $1 million of principal, whether they file separate returns or not. Unmarried taxpayers are separate taxpayers who must file individual tax returns, even if they are legally united in a civil union. Same-sex couples, even if they are married under state law, are not considered married under federal law.[61] Thus, arguably, two people who are not related in the eyes of the federal government could join together to purchase a house and each take

---

54. *See* Report of the President's Advisory Panel on Tax Reform, Simple, Fair, and Pro-Growth: *Proposals to Fix America's Tax System*, Chapter 5, at 61 (Nov. 2005), available at http://govinfo .library.unt.edu/taxreformpanel/final-report/index.html, last visited June 12, 2012, (and on file with author) (proposing to replace the home mortgage interest deduction with a 15% credit available to all taxpayers, limited to the average regional price of housing).

55. I.R.C. §32. *See also* Lily L. Batchelder et al., *Efficiency and Tax Incentives: the Case for Refundable Tax Credits*, 59 Stan. L. Rev. 23 (2006).

56. I.R.C. §63(e); 67(b)(1). IRS Publication 1204, *Individual Income Tax Returns, Complete Report 2006*, Table 1.2, row 1 (138 million returns), and Table 1.3, row 55 (86 million returns with standard deduction).

57. *See, e.g.*, Anthony C. Infanti, *Tax Equity*, 55 Buffalo L. Rev. 1191 (2008); Patricia A. Cain, *Federal Tax Consequences of Civil Unions*, 30 Cap. U.L. Rev. 387 (2002).

58. *See* Theodore P. Seto, *The Unintended Advantages of Gay Marriage*, 65 Wash. & Lee L. Rev. 1529, 1571 (2008).

59. I.R.C. §163(h)(3)(B)(ii).

60. I.R.C. §163(h)(1).

61. The Defense of Marriage Act (DOMA), 1 U.S.C. section 7 (1996), prevents even married same-sex couples from being treated as spouses under federal law, including the Internal Revenue Code. DOMA has been challenged in several courts and is being considered by the Supreme Court. *See* Abby Goodnough, *Appeals Court Hears Arguments on Gay Marriage Law*, NY Times A12 (Apr. 5, 2012).

a QRI deduction for interest on up to $1 million in acquisition debt. Patricia Cain points out that in many areas of the country, such as northern California, it can be hard to find a home costing less than $1 million.[62] However, in an internal document, the Internal Revenue Service (IRS) has taken the view that the QRI deduction applies on a per residence basis.[63] If the QRI deduction should be reformed, its replacement should apply in a consistent manner to same-sex couples.

Religious Impact

Religion has little impact on the QRI deduction, unless the taxpayer happens to believe in a religion that forbids the use of debt. This, like other problems with the QRI deduction, may be evolutionary in nature. The deduction for interest has been in the IRC since 1913. The deduction for personal interest has been limited to homeowners only since 1986.[64] Social norms and the demographic makeup of the United States have changed significantly since 1913. For example, in 2010, the U.S. population was 28 percent nonwhite, whereas in 1910, the U.S. population was 12 percent nonwhite.[65] If the federal government had set out to design a tax subsidy for housing from scratch, would it have based it on debt? We will never know, but many Muslims and Orthodox Jews refuse to enter into debt for religious reasons and, consequently, cannot benefit from the governmental housing benefit provided by the QRI deduction.[66]

Banks have designed home financing alternatives that comply with Islamic prohibitions against debt.[67] Although it could be argued that, in substance, such financing alternatives did result in payments that are the economic equivalent of interest, it is not clear that such arguments would result in deductibility of the payments.[68] The apparent discriminatory effect of the QRI deduction does not rise to the level of a violation against the constitutional guarantee of freedom of religion,[69] but in light of the significance of the government benefit provided by the QRI deduction, it is another reason why the QRI deduction is ripe for reform.

---

62. Patricia Cain, *Unmarried Couples and the Mortgage Interest Deduction*, 122 Tax Notes 473, 473 (2009).

63. ILM 200911007 (Nov. 24, 2008). Cain disputes the conclusion of this document. *See* Cain, *id.* at 476. Martin McMahon agrees with the IRS's interpretation. Martin J. McMahon Jr., *Counterpoint: CCA 2009211007: Trying to Make Sense of the $1,000,000 Ceiling in the Home Mortgage Interest Deduction Rules*, ABA Section of Taxation News Quarterly 21 (Summer 2009).

64. I.R.C. §163(h)(3). *See* Mann, *Prairie*, *supra* note 53, at 1352.

65. *See* http://www.census.gov/prod/cen2010/briefs/c2010br-05.pdf and http://www.census. gov/population/www/documentation/twps0056/twps0056.html (last visited June 12, 2012).

66. *See* Joel S. Newman, *Islamic and Jewish Perspectives on Interest*, 89 Tax Notes 1311, 1318 (2000).

67. *See* Roberta Mann, *Is Sharif's Castle Deductible? Islam and the Tax Treatment of Mortgage Debt*, 17 Wm. & Mary Bill of Rts. J. 1139, 1147–50 (2009) (describing Islamic financing transactions) (hereinafter Mann, *Islam*).

68. *Id.* at 1150–53.

69. *Id.* at 1156–58 (tax provisions of general application do not violate the free-exercise clause).

OVERINVESTMENT IN HOUSING AND INFLUENCING DECISION MAKERS

It is axiomatic that "housing is the cornerstone of household net worth."[70] Since 1970, the real estate share of household sector wealth has usually exceeded that of other assets, remaining at above 30 percent in recent years.[71] When the economy is in a downturn, even well-off homeowners suffer from housing cost burden. The Harvard Joint Center for Housing Studies determined that "[f]or homeowners earning more than the median income, the likelihood of being cost burdened nearly doubled between 2001 and 2006."[72]

If the loose lending standards and increased homeownership rates did not benefit American homeowners, then who did benefit? Perhaps the whole focus on benefiting homeowners is naive. As Watergate informant "Deep Throat" said to Bob Woodward, "follow the money."[73] It is probably no coincidence that President Ronald Reagan announced his firm support for the mortgage interest deduction at a convention of the National Realtors'Association.[74] Although there has been a personal interest deduction in the tax laws since 1913, it was not limited to homeowners until 1986.[75] Professor Dennis Ventry noted that policymakers and taxpayers did not consider the interest deduction as "an integral part of national housing policy" until about 1960.[76] However, the politics of the mortgage interest deduction were about to come alive. In 1961, Stanley Surrey became the Treasury Department's Assistant Secretary for Tax Policy and began his crusade to end subsidies through the tax system.[77] A 1963 Treasury Department proposal to reduce itemized deductions by 5 percent of adjusted gross income was strongly opposed by, among others, the real estate lobby.[78] Later, Surrey noted that "Congress appears decidedly to favor assisting homeownership, and apparently is not about to consider the question whether this should be done under the tax system or through direct expenditure policies."[79] Further efforts to reform housing tax subsidies continued to meet with opposition from the housing lobby.[80] The 2005 tax reform panel had a mandate to preserve tax benefits for homeowners.[81]

---

70. Belsky, *supra* note 46, at 3.

71. *Id.*

72. *The State of the Nation's Housing 2008*, at 28, available at http://www.jchs.harvard.edu/research/publications/state-nations-housing-2008, last visited June 12, 2012.

73. *All the President's Men* (Warner Bros. Pictures, 1976).

74. *See* Jeffrey H. Birnbaum and Alan S. Murray, *Showdown at Gucci Gulch: Lawmakers, Lobbyists, and the Unlikely Triumph of Tax Reform* (Random House, 1987), 57 (describing President Reagan's May 10, 1984, speech).

75. I.R.C. §163(h)(3). *See* Mann, *Islam*, *supra* note 67, at 1352.

76. Dennis J. Ventry Jr., *The Accidental Deduction: A History and Critique of the Tax Subsidy for Mortgage Interest*, 73 Law & Contemporary Problems 233, 251 (2010).

77. *Id.* at 259–60.

78. *Builders Oppose Exemption Limit, Assail New Tax Plan to Cut Home-Owner Deductions*, NY Times A9 (Feb. 12, 1963).

79. Stanley S. Surrey, *Pathways to Tax Reform: The Concept of Tax Expenditures* (Harvard University, 1973), 234.

80. *See Focus on Treasury, Limitation on Mortgage Interest Deduction Would Have "Devastating Impact," Attorney Says*, 12 Tax Notes 744, 744 (1981).

81. George W. Bush, Announcement (Jan. 7, 2005), "The Advisory Panel will submit to the Secretary of the Treasury a report containing revenue neutral policy options for reforming the Federal Internal Revenue Code as soon as practicable, but not later than November 1, 2005.

The Obama administration encouraged a number of tax reform and simplification efforts, all of which addressed housing in one way or another.[82] The President's Economic Recovery Advisory Board (PERAB), chaired by Paul Volcker, was instructed not to consider options that involve raising taxes on families making less than $250,000 per year, while considering ideas on tax simplification, better enforcement of tax law, and reforming corporate taxes.[83] The PERAB report suggested indexing the exclusion of capital gains on the sale of principal residence for inflation, but did not mention the QRI.[84] The bipartisan National Commission on Fiscal Responsibility and Reform, co-chaired by Erskine Bowles and Alan Simpson, proposed changing the QRI to a nonrefundable 12 percent credit, capped at $500,000 principal amount and limited to one home.[85] The Debt Reduction Task Force, chaired by Alice Rivlin and Pete Domenici, proposed changing the QRI to a 15 percent refundable credit on the first $25,000 of mortgage interest paid on the principal residence.[86]

Real estate and home building groups are still paying devoted attention to tax issues. The National Association of Realtors (NAR) spent more on lobbying in 2008, $17.3 million, than in any previous year.[87] The second largest spender in the real estate category, after NAR, was the National Association of Mortgage Brokers, at $1.5 million.[88] From 1998 to 2009, the industry sector of finance, insurance, and real estate was the top lobbying spender, spending an aggregate $3.7 billion.[89] Total contributions to Congress from the real estate industry in 2008 totaled $135.9 million, ranking fourth among industries in total contributions, behind lawyers, retirees, and investments.[90] It will be difficult to draw a direct relationship between lobbying dollars and the survival of the QRI deduction. The QRI deduction directly benefits homeowners—but surely much of that benefit flows to the real estate and finance industry. Economists

These options should . . . share the burdens and benefits of the Federal tax structure in an appropriately progressive manner while recognizing the importance of homeownership and charity in American society." http://govinfo.library.unt.edu/taxreformpanel/, last visited June 12, 2012.

82. *See* Exec. Order 13501, 74 Fed. Reg. 6983 (Feb. 11, 2009) (creating President's Economic Recovery Advisory Board); Exec. Order 13531, 75 Fed. Reg. 7927 (Feb. 23, 2010) (creating the National Commission on Fiscal Responsibility and Reform).

83. PERAB Tax Reform Subcommittee, *Tax Reform Subcommittee Requests Ideas* (posted Sept. 29, 2011), available at http://www.whitehouse.gov/blog/Tax-Reform-Subcommittee-Requests-Ideas/, last visited June 12, 2012.

84. President's Economic Recovery Advisory Board (PERAB), *The Report on Tax Reform Options: Simplification, Compliance, and Corporate Taxation* 41 (2010), available at http://www.whitehouse.gov/administration/eop/perab/blog, last visited June 12, 2012.

85. *Report of the Nat'l Comm'n on Fiscal Resp. and Reform, The Moment of Truth* (2010), 30–31, available at http://www.fiscalcommission.gov/, last visited June 12, 2012).

86. Debt Reduction Task Force, *Restoring America's Future* (2010), 35–36, available at http://bipartisanpolicy.org/projects/debt-initiative/about, last visited June 12, 2012.

87. Center for Responsive Politics, *Lobbying Top Spenders* (2008), available at http://www.opensecrets.org/lobby/top.php?showYear=2008&indexType=s, last visited June 12, 2012 (ranking 12th in terms of top spenders in 2008).

88. Center for Responsive Politics, *Lobbying: Nat'l Assoc. of Mtg. Brokers* (2008), available at http://www.opensecrets.org/lobby/clientsum.php?id=D000022130&year=2008, last visited June 12, 2012.

89. Center for Responsive Politics, *Lobbying: Finance, Insurance and Real Estate, Sector Profile 2009*, available at http://www.opensecrets.org/lobby/indus.php?id=F&year=2009, last visited June 12, 2012.

90. Center for Responsive Politics, *Top Industries Giving to Members of Congress, 2008 Cycle*, available at http://www.opensecrets.org/industries/mems.php?party=A&cycle=2008, last visited June 12, 2012.

note that the mortgage interest deduction has the effect of increasing the price of housing.[91] As real estate agents' commissions are based on the price of housing, that would also increase commissions. If the QRI deduction encourages home purchasing, that would lead to more agent commissions. More mortgages also lead to more commissions for mortgage brokers. The 2005 President's Tax Reform Panel report concluded that the tax preferences for housing lead to excessive investment in housing.[92]

ENVIRONMENTAL EFFECTS

As noted, the wealthier taxpayer gets more assistance from the QRI deduction because he will have a higher mortgage payment because he purchased a more expensive house. It is also likely that the more expensive house is larger than the less expensive house. It is possible that the more expensive house is farther away from work, resulting in a longer commute. Harvard economist Edward Glaeser commented on the utility of the QRI deduction:

> The tax subsidy does modestly encourage homeownership. But it specifically encourages borrowing to invest in expensive homes, which are risky assets that can crash as well as boom. We had housing bubbles long before the federal government got into the subsidy business, but encouraging homeowners to buy with borrowed money certainly did nothing to moderate extreme price swings. . . . We are essentially spending federal money to encourage people to live in 3,000-square-foot houses instead of 2,500-square-foot houses.[93]

Although some predicted that the fuel price increases experienced in the summer of 2008 would spell the death of suburbia, reports of its demise may have been premature.[94] From 1985 to 2003, the United States experienced a slight population shift to the suburbs and increased preferences for larger, single-family housing.[95] The total number of single-family, owner-occupied

---

91. *See, e.g.,* Congressional Research Service, *Effect of Flat Taxes and Other Proposals on Housing: Full Report* 9 (Jane G. Gravelle, Apr. 29, 1996), and William G. Gale, Jonathan Gruber, and Seth Stephens-Davidowitz, *Encouraging Homeownership Through the Tax Code*, 115 Tax Notes 1171, 1171 (2007).

92. The President's Advisory Panel on Federal Tax Reform, *Final Report* 71 (Nov. 2005), available at http://govinfo.library.unt.edu/taxreformpanel/, last visited June 12, 2012.

93. Edward Glaeser, *This Old House Policy*, Boston Globe (Nov. 2, 2008), available at http://www.boston.com/bostonglobe/ideas/articles/2008/11/02/this_old_house_policy/, last visited June 12, 2012.

94. *See* Christopher B. Leinberger, *The Next Slum?*, Atlantic Online (Mar. 2008) (describing the rise of the American dream of housing in the suburbs and predicting a demographic shift of the wealthy to the cities and the poor to the suburbs), available at http://www.theatlantic.com/doc/200803/subprime, last visited June 12, 2012, and Joel Kotkin, *Suburbia's Not Dead Yet*, L.A. Times (July 6, 2008) (noting that many jobs have migrated to the suburbs, and in Los Angeles, less than 3 percent of regional jobs are in the central city), available at http://www.latimes.com/news/print edition/opinion/la-op-kotkin6-2008jul06,0,1038461.story, last visited June 12, 2012.

95. HUD User — Policy Development and Research Information Service, *American Households and Their Housing: 1985 and 2003*, available at http://www.huduser.org/periodicals/ushmc/winter04/article_USHMC_04Q4.pdf, last visited June 12, 2012. *See also* Les Christie, *The Rich: Still Bullish on Real Estate* (June 18, 2007) ("The wealthy also appear to want more space; 61 percent

homes in the suburbs has increased from 30.8 million in 1997[96] to 34.3 million in 2007.[97] Suburbs are defined as the portion of each metropolitan area that is not in any central city. Any city with at least 250,000 population or at least 100,000 people working within its corporate limits qualifies as a central city. Metropolitan areas are composed of whole counties that have significant levels of commuting and contiguous urban areas in common.[98] Strikingly, the average lot size for suburban homes constructed in the past four years has increased from 0.39 acres in 1997[99] to 1.75 acres in 2007.[100] The larger the lot size, the lower the density. Low-density development outside the central city is the definition of sprawl.[101] Sprawl development results in automobile dependence because low-density development discourages walking and use of public transportation.[102]

New single-family homes continue to increase in size. In 1987, the average single-family home in the United States contained 1950 square feet.[103] In 1997, the average single-family home contained 2150 square feet.[104] In 2007, the average single-family home contained 2521 square feet.[105] While one might think that increasing home sizes would increase energy usage, the Department of Energy found that over the past three decades, homes have become larger and more energy-efficient.[106] The National Association of Home Buildings (NAHB) draws a similar conclusion.[107] Various tax credits encourage energy efficiency in residential property.[108] However, as fewer people are living in those larger homes—down to 2.6 people per household in 2010 from 3.7 people in 1940—energy usage per occupant is increasing.[109]

of those moving this year plan to buy a bigger house," citing the Coldwell Banker Previews International Luxury Survey), available at http://money.cnn.com/2007/06/15/real_estate/the_wealthy_bullish_on_real_estate/index.htm?postversion=2007061812, last visited June 12, 2012.

96. American Housing Survey National Tables: 1997, *Size of Unit and Lot – All Housing Units – Suburbs*, Table 1C-3, at 22, http://www.census.gov/prod/99pubs/h150-97.pdf, last visited June 12, 2012 (hereinafter 1997 Housing Table 1C-3).

97. American Housing Survey for the United States: 2007, *Size of Unit and Lot – All Housing Units – Suburbs*, Table 1C-3, at 26, available at http://www.census.gov/housing/ahs/files/ahs07/h150-07.pdf, last visited June 12, 2012 (hereinafter 2007 Housing Table 1C-3).

98. *Id.*

99. 1997 Housing Table 1C-3, *supra* note 96, at 22.

100. 2007 Housing Table 1C-3, *supra* note 97, at 26.

101. Mann, *Prairie*, *supra* note 53, at 1370. *See also* The Sierra Club, *The 1998 Sprawl Report*, at http://www.sierraclub.org/sprawl/report98/report.asp#about, last visited June 12, 2012.

102. GAO, *Community Development: The Extent of Federal Influence on "Urban Sprawl" is Unclear* 1 (Apr. 30,1999), available at http://www.gao.gov/products/RCED-99-87, last visited June 12, 2012.

103. U.S. Census Bureau, *Median and Average Square Feet of Floor Area in New Single-Family Houses Completed by Location*, available at http://www.census.gov/const/C25Ann/sftotalmedavgsqft.pdf, last visited June 12, 2012.

104. *Id.*

105. *Id.*

106. Energy Information Administration, *What's New in Our Home Energy Use* (Mar. 28, 2011), available at http://www.eia.gov/consumption/residential/reports/2009overview.cfm, last visited June 13, 2012.

107. Yingchun Liu, *Home Operating Costs* (Feb. 8, 2005) (noting that fuel costs per square foot are substantially lower for newer homes), http://www.nahb.org/generic.aspx?sectionID=734&genericContentID=35389, last visited June 12, 2012.

108. *See* Roberta F. Mann, *Back to the Future: Recommendations and Predictions for Greener Tax Policy*, 88 Or. L. Rev. 355, 391–95 (2010).

109. *See* http://2010.census.gov/news/releases/operations/cb11-cn144.html. *See also* Tommy Unger, *Smaller Families Living in Larger Homes* (Feb. 20, 2007), available at http://www.zillow.com/blog/smaller-families-living-in-larger-homes/2007/02/, last visited June 13, 2012.

PROPOSALS FOR REFORM

In the author's view, the ideal tax benefit for housing would be equitably distributed, would not unduly influence housing prices, would not encourage excessive debt, and would respect environmental as well as social goals. Since 1963, scholars and policymakers have been considering how the tax system should deal with homeownership. This section will consider five main alternatives to current law: (1) making the QRI deduction an add-on to the standard deduction, (2) capping the benefit from the QRI deduction for upper-bracket taxpayers, (3) keeping the existing QRI deduction but taxing imputed rents, (4) converting the QRI deduction to a tax credit, and (5) creating a tax benefit for housing irrespective of debt status.

QRI AS AN ADD-ON TO THE STANDARD DEDUCTION

If the QRI deduction were an add-on to the standard deduction rather than an itemized deduction, it would be available to all taxpayers, not only the 38 percent of taxpayers who elect to itemize their deductions.[110] If it followed the model of existing add-ons to the standard deduction, like the additional standard deductions for the aged or the blind, it would be a flat amount, which could be tailored to the median house price and be indexed for inflation.[111] In 2008 and 2009, the real property tax deduction could be used by nonitemizers as an add-on to the standard deduction, but this was calculated in a different way and was capped at $500 ($1,000 for a joint return).[112] As the standard deduction is an alternative to itemizing deductions, this proposal would add some benefit to lower-income taxpayers, but the majority of higher-income taxpayers would continue to itemize and receive disproportionate benefits due to the upside-down nature of the deduction benefit. To achieve optimal fairness, the benefit should be restricted on the upper end as well as enhanced on the lower end.

CAPPING THE BENEFIT FOR UPPER INCOME TAXPAYERS

President Obama's 2011 Plan for Economic Growth and Deficit Reduction proposes capping the benefit of itemized deductions, including the QRI deduction, to the equivalent of the 28 percent rate tax bracket.[113] The $1 million principal amount would remain unchanged. Under the proposal, taxpayers now subject to 33 percent and 35 percent rates would be able to claim

---

110. Author's own proposal, inspired by Stanley Surrey's 1963 Treasury Department proposals.
111. I.R.C. §63(f).
112. I.R.C. §63(c)(7) defines the real property tax deduction as the lesser of

> (A) the amount allowable as a deduction under this chapter for State and local taxes described in section 164(a)(1), or

> (B) $500 ($1,000 in the case of a joint return).

113. Office of Management & Budget, *Living Within Our Means and Investing in the Future: The President's Plan for Economic Growth and Deficit Reduction* 47 (2011), available at http://www.whitehouse.gov/sites/default/files/omb/budget/fy2012/assets/jointcommitteereport.pdf, last visited June 13, 2012.

deductions only at a 28 percent rate. So, for every $1,000 in deductions, a top-bracket household would save $280 in taxes, down from $350. This proposal does modestly restrict the upper income bracket taxpayers' benefit from the QRI, although the benefit is still upside-down. It could be combined with an enhanced standard deduction to provide benefit to lower-income taxpayers. Unfortunately, even President Obama's modest proposal faces significant political opposition, with affected industry groups planning to lobby heavily against the proposal.[114]

KEEPING THE QRI DEDUCTION AND TAXING IMPUTED RENTS

Professor Calvin Johnson's proposal to tax imputed rents from owner-occupied housing while retaining the QRI would make both the tax treatment of mortgage debt and the decision to invest in a home more rational.[115] The IRC generally disallows the deduction of interest incurred to produce tax-exempt income.[116] It also limits an individual's interest deduction on debt incurred for investment to the amount of the income from the investment.[117] Logically, therefore, if the imputed income from owner-occupied housing is not taxed, then the mortgage interest should not be deductible. However, Johnson's proposal is less draconian: he proposes initially to tax only the imputed rental value of housing computed only "at the excess by which a family's aggregate personal-use property exceeds $1 million."[118] This $1 million exemption threshold would be reduced annually by $50,000, providing transitional relief for wealthy families.[119] Johnson contemplates this proposal primarily as a revenue raiser.[120] Johnson considered, but rejected, the idea of eliminating the QRI.[121] He reasons that eliminating the QRI would have "no impact on the richest taxpayers, who can substitute equity for debt-financing of houses."[122] Johnson's proposal has appeal, but little political viability. Exclusion of imputed income is deeply ingrained in the U.S. tax system.

CONVERTING THE QRI DEDUCTION INTO A TAX CREDIT

Variations on this proposal have been popular. Unlike a deduction, a tax credit has an even impact on taxpayers irrespective of their tax bracket, thus mitigating charges of unfairness. The Congressional Budget Office's 2007 Budget Options report suggested reducing the maximum mortgage on which interest can be deducted from $1 million to $400,000 or converting

114. *See, e.g.*, Richard Rubin et al., *Obama Proposes Tax on Bonds, Carried Interest for Wealthy*, Business Week (Sept. 13, 2011), available at http://www.businessweek.com/news/2011-09-13/obama-proposes-tax-on-bonds-carried-interest-for-wealthy.html, last visited June 13, 2012.

115. Johnson, *supra* note 31, at 918.

116. I.R.C. §265.

117. I.R.C. §163(d).

118. Johnson, *supra* note 31, at 920.

119. *Id.*

120. *Id.* at 918 ("Taxing the return in personal use is justified because the federal government needs the money").

121. *Id.* at 921–22.

122. *Id.* at 921.

the mortgage interest deduction to a credit.[123] The 2005 Tax Reform Panel recommended that the QRI deduction be replaced with a "Home Credit available to all taxpayers equal to 15 percent of interest paid on a principal residence."[124] The panel applied a limit to the home credit based on the average cost of housing in the region of the country where the home is located.[125] The panel also would have eliminated any tax benefit for second homes or home equity loans.[126] The panel reasoned that the home credit would "encourage home ownership, not big homes."[127] The panel also noted that lower-income taxpayers would do better under its recommendations than under current law.[128] As noted above, the 2010 National Commission on Fiscal Responsibility and Reform advocated changing the QRI to a nonrefundable 12 percent credit, capped at $500,000 principal amount and limited to one home,[129] while the Debt Reduction Task Force proposed changing the QRI to a 15 percent refundable credit on the first $25,000 of mortgage interest paid on the principal residence.[130]

Critics of the 2005 Panel's recommendations on the QRI should be pleased with the Debt Reduction Task Force's proposal.[131] A nonrefundable tax credit can benefit only homeowners with current tax liability. To benefit a significant portion of lower-income Americans, the credit would have to be refundable like the earned income tax credit.[132] A 2006 article written by Lily Batchelder, former IRS Commissioner Fred T. Goldberg Jr., and Peter R. Orzag—who later held the position of Director of the Office of Management and Budget—advocates that the default structure for any tax incentive should be a refundable tax credit.[133] Batchelder et al. base their argument on economic efficiency grounds, but also note that refundable credits can help smooth income at a household level.[134] Although income smoothing can be justified on the basis of economic efficiency, it is also significant from an equity perspective, as it enables taxpayers to withstand economic shocks, such as recession.

Professor Dorothy Brown envisions the ideal housing tax benefit as a refundable credit with special antidiscrimination features. Her credit seeks to overcome the market externalities faced by homeowners in predominantly

---

123. CBO, *Budget Options 2007*, at 267 (Option 7), available at http://www.cbo.gov/sites/default/files/cbofiles/ftpdocs/78xx/doc7821/02-23-budgetoptions.pdf, last visited June 13, 2012.
124. The President's Advisory Panel on Federal Tax Reform (2005), *supra* note 92, at 73.
125. *Id.*
126. *Id.*
127. *Id.*
128. *Id.* at 74 ("[T]he percentage of taxpayers with adjusted gross incomes between $40,000 and $50,000 who have mortgages and receive a tax benefit for mortgage interest paid would increase from less than 50 percent to more than 99 percent").
129. Report of the Nat'l Comm'n on Fiscal Resp. and Reform, *supra* note 85, at 30–31.
130. Debt Reduction Task Force, *supra* note 86, at 35–36 (2010).
131. In a practical sense, the recommendations didn't go anywhere, since they were generally ignored by policymakers. *See* Rosanne Altshuler, *Tax Reform 2.0* (Mar. 26, 2009), available at http://taxvox.taxpolicycenter.org/blog/_archives/2009/3/26/4134714.html.
132. I.R.C. §32. *See* Peter Dreier, *The New Politics of Housing*, 63 J. Am. Plan. Ass'n 5, 18 (1997) (proposing eliminating the QRI deduction and replacing it with a refundable homeowner tax credit).
133. Batchelder et al., *supra* note 55, at 26 (2006).
134. *Id.* at 30.

minority neighborhoods. Any homeowner, regardless of race, would be eligible for the refundable credit, which would apply to both mortgage interest deductions and property deductions on homes in neighborhoods that are more than 10 percent black.[135]

A refundable tax credit could also address the environmental concerns posed by the QRI deduction. Changing the structure of the tax benefit from a deduction to a credit would eliminate the incremental incentive to buy larger and larger homes. Limiting the basis of the credit to the average regional housing cost would also encourage more modest home purchases. The housing credit could contain a "location efficiency premium" (LEP).[136] The amount of the credit would be increased for homes located close to public transportation, thereby reducing traffic, automobile dependency, and greenhouse gas emissions.[137]

The shelter credit would apply to renters and homeowners alike.[138] Renters would receive matching funds for saving for home ownership. For home-owners, the credit would be determined by multiplying the median national home price by the annualized long-term tax exempt interest rate and then multiplying that product by the lowest marginal tax rate. This structure would eliminate the upside-down nature of the subsidy provided by the mortgage interest deduction, and it would also reduce the incentive to buy a larger, more expensive home.

TAKING DEBT OUT OF THE EQUATION

All the previously discussed proposals still tie the tax benefit for housing to debt, as the tax benefit is available only to those who borrow to acquire their homes.[139] Tying the tax benefit to debt has a number of disadvantages. The recession of 2008–2009 was deepened, if not originated, by excessive levels of debt in the housing market. Having the government share payments encourages prospective home purchasers to acquire a more costly home than they could afford without the subsidy. Finally, the biggest obstacle for first-time homebuyers is coming up with the cash for a down payment and closing costs.[140] The temporary first-time homebuyer's credit is aimed at over-coming that obstacle, but it is not well designed for the purpose. First, the credit is claimed on the homebuyer's tax return for the year of purchase. The tax return is filed in April or October of the following year. Thus, the credit is not available when it is needed, when the homebuyer closes on the house.

---

135. Brown, *supra* note 32, at 44.

136. *See* Mann, *Prairie*, *supra* note 53, at 1395.

137. *See* John Holtzclaw, Natural Resources Defense Council, *Using Residential Patterns and Transit to Decrease Auto Dependence and Costs* (NRDC, 1994), 2.

138. *See* Mann, *Prairie*, *supra* note 53, at 1393–97.

139. Admittedly, over two-thirds of homeowners have a mortgage. Author calculations from U.S. HUD & U.S. Census Bureau, *American Housing Survey 2009*, Table 3-15 at 65, available at http://www.census.gov/prod/2011pubs/h150-09.pdf, last visited June 13, 2012.

140. Sara Weiss, *Downpayment, Closing Costs Still Greatest Obstacles to Homeownership, NAR Survey Shows* (July 9, 2009), available at http://www.realtor.org/press_room/news_releases/2009/07/obstacles_homeownership.

Second, the credit is not refundable and does not help homebuyers without tax liability. Finally, the credit has been shown to be vulnerable to fraud.[141]

Helping citizens to save for a home would be a better way to get over the down payment obstacle. Americans' low savings rate may have also contributed to the recession, and providing a tax benefit for saving for the first home purchase could increase savings rates and help with down payments. Under current law, taxpayers can avoid the penalty for early withdrawal from an individual retirement account (IRA) if the distribution is a "qualified first-time homebuyer distribution."[142] Using an IRA to fund a home purchase has a number of disadvantages. First, an IRA is designed to provide funding for the taxpayer's retirement, an important goal that may not be perfectly aligned with home purchase. Second, only a relatively small amount may be contributed to an IRA annually.[143] Finally, renters who are trying to save for home purchase still have to pay rent. The author suggests a refundable shelter tax credit, based on a percentage of annual average rents and capped by actual rental payments. For example, if average rents in Houston were $1,200 per month and the renter paid $1,000 per month, a 20% credit would entitle the renter to receive a $2,400 credit.[144] The renter would be required to deposit the credit in a housing investment account (HIA). As with a Roth IRA, the account's earnings would not be taxed upon withdrawal to purchase a home.[145]

CONCLUSION

Like Goldilocks looking for a comfortable bed, it is hard to find the perfect alternative to the QRI deduction. The QRI deduction is politically entrenched, and changing it would face fierce opposition. Realtors and banks fear the impact on their businesses. Current homeowners would be concerned about the impact of repeal on the value of their homes. Hopeful future homeowners look forward to having the government share their mortgage payments. The QRI deduction is the sacred cow of tax policy.[146] However, its deficiencies are clear: the QRI deduction is neither efficient nor fair. Tax reformers have long had it in their sights as a target for change. This chapter explored some of the possibilities: changing the QRI deduction to an add-on to the standard deduction, capping the benefit for upper-income taxpayers, taxing imputed rent from housing, converting the QRI deduction to a credit and delinking the tax subsidy for housing from debt. Discussing the reform of tax benefits for housing is a conversation worth having, and it will continue.

---

141. GAO, *First-Time Homebuyer Tax Credit: Taxpayers' Use of the Credit and Implementation and Compliance Challenges* (Oct. 22, 2009), available at http://www.census.gov/prod/2011pubs/h150-09.pdf, last visited June 13, 2012.
142. I.R.C. §72(t)(2)(F).
143. I.R.C. §219(b)(5).
144. $1,000 rent × 12 months = $12,000 × 20% = $2,400.
145. I.R.C. §408A.
146. *See* Nick Timiraos, *Mortgage Deduction Looks Less Sacred*, WSJ (Feb. 27, 2009), available at http://online.wsj.com/article/SB123569898005989291.html, last visited June 13, 2012.

VI
TAXATION AS REGULATION

CHAPTER 8

CARBON TAX, HEALTH CARE TAX, BANK TAX, AND OTHER REGULATORY TAXES

Reuven S. Avi-Yonah, University of Michigan Law School

""[A] tax is a pecuniary burden laid upon individuals or property for the purpose of supporting the Government"[1]"

""[A] tax is not any less a tax because it has a regulatory effect"[2]"

The momentous decision of the U.S. Supreme Court to uphold the constitutionality of the Patient Protection and Affordable Health Care Act (PPACA) took sides in a long-running dispute about whether taxation can legitimately be used for purposes other than raising revenue for the government. The context was the imposition by Congress of a monetary penalty on individuals who refuse to buy health insurance. Opponents of the Act argued that calling this levy a tax added nothing to its constitutional validity since "the noncompliance penalty . . . does not meet the historical criteria for a tax" because "the clear purpose of the assessment is to regulate conduct, not generate revenue for the government."[3] On the other hand, the Federal Government argued that taxation has frequently been used for regulatory purposes, and that "[i]t is beyond serious question that a tax does not cease to be valid merely because it regulates, discourages, or even definitely deters the activities taxed."[4] In his controlling opinion for the U.S. Supreme Court, Chief Justice Roberts took the latter view, writing that while "the essential feature of any tax [is that] it produces at least some revenue for the Government," "taxes that seek to influence conduct are nothing new," citing Justice Story for the proposition that "the taxing power is often, very often, applied for other purposes, than revenue."[5] Indeed, Roberts went further and stated that "[e]very tax is in some measure regulatory. To some extent it interposes an economic impediment to the activity taxed as compared with others not taxed."[6] Is this view correct?

---

1. *United States v. Reorganized CF&I Fabricators of Utah, Inc.*, 518 U.S. 213, 224 (1996).
2. *Sonzinsky v. United States*, 300 U.S. 506, 513 (1937).
3. *Virginia v. Sebelius*, Civil Action No. 3:10CV188-HEH, mem. op. at 26–27 (E.D. Va. Aug. 2, 2010).
4. *Id.* at 29 (citing *United States v. Sanchez*, 340 U.S. 42, 44 (1950)).
5. *National Federation of Independent Businesses v. Sebelius*, 132 S.Ct. 2566, 2594, 2596 (2012).
6. *Id.* at 37 (citing *Sonzinsky, supra*).

Taxation has two well-known goals.[7] Undoubtedly, as suggested by the first quotation at the beginning of this chapter, the first and most widely accepted one is to raise revenue for necessary government functions. Although there is a broad debate about which governmental functions are truly indispensable, most commentators would agree that raising revenue is an indispensable feature of governments and that a government that is unable to collect taxes, as the Russian government almost was in 1998, is unlikely to survive.

A second and more controversial goal of taxation is redistribution. Most developed countries see the tax system as a way to redistribute income from the rich to the poor. The desirability of redistribution has been controversial, but most commentators agree that if redistribution is a legitimate government goal, then taxation may be the most effective way to achieve that goal.

But taxation has a third goal that has not been noticed as widely: a regulatory goal. In most developed countries, governments use the tax system to change the behavior of actors in the private sector, by incentivizing (subsidizing) activities they wish to promote and by disincentivizing (penalizing) activities they wish to discourage. This is the point of the second quotation at the beginning of this chapter.

This regulatory function of the tax system is quite well established. Indeed, it can be argued that some types of taxes, such as Pigouvian taxes (designed to deter certain activities by forcing private actors to internalize their social costs), are entirely regulatory in nature. In other cases, such as the corporate income tax, much of the complexity of the current tax structure stems from the government's attempting to use it to achieve regulatory aims. If the U.S. income tax were purely a revenue-raising and redistributive tax, most of the complexity of the current tax code could be eliminated.

Precisely for this reason, most commentators have decried the use of taxation for regulatory purposes. Either, they argue, regulation should be done directly, or, if it is desirable that it be done via subsidies or penalties, those should be delivered directly as well by other government agencies. The Internal Revenue Service (IRS) should be left to its proper role of collecting revenues, with a possible side role in achieving redistribution.

This argument underlies the long debate over the U.S. tax expenditure budget. As originally conceived by Stanley Surrey in the 1960s, the tax expenditure budget (which has been a feature of U.S. budgets since 1974) was intended to single out all the instances in which the tax code is used for regulatory purposes. However, the tax expenditure budget has been controversial from the beginning, with critics charging that it is impossible to define an objective, nonpolitical baseline against which to measure tax expenditures. Recently, this has led the Joint Committee on Taxation to redefine tax expenditures as any deviation not from an objective baseline but from the language of other provisions of the code.[8] The committee eventually reversed course and returned to the original definition of tax expenditures, but the debate will continue.

---

7. For a longer discussion, *see* Avi-Yonah, *The Three Goals of Taxation*, 60 Tax L. Rev. 1 (2007).

8. Edward Kleinbard, *Tax Expenditure Framework Legislation*, 63 National Tax J. 353 (2010); *see also* Edward Kleinbard, *The Congress Within a Congress: How Tax Expenditures Distort Our Budget and*

This chapter will discuss the regulatory role of taxation. First, it will argue that regulation is a legitimate role of taxation and that in some cases taxes are a superior vehicle compared to other regulatory techniques. Second, it will ask which of the current taxes in developed countries are best suited for achieving regulatory goals. Finally, it will argue that in general, using only one form of tax for each goal should permit us to simplify the others. In conclusion, we will examine two current proposals for regulatory taxation in the context of financial and health care reform, and argue that while one is a proper use of taxation as regulation, the other is not.

IS REGULATION A LEGITIMATE GOAL FOR TAXATION?

This essay will argue that in some cases regulation is a legitimate goal of taxation. In general, the choice between taxation and other forms of regulation, such as command and control regulation or direct subsidies, depends on the particular policy context. In some instances, taxation is the most effective way to achieve a specific regulatory goal.

A good example of this is combating global climate change. There are three broad methods that have been advanced for government to reduce greenhouse gas emissions: command and control regulation, cap and trade, and carbon taxes. Of these, there is a broad consensus among commentators that carbon taxes are the most effective.[9]

Command and control regulation of greenhouse gas emissions has generally been rejected because of a wide consensus that the government does not have the necessary information to ensure that the emissions targets are distributed most effectively among private market actors. The solution to the climate change problem depends on technological innovation in the private sector, and governments are ill suited to picking winners to develop such technologies. In addition, existing command and control regimes are sector-specific, while the climate change problem applies to the entire economy.

This leaves cap and trade and carbon taxes as the two leading market-based solutions. However, a carbon tax is much simpler than cap and trade. A tax is imposed at $x per ton of carbon content on the main sources of carbon dioxide emissions in the economy—namely, coal, oil, and natural gas. The tax is imposed "upstream"—that is, at the point of extraction or importation—which means that it can be imposed on only 2,000 taxpayers (500 coal miners and importers, 750 oil producers and importers, and 750 natural gas producers and importers). Credits can be given to carbon sequestration projects and to other projects that reduce greenhouse gas emissions, and exports are exempted.

Our Political Process, 36 Ohio Northern Univ. L. Rev. 1 (2010). *But see* Robert Peroni and J. Clifford Fleming Jr., *Can Tax Expenditure Analysis Be Divorced from a Normative Tax Base? A Critique of the 'New Paradigm' and Its Denouement*, 30 Va, Tax Rev. 135 (2010).

9. *See* Reuven S. Avi-Yonah and David M. Uhlmann, *Combating Global Climate Change: Why a Carbon Tax Is a Better Response to Global Warming Than Cap and Trade*, 28 Stan. Envir. L. J. 3 (2009).

Cap and trade, on the other hand, is inherently more complicated. While the cap can also be imposed "upstream," it has several features that require complexity. First, the proposal needs to determine how allowances will be created and distributed, either for free or by auction. Free distribution requires deciding which industries receive allowances, while an auction requires a complex monitoring system to prevent cheating. Second, the trading in allowances needs to be set up and monitored: a system needs to be devised to prevent the same allowance from being used twice, and penalties need to be established for polluters who exceed their allowances. Third, if allowances are to be traded with other countries, the international trading of allowances would need to be monitored as well. Fourth, to prevent cost uncertainty, cap and trade proposals typically have complex provisions for banking and borrowing allowances, and some of them provide for safety valves. Fifth, offsets are needed for carbon sequestration and similar projects, and those are more complicated than credits against a carbon tax liability. Finally, most cap and trade proposals involve provisions for coordinating with the cap and trade policies of other countries and for punishing countries that do not have a greenhouse gas emission reduction policy.

In addition to its inherent complexity, cap and trade is also more difficult to enforce. An elaborate mechanism needs to be set up to distribute and collect allowances and to ensure that allowances are real (a difficult task, especially if allowances from non-U.S. programs are permitted) and that polluters are penalized if they emit greenhouses gases without an allowance. A new administrative body needs to be set up for this purpose, or at least a new office within EPA, and new employees with the relevant expertise need to be hired. A carbon tax, on the other hand, can be enforced by the IRS with its existing staff or a small number of additional staff, which has the relevant expertise in enforcing other excise taxes.

Cap and trade also raises collateral issues that are not present in a carbon tax, such as the need for the SEC to enforce rules regarding futures trading in allowances. A good example is the tax implications of both policies. A carbon tax, as a federal tax, has no tax implications: it is simply collected and is not deductible. Allowances under cap and trade, on the other hand, raise a multitude of tax issues: What are the tax implications of distributing allowances for free? What are the tax implications of trading in allowances? Should allowance exchanges be permitted to avoid the tax on selling allowances? What amount of the purchase price of a business should be allocated to its allowances? If borrowing and banking occur, what are the tax consequences? Can allowances be amortized? None of these issues arises under a carbon tax.

It can in fact be argued that tax complexity is inconsistent with the basic premise of the cap and trade system. The theory behind cap and trade posits that permits to emit CO_2 will be traded freely among private market participants, so that they end up distributed in the most efficient way (i.e., in the hands of companies whose costs of abating emissions are the highest). This is consistent with the Coase theorem, because, in the absence of transaction costs, the initial allocation of permits does not matter. However, there are likely to be significant transaction costs, including the application of the corporate tax. Under current tax rules, companies are likely to face a tax burden when they (a) receive permits, (b) sell permits, (c) borrow permits, and (d) bank permits and (e) when a business that has permits is bought or sold. These barriers mean that the Coase theorem does not apply and the initial allocation matters.[10] This problem can be mitigated by changing the Internal Revenue Code (IRC, the Code) to provide for tax-free trading in permits, but other tax-related transaction costs are likely to persist in any cap and trade regime. Therefore, a carbon tax emerges as the superior price mechanism to restrict carbon emissions.

This example illustrates that at least in one important policy context, taxation is not just an acceptable vehicle for regulation, but also the regulatory technique that is preferred by most commentators (even though it may be less realistic politically). Another example of a preference for taxation is Pigouvian taxes on items like tobacco and alcohol, which are designed to reduce behavior that has important negative externalities. The experience with Prohibition in the early part of the twentieth century has clearly demonstrated that taxation is superior to direct regulation in reducing alcohol consumption, and taxation of cigarettes has been the most effective technique in reducing smoking.

These taxes are relatively marginal in the tax systems of developed economies. But it is also clear that developed countries also use their main taxes, which are the individual and corporate income taxes and the value-added tax (VAT), to achieve regulatory goals. Given that regulation via taxation is legitimate in some cases, the next section will address which of these taxes is best suited to achieve regulatory goals.

WHICH TAX IS BEST SUITED FOR REGULATION?

One of the remarkable examples of convergence in comparative taxation is that most countries rely primarily on three types of tax—the individual income tax, the corporate income tax, and the VAT. While the weight of each tax in total revenue varies (in general, developing countries rely more on the VAT and the corporate tax than on the individual income tax), the vast majority of countries have all three taxes.

The reason for this phenomenon is that each tax is best suited to one of the three aforementioned goals of taxation and that most countries adopt all three goals. If your main goal is raising revenue to fund the government, the best instrument is the VAT. Because an invoice-credit, destination-based VAT relies heavily on the private sector to monitor its collection, even developing countries with weak tax administrations can collect significant revenues from the VAT. Much of it is collected at the border on imports, and the rest is collected on business-to-business transactions in which the buyer has an interest in making sure that the seller paid tax to obtain input credits.

---

10. Ethan Yale has argued that the tax on selling permits can be offset by deducting the costs of avoiding pollution when permits are sold. *See* Ethan Yale, *Taxing Cap and Trade Environmental Regulation*, 37 J. of Legal Studies 535 (2008). However, this only applies when the practice of borrowing and banking permits is not permitted, which seems unlikely, and it assumes that all pollution avoidance costs are currently deductible, which would also require changes in current law.

By contrast, the corporate income tax and the individual income tax are less effective at raising revenue. Corporate income taxation requires a sophisticated tax administration and is open to avoidance by techniques such as thin capitalization and transfer pricing. In addition, most corporate income tax is collected from multinational enterprises, and countries that wish to attract multinational enterprises (MNEs) use tax incentives, a form of tax competition that reduces revenues. As for the individual income tax, most developing countries are unable to enforce it on anyone except wage earners, and even developed countries have a hard time preventing tax evasion by taxpayers with mobile income.

For redistributive purposes, however, the individual income tax is best, and redistribution is the main reason this tax is used by developed countries and nominally even by developing countries (although they may not be able to enforce it, the tax has an important symbolic value). The VAT is inherently regressive and cannot reach wealth that is not consumed, while the corporate tax is a poor vehicle for redistribution because of the uncertainty about its incidence. This leaves the individual income tax as the main vehicle for redistribution in developed countries, and U.S. data indicate that the tax is in fact quite progressive and able to achieve significant redistribution.

This leaves the regulatory function of taxation, and here it is the corporate tax that is best suited to fulfill this function. The main reason is that corporations are major players in the economy of every country, and that there are relatively few of them, so that it is possible to achieve regulatory goals with minimal administrative efforts by focusing on the corporate sector. The carbon tax, for example, is to be levied only on about 2000 oil, gas, and coal producers and importers, all of whom are corporations. These 2000 corporations will pass the tax burden downstream, where it will ultimately influence consumer behavior, but the regulatory structure that is needed to police the tax is much simpler than it would be if the government attempted to monitor consumers directly.

Thus, because each tax is best suited to fulfill one of the three goals of taxation, most countries use all three. As the United States is now finding out, it is very difficult to collect sufficient revenue from taxation without using a VAT, which is why the VAT has now been adopted by every other member of the Organisation for Economic Co-operation and Development (OECD). Redistribution is very difficult without an effective personal income tax, and that is a major reason for the greater income inequality in developing than in developed countries. And the persistence of the corporate tax despite widespread calls to abolish it stems from its effectiveness as a regulatory vehicle. We could easily replace the revenue of our corporate tax by a small VAT, and it is not effective for redistribution because its incidence is unknown and probably shifting. But we are very unlikely to be able to achieve the regulatory goals of taxation without a corporate tax.

ALLOCATING ONE GOAL PER TAX?

Would it be possible to go further and simplify each tax if we were clear about its main goal? I believe the answer is yes, at least to a significant extent.

The clearest example of goal confusion is the individual income tax in the United States. Because we do not have a VAT, we must rely on the individual tax for most of our revenue. In addition, Congress in recent years has added a multitude of special credits to the individual tax to incentivize a myriad of desirable activities such as education, energy saving, saving for retirement, and the like.

We could achieve significant simplification of the individual tax if we gave up on its revenue and regulatory potential. For revenue, as Michael Graetz has suggested, we could substitute a VAT and exempt from tax anyone but the rich.[11] Anyone earning below $100,000 consumes most of his or her income and would benefit from elimination of the income tax.

In addition, most of the criticism of tax expenditures is focused on the individual tax provisions. They are very complex, difficult for ordinary taxpayers to use, and cumbersome for the IRS to administer. In most cases, we would save transaction costs by converting the tax expenditure to a direct subsidy—e.g., for tuition or for energy-saving equipment. These subsidies could be delivered to colleges and producers, rather than funneled via the individual tax system.

Similarly, the VAT in many countries is made needlessly complex by an attempt to mitigate its regressivity by exempting certain products such as food, clothing, or medicine or by having multiple rates. Once the VAT is conceived as a pure revenue raiser, it can be made as broad as possible with a single rate. Regressivity should be addressed via the income tax system or by sending low-income taxpayers rebate checks, as well as through the expenditure side of the budget.

Finally, a lot of the trouble people have with the corporate tax system stems from a misunderstanding of its primarily regulatory nature. Once we understand that the main purpose of the corporate tax is to regulate corporate behavior, the key issue becomes not how much revenue is raised, or what the incidence of the tax may be, but rather whether the tax is effective in achieving its regulatory goals. It may be, for example, perfectly acceptable for a large corporation to pay no tax, as long as the reason for this is consistent with Congress's intent in allowing it certain exemptions or deductions. The newly codified economic substance doctrine, for example, is misguided because it focuses on the business purpose of the corporate taxpayer, rather than on congressional intent.

CONCLUSION: THE BANK TAX AND THE HEALTH CARE TAX

Two current examples illustrate the distinction between effective and less effective uses of taxation as a regulatory instrument: the proposed bank tax and the enacted health care tax.

---

11. Michael J. Graetz, *100 Million Unnecessary Returns: A Simple, Fair, and Competitive Tax Plan for the United States* (Yale University, 2007).

The bank tax falls squarely within the realm of effective uses of taxation to regulate. It would be imposed on financial institutions' capital at risk, excluding federally insured deposits, and it is designed to deter banks from taking excessive risks. The bank tax is imposed on a relatively small number of sophisticated taxpayers and is not particularly complicated. It can serve as an offset to the numerous ways in which banks are currently subsidized by the tax system, including the ability to deduct bad loan reserves, to defer tax on interest earned overseas, and to acquire other banks to use their losses to offset future income. If enacted, the bank tax would represent a small repayment of the funds expended by taxpayers to rescue the major banks during the crisis of 2008, and it is well designed to target only those institutions that are deemed "too big to fail."

The health care tax, on the other hand, stems primarily from the desire to ensure the constitutionality of the individual health insurance mandate. It is really a penalty for individuals who do not purchase health insurance. It is relatively complex, with difficult definitions that govern the level of the penalty. It applies to many taxpayers but exempts those who are covered through their employers, so that it falls disproportionately on the poor. For the same reason, it is likely to be as difficult to enforce as the earned income tax credit.

Moreover, the two taxes have different signaling effects. Calling the bank tax a tax rather than a fee or premium is reasonable, because it does not represent payment for insurance. Calling the health insurance penalty a tax, however, may dilute its effect, because people tend to have a different reaction to not paying taxes than to avoiding penalties. One of the main concerns regarding the health care tax is that people would prefer to pay it rather than obtain insurance, and calling it a tax does nothing to mitigate this concern.

In general, taxation as regulation makes sense when (1) it is applied to small numbers of taxpayers, (2) the taxpayers are sophisticated and able to deal with complex tax incentives, and (3) the regulatory goal is clear and related to the level of the tax. The bank tax, the carbon tax, and other forms of corporate taxation meet these criteria, but the health care tax and many tax expenditures of the individual income tax do not. In general, Congress should limit its regulatory activities to the corporate tax, apply the individual income tax to the rich as a vehicle for redistribution, and enact a VAT to raise revenue.

UNIT VII

THE ROLE OF WEALTH

CHAPTER 9

BALANCING GREATER PROTECTION WITH INDIVIDUAL CHOICE IN 401(K) PLANS

Regina T. Jefferson, Catholic University of America, Columbus School of Law

Regarding some of the most critical issues facing society today, policymakers struggle to balance traditional values of collective protection with recently emerging preferences for individual choice and responsibility. Indeed, whether it is health care insurance, Social Security, or private retirement savings, workers increasingly are asked, or face the prospect of being asked, to make decisions that were once made by employers or professionals. In many instances, individuals are asked to make these decisions without a safety net in the event that miscalculations or losses occur. Accordingly, the shift from collective protection to individual responsibility has enormous economic and societal implications. In the retirement arena, the developing trend of individual choice is particularly complex and controversial. It challenges not only traditional views regarding protection against the risk of old age, but also the structure and effectiveness of the existing private retirement system.

Each year the United States Treasury forgoes billions of dollars in tax revenue as a result of the tax-favorable treatment of private pension plans.[1] The tax expenditure estimate for employer-based retirement plans for fiscal year 2011 was $380.3 billion.[2] Because of the magnitude of this expense, it is reasonable for taxpayers to expect participants covered by qualified retirement plans to have greater retirement security than they would saving on their own, regardless of the type of plan that is offered. However, this result does not always occur.

---

1. *See* Employee Benefit Research Institute, *Tax Expenditures and Employee Benefits: Estimates from the FY 2011 Budget* (March 2010), 1, http://www.ebri.org/pdf/publications/facts/FS-209_Mar10_Bens-Rev-Loss.pdf (the employee benefit-related tax expenditure for fiscal year 2011 will account for 36 percent of all tax expenditures in the budget); Regina T. Jefferson, *Redistribution in the Private Retirement System: Who Wins and Who Loses?*, 53 How. L.J. 283, 287 (2010) [hereinafter Jefferson, *Redistribution in the Private Retirement System*] (providing a detailed explanation of the redistribution efforts of tax expenditures).
2. *Id.*

Participants in the increasingly popular 401(k) plans are exposed to essentially the same risks that personal savings arrangements such as passbook savings accounts and certificates of deposit (CDs) present. Without the assistance of the employer or financial experts, participants in such plans must decide whether and to what extent contributions are to be made on their behalf.[3] As a result, many individuals fail to save adequately for retirement. Also, because benefits in 401(k) plans typically are paid in the form of lump sums as opposed to life annuities, tax-subsidized savings set aside for retirement regularly are used for current consumption.[4]

Participant-directed 401(k) plans pose even greater challenges for retirement security. Participants in these plans are required not only to elect whether to participate and the level at which to contribute, but also the manner in which to invest the funds in their accounts.[5] They also have no protection against shortfalls in their account balances in the event of sudden market fluctuations.[6] Consequently, participants in such plans often receive retirement benefits significantly smaller than those they expect and on which they have relied.[7]

Thus, at every stage of the savings process, participant-directed 401(k) plans present substantial risks to plan participants. From the decision of whether to make a contribution, to the determination of how to allocate investments, to selections regarding the time and form of distribution, participants are required to make choices that will significantly impact their retirement security. Notwithstanding the importance of these decisions, however, plan sponsors are not required to offer financial training or education to enable individuals to make prudent investment decisions.[8] Also, in the event of miscalculations or sudden market fluctuations, participants are provided no means of protecting themselves against plan losses.[9]

Without such measures of protection, participant-directed 401(k) plans are functionally equivalent to personal savings and bear very little resemblance to traditional retirement plans. Yet, for tax purposes, 401(k) plans are treated very differently than personal savings, receiving the same special tax treatment as other qualified retirement savings plans.[10] However, the similarity in risk exposure between participant-directed 401(k) plans and personal savings arrangements makes it difficult to justify the preferential tax treatment that these plans receive.

Prior to the passage of the Employee Retirement Income Security Act of 1974 (ERISA), defined contribution plans were used primarily as supplemental

---

3. See infra "Section 401(k) Plans."
4. See infra 'Current Law" under "Proposals to Provide Greater Retirement Security in 401(k) Plans."
5. ERISA §404 (c), 29 U.S.C. §1104(c) (2006).
6. Regina T. Jefferson, Rethinking the Risk of Defined Contribution Plans, 4 Fla. Tax Rev. 4, 607, 637 n.137 (2000) [hereinafter Jefferson, Rethinking the Risk].
7. Id.
8. See infra "Financial Education Requirement" under "Proposals to Provide Greater Retirement Security in 401(k) Plans."
9. See infra "Required Option for Annuitization" under "Proposals to Provide Greater Retirement Security in 401(k) Plans."
10. See infra notes 21–25 and accompanying text (describing the tax treatment of qualified plans).

plans; consequently, ERISA as originally drafted placed little emphasis on providing protection against losses in these types of plans.[11] Since the passage of ERISA, the pension landscape has changed dramatically. Thus, as 401(k) plans increase in popularity, it is unclear why policymakers have not amended the legislation to address the inherent risks associated with these plans.[12] The failure of ERISA to provide adequate protection against 401(k) plan losses seriously compromises the financial security of many retirees and also undermines the primary objectives of the private retirement system. The potential harm resulting from this omission will only intensify as greater numbers of employers offer 401(k) plans as primary retirement savings vehicles. Moreover, the tax expenditure for the private retirement system will become increasingly difficult to justify as retirees who are inadequately protected from plan losses require additional governmental assistance in their old age.[13]

Accordingly, this chapter argues for greater protection against losses in 401(k) plans. Specifically, the next section explains the goals and objectives of the existing private retirement system and analyzes the impact of 401(k) plans on existing pension policy. The subsequent section identifies the weaknesses in current pension law as it relates to the role of 401(k) plans. The section following proposes several measures to increase retirement security in 401(k) plans and to justify the tax subsidies that they receive: (1) all sponsors of participant-directed 401(k) plans should be required to provide financial education; (2) all 401(k) plans should be required to offer annuitized retirement benefits; and (3) all 401(k) plans should be required to offer a minimum guaranteed benefit as an optional form of payment.

THE PRIVATE RETIREMENT SYSTEM

CHARACTERISTICS OF THE PRIVATE RETIREMENT SYSTEM

The private retirement system is voluntary, employment-based, and tax-subsidized.[14] Each of these characteristics is believed to enhance the private retirement program, and each of these characteristics significantly impacts the structure and effectiveness of the program. Because the private retirement system is voluntary rather than mandatory, it is necessary to provide tax incentives to employers to maintain retirement plans that advance established

---

11. *See* ERISA, Pub. L. No. 93-406, 88 Stat. 829 (codified as amended in scattered sections of I.R.C. and Titles 26 and 29 U.S.C.). ERISA is a massive piece of legislation that governs employee benefits. *Id.* It originated as early as 1962, when President John F. Kennedy commissioned a special cabinet level task force to evaluate the impact of private retirement programs on the nation's economy. *Rethinking the Risk supra* note 6, at 609.

12. *See infra* note 68 (listing some of the amendments to ERISA).

13. Dennis Cauchon, *Senior Benefit Costs Up Sharply*, USA Today, Feb. 14, 2008, at A1. A significant portion of the federal budget is devoted to programs that support the elderly. *See id.* (indicating that the federal government now spends $952 billion a year, or $27,289 per senior citizen, on programs that support the elderly such as Social Security and Medicare; this equates to 35% of the federal budget).

14. *See generally* John H. Langbein et al., *Pension and Employment Benefit Law* (5th ed., Foundation, 2010) (providing a general description of the development of ERISA and the private retirement system).

pension and public policies.[15] These plans, referred to as "qualified plans," receive the full range of tax benefits available to retirement savings.[16]

The private pension system is also employment-based. This means that individuals are not free to establish retirement plans on their own, and they can benefit from the tax preferences for private retirement plans only if their employers decide to establish and maintain such arrangements.[17] The rationale for the employment-based characteristic of the private retirement system is that historically there have been comparative advantages from saving in employer-sponsored plans as compared to personal savings instruments.[18] One advantage is that employers who invest large sums of money can benefit from economies of scale. Accordingly, investment returns are typically higher and average administrative costs lower in employer-sponsored plans.[19] Another reason it is believed that employer-sponsored arrangements are advantageous relative to personal savings is that presumably employers are in a better position than most employees to retain the services of financial experts to optimize investment returns.[20] However, in participant-directed plans, it is questionable whether either of these advantages actually exists because participants, not employers or financial experts, make the investment decisions regarding the plan assets.

Finally, qualified retirement plan savings receive substantial tax benefits.[21] The first tax advantage allows the employee to defer the payment of the taxes on contributions to qualified plans until the funds are actually received.[22] This deferral is a departure from the general rule that income is taxed upon receipt, whether actual or constructive, and it provides significant tax savings to individuals in higher income tax brackets.[23] The second tax advantage allows the income earned on the contributions to accumulate tax-free.[24] This

---

15. *See* I.R.C. §§401(a)(4), 410(b) (establishing coverage and nondiscrimination rules). To ensure that tax preferential treatment of qualified plans benefits a cross section of the population, rather than disproportionately favoring highly compensated employees, there are coverage and nondiscrimination rules. *Id.* These rules have two distinct functions: (1) the rules establish minimum coverage and participation standards that limit the employer's ability to exclude certain employees from the plan; (2) the rules limit the extent to which plan contributions and benefits can vary among plan participants. *Id.*

16. I.R.C. §401(a). Although the term "qualified plan" does not actually appear in the Internal Revenue Code, it is commonly used to describe employer sponsored plans that meet the requirements of I.R.C. §401(a) and the accompanying regulations. *See* Langbein et al., *supra* note 14, at 329 (explaining that qualified plans must meet strict requirements including minimum participation, vesting, and funding standards in order to receive favorable tax treatment).

17. *See* I.R.C. §§408, 408A (granting an exception for favorable tax treatment on amounts saved for retirement outside the employment-based regime). Individuals can receive tax preferences on saved amounts contributed to an Individual Retirement Arrangement (IRA); however, the contribution limits for IRAs are relatively low compared to employer sponsored plans. *See id.* (establishing limits on IRA contributions).

18. *See* Langbein et al., *supra* note 14, at 29–34.

19. *Id.*

20. *Id.*

21. *Id.* at 329 (discussing the tax treatment of qualified plans).

22. *See* I.R.C. §402(a).

23. *See* I.R.C. §61 (providing that all income regardless of the source is included in gross income).

24. *See* I.R.C. §501(a) (providing that the plan trust is exempt from paying tax on its investment income).

treatment results in a tax-free build-up of the investment income and is the essence of the favorable tax treatment of qualified pension plans.[25] One effect of the preferential tax treatment of qualified plans on employers is that they can deliver a dollar of retirement income at a lower cost than they can deliver a dollar of current wages to their employees.[26] Accordingly, an employer is able to reduce current levels of compensation by more than the actual amount of contributions made to the plan.

PLAN TYPES

In the private pension system, there are two broad classifications of retirement plans: defined benefit and defined contribution.[27] Both types of plans can have similar income replacement objectives and, theoretically, can be used equally effectively for retirement savings purposes.[28] The distinguishing characteristic between the two types of plans is risk allocation.[29]

In defined benefit plans, assets are pooled in an aggregate trust fund and the participants are guaranteed fixed benefits at retirement.[30] The benefit generally is accrued on the basis of compensation and service and is paid in the form of an annuity over the life of the participant, or the joint lives of the participant and a surviving spouse.[31] The employer is required to fund the plan sufficiently to pay the promised benefits and is liable for payment despite the investment performance of the plan assets. Thus, the employer bears the risk of investment loss in defined benefit plans. The employer also is required to insure the accrued benefit through the Pension Benefit Guarantee Corporation (PBGC) in order to protect plan participants in the event of employer insolvency.[32]

---

25. *See generally* Daniel I. Halperin, *Interest in Disguise: Taxing the "Time Value of Money,"* 95 YALE L.J. 506 (1986) (explaining that the timing of the deduction and the inclusion of income do not necessarily have advantageous effects if the rates remain constant).

26. *See* Jefferson, *Rethinking the Risk, supra* note 6, at 637 n. 137 (discussing the effects of the preferential tax treatment of qualified plans). For example, an employee with a marginal tax rate of 25% may be willing to accept a lesser-valued plan contribution of $4,500 in lieu of $6,000 of current taxable compensation because of a tax deferral; thus the employer's out-of-pocket cost for the employee's compensation would be reduced. *Id.*

27. ERISA §§3(34)–(35), 29 U.S.C. §1002(34)–(35) (2006); *see* Edward A. Zelinsky, *The Defined Contribution Paradigm*, 114 Yale L.J. 451, 455–57 (2004) (describing the difference between defined benefit plans and defined contribution plans).

28. Jefferson, *Rethinking the Risk, supra* note 6, at 610 (citing Daniel I. Halperin, *Tax Policy and Retirement Income: A Rational Model for the 21st Century*, in Jack L. VanDerhei, ed., *Search for a National Retirement Income Policy* (University of Pennsylvania, 1987), 184).

29. *Id.* There are some other differences, such as the availability of loans and hardship distributions, but these differences are optional rather than inherent. *Id.*

30. *See* ERISA §3(35), 29 U.S.C. §1002(35) (2006) (defining "defined benefit plans" as a "pension plan . . . which is not an individual account plan and which provides a benefit derived from employer contributions").

31. *See* ERISA §§203–05, 29 U.S.C. §§1053–55 (2006) (describing vesting standards, benefit accruals, and joint and survivor annuities).

32. *See* ERISA §1302(a) (2006) (describing one of the stated purposes of the PBGC as "to provide for the timely and uninterrupted payment of pension benefits to participants and beneficiaries"). *See also* 29 C.F.R. §4022.22 (2007) (indicating that when plans terminate with insufficient assets, the PBGC is required to pay accrued, vested benefits to plan participants up to the guaranteed amounts).

In contrast to the single trust that characterizes the defined benefit plan, defined contribution plans assign each employee an individual account.[33] The employer makes annual contributions to the participants' accounts but does not guarantee specific benefits.[34] At retirement, participants receive the balances in their accounts, usually in the form of lump sum payments.[35] Therefore, the success or failure of the defined contribution plan depends on the level of contribution made to the plan accounts, the investment experience of the assets, and the length of time the funds remain in the accounts prior to distribution. In the event of plan losses or employer insolvency, there is neither employer liability nor PBGC insurance.[36] Accordingly, in defined contribution plans the employee alone bears the risk of investment loss.[37]

SECTION 401(K) PLANS

Over the last twenty-five years, there has been a discernable shift from the use of traditional defined benefit plans as primary retirement savings vehicles toward the use of defined contribution plans for this purpose, with 401(k) plans dominating new plan offerings.[38] As of 2009, approximately 67 percent of all employers maintaining retirement plans offered section 401(k) plans as their primary retirement savings vehicles, as compared to 35 percent ten years earlier.[39] Recent data shows that contributions made to 401(k) plans alone

---

33. *See* ERISA §3(34), 29 U.S.C. §1002(34) (2006) (defining a "defined contribution plan" as a "pension which provides for an individual account for each participant and for benefits based solely upon the amount contributed to the participant's account, and any income . . . which may be allocated to such participant's account").

34. *See id.*

35. *See infra* text accompanying notes 132–38 (discussing lump sum distributions). Subject to the specific provisions of the plan, participants may be able to access the funds prior to retirement on account of hardship or termination of employment or through loans. *See* I.R.C. §§401(k)(2)(B), 403(b)(11)(B) (establishing the provisions relating to hardship and termination of employment); *see* ERISA §408(b)(1); 29 U.S.C. 1108(b)(1) (2006) (establishing the provisions relating to loans); *see also* I.R.C. §4975(d)(1).

36. *See supra* note 32 (describing PBGC protection).

37. Zelinsky, *supra* note 27, at 455–57; *see also* Jefferson, *Rethinking the Risk*, *supra* note 6, at 610–11; Regina T. Jefferson, *Post-Enron Pension Reform: Where Do We Go From Here?*, in Alvin D. Lurie, ed., *New York University Review of Employee Benefits and Executive Compensation 2003* (Lexis-Nexis, 2003), 8 [hereinafter Jefferson, *Pension Reform*].

38. *See* U.S. Gov't Accountability Office, GAO-10-632R, *Retirement Income: Challenges for Ensuring Income Throughout Retirement* (GAO, 2010), 6 [hereinafter *Challenges for Ensuring Income Throughout Retirement*] (discussing the growth of defined contribution plans in the last three decades). Section 401(k) legislation was not adopted until 1978 and did not become effective until three years later. Employee Benefits Research Institute, *Facts from EBRI: History of 401(k) Plans: An Update* (EBRI, 2005), http://www.ebri.org/publications/facts/. Although the legislation merely codified the position that many employers had taken prior to that time, there was a sharp increase in the number of 401(k) plans offered as more cautious employers, who were once reluctant to offer the plans as primary retirement savings vehicles, became more comfortable when the legislation became effective. *Id.*

39. *See* Hewitt Associates LLC, *Trends and Experience in 401(k) Plans* (Hewitt Associates, 2009), 2, available at http://www.retirementmadesimpler.org/Library/Hewitt_Research_Trends_in_401k_Highlights.pdf [hereinafter Hewitt Associates, *Trends and Experience*] (noting that the rate of 401(k) plans being offered has leveled off after rising over the previous ten years).

currently exceed contributions made to traditional defined benefit and all other types of defined contribution plans combined.[40]

Section 401(k) plans require participants to make elections between receiving amounts in cash as current compensation or having the employer make pretax contributions to a qualified retirement plan on their behalf as deferred compensation.[41] Participant-directed plans, which represent the fastest growing type of 401(k) plan, additionally require participants to decide the manner in which their accounts are to be invested.[42]

THE 401(K) DEBATE

Notwithstanding their popularity, section 401(k) plans have sparked considerable debate among policymakers as to whether the function of these plans is consistent with the primary objective of the private retirement system. At the crux of the debate are conflicting views about the purpose of participant-directed 401(k) plans and the rules that govern them. There are those who believe that the primary purpose of tax-subsidized retirement savings plans, including 401(k) plans, is to provide greater retirement security.[43] Accordingly, in view of the increased risks that 401(k) plans present, these individuals advocate tighter regulations and more protection to ensure that such plans provide adequate retirement security to plan participants.[44]

At the other end of the spectrum are policymakers who prefer the wider choice and greater flexibility in 401(k) plans to what is available in traditional plans. They maintain that 401(k) plans are no different from any other personal savings instruments. Accordingly, they argue it is unnecessary to subject these savings arrangements to greater regulation and control, believing it is sufficient that the plans merely give participants "a chance to hit the jackpot."[45]

---

40. Investment Company Institute, *401(k) Plans: A 25-Year Retrospective*, 12 Research Perspective, No. 2, Nov. 2006. At the end of 2009, there were 20.7 million participants in plans with a 401(k) feature and the total assets of the plans were estimated to be $1.2 trillion. Jack VanDerhei et al., *401(k) Plan Asset Allocation, Account Balances, and Loan Activity in 2009*, 350 Emp. Benefit Res. Inst. 6 (Nov. 2010).

41. *See* I.R.C. §402(e)(3) (section 401(k) plans are also known as cash or deferred arrangements (CODAs)). In §401(k) plans, the salary voluntarily deferred by the employee is excluded from income and is treated as an employer contribution for tax purposes. *Id.* To encourage greater participation, employers sponsoring 401(k) plans frequently match employee contributions in some proportion, with the most common match being $.50 per $1.00, up to a specified percentage of pay. Hewitt Associates, *Trends and Experience, supra* note 39, at 4.

42. I.R.C. §401(k). Approximately 40 million Americans participate in defined contribution plans. Patrick Purcell, *Retirement Savings and Household Wealth in 2007*, RL 30922 (Congressional Research Service, 2009). As of 2009, 78 percent of the $9.7 trillion in pension assets were held in participant-directed plans. Testimony of J. Mark Iwry, Senior Adviser to the Secretary of the Treasury and Deputy Assistant Treasury Secretary for Retirement and Health Policy, *Senate Special Committee on Aging on Lifetime Income Options for Retirement* (2010), 3.

43. Jefferson, *Pension Reform, supra* note 37, at 21; *see also* Susan J. Stabile, *Is It Time to Admit the Failure of an Employment-Based Pension System?*, 11 Lewis & Clark L. Rev., 305, 310–17 (2007) (discussing the "Major Problems Associated with 401(k) Plans").

44. *See* John Morgan, *Investors Learn Not to Gamble with Life Savings*, 23 Employee Benefit News 6, 54 (2009) (discussing the need for additional tools to protect retirees from outliving their assets).

45. Albert Crenshaw, *401(k) Debate: The Jackpot Versus the Sure Thing*, Wash. Post, Mar. 24, 2002, at H04.

To appreciate the complexity of the debate better, it is useful to understand the present pension landscape and the factors responsible for the shift from traditional defined benefit plans to 401(k) plans in the private retirement system.[46] First, changes in the labor market have impacted significantly the demand for defined benefit plans. Historically, large, unionized firms in the manufacturing industry selected traditional defined benefit plans as their primary retirement savings instruments; however, the number of unionized firms has declined precipitously in recent years.[47] As a result, the number of defined benefit plans also has fallen. In contrast, the number of small, non-unionized companies in the service industry has risen over the last two decades.[48] Smaller employers tend to prefer defined contribution plans because they are simpler and their costs are more predictable; thus, the number of defined contribution plans has risen sharply in recent years.[49]

Second, over the last two decades, the cost of maintaining traditional defined benefit plans has increased disproportionately relative to that of defined contribution plans as a result of more frequent and burdensome regulations.[50] Therefore, employers concerned about the cost of maintaining retirement plans are more likely to offer defined contribution plans.

Third, a bull market in the 1990s made it possible for inexperienced investors, both inside and outside the private pension system, to experience tremendous success in the stock market.[51] This environment, coupled with the emerging desire for individual choice, continues to cause some workers to clamor for participant-directed 401(k) plans, apparently believing that a turn-around in the market will once again yield very high returns.

Finally, because retirement funds have grown rapidly relative to the economy as a whole, there is heightened interest in these assets by financial institutions. As of 2010, pension assets exceeded $17 trillion.[52] Financial institutions and insurance companies have particularly marketed their financial and management services to 401(k) plans because of their fee

---

46. Regina T. Jefferson, *Striking a Balance in the Cash Balance Debate*, 49 Buff. L. Rev. 513, 524 (1993) [hereinafter Jefferson, *Striking a Balance*].

47. *Id.* (citing John R. Keville, Note, *Retire at Your Own Risk: ERISA's Return on Your Investment?*, 68 St. John's L. Rev. 527, 543–53 (1994) and Richard Ippolito, *Pension Plans and Employee Performance: Evidence Analysis and Policy* (University of Chicago, 1997), 4–5).

48. *Id.* (citing Ippolito, *supra* note 47).

49. *Id.* The financial obligations of the employer are also immediately dischargeable in defined contribution plans. *Id.* This is not the case in defined benefit plans, where annual costs vary from year to year depending on plan experience; consequently, large unfunded liabilities can occur. *Id.* at 524–25.

50. *See* Stabile, *supra* note 43, at 309 n. 15; *see also* Jefferson, *Striking a Balance*, *supra* note 46, at 524–25.

51. *See infra* note 152–53 and accompanying text.

52. Investment Company Institute, *Investment Company Fact Book: A Review of Trends and Activity in the Investment Company Industry* (51st ed., ICI, 2011), 8, http://www.ici.org/pdf/2011_factbook.pdf. Significant portions of pension assets are held in section 401(k) and 403(b) plans. Langbein et al., *supra* note 14, at 21. As of year end 2010, the nation's largest pension fund, Teachers Insurance and Annuity Association—College Retirement Equities Fund (TIAA-CREF), the college teachers' fund, held $453 billion in assets. TIAA-CREF, *Company Stats and Facts*, http://www.tiaa-cref.org/public/about/press/about_us/overview/index.html (last visited Aug. 10, 2011).

structure.[53] As a result of such promotions, 401(k) plans have been given greater visibility relative to traditional retirement plans.[54]

For all these reasons, the trend of using 401(k) plans as primary retirement savings vehicles is well under way and is unlikely to change in the near future. Regardless of the risks that these plans present, they are more popular than traditional defined benefit plans because they are cheaper, simpler, and less risky for employers to maintain. Consequently, the imposition of mandatory measures by policymakers to provide protection against losses in these plans is likely to be unsuccessful and may generate tremendous opposition from employers and various interest groups that support 401(k) plans in their current form.[55]

To preserve the integrity of the private retirement system, it is thus incumbent upon policymakers to balance the concerns of each side of the debate. In doing so, they must seek to advance pension laws and policies that preserve some of the features of traditional defined benefit plans that have proven to be essential to retirement security and, at the same time, retain some of the flexibility, simplicity, and administrative ease that 401(k) plans currently provide.

WEAKNESS IN EXISTING PENSION LAW

LACK OF PROTECTION AGAINST LOSSES IN DEFINED CONTRIBUTION PLANS

ERISA established a federal insurance program administered by the PBGC that provides substantial protection against losses, including those attributable to market fluctuations, in defined benefit plans.[56] However, section 3(34) of ERISA specifically provides that PBGC protection is not available for individual account plans.[57] Accordingly, section 401(k) plans are excluded from ERISA's insurance program.[58]

---

53. Karen Pence, *Nature or Nurture: Why Do 401(k) Participants Save Differently Than Other Workers?* (Federal Reserve Board of Governors, June 2002), 5, http://www.federalreserve.gov/ Pubs/feds/2002/200233pap.pdf [hereinafter Pence, *Nature or Nurture*]; *also see generally* Matthew D. Hutcheson, *Uncovering and Understanding Hidden Fees in Qualified Retirement Plans*, 15 Elder L.J. 323 (2007) (discussing 401(k) and 403(b) plan fees and the concerns these fees present when they are overly large).

54. *See* Pence, *Nature or Nurture, supra* note 53, at 5.

55. *See* Jefferson, *Pension Reform, supra* note 37, at 21 (citing Albert Crenshaw, *White House Opposes Stock Cap,* Wash Post, Feb. 7, 2002, at El).

56. *See supra* note 32 and accompanying text (discussing the PBGC); *see also* Jefferson, *Rethinking the Risk, supra* note 6, at 644 (discussing PBGC liability in the event of erroneous interest rate assumptions).

57. *See* ERISA §3(34), 29 U.S.C. §1002(34) (2006) (defining a defined contribution plan as a plan providing an individual account for each participant). The statute defines individual account plans as plans in which the level of benefit for each employee fluctuates depending on the experience of the account. *Id. See also* ERISA §4021(b)(1), 29 U.S.C. §1321(b)(1) (2006) (providing that PBGC protection is unavailable to "[any plan] which is an individual account plan as defined in [ERISA §3(34)]").

58. ERISA §4021(b)(1), 29 U.S.C. §1321(b)(1) (2006).

ERISA not only excludes defined contribution plans from its pension insurance program, but it also places little emphasis on the prevention and recovery of losses in such plans. While there are complex fiduciary rules that focus on the mismanagement of plan assets held in common trust by employers and other plan fiduciaries associated with defined benefit plans, there is less emphasis on similar matters regarding individual account plan assets.[59] Even to the extent that existing ERISA remedies could be interpreted to apply to defined contribution plans, uncertainty remains about how expansively or narrowly Congress intended for ERISA to be read regarding the scope of remedies available to 401(k) plan participants when losses occur due to asset mismanagement.[60] Making it even more difficult for participants in this situation, in recent years the Supreme Court has adopted a very narrow reading of the applicability of the remedies available under ERISA as they apply to defined contribution plans.[61] Thus, under current law, when losses occur in 401(k) plans, participants can expect relief neither from the statute nor from the courts.

NEED FOR PENSION REFORM

The heavy use of 401(k) retirement plans in the private sector as primary retirement savings vehicles has created a retirement system that fails to provide participants with adequate protection against benefit losses and, at the same time, encourages them to take risks with their retirement savings. This contradiction was less problematic during the 1990s bull market, when many 401(k) plan participants experienced double-digit returns, even when they used nonconventional investment strategies.[62] However, in more recent times, the slumping stock market has decimated the retirement savings of millions of Americans.[63] The Congressional Budget Office reported that more than $2 trillion in retirement savings was lost in the fifteen-month period following the stock market collapse of 2008.[64] Data collected by the University of Michigan Health and Retirement Study reported that approximately $678 billion in retirement savings was lost in the three-year period after the market downturn of 2002.[65] As a result, over the last ten years, many workers have postponed their retirements, causing the population of Americans between the ages of 55 and 65 working or seeking

---

59. ERISA §§401–414, 29 U.S.C. §§1101–14 (2006).

60. Warren Richey, *Can You Sue If Your 401(k) Nest Egg is Mishandled?*, Christian Sci. Monitor, Nov. 26, 2007, at 1.

61. *LaRue v. DeWolff, Boberg & Associates, Inc.*, 552 U.S. 248, 255–56 (2008).

62. Langbein et al., *supra* note 14, at 49.

63. *See* Emily Brandon, *Retirement Savers Lost $2 Trillion in the Stock Market, Planning to Retire*, U.S. News (Oct. 8, 2008), http://money.usnews.com/money/blogs/planning-to-retire/2008/10/08/retirement-savers-lost-2-trillion-in-the-stock-market (describing sudden financial straits affecting many retirees); *see also* Committee on Education and Labor, U.S. House of Representatives, *Retirees Facing a 401(k) Savings Crisis, Witnesses Tell House Panel in San Francisco U.S. Pension Agency Lost 3 Billion in Assets, Chairman Miller Announces* (press release, Oct. 22, 2008), available at http://www.house.gov/apps/list/speech/edlabor_dem/102208SanFranHearing.html.

64. Robert Gavin, *Back to Work Reluctantly*, Wall St. J., Mar. 3, 2003, at B1 (describing sudden financial straits affecting many retirees).

65. Brandon, *supra* note 63; Committee on Education and Labor U.S. House of Representatives, *supra* note 63.

employment to escalate.[66] This development in the workforce has been described as "unprecedented in post war United States economic history."[67] Not surprisingly, many participants now desire more security from their retirement plans.

There have been numerous amendments to ERISA since its passage in 1974; however, the increased risk to plan participants posed by the use of 401(k) plans as primary retirement savings vehicles has not been addressed in any meaningful way by the legislature.[68] The Pension Protection Act of 2006 introduced various rules designed to enhance retirement savings in defined contribution plans.[69] The rules include provisions that encourage automatic rollovers in 401(k) plans,[70] require faster vesting for certain employer contributions,[71] and create safe harbors for automatic enrollment.[72] These changes are very likely to have a positive effect on contribution and participation rates in 401(k) plans. However, the changes are insufficient to increase overall retirement security for 401(k) plan participants, because they neither address the inherent risks presented by 401(k) plans nor help to prevent plan losses in such plans. In failing to do so, the pension law continues simultaneously to underplay the risks of 401(k) plans and to overestimate participants' abilities to protect themselves adequately against plan losses.

PROPOSALS TO PROVIDE GREATER RETIREMENT SECURITY IN 401(K) PLANS

FINANCIAL EDUCATION REQUIREMENT

In non-participant-directed plans, plan administrators or investment professionals typically control the investment of plan assets.[73] ERISA's fiduciary rules mandate "fiduciary responsibility" for plan trustees, investment managers, and other persons with control of pension assets.[74] These rules make all plan fiduciaries responsible for the performance of plan assets and require

---

66. Brandon, *supra* note 63; Committee on Education and Labor U.S. House of Representatives, *supra* note 63. Deb Riechmann, *Older Workers, Hurt by Recession, Seek New Jobs*, SeacoastOnline.com, (April 5, 2009), http://www.seacoastonline.com/articles/20090405-BIZ-904050327.

67. Gavin, *supra* note 64, at B1. *See* Brandon, *supra* note 63 (describing solutions for losses in retirement accounts).

68. *See* Langbein et al., *supra* note 14, at 92–96 (listing and describing amendments to ERISA and other areas of federal law affecting ERISA). For example, the Retirement Equity Act of 1984 (REA or REAct) addressed issues of special concern to women, and the Small Job Protection Act of 1996 created the savings incentive math plan (SIMPLE), a new type of plan available to small businesses. Most recently, the Pension Protection Act of 2006 (PPA) changed the funding rules for single employer-defined benefit plans and established safe harbors in 401(k) plans for employers to provide investment advice and automatic enrollment. *Id.*

69. Pension Protection Act of 2006, Pub. L. 109-280, 120 Stat. 780 (codified as amended in scattered sections of 26 and 29 U.S.C.A.).

70. 26 U.S.C.A. §402(c)(2)(A) (2006).

71. *Id.* §411(a)(2).

72. *Id.* §401(k)(13).

73. *See* Jefferson, *Rethinking the Risk*, *supra* note 6, at 627–29 (discussing investment practices in participant-directed plans).

74. ERISA §402, 29 U.S.C. §1102 (2006).

them to allocate investments in a manner that offers protection against inflation, market fluctuations, and unfavorable market performance.[75] Although employers who sponsor participant-directed plans remain liable as ERISA fiduciaries, the fiduciary standards are applied much less strictly. Employers generally are obligated to exercise only procedural prudence regarding the investment decisions made by plan participants.[76]

As a method of further minimizing liability for the employees' investment decisions in participant-directed 401(k) plans, many employers adopt 404(c) "safe harbor" plans.[77] When plans comply with the rules of section 404(c) and the accompanying regulations, the employers' exposure to fiduciary liability is substantially reduced.[78] These rules require employers to give participants only a broad range of investment options and reasonable instructions regarding the significance of the options.[79] In contrast to non-participant-directed 401(k) plans, where plan fiduciaries retain some obligation to ensure that plan assets are protected against losses, there is essentially no residual liability in section 404(c) plans.[80] Thus, regardless of how plan participants allocate their assets, employers and other plan fiduciaries generally are not liable for any losses that may result from poor investment returns.

Without having the benefit of financial professionals to assist in their investment choices, participants generally fail to diversify their retirement accounts sufficiently, and they invest disproportionately in low-risk, low-yield instruments.[81] High concentrations of stable value funds are unlikely to produce enough investment income over an employee's working life to provide an adequate source of retirement income.[82] Inexperienced investors are not only less likely to adequately diversify their accounts, but are also less

---

75. 29 C.F.R. §2550.404a-1 (2007).

76. *See DiFelice v. U.S. Airways, Inc.*, 497 F.3d 410, 421 (4th Cir. 2007) (finding that the plan fiduciary engaged in a reasonable duty of procedural prudence). *See also* Fred Reish and Bruce Ashton, *401(k) Investment Issues: What It Means to Be Prudent Under ERISA*, 12 J. of Pension Benefits 67 (2005) (describing the procedural prudence standard).

77. 29 C.F.R. §2550.404c-1 (2007). The §404(c) regulations were issued in October 1992. 57 Fed. Reg. 46932 (1992). The regulations define an ERISA §404(c) plan as, generally, a defined contribution plan that provides participants with the opportunity to "exercise control over assets" in their accounts and provides the participants with "an opportunity to choose, from a broad range of investment alternatives." 29 C.F.R. §2550.404c-1(b)(i)–(ii) (2007).

78. ERISA §404(c), 29 U.S.C. §1104(c) (2006). This section provides that "[i]n the case of a pension plan which provides for individual accounts and permits a participant or beneficiary to exercise control over assets in his account, if a participant or beneficiary exercises control over the assets in his account (as determined under regulation of the Secretary)—(i) such participant or beneficiary shall not be deemed to be a fiduciary by reason of such exercise, and (ii) no person who is otherwise a fiduciary shall be liable under this part for any loss, or by reason of any breach, which results from such participant's or beneficiary's exercise of control." *Id.* Section 404(c) of ERISA is elective and applies only to defined contribution plans, such as 401(k) plans, where participants control the investment of their assets. *Id.*

79. 29 C.F.R. §2550.404c-1 (2007).

80. *Id.*

81. *See* Alicia H. Munnell and Anika Sunden, *401(k) Plans Are Still Coming Up Short* 4 (Center for Retirement at Boston College, Issue in Brief 43, Mar. 2006), available at http://crr.bc.edu/briefs/401_k_plans_are_still_coming_ip_short.html.

82. Jefferson, *Rethinking the Risk*, *supra* note 6, at 629; *see also* Susan J. Stabile, *Paternalism Isn't Always a Dirty Word: Can the Law Better Protect Defined Contribution Plan Participants?*, 5 Emp. Rts. & Emp. Pol'y J. 491, 498-501 (2001) (noting that "[m]any defined contribution plan participants invest too conservatively to ensure sufficient benefits at retirement—disproportionately investing in fixed income alternatives").

likely to recognize financial indicators that investment professionals rely upon to determine when to shift funds from one investment to another.[83] Accordingly, some participants may fail to make appropriate changes when they are indicated by market conditions, reacting either too slowly or too hastily.[84]

Therefore, because of the importance and complexity of investment decisions, all employers sponsoring qualified participant-directed 401(k) plans should be required to provide plan participants a minimum level of investment education to enable them to make informed decisions regarding the assets in their accounts.[85] Requiring the employer to assist participants in making prudent investment decisions not only would reduce the risk of loss in participant-directed plans but also would justify the tax subsidy that these plans receive. Additionally, an education requirement would advance existing pension policy by ensuring that participants actually receive some advantage from the employment-based characteristic of the private pension system.

The education requirement for 401(k) plans proposed in this chapter would apply to all participant-directed 401(k) plans. The proposed requirement mandates uniform standards for the content, frequency and method of communication. Financial education would be provided at the employer's expense as a trade-off for the reduction of fiduciary responsibility that it enjoys.[86] The cost of the required financial training program would be deductible by the employer as an ordinary and necessary business expense only if the training complied with the specified terms and conditions for qualifying programs.[87]

CURRENT LAW

Prior to the enactment of the Pension Protection Act of 2006 (PPA), the fiduciary rules of ERISA deterred employers from providing assistance to employees in making investment decisions.[88] Under the prohibited transaction rules of both ERISA and the Internal Revenue Code (IRC), employers and their intermediaries that provide specific "investment advice" can be held liable as ERISA fiduciaries if participants relying on the advice lose money.[89] The rules, however, do not treat the provision of general investment

---

83. Jefferson, *Rethinking the Risk, supra* note 6, at 629.

84. *Id.*

85. *Id.* at 636–40.

86. U.S. Gov't Accountability Office, GAO-08-774, *Fulfilling Fiduciary Obligations Can Present Challenges for 401(K) Plan Sponsors, Report to the Chairman, Committee on Education and Labor, House of Representatives* (July 2008), 7.

87. *See* I.R.C. §162 (permitting the deduction of ordinary and necessary business expenses).

88. *See* ERISA §3(21)(A)(ii), 29 U.S.C. §1002 (21)(A)(ii) (2006) (providing that a fiduciary is any person who "renders investment advice for a fee or other compensation, direct or indirect, with respect to any money or other property of such plan, or has any authority or responsibility to do so"). Thus, prior to the PPA exemption, any employer providing investment advice could have been liable as an ERISA fiduciary if losses occurred as a result of the advice. *Id.*

89. *See* 29 C.F.R. §2510.3-21(c) (2007) ("A person shall be deemed to be rendering 'investment advice' . . . only if (i) Such person renders advice to the plan as to the value of securities or other property, or makes recommendation as to the advisability of investing in, purchasing, or selling securities or other property; and (ii) Such person either directly or indirectly . . . (A) Has discretionary authority or control . . . with respect to purchasing or selling securities or other property for the plan; (B) Renders any advice . . . on a regular basis to the plan pursuant to a mutual

information as a fiduciary function.[90] Thus, unlike providing "investment advice," providing "investment education" is risk-free to employers and other plan fiduciaries.[91] As a practical matter, however, it is difficult to distinguish financial education from financial advice.[92] Accordingly, prior to PPA, employers often were advised that the risk of providing bad investment advice exceeded the risk of providing insufficient investment education.[93] Consequently, many employers did not offer any form of investment education.

The PPA addressed this concern by amending ERISA to include an exemption from fiduciary liability for plans that provide investment advice to participants and their beneficiaries under eligible investment advice arrangements (EIAAs), as defined in section 408(g) of ERISA, and section 4975 of the IRC.[94] The exemption permits employers that sponsor participant-directed plans to provide investment advice under circumstances that, prior to the passage of PPA, would have been considered a prohibited transaction.[95] The rule makes it clear that plan sponsors and other fiduciaries do not have a duty under ERISA to monitor the specific investment advice given by a fiduciary advisor to a particular participant; however, the rules continue to place a duty on them for the prudent selection and periodic review of the fiduciary advisors.[96]

To be exempted under the PPA, the investment advice must be provided in one of two ways. First, the advice may be offered pursuant to a fee-neutral arrangement, such that the fees charged by the fiduciary advisor do not depend on the investment options selected by the plan participant.[97] Alternatively, the advice may be based on a computer program that is certified by an independent third party to satisfy the statutory requirements.[98] The computer program must apply generally accepted investment theories and use relevant information regarding specific participants.[99] The program also must operate in an unbiased manner, taking into account all of the

---

agreement, arrangement, or understanding, . . . that such services will serve as a primary basis for investment decisions with respect to plan assets, and that such person will render individual investment advice to the plan based on the particular needs of the plan.)".

90. *See* Mary Rowland, *Educate-or Litigate: Educating Pension Plan Participants*, Inst. Inv., Mar. 1, 1995, at 87. If the information were considered investment advice, those providing the information (e.g., employers, plan sponsors, service providers) would be deemed fiduciaries, subject to liability under ERISA. *See* Frederick C. Kneip, *Section 404(c): Basic Principles*, 397 PLI Tax 43 (1997); *see also* Roger C. Siske et al., *What's New in Employee Benefits: A Summary of Current Cases and Other Developments*, SB66 A.L.I.-A.B.A. 1, 78–79 (1997).

91. Kneip, *supra* note 90, at 51–53.

92. Leah Carlson Shephard, *How to Tell the Difference Between Financial Education and Advice*, ebn.benefitnews.com, (July 1, 2007), http://ebn.benefitnews.com/news/tell-difference-between-financial-education-and-107408-1.html. *See* Dana M. Muir, *The Dichotomy Between Investment Advice and Investment Education: Is No Advice Really the Best Advice?*, 23 Berkeley J. Emp. & Lab. L. 1, 18–20 (2002) (discussing the tension between investment advise and investment education prior to the passage of the Pension Protection Act of 2006).

93. *Id.*

94. *See* ERISA §408(g), 29 U.S.C.A. §1108 (2006) and I.R.C. §4975(f)(8) (specifying that the provision of investment advice, the investment strategy entered into pursuant to the advice, and the receipt of fees and commissions by the investment advisor are exempt under §408(b)(14) from the prohibited transaction rules).

95. *See supra* notes 88–91 and accompanying text.

96. ERISA §408(g), 29 U.S.C.A. 1108 (2006).

97. *Id.* §408(g)(2)(A).

98. *Id.* §408(g)(3).

99. *Id.*

investment options under the plan and utilizing objective criteria in its asset allocation function.[100]

Although the new provisions enacted by PPA may encourage more employers who sponsor participant-directed plans to provide investment advice, they do not impose a requirement on them to do so. Consequently, many cost-conscious employers may remain reluctant to invest the resources necessary to provide quality education programs.[101] Therefore, to ensure that all participants have access to financial education, it is necessary that employers sponsoring participant-directed plans be required to provide financial training. In the absence of such a mandate, many 401(k) plan participants will continue to be forced to make important investment decisions without the benefit of investment education.

Specific Requirements for Qualifying Education

The success of an education program is determined not only by its availability but also by the quality of instruction. Thus, the proposed education requirement regulates the timing, type, and content of the information provided in the following manner.[102]

First, qualifying education programs would be required to utilize a variety of educational media, including a complement of written materials and seminars as well as financial planning software. This approach is responsive to evidence showing that printed information is less effective than other modes of communication in aiding the investment education of plan participants.[103]

Second, in addition to requiring that investment information be tailored to individual participants, the proposed education program would require that financial education be made available on a regular basis to all plan participants throughout their employment, regardless of age. Currently, some employers offer one-time planning sessions to older employees, believing that only those near retirement need financial education. However, this is not the case. Imprudent investment decisions can be just as devastating — if not more so — for younger employees. This result occurs because younger employees have longer investment horizons; consequently, the negative effects of their mistakes are compounded over greater periods.[104] Thus, to ensure that not only older workers but also younger workers have access to financial training, under the proposed education program, employers would be required to provide investment information periodically to all participants.

---

100. *Id.*

101. *See* Hewitt Associates, *Trends and Experience, supra* note 39, at 5–6 (explaining that currently only 50 percent of employers provide outside investment advisory services to their employees, and that employers not providing such services indicated that cost prohibited them from doing so). Outside investment services include "advice, guidance, and managed accounts." *Id.*

102. *See supra* notes 98–100 and accompanying text (explaining the current requirements).

103. *See* Jefferson, *Rethinking the Risk, supra* note 6, at 639 (citing Ed Peratta, *401(k) Communication That Works*, Pens. Mgmt., Dec. 1995, at 32; *EBRI Releases Report on Participant Education for Improved Retirement Savings*, 95 Tax Notes Today 86–51 (May 3, 1995)).

104. *See* Jefferson, *Rethinking the Risk, supra* note 6, at 629 (citing James E. Graham, *Does 404(c) Provide More Questions Than Answers?*, Pension World, July 1994, at 48).

Finally, the goal of the private retirement system is not only to assist workers in saving for retirement but also to assist them in managing their assets to last throughout retirement. For this reason, there are rules that encourage some forms of distribution over others, and rules that restrict early access to retirement plan assets.[105] Therefore, financial education programs should emphasize the importance of investment allocation as well as the timing and forms of distribution. This information is essential to financial training because decisions regarding these matters are complex and have long-term effects.[106]

In order to make meaningful comparisons of different forms of payment, numerous contingencies must be considered. For example, it is necessary for participants to predict investment rates of return accurately over extended periods of time, the effects of inflation and their own life expectancies. In making decisions regarding the forms of distribution, it also is useful to consider the cost of purchasing annuities outside the plan when lump sum options are selected. Numerous studies show that when given a choice, most individuals choose lump sum payments.[107] This is the case even when the annuitized payments are subsidized by the employer or when substantial tax penalties for early distributions apply.[108] Undoubtedly, the complexity of relative-value calculations, coupled with the inability to appreciate fully the value of annuity options, causes many participants to make this selection.[109]

When traditional defined benefit plans dominated the private pension system, it was less critical for plan participants to understand the relative value of annuities, because they were the normal form of distribution in such plans. However, this is no longer the case. In the current pension landscape, 401(k) plans dominate, and annuities often are provided only as optional forms of benefit. Thus, it is necessary for participants to make choices affirmatively regarding the form of payments that they will receive. Accordingly, the proposed education requirement mandates that training on the advantages and disadvantages of various forms of distribution be included in the financial training that participant-directed plans must provide.[110]

---

105. See Langbein et al., *supra* note 14, at 481–82 (describing limitations on distributions from qualified plans). ERISA and the IRC both impose limitations on the timing and type of distributions from qualified plans designed to protect participants or their spouses; for example, plans may not postpone distributions beyond a specified date without the participants' consent. I.R.C. §401(a)(14); ERISA 206(a), 29 U.S.C. §1056(a) (2006). Vested accrued benefits worth more than $5,000 may not be "cashed out" of the plan prior to normal age without the participant's consent. I.R.C. §411(a)(11); ERISA 203(e), 29 U.S.C. §1053 (2006). Qualified plans must also provide benefits in the form of "qualified joint and survivor annuities," unless the participant and the participant's spouse elect otherwise in writing. I.R.C. §§401(a)(11), 417; ERISA 205(a), 29 U.S.C. §1055(a) (2006). Additional rules also affect the time of distributions and require certain types of plans to limit early distributions. I.R.C. §72(t).

106. See *infra* notes 116–29 and accompanying text.

107. See Christine Dugas, *Many Retirees Select Lump Sum*, USA Today, Aug. 8, 2003, at B3 (noting that many participants choose to receive a lump sum rather than an annuity).

108. *Id.*

109. See *infra* notes 116–29 and accompanying text.

110. See *infra* notes 116–29 and accompanying text (proposing to extend relative value regulations to all 401(k) plans, and require the use of participant-specific calculations and the provision of all other financial information to employees throughout their lives).

Under current law, the relative value regulations require that plan administrators disclose to participants the relative values and monthly payments for optional forms of benefit available in the plan, using the plan's single life annuity and qualified joint and survivor annuity (QJSA) as the basis of comparison.[111] The regulations generally apply to defined benefit plans and were issued to enable participants to make fully informed choices about their available benefits.[112] The regulations require that information regarding the relative value of the optional forms of benefits be given to terminating participants when they make their benefit election.[113] Explanations of the benefits must be written in a manner calculated to be understood by the average participant and must contain either participant-specific information or general information based on a hypothetical participant at representative ages.[114]

However, for many participants, waiting until they reach retirement age to understand the significance of such decisions may be too late. Once participants have anticipated and relied upon the receipt of a lump sum payment, they may be less receptive to choosing a life annuity, even if they appreciate its value. Accordingly, it is important for participants to be educated on the value of their benefits long before reaching retirement age so that this information can be considered in the early stages of their financial planning.

For this reason, the education program proposed in this article would amend the existing law in the following manner. First, it would extend the application of the relative value regulations to all participant-directed 401(k) plans. Second, it would eliminate the generalized information alternative and require that only participant-specific calculation be used. Third, unlike the relative value regulations, which currently are satisfied by a single disclosure prior to retirement, the proposed education program would require that all financial information, including that pertaining to the values of the optional forms of benefit, be provided throughout the participants' working lives.[115] For administrative ease, the employer could select annually a particular day, or dates, for this purpose.

111. Treas. Reg. §1.417(a)(3)-1 (as amended in 2006). Prior to the issuance of the relative value regulations, plans were permitted to describe different forms of benefits as being equal in value; however, under the new regulations, plans must actually calculate, and disclose to retirees, the relative actuarial values of the different forms of benefits using reasonable actuarial assumptions. *Id.*

112. *See id.* (providing that defined benefit plans, money purchase pension plans, and certain other defined contribution plans are subject to IRC §401 (a)(11) joint and survivor annuity, and preretirement survivor annuity requirements).

113. *Id.* The regulations specifically provide that explanations of QJSA benefits must be given to participants no later than 30 days and no earlier than 90 days prior to the annuity starting date. *Id.* §1.417(e)-1(b)(3)(ii).

114. *Id.* §1.417(a)(3)-1.

115. *See supra* notes 111–14 and accompanying text (discussing the relative value regulations).

REQUIRED OPTION FOR ANNUITIZATION

Protection Against Unexpected Longevity

Life annuities are the most effective method by which individuals can protect themselves against the risk of outliving their assets, because these forms of payment provide a stream of income over the life of the annuitant.[116] To illustrate the value of a life annuity, consider an individual who owns significant assets and is preparing for retirement. Assume that there will be no other sources of income, such as Social Security or private pension payments. If the individual knew her exact date of death, rate of investment return, and inflation index over the years prior to retirement, it would not be difficult to determine how much to spend annually in order not to deplete her assets before death.[117] However, without this information it is almost impossible for her to allocate her resources to achieve this goal. As a result, most individuals in this situation will either significantly over- or undersave for their retirements.

Although life expectancy tables are useful in determining how to allocate resources, they are merely estimates, and therefore they are inexact. Furthermore, there are substantial variations from group to group as well as within groups that diminish the reliability of actuarial predictors for individual use. For example, the average 65-year-old male in 2010 could expect to live until age 85, but the average 65-year-old female could expect to live to age 87.[118] However, the average 65-year-old male has a 30 percent chance of living past age 90, whereas the average 65-year-old female has a 40 percent chance.[119] There also are disparities in life expectancies relative to nationality and race. For example, Japan has the world's greatest life expectancy for women and San Marino has the greatest one for men, and life expectancies in the United States vary between African Americans and whites.[120] Therefore, despite the use of tools such as life expectancy tables, interest rate assumptions, and family histories regarding longevity, life annuities are the most reliable way of solving the wealth allocation problem for retirees.[121]

Annuities come in many variations and address a myriad of concerns about longevity-related issues. If, for example, an individual wished to protect her beneficiaries in the event of premature death, she could purchase a life annuity with a certain feature that guarantees payment for a fixed amount of years. To illustrate, assume she purchased a ten-year certain and life annuity. If she dies one year after payments begin, under the terms of the ten-year certain and life annuity, her beneficiaries would receive payments for nine years after her death.

---

116. *See* Jefferson, *Striking a Balance, supra* note 46, at 532–38 (discussing annuity payments).
117. *Id.* at 532–33.
118. American Academy of Actuaries, The News Monthly of the Am. Acad. of Actuaries, June 2010, at 3, available at http://www.actuary.org/update/pdf/0610.pdf.
119. *See* Miranda Hitti, *Living Longer: Life Expectancy Hits New High*, WebMD 50+ Live Better, Longer 1 (2007), http://www.webmd.com/healthy-aging/news/20070912/living-longer-life-expectancy-hits-new-high.
120. *Id.*
121. Jefferson, *Striking a Balance, supra* note 46, at 533.

If another individual believed that she had sufficient assets to last over the earlier years of retirement but was concerned about the later years, she could invest in a longevity annuity.[122] These arrangements pay lifetime income once individuals reach superannuated ages. For example, under the longevity annuity marketed by MetLife Retirement Income Insurance, for $50,000, a 60-year-old male would receive $21,741 per year, starting at age 85.[123] The reason the insurance company can offer such a generous return is that these arrangements are very risky for the annuitant. First, it is unlikely that participants will ever reach the triggering age; and second, these arrangements typically do not provide survivor benefits.[124]

Because of the importance of life annuities to retirement security, the pension law requires that defined benefit plans offer them as a form of payment.[125] However, 401(k) plans are not required to do so.[126] As a result, lump sum payments are the most common form of distribution in 401(k) plans, with only 15 percent of the 401(k) plans in existence in 2007 offering life annuities as an optional form of payment for final distribution.[127] Thus, millions of plan participants in 401(k) plans are unable to receive their retirement benefits in the manner that protects them against unexpected longevity, even if annuitization is their preferred form of payment. This omission is a serious deficiency in the existing pension law. With life expectancies increasing, it is more important than ever for individuals to protect themselves against the risk of outliving their assets.[128] For this reason, many economists maintain that life annuities are an essential component of any properly structured retirement portfolio.[129]

Leakage and the Value of Annuitization

Life annuities resolve not only issues concerning longevity but also those concerning leakage. "Leakage" is the term used to refer to the use of retirement funds for purposes other than retirement.[130] Because section 401(k) plans provide lump sum payments not only when participants retire, but also when they terminate employment prior to retirement, it is possible for many individuals participating in these plans to spend the funds long before reaching retirement

---

122. Kimberly Lankford, *Retirement Income You'll Never Outlive*, Kiplinger's Pers. Fin., July 2007, at 80.

123. MetLife Investors Insurance Company, *Longevity Income Guarantee*, http://www.metlife.com/assets/investments/products/annuities/Longevity-income-guarantee.pdf (last visited Sept. 25, 2011).

124. *Id.*

125. ERISA §205, 29 U.S.C. §1055 (2006).

126. *See id.* (noting that other types of defined contribution plans are also not generally required to offer life annuities).

127. Hewitt Associates, *Trends and Experience*, *supra* note 39, at 7.

128. *See* Lankford, *supra* note 122, at 80.

129. Jeffrey R. Brown, *How Should We Insure Longevity Risk in Pensions and Social Security?* (Center for Retirement Research at Boston College, Issue in Brief No. 4, Aug. 2000), 5, available at http://cr.bc.edu/briefs/how_should_we_insure_longevity_risk_in_pensions_and_social_security_.html.

130. *See generally* Saving Smartly for Retirement: Are Americans Being Encouraged to Break Open the Piggy Bank?, testimony of Mark Iwry and David John, Retirement Security Project, before the Senate Special Committee on Aging, 11th Cong. (2008) [hereinafter Iwry and John, Saving Smartly] (discussing strategies to decrease leakage in 401(k) plans).

age.[131] Thus, another important benefit that life annuities provide is the assurance that tax-preferred money set aside for retirement will not be used prematurely for current consumption.

The law permits individuals who received lump sum distributions prior to retirement to rollover the funds without penalty into IRAs or other qualified retirement plans that accept them.[132] However, many individuals do not reinvest their pre-retirement distributions in either of these ways.[133] Reports from the Employee Benefit Research Institute show that as few as 38 percent of individuals under age 35 who receive lump sum distributions prior to retirement reinvest them in other retirement savings vehicles.[134] Employers report that when participants leave their companies prior to retirement, they choose lump sum payments even when the values of the annuities are significantly higher than the lump sum payments.[135] Other employers report that terminating employees often ask that their lump sum payments be distributed directly to businesses such as auto repair shops.[136] These reports are troubling but consistent with findings that show that workers who receive lump sum distributions are more likely to spend the funds.[137] Participants who spend their retirement savings for current consumption will have fewer remaining assets to grow tax-free as retirement savings and, ultimately, will have less retirement security.[138]

Proposed Annuity Option Requirement

To provide greater retirement security, all qualified 401(k) plans should be required to offer single life annuities for unmarried participants and 50 percent qualified joint and survivor annuities (QJSAs) for married participants. Additional forms of annuitized payments also would be encouraged to address the financial needs of different participants. In order to avoid imposing undue financial hardship on smaller employers, however, it would be necessary to have an exception for plans with fewer than a specified low number of participants.

The waiver rules under this proposal for the QJSA would be consistent with those existing presently for other qualified defined contribution

131. I.R.C. §401(k)(2); *See* Iwry and John, *Saving Smartly, supra* note 130.

132. Employee Benefit Research Institute, *Lump-Sum Distributions and Rollovers*, in *EBRI Databook on Employee Benefits* (EBRI, 2006), http://www.ebri.org/publications/books/index.cfm?fa=databook.

133. *Id.* Not surprisingly, younger workers are less likely than older workers to reinvest such payments in other retirement instruments. *See id.* (noting that only 49 percent of workers between the ages of 35 and 44 reinvest their retirement funds in other qualified retirement savings vehicles, as compared to 50 percent of workers between the ages of 45 and 54 who do so). The size of the distribution also affects the propensity to roll it over; distributions of smaller amounts are less likely to be rolled over than distributions of larger amounts. *Id.*

134. *Id.*

135. U.S. Government Accountability Office, *GAO/HEHS-00-207, Cash Balance Plans, Implications for Retirement Income* (GAO, 2000), 31.

136. *Id.*

137. Jefferson, *Striking a Balance, supra* note 46, at 534 (citing Leonard Burman et al., *What Happens When You Show Them the Money? Lump-Sum Distributions, Retirement Income Security, and Public Policy* (Urban Institute, 1999)).

138. *See* I.R.C. §72(t), 401(a).

plans.[139] Accordingly, the QJSA form of payment could not be waived unless the participant, with the consent of the nonparticipant spouse, elected to do so in writing.[140] Also, consistent with existing rules, all waivers of the QJSA option would need to be notarized or witnessed by a plan representative.[141]

Although the employer would be required to offer at least two options for annuitized payments, the employer would not be required to subsidize these forms of payment.[142] Even without the subsidy, however, participants would be better off than under current law, because requiring employers that sponsor 401(k) plans to offer life annuities would make this form of protection more readily available and more affordable to plan participants.

Insurance companies typically charge significantly higher premiums for life annuities when individuals independently purchase them because of concerns about adverse selection.[143] In other words, because life annuities are more beneficial to those who live longer, insurance companies assume that individuals who independently purchase them are extremely healthy and, based on predictors such as family history, expect to live longer than average lives. Accordingly, insurance companies charge higher premiums for such products under these circumstances.[144] If, however, employers were required to offer life annuities to all plan participants, regardless of health and longevity predictors, the risk pool would be larger. Presumably, a larger pool would minimize the selectivity problem, so that the group rates offered by the plan for life annuities would be significantly less expensive than individual rates. Thus, the primary advantages to participants of requiring plans to offer annuitized payments would be lower cost and greater convenience.

REQUIRED OPTION FOR MINIMUM GUARANTEED BENEFITS

Finally, in order to reduce the risk of benefit losses, all qualified 401(k) plans would be required to offer an option for a guaranteed minimum retirement benefit.[145] As with the annuitized payment option described in the

---

139. *See* ERISA §205(d), 29 U.S.C. §1055 (2006) (revised by REAct, previously §205(g)(3))(defining QJSA as an annuity payable for the life of the participant with a survivor annuity for the life of the nonparticipant spouse). The value of the survivor annuity must be no greater than 100 percent and no less than 50 percent of the annuity payable over their joint lives. *Id. See* Langbein et al., *supra* note 14, at 274–80 (for a detailed discussion of QJSAs and the waiver rules).

140. *Id.* §205(c)(2)(A)(i).

141. *Id.* §205(c)(2)(A)(iii).

142. *See supra* notes 122–26 and accompanying text (discussing different forms of annuitized payments).

143. *See* Olivia S. Mitchell et al., *New Evidence on the Money's Worth of Individual Annuities* 89 Am. Econ. Rev. 1299, 1299 (1999) ("Research has shown that inefficiencies exist in the annuity market due to a lack of competition and adverse selection among those who purchase annuities. Adverse selection in the annuities market occurs because people who buy annuities also tend to live longer, which is adverse to the insurer.").

144. *See id.* ("those who voluntarily purchase annuities may tend to live longer than average; insurance premiums therefore must be set high enough to compensate insurers for the longer life expectancies of purchasers").

145. *See generally* Jefferson, *Redistribution in the Private Retirement System, supra* note 1 (discussing the structure of guarantees for defined contribution plans in greater detail). *See also infra* notes 154–59 and accompanying text (discussing the guaranteed minimum retirement benefits that are currently offered by mutual fund companies).

previous section, the employer would be required to offer the minimum guaranteed benefit as an optional feature but would not be required to subsidize it. The objective of the guaranteed benefit would be to provide participants some form of protection against the risk of market fluctuations and other factors contributing to shortfalls in the expected retirement benefits, while allowing them to retain the right of self-direction.[146] As an elective feature, participants not desiring such protection would not be compelled to purchase it.

Skeptics may argue that it is unnecessary to have such an option because participants can protect themselves against the risk of loss in 401(k) plans less expensively by investing in mutual funds that achieve optimum diversification.[147] It is true that investing in mutual funds, compared to the purchase of individual stocks or bonds, can provide certain advantages to plan participants that otherwise would not be available.[148] One reason for this result is that mutual funds invest in a broad range of assets that include stocks, bonds, and money market instruments. Thus, mutual funds enable individuals to diversify their investments more easily and less expensively than they can by investing in these instruments independently.[149] Another reason mutual funds are advantageous is that they provide professionally managed portfolios. This feature is particularly valuable for individuals in participant-directed plans, where often there is no professional advice available.[150]

However, investment in mutual funds is not fail-safe. Mutual funds are particularly problematic for older individuals because stocks present substantial risks over the short run.[151] For this reason, when individuals close to retirement invest in mutual funds, they are more vulnerable to sudden fluctuations in the stock market. This is because, unlike their younger counterparts, who will have more time for market corrections to occur, older employees have insufficient time before reaching retirement to recover from setbacks in the performance of their retirement savings accounts.[152] During the bull markets of the 1980s and 1990s, older individuals, like most investors, were enticed to overinvest in equity funds relative to bond funds. When investors suffered sudden and severe losses after the stock market took a downturn, the disparate impact on older workers was apparent, as they were the ones who were forced to postpone their retirements indefinitely.[153]

---

146. *See* Jefferson, *Rethinking the Risk, supra* note 6, at 644–45.

147. *See* J. Michael McGowan, *Watching Your Basket: Keys to Nurturing a Successful Investment Portfolio*, 78 A.B.A. J. 97 (Nov. 1992) (discussing the modern portfolio theory (MPT) of investment, which rests on understanding the importance of broad diversification within and across asset classes; thus, an adequately diversified portfolio should include an appropriate balance of stocks, bonds, and stable value funds as well as market, industry, and firm risks).

148. *See* Investment Company Institute, *A Guide to Understanding Mutual Funds*, (Sept. 2006), at 3–4, available at http://www.ici.org/brounderstandingmfsp.pdf (last visited September 6, 2008).

149. *See id.*

150. *See id.*

151. Jeremy J. Siegel, *Stocks for the Long Run* (3d ed., McGraw-Hill, 2002), 26–29.

152. John Waggoner, *Over-50s Have Little Time to Fix Portfolios*, USA Today, Oct. 23, 2002, available at http://www.usatoday.com/money/2002-10-23-over-usat_x.htm.

153. *Id. See also* Gabor Kezdi and Purvi Sevak, *Economic Adjustment of Recent Retirees to Adverse Wealth Shocks*, Michigan Retirement Research Center, April 2004, available at http://deepblue.lib.umich.edu/bitstream/2027.42/50544/1/wp075.pdf (explaining the effects of "adverse wealth shocks" on older workers).

Numerous mutual fund companies currently offer products that provide guaranteed minimum retirement benefits.[154] These products generally allow investors to pay an additional fee in exchange for a guaranteed minimum investment return.[155] The fees vary depending on the age of the insured and the type of guarantee selected. Investors pay the extra fee for the guarantee in addition to the regular fund management fees that are charged.[156] Since introducing the basic product, mutual companies have added enhancements such as bonuses and special options.[157] The continued promotion and upgrade of these arrangements suggests that there is a demand for the product. Thus, many individuals are, in fact, willing to accept lower rates of return on their retirement investments in exchange for guaranteed minimums.[158]

Although guaranteed minimum benefits are currently available to individual participants in 401(k) plans if purchased independently in the private sector, as is the case with annuities discussed in the previous section, the premiums and fees associated with these products are likely to be significantly less if offered by the plan. This is because economies of scale should both lower the cost of the group rate for minimum guaranteed benefits and raise the rates of return on such products.[159] Furthermore, the additional cost of conducting research for such products by individual participants would be eliminated entirely.

CONCLUSION

Reliance on self-help measures does not go far enough in advancing the goal of retirement security in the private pension system. The availability of self-help measures such as the independent purchase of annuities, mutual funds, and investment guarantees in the private market furnishes no safety net for many individuals, who may fail to obtain protection through no fault of their own. They may be unaware of which products to purchase, where to go to purchase the products, or the benefits that such products provide. It is for this very reason that the private retirement system was established as a tax-subsidized, employment-based program. It also is for this reason that the program was designed to provide retirement security to individuals who may not choose to save as well as for those who may have difficulty achieving retirement security on their own.[160] Thus, to enable participants to make fully informed

---

154. Kaja Whitehouse, *Family Finance; Insurers Expand Annuity Products For 401(k) Plans*, Wall St. J., Mar. 16, 2005, at D2. *See* Jane Birnbaum, *An Alternative to Annuities for Retirees Seeking Income*, N.Y. Times, November 22, 2007, available at http://www.nytimes.com/2007/11/22/business/22retire.html?pagewanted=all.

155. *See* U.S. Securities and Exchange Commission, *Variable Annuities: What You Should Know*, http://www.sec.gov/investor/pubs/varannty.htm (last visited Sept. 25, 2011) (general description of variable annuities).

156. *Id.*

157. *See id.* (describing the bonus credit options offered by their company).

158. *Id.*

159. *See supra* notes 18–20 and accompanying text.

160. *See* Langbein et al., *supra* note 14, at 378–81 (describing the purpose of ERISA's discrimination rules).

investment decisions, all employers sponsoring participant-directed 401(k) plans should be required to provide financial education. Additionally, as a method of providing greater security to participants who desire more protection against the risk of accumulating insufficient retirement assets, employers sponsoring qualified 401(k) plans should also be required to offer life annuities and minimum guaranteed benefits as optional forms of payment.

Ensuring that workers have adequate retirement savings is beneficial not only to individual investors but also to employers. The removal of superannuated workers who have failed to amass sufficient assets for retirement presents a difficult dilemma for the employer. On the one hand, if the employer retains the workers out of compassion, productivity may suffer. On the other, if the employer dismisses the workers, the organization may suffer from morale problems associated with the termination of loyal and previously productive members of the community.[161] The employer-based private retirement system is designed to avoid both of these potential problems.[162] However, to the extent that workers fail to protect themselves adequately against the risk of benefit losses in 401(k) plans because they are either unlucky or make mistakes in the management of their pension portfolios, these problems will re-emerge.

Requiring the employer to provide investment education and optional forms of the retirement benefit provide protection against unexpected longevity, leakage, and market fluctuations. These measures accordingly address numerous concerns regarding the existing private pension system and the role of 401(k) plans. Furthermore, the proposals in this chapter significantly increase retirement security without eliminating participant choice or unduly burdening plan sponsors. Equally important, each of the measures requires employers that sponsor 401(k) plans to assume responsibility to provide some level of protection against plan losses as a trade-off for the tax benefits they receive by maintaining qualified retirement savings arrangements.

---

161. *See* Douglas A. Wolf and Frank Levy, *Pension Vesting, and the Distribution of Job Tenures,* in H. J. Aaron and G. Burtless, eds., *Retirement and Economic Behavior* (Brookings Institution, 1984), 23, 27 (discussing employer motivations for maintaining pension plans).
    162. *See id.*

10

EIGHTEENTH-CENTURY MORAL SENTIMENTS IN DEFENSE OF THE TWENTY-FIRST CENTURY ESTATE TAX: WHAT ADAM SMITH AND JANE AUSTEN CAN TEACH US

Mary Louise Fellows, University of Minnesota Law School

> ""*The rich man is able better to fulfil his desire, and also to endure a great calamity if it fall upon him; whereas the other [a poor man] has these advantages over him: — he is not indeed able equally with the rich man to endure a calamity or to fulfil his desire, but these his good fortune keeps away from him, while he is sound of limb, free from disease, untouched by suffering, the father of fair children and handsome himself. If in addition to this he shall end his life well, he is worthy to be called that which you seekest, namely a happy man; but before he comes to his end it is well to hold back and not to call him happy yet but only fortunate.*"
>
> " . . . . *[N]o single person is complete in himself, for one thing he has and another he lacks; but whosoever of men continues to the end in possession of the greatest number of these things and then dies with grace, he is by me accounted worthy, O king, to receive this name. But we must for every thing examine the end and how it will turn out at the last, for to many god shows but a glimpse of happiness and then plucks them up by the roots and overturns them.*"[1]"

The federal government enacted the modern estate tax in 1916.[2] Over the years since, Congress has sought to prevent avoidance of the estate tax by expanding the types of transfers of wealth subject to tax. In 1932, it enacted a gift tax, and

1. Herodotus provides us the famous story of the encounter between the last Lydian king, Croesus, reckoned as one of the richest men in the world, and the Athenian statesman and poet Solon (circa 6th century B.C.E.). The epigraph contains a portion of Solon's response to Croesus's angry reaction to Solon's failure to name Croesus as the happiest man in the world. Herodotus, *The Histories* (G.C. Macaulay, trans., Donald Lateiner, rev., 1890; Barnes & Noble Classics, 2004), 12–13.

2. Revenue Act of 1916, ch. 463, §§200–212, 39 Stat. 765, 777–80. The federal government had enacted an estate tax three previous times to provide a source of revenue on a short-term basis

in 1976, it enacted a generation-skipping transfer (GST) tax.[3] Wealth transfer taxes have undergone major changes since their initial inception, but not until 2001 did Congress seriously consider their repeal.[4] At that time, Congress provided for a ten-year phaseout of the estate and GST taxes, their repeal in 2010, and their reinstatement in 2011. They further provided that, upon reinstatement, the wealth transfer tax rules in effect prior to the enactment of the 2001 Act would apply.[5] A compromise occurred in late 2010 that temporarily reinstated the estate and GST taxes through 2012. It provides for far more generous exemptions and substantially lower rates than those that were in effect prior to the 2001 Act.[6] The continuing controversy surrounding the federal transfer tax system animates reexamination of it. Many scholars and policy makers have analyzed the costs and benefits of federal wealth transfer taxes.[7] This chapter distinctively demonstrates the costs of unchecked inheritance by relying primarily on the discussion of wealth by the late eighteenth-century political theorist, Adam Smith, and the humanist and novelist of the same era, Jane Austen.

Smith and Austen would seem, at first glance, to have little in common with each other and little to teach us about wealth transfer taxes. Smith, renowned today primarily for his commitment to the free market, and Austen, known more for her attention to manners and decorum and less for her political and economic commentary, in fact, provide excellent instruction about the potential wealth transfer taxes have to address the tensions between market and nonmarket sentiments. Smith makes clear in his *Theory of Moral Sentiments* (*TMS*) that pursuit and retention of wealth are part, but not the whole, of what society should judge as virtuous conduct.[8] An analysis of *Pride and Prejudice* (*PP*) shows the relationship of this novel to Smith's concerns.[9] Through her consideration of the marriage market at the turn of the

---

to support its wars. Act of July 6, 1797, ch. 11, §1, 1 Stat. 527, 527 (raising money for the Navy during the period of tension with France); Act of July 1, 1862, ch. 119, §94, 12 Stat. 432, 475 (supporting the Civil War); Act of June 13, 1898, ch. 448, §§29–30, 30 Stat. 448, 464–66 (supporting the Spanish-American War); Staff of J. Comm. on Taxation, 107th Cong., *Description and Analysis of Present Law and Proposals Relating to Federal Estate and Gift Taxation* (Comm. Print 2001), 11–12.

3. Tax Reform Act of 1976, Pub. L. No. 94-455, §§2001–2010, 90 Stat. 1520, 1846–97.

4. Major legislation affecting the federal transfer tax law occurred in 1948, 1976, 1981 and 1986. *See* Revenue Act of 1948, ch. 168, §§351–66, 62 Stat. 110, 116–25; Tax Reform Act of 1976, Pub. L. No. 94-455, §§2001–2010, 90 Stat. 1520, 1846–97; Economic Recovery Tax Act of 1981, Pub. L. No. 97-34, §§401–29, 95 Stat. 172, 299–319; Tax Reform Act of 1986, Pub. L. No. 99-514, §§1401–1433, 100 Stat. 2085, 2711–32 (1986).

5. *See* Economic Growth and Tax Relief Reconciliation Act of 2001, Pub. L. No. 107-16, §§501–73, 115 Stat. 38, 69–94 (codified as amended in scattered sections of I.R.C.). The gift tax remained in place. In 2010, the gift tax was subject to a maximum rate of 35 percent and enjoyed a unified credit equivalent amount of $1 million. For a description of the phaseout, repeal, and return of the estate and GST taxes under the 2001 Act, *see* Karen C. Burke and Grayson M. P. McCouch, *Estate Tax Repeal: Through the Looking Glass*, 22 Va. Tax Rev. 187, 188–89 (2002).

6. Tax Relief, Unemployment Insurance Reauthorization, and Job Creation Act of 2010, Pub. L. No. 111-312, §302, 124 Stat. 3296, 3301–02 (2010) (codified at I.R.C. §§2001, 2010, 2502, 2505, 2511).

7. *See, e.g.*, Henry J. Aaron and Alicia H. Munnell, *Reassessing the Role of Transfer Taxes*, 45 Nat'l Tax J. 119–44 (1992); William G. Gale et al., *Rethinking Estate and Gift Taxation* (Brookings Institution, 2001).

8. Adam Smith, *The Theory of Moral Sentiments* (1759; Oxford University, 1976), 212–17.

9. Jane Austen, *Pride and Prejudice* (1813; Oxford University, 1990). All page number references to *PP* in the text and footnotes refer to this edition of her novel.

nineteenth century in England, Austen rejects an ethos that places the retention and further accumulation of wealth above all other moral sentiments, and she also objects to habits that ignore financial prudence. The parallels between *PP*'s marriage market and the U.S. wealth transfer tax regime suggest the need to dislodge the conventional economic arguments offered by opponents and proponents of wealth transfer taxes. It further suggests that Congress should repeal the current transfer tax system and introduce a new tax explicitly designed to address the tension between market and nonmarket sentiments.

The terminology used throughout the remainder of this chapter deserves explanation. The opponents of the federal wealth transfer tax regime prefer to refer to it as the *death tax* for two reasons. First, the label "death tax" emphasizes the seeming harshness of a government that would impose a tax at a time when friends and family are grieving a person's death. Second, it obscures the fact that the tax is an assessment on the lifetime accumulation of significant wealth.[10] The epigraph provides alternative, and for purposes of this analysis, illuminating grounds for a reconsideration of the sobriquet "death tax." It is an excerpt of the response Solon, the renowned Athenian statesman and poet, gave to Croesus, the last Lydian king, known widely for his exceptional wealth. To Solon, death serves as a fulcrum in which survivors look back to judge a deceased person at the same time that they incorporate the lessons learned from that deceased person into their own lives. "Death tax," as a popular term, rather than obscuring a tax on significant wealth, can emphasize that a life well-lived encompasses more than the accumulation of wealth. As Solon advises Croesus, wealth does not determine happiness, and any judgment concerning happiness must be delayed until death. This chapter embraces the label "death tax" throughout the following analysis, because it shows how and why taxation at death reflects the social and cultural ideals embodied in Solon's response to Croesus.[11]

The first of the following sections describes the major arguments that scholars and policy makers put forward in opposition to and in defense of the current death tax system. It shows that both sides make heavy use of economic theories, econometric models, and empirical studies of economic conduct to argue their cases. It concludes that within the current political environment where wealth maximization has talismanic dimensions, so long as the opponents to the death tax plausibly can argue that the tax may

---

10. *See* Michael J. Graetz and Ian Shapiro, *Death by a Thousand Cuts: The Fight over Taxing Inherited Wealth* (Princeton University, 2005), 76–78.

11. Notwithstanding that the federal transfer tax system includes a gift tax, a GST tax, and an estate tax, this chapter uses the term "death tax" to refer to the taxing regime. Congress enacted the gift tax and GST tax to prevent easy avoidance of the estate tax; therefore, the justification for these other two taxes rests primarily on the justification of the tax assessed at the death of a wealth holder. *See* Joseph M. Dodge, *Beyond Estate and Gift Tax Reform: Including Gifts and Bequests in Income*, 91 Harv. L. Rev. 1177, 1188 (1978). Congress, in fact, decided to retain the gift tax even after repeal of the other two taxes to protect the progressivity of the income tax against tax-free assignment of income through wealth transfers. That rationale has only tangential relevance to the force and reasoning in this chapter. For criticism of Congress's decision to retain the gift tax and alternative responses to the income tax concerns leading to its retention, *see* Task Force on Federal Wealth Transfer Taxes, *Report on Reform of Federal Wealth Transfer Taxes* (2004), 21–28 [hereinafter Task Force].

produce inefficiencies and interfere with economic growth, their arguments have political salience.

The next section relies on the writings of Adam Smith and Jane Austen to argue that pursuit and retention of wealth are part, but not the whole, of what society should judge as virtuous conduct. In *TMS*, Adam Smith demands that we make a distinction between self-interest and selfishness and prescribes conduct motivated by a complex web of moral sentiments. The possibility of a death tax that addresses the tension between market and nonmarket sentiments emerges out of *PP*, which reveals Austen's own ambivalence and anxiety about a commercial culture engrossed in the desire for wealth. The writings of Robin West, a long-time leader in the law and literature movement, also inform this discussion. She provides a framework for a discussion of *TMS* and *PP*. West characterizes *economic man* as a "Herculean rationalist" but an "empathic weakling" and *literary woman* as "multimotivational" with "virtually infinite empathic potential."[12] Part II uses this classification scheme to show how Smith and Austen advocate for a social being that reflects the strengths of both economic man and literary woman.

The subsequent section recognizes that Smith and Austen stress voluntary compliance based on collective social controls as opposed to governmental intervention. It examines whether government, through some form of a death tax, can or should have a role in instilling justice, beneficence, and prudence into civil society. It concludes that, given the current emphasis on market sentiments and the absence of sustained consideration of nonmarket sentiments, U.S. society needs a death tax in some form. It then considers alternative death tax regimes that have the potential to achieve the equivalent of Austen's experiment that melds economic man and literary woman.

The Conclusion places the death tax within the context of other testamentary restrictions—most notably, statutory spousal protections and the common law rule against perpetuities (RAP). The Conclusion relies on the Solon–Croesus legend, Smith's ideal virtuous social being, and *PP*'s marriage market in Hertfordshire to demonstrate how much each has to teach about our building a strong civil society.

THE DEATH TAX DEBATE

Congress's Joint Economic Committee's study of the death tax in 2006 paradigmatically demonstrates the prevalence of economic arguments in opposition to the death tax.[13] As it focuses almost exclusively on the death tax's economic impact, the study emphasizes five of the tax's negative effects. According to the study, the death tax "inhibits capital accumulation and

---

12. Robin West, *Economic Man and Literary Woman: One Contrast*, 39 Mercer L. Rev. 867, 871–72 (1988).

13. Joint Economic Committee, 109th Congress, *Costs and Consequences of the Federal Estate Tax: A Joint Economic Committee Study* (2006). There are, of course, many expositions of why Congress should repeal the death tax. For example, Edward J. McCaffery opposes it within a broader argument favoring a consumption tax. Edward J. McCaffery, *Fair Not Flat: How to Make the Tax System Better and Simpler* (University of Chicago, 2002), 62–77.

economic growth; threatens the survival of family businesses and depresses entrepreneurial activity; hinders income and wealth mobility; violates the principles of good tax policy, such as simplicity and fairness; and adversely impacts the conservation of environmentally sensitive land."[14] The study's thesis is unmistakable: the death tax, which the Committee estimates at that time to "cost the economy roughly $850 billion in capital stock," interferes with and distorts economic growth.[15] To the extent that the study shows particular concern for small family businesses, social mobility, racial justice, and tax equity, its arguments remain economically based. For example, on the issues of social mobility and racial justice, the study emphasizes entrepreneurship and specifically how the death tax interferes with the creation and perpetuation of family-owned businesses.[16] Even when it discusses the "inappropriate" timing of the tax —"the death of a loved one"—the study returns to market considerations. "As if mourning [the loss of a loved one] were not enough, the federal government worsens the pain by seeking to confiscate up to one-half of all the decedent's savings, very often accumulated through hard work, frugality, deferred consumption and entrepreneurship."[17]

The proponents of the death tax also largely have embraced an economic analysis as they affirm the tax's benefits and respond to challenges to it. In recent and not so recent years they have justified the tax with arguments that it encourages charitable giving, provides needed revenue to the government, adds progressivity to the federal tax system, and prevents wealth concentration.[18] The charitable-giving argument relies on the fact that the current income and death taxes create substantial economic incentives for taxpayers to make gifts to charitable organizations. The proponents of the tax argue that

---

14. Joint Economic Committee, *supra* note 13, at 16.

15. *Id.* at 28.

16. *Id.* at 22–25. The study's argument about the detrimental effects of the death tax on the environment moves beyond the preservation and growth of capital. It argues that the substantial tax liability imposed on real estate leads to development of land that the owners otherwise would have preserved for natural habitats for fauna and flora. In order to raise the funds necessary to pay death taxes, landowners break up large, environmentally beneficial parcels and either sell or otherwise use the smaller acreages for more profitable enterprises. *Id.* at 26–27. It refers to other analyses that show that "approximately 2.6 million acres of forest land must be harvested each year to pay for the estate tax" and that "another 1.3 million acres must be sold to raise funds to pay estate taxes, of which close to one-third (29 percent) is either developed or converted to other uses." *Id.* at 27. The inclusion of this argument undoubtedly helps to broaden the coalition of groups interested in death tax repeal. By gaining the support of groups, such as environmentalists, who generally have not been associated with efforts to repeal the death tax, the opponents strengthen their own appeal and politically weaken proponents of the death tax. *See* Graetz and Shapiro, *supra* note 10, at 15–16 (describing how Frank Blethen, owner and publisher of the *Seattle Times*, had been the first to see "the value of involving minorities, gays, environmentalists and other unlikely groups in the repeal campaign"); *see also id.* at 50 (describing a Heritage Foundation analyst's use of a story about a family in Florida whose sale of 12,000 of their 17,000 "acres to pay estate taxes threatened the habitat of the Florida panther, an endangered species"). Notably, the study does not explore alternative responses to social concerns about the loss of forest land other than repeal of the death tax. *See* Joint Economic Committee, *supra* note 13, at 27–28 (discussing the estate tax relief currently available for conservation easements).

17. Joint Economic Committee, *supra* note 13, at 29.

18. *See, e.g.,* Charles Davenport and Jay A. Soled, *Enlivening the Death-Tax Death-Talk*, 84 Tax Notes 591 (1999); William G. Gale and Joel B. Slemrod, *Policy Watch: Death Watch for the Estate Tax?*, 15 J. Econ. Persp. 205 (2001); Michael J. Graetz, *To Praise the Estate Tax, Not to Bury It*, 93 Yale L.J. 259 (1983); Glendell Jones Jr. *Repeal the Estate Tax Bad Move: The Transfer Tax System Paradigm*, 89 Tax Notes 793 (2000).

charitable giving will decline if contributions do not result in tax savings.[19] The revenue-raising argument recognizes that large budget deficits and the increased need for both discretionary and nondiscretionary governmental expenditures make the revenue generated by the death tax, more than $25 billion a year, important, notwithstanding that it is a small percentage of the total revenue raised by the federal government.[20] Regarding the progressivity argument, proponents provide evidence that it applies to those who have substantial accumulations of wealth.[21] Finally, proponents raise concerns about the social harms created by wealth concentration.[22]

Two of these justifications rely on many of the same economic assumptions that influence the tax's opponents. The charitable-giving argument embraces private market theory when it focuses on the reduction of out-of-pocket costs to individual taxpayers who make charitable gifts. Notwithstanding the opponents' commitment to private markets and economic incentives, they counter concerns that repeal of the death tax will lead to a reduction of contributions to charities with studies that show little or no impact of the tax on charitable giving. They also argue that the repeal will provide greater resources to allocate between heirs and charities. In other words, they claim that the increase in after-tax wealth will override any increase in the after-tax price of the donor's making a charitable gift.[23] Charges and countercharges supported by microeconomic analyses ultimately have raised doubts about the proponents' claims and have allowed opponents to minimize the potential costs of repeal.

Those same debate dynamics operate in consideration of the revenue-raising aspect of the tax. The death tax opponents rely on economic theories and models to argue that the tax reduces income tax revenues to the federal government because it discourages asset accumulation. They also argue that income tax reform providing for the taxation of appreciation, which otherwise escapes taxation under the current tax law, would accompany repeal of the death tax and limit any loss in tax revenue.[24] Again, merely by raising doubts about the tax proponents' concerns about revenue losses generated by repeal

---

19. *See* Gerald E. Auten et al., *Taxes and Philanthropy Among the Wealthy*, in Joel B. Slemrod, ed., *Does Atlas Shrug? The Economic Consequences of Taxing the Rich* (Harvard University, 2000), 392, 418 (after evaluating all federal taxes, concluding that tax deductions for charitable contributions do not cause people to make contributions, but "induce people to give more than they would have otherwise"); Jon M. Bakija et al., *Charitable Bequests and Taxes on Inheritances and Estates: Aggregate Evidence from Across States and Time*, 93 Am. Econ. Rev. 366, 369 (2003) (using estate tax return data for most of the twentieth century, estimating "a decline in charitable bequests" in response to repeal of the death tax).

20. *See* J. Richard Aronson and Vincent G. Munley, *Wealth-Transfer Taxes in U.S. Fiscal Federalism: A Levy Still in Need of Reform*, 31 Publius: J. of Federalism 151, 158–60 (2001) (setting forth federal transfer tax revenues between 1936 and 1999). *See also* Mark L. Ascher, *Curtailing Inherited Wealth*, 89 Mich. L. Rev. 69, 76 (1990) (looking to the growing federal deficit as a significant justification for the government's enacting a taxing regime that severely curtails inheritance).

21. *See* Graetz, *supra* note 16, at 272–73.

22. *See* James R. Repetti, *Democracy, Taxes, and Wealth*, 76 N.Y.U. L. Rev. 825, 849 (2001); Dennis J. Ventry Jr., *Straight Talk About the "Death" Tax: Politics, Economics, and Morality*, 89 Tax Notes 1159, 1166–68 (2000).

23. Joint Economic Committee, *supra* note 13, at 8-12.

24. *Id.* at 12-16. Under the current death tax system, I.R.C. §1014 generally provides that property included in a decedent's gross estate for estate tax purposes enjoys a step-up in basis. The effect of this provision is that unrealized appreciation on property owned by the decedent at death escapes income taxation. The current legislation providing for death tax repeal includes only

of the death tax, the opponents have found recent political success. Economic-centered arguments by death tax proponents just have not succeeded, no matter how well-conceived and supported.

The progressivity and wealth concentration arguments seem to go beyond conventional economic analysis and embrace moral sentiments of equity, fairness, and community responsibility. The proponents of the death tax nevertheless supplement these arguments with economic analysis. They do so in an effort to counter their opponents' charges that a death tax leads to excessive consumption, at the same time that it discourages the highly desirable behavior of work and thrift. They also address the opponents' allegations that inheritance does not contribute significantly to wealth inequality and, in any case, that inequality persists notwithstanding governmental efforts, such as the death tax, to rectify it.[25] Moreover, some proponents of the tax even use economic analysis to make their case about social harms. For example, James R. Repetti explains how "wealth concentration correlates with *poor economic growth* in the long run because of educational disadvantages for the poor and because of sociopolitical malaise generated by disparities in wealth."[26] He expands the argument to encompass the disproportionate political influence of the wealthy.[27] This aspect of the argument also is tinged with economic concerns, of course, because it outlines how local, state, and federal officials favor businesses interested in maximization of profits.

Both sides engaged in the debate about death taxes start from the basic assumption that the government must minimize interference with private markets and economic growth. As a consequence, any doubt about the adverse impact of the death tax on economic incentives inevitably gets resolved in favor of repeal.[28] When the proponents and opponents arm themselves for battle with economic theories, econometric models, and empirical studies of economic conduct, they end up describing a capitalist democracy populated exclusively by wealth-maximizing robots. Michael J. Graetz and Ian Shapiro's book *Death by a Thousand Cuts: The Fight over Taxing Inherited Wealth*, which analyzes the politics behind the thirty-year effort to repeal the death tax, demonstrates the extent to which the death tax debate has degenerated.[29]

---

a limited step-up in basis rule, thus exposing appreciation that occurred in the hands of the decedent to taxation in the hands of the decedent's heirs if and when they decide to sell the property. *See* I.R.C. §1022.

25. *Costs and Consequences of the Federal Estate Tax: A Joint Economic Committee Study* sets forth the economic arguments to counter the claim that the death tax reduces income and wealth inequality. Joint Economic Committee, *supra* note 13, at 4–8. For examples of death tax proponents' responses to these concerns, *see* Davenport and Soled, *supra* note 18, at 602–09; Gale and Slemrod, *supra* note 18, at 210–12; Graetz, *supra* note 18, at 278–83.

26. Repetti, *supra* note 22, at 849 (emphasis added).

27. *Id.* at 841–50.

28. *Contra* Ascher, *supra* note 20 (arguing for a limited right to inheritance based on the United States' commitment to equality of opportunity, although bolstering his arguments with concerns about the growing federal deficit). An exceptionally fine collection of conference papers edited by William G. Gale, James R. Hines Jr., and Joel Slemrod provides an excellent example of the futility of a debate centered on economics. *See* Gale et al., *supra* note 7. It presents sophisticated analyses challenging the economic arguments against the death tax. Nevertheless, the collection has failed to change the debate in any fundamental way. *See* Graetz and Shapiro, *supra* note 10, at 226.

29. Graetz and Shapiro, *supra* note 10.

They document the personal stories told by opponents of the death tax that portray "model citizens who fulfilled the American Dream through their efforts and ingenuity."[30] Graetz and Shapiro argue that with the stories of these people "the repealers had the fairness angle covered. They had gained the high moral ground."[31] What we should not overlook, however, is that the "repealers" gain "the high moral ground," through their portrayals of wealth-maximizing robots, which rely on a body politic eager to equate virtue with preservation of private wealth. It surely makes sense to consider economic arguments in discussions of a tax on wealth. The more pertinent question is whether it makes sense for our political leaders to treat economic arguments as determinative of good tax policy. The rest of this chapter makes a case for why we should answer that question with a resounding no.

THE TENSION BETWEEN MARKET AND NONMARKET SENTIMENTS

ADAM SMITH'S VIRTUOUS SOCIAL BEING

With ironic satisfaction, I look to Adam Smith, a twenty-first-century icon of free and unregulated markets, to challenge the anemic economic debate surrounding the death tax.[32] In his famous collection of lectures published familiarly under the title *Wealth of Nations* (*WN*), he sets forth his economic theory and uses the now oft-repeated phrase—"the invisible hand."[33] The term has come to refer to a dynamic market in which individual actors pursuing their own self interests benefit the entire community. In *WN*, Smith also specifically, but unpersuasively, criticizes taxation of wealth transfers.

> All taxes upon the transference of property of every kind, so far as they diminish the capital value of that property, tend to diminish the funds destined for the maintenance of productive labour. They are all more or less unthrifty taxes that increase the revenue of the sovereign, which seldom maintains any but unproductive labourers; at the expence of the capital of the people, which maintains none but productive.[34]

Even death tax opponents must recognize the flaw in his reasoning. At the least, his attack on a death tax fails if the government uses the tax revenue to reduce national debt or other taxes.[35]

---

30. *Id.* at 229.
31. *Id.*
32. Sagit Leviner's approach to taxation complements the approach I am advocating. She embraces a "community-oriented" view of society in her analysis of the tax system. Her conclusion, relying on John Rawls, John Stuart Mill, and Robert Nozick, advocates taxation of wealth at death. *From Deontology to Practical Application: The Vision of a Good Society and the Tax System*, 26 Va. Tax Rev. 405, 442–45 (2006).
33. 1 Adam Smith, *An Inquiry into the Nature and Causes of the Wealth of Nations* (1776; Oxford University, 1976), 456.
34. 2 *Id.* at 862 (editorial note and footnote omitted).
35. *See* Graetz, *supra* note 18, at 282–83.

Of more concern is how subsequent generations of free market advocates have distorted Smith's invisible hand principle by equating self-interest with selfishness.[36] The error comes in part by their general failure to consider Smith's *TMS*, which sets forth his moral philosophy.[37] They ignore that Smith used his famous metaphor (invisible hand) in *TMS* when discussing the distribution of the means for everyone to achieve happiness.

> [The rich] are led by an *invisible hand* to make nearly the same distribution of the necessaries of life, which would have been made had the earth been divided into equal portions among all its inhabitants, and thus without intending it, without knowing it, advance the interest of the society, and afford means to the multiplication of the species. . . . In what constitutes the real happiness of human life, they [the poor] are in no respect inferior to those who would seem so much above them.[38]

In *WN* Smith refers to the invisible hand to describe wealth maximization, whereas in *TMS* he refers to wealth distribution. In both instances, Smith's central concern is to promote the interest of society.

Free marketers also ignore Smith's antipathy toward undue wealth and the admiration of it.

> We frequently see the respectful attentions of the world more strongly directed towards the rich and the great, than towards the wise and the virtuous. We see frequently the vices and the follies of the powerful much less despised than the poverty and weakness of the innocent. To deserve, to acquire, and to enjoy the respect and admiration of mankind, are the great objects of ambition and emulation. Two different roads are presented to us, equally leading to the attainment of this so much desired object; the one, by the study of wisdom and the practice of virtue; the other, by the acquisition of wealth and greatness. Two different characters are presented to our emulation; the one, of proud ambition and ostentatious avidity; the other, of humble modesty and equitable justice.[39]

His antagonism toward avarice obviously tempers his commitment to commercial expansion.

For the chase for wealth to remain virtuous within Smith's private market theory, market actors have to be more than economic automatons. They have

---

36. *See* D. D. Raphael and A. L. Macfie, *Introduction* in Smith, *supra* note 8, at 8, 20–22.

37. Smith, *supra* note 8. Attempts to dismiss *TMS* as unrepresentative of his more mature views found in *WN* fail as a matter of both chronological record and related content. *See* Raphael and Macfie, *supra* note 36, at 20–25. *See also* Emma Rothschild, *Economic Sentiments: Adam Smith, Condorcet, and the Enlightenment* (Harvard University, 2001), 116–56 (providing the intellectual history of the term invisible hand, demonstrating Smith's ironic usage of the term and explaining why twentieth-century commentators have overestimated it). For a recent analysis of the federal tax system that focuses primarily on *WN*, while acknowledging *TMS*, *see* Beverly Moran, *Adam Smith and the Search for an Ideal Tax System*, in Isaac William Martin et al., eds., *The New Fiscal Sociology: Taxation in Comparative and Historical Perspective* (University of California, 2009), 210–15.

38. Smith, *supra* note 8, at 184–85 (emphasis added). *See also id.* at 184 n.7 (discussing Smith's use of "invisible hand" throughout his writings).

39. *Id.* at 62. *See generally* Herbert Gintis et al., *Moral Sentiments and Material Interests: The Foundations of Cooperation in Economic Life* (MIT, 2005) (with *WN* and *TMS* as a starting point, using transdisciplinary research to challenge economic models relying on the "self-regarding human actor" with evidence of "non-self-regarding motives" (8) and to indicate the importance of this research to social policy).

to take account of social connections, which require that a person act according to the dictates of prudence, justice, and beneficence.

> In our approbation of the character of the prudent man, we feel, with peculiar complacency, the security which he must enjoy while he walks under the safeguard of that sedate and deliberate virtue. In our approbation of the character of the just man, we feel, with equal complacency, the security which all those connected with him, whether in neighbourhood, society, or business, must derive from his scrupulous anxiety never either to hurt or offend. In our approbation of the character of the beneficent man, we enter into the gratitude of all those who are within the sphere of his good offices, and conceive with them the highest sense of his merit. In our approbation of all those virtues, our sense of their agreeable effects, of their utility, either to the person who exercises them, or to some other persons, joins with our sense of their propriety, and constitutes always a considerable, frequently the greater part of that approbation.[40]

A fair reading of both *WN* and *TMS* together demands that Smith's adherents distinguish self-interest from selfishness. They must recognize that Smith's theory of social behavior depends upon self-interest and also *sympathy*, meaning "our fellow-feeling with any passion whatever."[41] Pursuit and retention of wealth are part, but not the whole, of what society should judge as virtuous conduct.

Smith's repulsion toward the materialistic society, which the growth of commerce in the late eighteenth century engendered, should force a reevaluation of the current death tax debate. Through a robust description of a social being motivated by a complex web of moral sentiments, *TMS* undermines the rhetorical power wielded by death tax opponents when they raise concerns about interference with economic growth. Robin West's taxonomy captures the parody of *WN* and also the force of *TMS*. She distinguishes the *economic man*, which emerges out of the law and economics movement and the *literary woman*, which she posits as the ideal for the law and literature movement.[42]

---

40. *Id.* at 264. Smith goes on to talk about self-command, which he divides into control of the passions of fear, anger, and other similar feelings and control of the "love of ease, of pleasure, of applause and of many other selfish gratifications." *Id.* at 238. For further discussion of Smith's views on the relationship of individual action with the community, *see* Keigo Tajima, *The Theory of Institutions and Collective Action in Adam Smith's* Theory of Moral Sentiments, 36 J. Socio-Econ. 578, 582 (2007) (showing that the "significance of *TMS* lies in Smith's conviction that human behavior in general, and selfish behavior in particular, should be subject to rules and norms of conduct so that some kind of social order may be established").

41. Smith, *supra* note 8, at 10. The principle of sympathy contradicts many economists who reject interpersonal comparisons. *See* Ralph Anspach, *The Implications of the* Theory of Moral Sentiments *for Adam Smith's Economic Thought*, 4 Hist. Pol. Econ. 176, 203 (1972). Sympathy has a central function in Smith's norms of conduct, which includes the emergence of the *spectator* ["what he himself would feel if he was reduced to the same unhappy situation" (Smith, *supra*, at 12)]. For further discussion of these aspects of Smith's moral theory, *see* Anspach, *supra*, at 183–88; Tajima, *supra* note 40, at 582–84.

42. West, *supra* note 12, at 867–68. West explains her decision to distinguish the two models based on gender.

> In the interest of rough justice, I use the word "woman" to include men as well as women, "she" to include the male pronoun, and "womankind" to include mankind. In the interest of accuracy, women's moral voice seems to be distinctively tied to the moral value of empathy I discuss in this paper, and the literary method of narrative.

West focuses on two significant attributes of the economic man, whom economists place at the center of their analytical work.

> First, economic man is an infallible "rational maximizer of his own utility." This attribute subdivides into two subparts, one "cognitive" and the other "motivational": economic man invariably knows what is best for himself, and he inevitably is motivated to seek it . . . . Thus, he relentlessly chooses what he prefers, prefers what he wants, wants what he desires, and desires what will maximize his subjective well-being. He is perfectly rational.

> The second distinguishing attribute of economic man is what I call his "empathic impotence." Although economic man is perfectly rational with respect to knowledge of his own subjective well-being, he is at the same time utterly incapable of empathic knowledge regarding the subjective well-being of others.[43]

She contrasts the hyper-rational and nonempathic stick figure of the law and economics movement to the literary woman.

> [T]he literary woman, emerging from our literary analysis of law is no Herculean rationalist. Her character is multimotivational, which is why it is worth exploring, and she does not know herself—her own subjectivity—as well as she might. She is sufficiently complex so that as a character, she is worth portraying, and as a reader, she is worthy of dialogue, she is educable. . . .

> Literary woman . . . , unlike economic man, may not be a Herculean rationalist, but nor is she an empathic weakling: she is fully able to make intersubjective comparisons of utility. Empathic ability is the very competence that is assumed—that *must* be assumed—by both writer and reader if narrative communication is to be meaningful. Indeed, the idealized literary person posited by literary legal theorists is distinctively capable in just this way—the literary person has a virtually infinite empathic potential.[44]

West's emphasis on empathy remarkably parallels the parts of *TMS* in which Smith concentrates on issues of intersubjectivity.[45] Literary woman's empathic competence connects her directly to *TMS*, because that very competence produces her "moral promise" as a model social actor.[46] West's uneasiness about the unrelenting influence of the efficient market place closely maps Smith's moral philosophy and apprehension about a singular focus on materialism. As the subsequent discussion of *PP* demonstrates, West's categories of

---

Id. at 867 n.2, *citing* Carol Gilligan, *In a Different Voice* (Harvard University, 1982); Sherry, *Civic Virtue and the Feminine Voice in Constitutional Adjudication*, 72 Va. L. Rev. 543 (1986).

43. West, *supra* note 12, at 868 69 (footnotes omitted).

44. *Id.* at 871–72.

45. Smith did not write in terms of *empathy*. Instead, he used the term *sympathy*, which carries a connotation of pity and sorrowfulness that is absent from empathy and has more to do with vicarious feeling. *See Webster's Third New International Dictionary of the English Language* (Merriam-Webster, 1961), 2317 (describing the distinction between the two terms and authoritative use of the two terms). For purposes of this discussion, the distinction between the two terms is not nearly as important as the fact that both Smith and West urge individuals to use their imaginations to place themselves in another person's circumstances and not to focus exclusively on the promotion of their own self-interest.

46. West, *supra* note 12, at 872.

economic man and literary woman correlate with Austen's characters and provide a useful analytical tool to explore Austen's own anxiety about hypermaterialism.

JANE AUSTEN'S VIRTUOUS SOCIAL BEING

The novels of Jane Austen reinforce the analytical work of Smith. The chronological proximity of Austen's writings to Smith's own work and other publications raising concerns about society's excessive attention to wealth supports a reading of her novels as reflecting an ambivalence toward and a suspicion about a commercial culture engrossed in the desire for wealth.[47] *PP* shows the dangers of both avarice and economic imprudence and imagines the potential benefits that could emerge when wisdom and virtue modulate wealth-maximization.[48] Austen's preference for complexities also introduces an alternative mode of reasoning about, as well as an alternative perspective on, inheritance and the taxation of it.[49] By tracking the operation of the Hert-fordshire marriage market, the reader has many opportunities to observe clashes between West's economic men and literary women. The characters who treat marriage as primarily a financial arrangement and shun concerns about love and compatibility (economic men) have great difficulty understanding and even negotiating with those seeking emotional attachment and self-fulfillment through marriage (literary women). Within these contentious encounters, the novel provides us crucial insights about what is at stake in the death tax debate. It helps to explain why the opponents of the tax demand repeal and refuse to leave it in place, even with high exclusions and low rates. It also suggests how the proponents of the tax could provide a vision of a civil society that requires prudence, justice, and beneficence to temper the desire for wealth.

The novel opens at the Bennets' home in Hertfordshire with the narrator setting the novel's theme in its first two sentences.

> It is a truth universally acknowledged, that a single man in possession of a good fortune, must be in want of a wife.

> However little known the feelings or views of such a man may be on his first entering a neighbourhood, this truth is so well fixed in the minds of the surrounding families, that he is considered as the rightful property of someone or other of their daughters (page 1).

---

47. *See* Elsie B. Michie, *Austen's Powers: Engaging with Adam Smith in Debates About Wealth and Virtue*, 34 Novel: A Forum on Fiction, Autumn 2000, at 5, 5 n.1.

48. Austen began *PP* in October 1796 under the original title of *First Impressions*. About a year later, her father offered it for publication, but the publishing house rejected it. She revised it after her successful publication of *Sense and Sensibility* (1811), retitled it *Pride and Prejudice*, and saw it published in 1813. In the interim, she had written *Northanger Abbey* and probably had started *Mansfield Park*, which she had published in 1814. *See* Paul Poplawski, *A Jane Austen Encyclopedia* (Greenwood, 1998), 10–18.

49. In her study of Austen's fiction in relation to other novelists writing around the same time, Mary Waldron concludes that Austen demonstrated "that the novel form was capable of containing more uncertainties and unanswered questions than had before been thought, and that it could still identify issues of principle without dealing in extremes of 'guilt and misery.'" Mary Waldron, *Jane Austen and the Fiction of Her Time* (Cambridge University, 1999), 14.

By tethering marriage to property and property to the neighborhood, this community at the turn of the nineteenth century has embraced acquisitiveness as a moral virtue and subverted, and perhaps even spurned, wisdom and the practices of beneficence.[50] Within this circumscribed society, property and marriage work in concert to bring respectability to families. For Austen, the setting permits examination of economic rationality, empathy, passion, and community responsibility. Her complex portrayal of the neighborhood and its inhabitants enables her to display (1) the defects of character in those who place wealth and the acquisition of wealth above other values, (2) the recklessness of those who overestimate romantic love and passion and underestimate financial security and family responsibility, and (3) the rewards that accrue to those who learn to temper acquisitiveness with emotional connectedness and to limit impetuousness and self-indulgence with economic prudence.

The encounter of Mrs. Bennet and Mr. Collins on one side and her husband and daughter Elizabeth on the other encapsulates the various moral strands and tensions hurtling around England at the turn of the nineteenth century. Mrs. Bennet is "a woman of mean understanding, little information, and uncertain temper. . . . The *business* of her life was to get her daughters married; its solace was visiting and news" (3, emphasis added). She and Mr. Bennet live comfortably on an estate in the small village of Longbourn (9), but with five daughters and no son, they face eventual eviction at Mr. Bennet's death when the fee tail passes to his nephew, Mr. Collins (23, 54–55).[51] Austen assuredly portrays Mrs. Bennet as a silly woman unable to discern the difference between the virtue of high character and the virtue of financial security. She also, however, provides considerable justification for Mrs. Bennet's anxiety about the future well-being of her family, especially in light of Mr. Bennet's

---

50. Austen reiterates the economic engine behind her fictional society by introducing characters through the source of their wealth. For example, consider her portrayal of Sir William Lucas. He "had been formerly in trade in Meryton, where he made a tolerable fortune and risen to the honour of knighthood" (14). She does the same when describing Mr. Bingley and his sisters. They "were of a respectable family in the north of England; a circumstance more deeply impressed on their memories than that . . . [their] fortune had been acquired by trade" (12). *See* Juliet McMaster, *Class*, in Edward Copeland and Juliet McMaster, eds., *The Cambridge Companion to Jane Austen* (Cambridge University 1997), 115, 129 (observing that "[i]n Jane Austen's world, human worth is to be judged by standards better and more enduring than social status; but social status is always relevant"). In addition, Austen situates the Bennets' Longbourn estate near the "small market town" of Meryton (14). Meryton became the temporary headquarters for a militia regiment (24). The Napoleonic Wars, to which Austen alludes in the novel, reduced the availability of men eligible for marriage considerably.

51. Mr. Bennet has not taken the family situation as seriously as he should have, even by his own estimation.

> Mr. Bennet had very often wished, before this period of his life, that, instead of spending his whole income, he had laid by an annual sum, for the better provision of his children, and of his wife, if she survived him. . . .

> When first Mr. Bennet had married, economy was held to be perfectly useless; for, of course, they were to have a son. This son was to join in cutting off the entail, as soon as he should be of age, and the widow and younger children would by that means be provided for. Five daughters successively entered the world, but yet the son was to come; and Mrs. Bennet, for many years after Lydia's birth, had been certain that he would. This event had at last been despaired of, but it was then too late to be saving. Mrs. Bennet had no turn for economy, and her husband's love of independence had alone prevented their exceeding their income (272).

indifference to that problem (100). Mr. Bennet absents himself in his library for much of the novel. He practices the art of keen observation, which allows him to judge the character of others well, without any perceptible recognition of his own failings. His disinterest in all but gentlemanly pursuits, in addition to his lack of interest in acquisitiveness, makes him a counterexample for those promoting the pursuit of commerce and trade as virtuous. Mr. Bennet, as little more than a literary buffoon, hardly provides an attractive alternative to the gracelessness by which Mrs. Bennet pursues the business of marriage for her daughters. Mr. Bennet's daughters, with the exception of Elizabeth and to a lesser extent his oldest daughter, Jane, come close to mirroring their father's fecklessness and irresponsible attitude.[52] His youngest daughters, Catherine and Lydia, display their irresponsibility by their impetuosity and irrepressible desire for male attention, and his middle daughter, Mary, takes bookishness and didacticism to the extreme (27, 53). They serve only to accentuate Mr. Bennet's failings.

Mr. Collins and Mrs. Bennet find common cause quite early in their dealings with each other, because both of them have similar views of and approaches to the marriage market. It is first and foremost an arrangement intended to provide financial security, however they may wrap their self-interested crass views of marriage in selfless sentiments. Mr. Collins's proposal to Elizabeth and her response exemplifies the core differences between an economic man and a literary woman, even when the former embraces some of the sentiments of the latter.

> [Mr. Collins says] "My reasons for marrying are, first, that I think it a right thing for every clergyman in easy circumstances (like myself) to set the example of matrimony in his parish. Secondly, that I am convinced it will add very greatly to my happiness; and thirdly—which perhaps I ought to have mentioned earlier, that it is the particular advice and recommendation of the very noble lady whom I have the honour of calling patroness [Lady Catherine de Bourgh]. . . . And now nothing remains for me but to assure you in the most animated language of the violence of my affection. To fortune I am perfectly indifferent, and shall make no demand of that nature on your father, since I am well aware that it could not be complied with . . ."
>
> "You are too hasty, Sir," she [Elizabeth] cried. . . . Accept my thanks for the compliment you are paying me. I am very sensible of the honour of your proposals, but it is impossible for me to do otherwise than decline them." . . .
>
> [Mr. Collins responds] . . . [I]n spite of your manifold attractions, it is by no means certain that another offer of marriage may ever be made to you. Your portion is unhappily so small that it will in all likelihood undo the effects of your loveliness and amiable qualifications . . . .
>
> [Elizabeth then says] ". . . I thank you again and again for the honour you have done me in your proposals, but to accept them is absolutely impossible.

---

52. Jane makes an art of passivity and at times seems naive. Yet, Elizabeth values highly Jane's "generous candour" and finds an alliance with her that she does not have with the rest of her family (185).

My feelings in every respect forbid it. Can I speak plainer? Do not consider me now as an elegant female intending to plague you, but as a rational creature speaking the truth from her heart" (95–98).

Mr. Collins cannot comprehend Elizabeth's acting so against what he considers her own financial interest. For him, "rational" and "heart" do not belong in the same sentence. He appreciates that one needs to speak to "affections," but those feelings, if they come at all, have little valence when it comes to marriage negotiations. Mrs. Bennet wholly concurs in Mr. Collins's understanding of the matter when she says "[b]ut depend upon it, Mr. Collins . . . that Lizzy shall be brought to reason. . . . She is a very headstrong foolish girl, and does not know her own interest; but I will *make* her know it" (99).

Elizabeth and her father shared a disregard for Mr. Collins and the conviction that he would be a bad match for her. Austen surely makes clear, through her irony, that she favors the sentiments that create this father-daughter alliance.[53] Nevertheless, Austen gives her readers a number of cues to deter them from their rejecting the economic man out of hand in favor of the literary woman. Mrs. Bennet's concerns about the financial security of her daughters and herself may be overwrought, but Mr. Bennet's apparent total disinterest in his daughters' marriage prospects (92), impatience with the invasions into his library by Mr. Collins (63) and Mrs. Bennet (101) respectively, and his penchant to remain a social observer (92) raise doubts about Mr. Bennet's own character. The Bennets' marriage, financially convenient, yet by all appearances loveless with moments of abusiveness on the part of Mr. Bennet toward his wife (e.g., 100–101), explains, perhaps more than anything else we learn about Elizabeth, why she values compatibility and love more than financial security. She has seen firsthand how a marriage based on financial security alone deforms the character of both husband and wife.

Mr. Collins's marriage proposal and Elizabeth's rejection of it, with only a bit of a stretch, provide an excellent metaphor for the death tax debate. Collins is an Austenian version of Grover Norquist and the other death tax opponents.[54] They claim moral superiority, because their sole motivation is protecting and maximizing the potential for further wealth and success for everyone concerned, and they do so with lengthy, seemingly rational arguments. Collins makes arguments that serve the economic aristocracy far more than himself. Indeed, he quotes the pinnacle of that aristocracy, Lady Catherine de Bourgh, as he makes his case for marriage to Elizabeth. That Mrs. Bennet should make these arguments, she who has paid dearly in the marriage market she defends and wants to perpetuate, reveals how enticing the "business of marriage" can be. Behind the scenes, many of the wealthy and exceptionally wealthy fund and

---

53. At the first dinner, Mr. Bennet measured Mr. Collins, took pleasure at this clergyman's "conceit," (101) and shared that pleasure with Elizabeth."Mr. Bennet's expectations were fully answered. His cousin was as absurd as he had hoped, and he listened to him with the keenest enjoyment, maintaining at the same time the more resolute composure of countenance, and except in an occasional glance at Elizabeth, requiring no partner in his pleasure" (60).

54. Grover Norquist is the president of the group Americans for Tax Reform, which is a coalition of groups working against higher taxes. His biography can be found at http://www.atr.org/home/about/ggnbio.html. *See also* Graetz and Shapiro, *supra* note 10, at 27–31, 213–14 (describing Norquist and the role he has played in the death tax repeal debate).

strategize the death tax repeal movement.[55] The superrich in the character of Lady Catherine take more overt action. When she arrives at Longbourn, she refuses mannerly discourse with the Bennet family and instead arranges a private walk with Elizabeth. Lady Catherine mimics the righteousness and certainty of the death tax opponents as she tries mightily to get Elizabeth to renounce any intention to marry her nephew, Mr. Darcy, whose mother and aunt had agreed years ago should marry Lady Catherine's daughter.[56]

> While in their cradles, we planned the union: and now, at the moment when the wishes of both sisters would be accomplished, in their marriage, to be prevented by a young woman of inferior birth, of no importance in the world, and wholly unallied to the family! . . .
>
> My daughter and my nephew are formed for each other. They are descended on the maternal side, from the same noble line; and, on the father's, from respectable, honourable, and ancient, though untitled families. Their fortune on both sides is splendid. They are destined for each other by the voice of every member of their respective houses; and what is to divide them? The upstart pretensions of a young woman without family, connections, or fortune. Is this to be endured! But it must not, shall not be. (315–16).

Lady Catherine's view of an appropriate marriage parallels the arguments of the death tax opponents. The death tax interferes with the wealth their owners "are destined" to control.

Elizabeth, as the literary version of the proponents of the death tax, has far less to say than Collins about the proposition of her marriage to him. She speaks and acts only on the certainty of "the truth from her heart" that the price of financial security is too high, if it means marriage to Collins. She has seen a future with Collins in the marital history of her parents and rejects it out of hand as hopelessly regressive and damaging to all involved. In the same way that the proponents of the death tax have not taken seriously the notion that public policy would retreat back to the early twentieth century, when wealth accumulation went unfettered, Elizabeth found marriage tethered exclusively to property and unrestrained by considerations of love, compatibility, and self-fulfillment "impossible" (113).[57] Elizabeth challenges the amassing of wealth

---

55. *See* Graetz and Shapiro, *supra* note 10, at 15–21 (describing how the coalition for repeal of the death tax developed in recent years).

56. Mr. Wickham, who acts dishonorably throughout the novel and causes Elizabeth a great deal of worry when he runs off with her sister Lydia, has earlier revealed to Elizabeth the import of the plan to merge the inherited wealth of Mr. Darcy and Miss De Bourgh through marriage. When the De Bourgh family name arises in conversation, he reports to Elizabeth that Lady Catherine's daughter "will have a very large fortune, and it is believed that she and her cousin [Mr. Darcy] will unite the two estates" (74).

57. *See* Graetz and Shapiro, *supra* note 10, at 107–17 (describing how the proponents of the death tax failed to mount a serious counter-argument to those arguing in favor of repeal). The certainty of her position and her frustration with the marriage market in general lead her to equate acts of prudence with acts of avarice in her discussion of marriage with her aunt, Mrs. Gardiner.

> Pray, my dear aunt, what is the difference in matrimonial affairs, between the mercenary and the prudent motive? Where does discretion end, and avarice begin? Last Christmas you were afraid of his [Wickham] marrying me, because it would be imprudent; and now, because he is trying to get a girl with only ten thousand pounds, you want to find out that he is mercenary (137).

when she defies Lady Catherine's entreaties (315–18). She also questions the deference owed the owners of those fortunes (318). In contrast to Elizabeth, Mr. Collins and Mrs. Bennet wish for access into Lady Catherine's world, have undue respect for her and the aristocracy she represents, and defend it.[58] Grover Norquist and his followers would seem to share an equivalent view of wealth and wealth holders in the twenty-first century.

Charlotte Lucas, a neighbor and dear friend of Elizabeth, appears to adopt a view of the marriage market quite similar to Mr. Collins and Mrs. Bennet when she readily accepts Mr. Collins's proposal for marriage after Elizabeth had turned him down.[59] In this complex character, Austen challenges the chasm she establishes between Mr. Collins and Elizabeth and, instead, portrays a literary woman forced to take actions according to the precepts of an economic man. Charlotte's appreciation of the marriage market deviates from Mr. Collins's and Mrs. Bennet's as much as it deviates from Elizabeth's. She has great respect for Elizabeth and, unlike Mr. Collins and Mrs. Bennet, understands why Elizabeth finds marriage to Mr. Collins impossible, even as she herself views marriage to him as her best opportunity for domestic contentment.[60] Importantly, the marriage market has not captured Charlotte in the way it has Mr. Collins and Mrs. Bennet.[61] She distances herself sufficiently from

---

58. In this regard, West may overstate economic man's inability to empathize. Mr. Collins and Mrs. Bennet reveal a good deal of empathy for the concerns of the wealthy. As to the prospect of Elizabeth's marriage to Mr. Darcy, Collins makes clear his appreciation of the De Bourgh family's situation when he writes the following in a letter to Mr. Bennet:

> This young gentleman, is blessed in a peculiar way, with everything the heart of mortal can most desire, — splendid property, noble kindred, and extensive patronage. Yet in spite of all these temptations, let me warn my cousin Elizabeth, and yourself, of what evils you may incur, by a precipitate closure with this gentleman's proposals, which, of course, you will be inclined to take immediate advantage of. . . .

> My motive for cautioning you, is as follows. We have reason to imagine that his aunt, Lady Catherine de Bourgh, does not look on the match with a friendly eye (322).

After learning of Elizabeth's engagement to Mr. Darcy, Mrs. Bennet, who previously described Mr. Darcy as "disagreeable" (333) and "tiresome" (333) when she thought he had no interest in any of her daughters, came to stand "in such awe of her intended son-in-law, that she ventured not to speak to him, unless it was in her power to offer him any attention, or mark her deference for his opinion" (337).

59. She is the daughter of Sir William, himself a tradesman who as mayor of Meryton had achieved a knighthood (14). The novel reveals Charlotte's attention to wealth and status when she cautions Elizabeth "not to be a simpleton and allow her fancy for Wickham to make her appear unpleasant in the eyes of a man of ten times his consequence" (81). Further evidence of Charlotte as an economic man comes when Charlotte agrees to a short courtship with Mr. Collins and a speedy wedding. "The stupidity with which he was favoured by nature, must guard his courtship from any charm that could make a woman wish for its continuance; and Miss Lucas, who accepted him solely from the pure and disinterested desire of an establishment, cared not how soon that establishment were gained" (110). She understood as well as her parents that "they could give little fortune" and that Collins's "prospects of future wealth were exceedingly fair" (110).

60. Charlotte values her friendship with Elizabeth "beyond that of any other person" (111).

61. Charlotte's explanation of her decision to Elizabeth reveals her clarity about what marriage has to offer her.

> "I see what you are feeling," replied Charlotte, — you must be surprised, very much surprised, — so lately as Mr. Collins was wishing to marry you. But when you have had time to think it all over, I hope you will be satisfied with what I have done. I am not romantic you know. I never was. I ask only a comfortable home; and considering Mr. Collins's character, connections, and situation in life, I am convinced that my

it to appreciate its destructive, as well as its productive, consequences. Charlotte supports the likes of Mr. Collins and Lady Catherine more as a matter of default. She has no enthusiasm for their way of thinking or behaving. She makes the best out of the possible and protects herself from disappointment by taking a dim view of men, marriage, and the opportunities available to women. Her counterpart in the death tax debate is the segment of society who appreciates the appropriateness of the death tax, but, feeling disheartened and pessimistic, accepts its repeal as inevitable, given the powerful forces behind the repeal.

In contrast to Charlotte's marriage to Collins, Elizabeth's marriage to Darcy suggests a possible transformation of the meaning and purpose of the death tax. The household they establish protects, nourishes, and inspires the moral sentiments of members of their respective families. This accomplishment required both Elizabeth and Darcy to reassess their market and nonmarket sentiments.

Darcy initially refuses to yield to his attraction for Elizabeth, because marriage to her contradicted all the rules of the market that supported his aristocratic status. Darcy's transformation progresses first from his willingness to listen to his heart. When he pays Elizabeth a surprise visit, he blurts out "[i]n vain have I struggled. It will not do. My feelings will not be repressed. You must allow me to tell you how ardently I admire and love you" (168). He is not yet willing to yield the habits of mind of the marriage market.

> He spoke well, but there were feelings besides those of the heart to be detailed, and he was not more eloquent on the subject of tenderness than of pride. His sense of her inferiority—of its being a degradation—of the family obstacles which judgment had always opposed to inclination, were dwelt on with a warmth which seemed due to the consequence he was wounding, but was very unlikely to recommend his suit (id.).

It took Elizabeth's refusal of this initial marriage proposal, accompanied by a litany of what she viewed as his failings of character, for him to begin to appreciate that his wealth neither could purchase her good will nor protect him from her harsh criticism (169–72). Her charge that in his speech to her he had not "behaved in a . . . gentleman-like manner" gave him a particular "start" (171). Having taken the first step of placing his attachment for Elizabeth above the demands of the marriage market, Darcy had to take the next step and see himself as Elizabeth saw him, which is to say he gained empathic competence as well as self-awareness.[62] For Elizabeth's part, her transformation also comes in two steps. It begins when she reads and rereads Darcy's letter in which

---

chance of happiness with him is as fair, as most people can boast on entering the marriage state (113).

62. He says as much to Elizabeth after she accepts his second proposal of marriage.

I have been a selfish being all my life, in practice, though not in principle. As a child I was taught what was *right*, but I was not taught to correct my temper. I was given good principles, but left to follow them in pride and conceit. Unfortunately, an only son . . . I was spoilt by my parents, who . . . allowed, encouraged, almost taught me to be selfish and overbearing, to care for none beyond my own family circle, to think meanly of all the rest of the world, to *wish* at least to think meanly of their sense and worth compared with my own. Such I was, from eight to eight and twenty; and such I might still have been but for you, dearest, loveliest Elizabeth! What do I now owe you! You taught me a lesson, hard indeed at first, but most advantageous. By you, I was

he defends himself against her charges that he had not acquitted himself well as a gentleman (174–86). That letter made her see that she did not have as much empathic competence as she pridefully had supposed.[63] Darcy initially believed his happiness and destiny were tied to his wealth. Elizabeth initially believed her happiness and destiny were tied to love. Once Darcy values his feelings of the heart above his wealth and the status it brings him, he attains empathic competence and self-awareness. In contrast, once Elizabeth learns greater empathic competence and self-awareness, she then gains appreciation of wealth and the joy that it can bring her.

> By portraying a transformation of sentiments for the quintessential economic man, Fitzwilliam Darcy, and the archetypal literary woman, Elizabeth Bennet, Austen strives to respond to the tension between market and nonmarket sentiments. The experiment of melding the sensibilities of an economic man and a literary woman into both husband and wife promises to change the meaning and experience of marriage.[64] This marriage includes a substantial role for economic prudence as a practice and a virtue. Elizabeth held her younger sister Lydia and her husband Wickham in low regard in part because of their unwillingness to abandon extravagances.[65] Although Lydia remained unaffected by

---

> properly humbled. I came to you without a doubt of my reception. You shewed me how insufficient were all my pretensions to please a woman worthy of being pleased (328).

Even as Darcy sheds the expectation of respect merely because he held considerable wealth — the very respect that Smith berates (*see supra* text accompanying note 39) — and gains empathic competence, it is noteworthy that he expresses his insights in economic terms, such as *owe, advantageous, insufficient,* and *worthy.*

63. After reading his letter, she admits her own failings.

> "How despicably have I acted!" she cried. — "I, who have prided myself on my discernment! — I, who have valued myself on my abilities — Who have often disdained the generous candour of my sister, and gratified my vanity, in useless or blameable distrust. — How humiliating is this discovery! — Yet, how just a humiliation! — Had I been in love, I could not have been more wretchedly blind. But vanity, not love, has been my folly. — Pleased with the preference of one [Wickham], and offended by the neglect of the other [Darcy], on the very beginning of our acquaintance, I have courted prepossession and ignorance, and driven reason away, where either were concerned. Till this moment, I never knew myself" (185).

Humility in her discernment of character enabled her to admire rather than disdain Darcy's wealth upon her visit to his estate.

> The rooms were lofty and handsome, and their furniture suitable to the fortune of their proprietor; but Elizabeth saw with admiration of his taste, that it was neither gaudy nor uselessly fine; . . .

> "And of this place," thought she, "I might have been mistress! With these rooms I might now have been familiarly acquainted! Instead of viewing them as a stranger, I might have rejoiced in them as my own . . . (216).

64. *See* Claudia L. Johnson, *Jane Austen: Women, Politics, and the Novel* (University of Chicago, 1988), 79–80, 92–93 (demonstrating the influence of Samuel Johnson's writings on the pursuit of happiness and describing Elizabeth's marriage to Darcy as a "provisional experiment, an effort to work through established forms[,] . . . in order to transform them into the purveyors of ecstatic personal happiness").

65. Lydia and Wickham apparently remained immune from the influences of Elizabeth and Darcy and the new kind of marriage they were establishing.

> As for Wickham and Lydia, their characters suffered no revolution from the marriage of her sisters [Jane Bennet's marriage to Mr. Bingley and Elizabeth's marriage to Mr. Darcy]. . . . Such relief, however, as it was in her [Elizabeth's] power to afford, by the practice of what might be called economy in her own private expenses, she frequently

Elizabeth's marriage, it seems this newly created household could have lifelong influences on Elizabeth's younger sister Kitty and Darcy's younger sister Georgiana (343, 345).[66] Austen's focus on these two young women at the end of the novel leaves the impression that Elizabeth and Darcy's marriage will not remain unique. Kitty and Georgiana and many other young women will use Elizabeth and Darcy's marriage as a model as they choose their own lifetime partners.

Smith and Austen offer us a critical perspective on the justice of an impending repeal of the death tax. They go far in giving us a vocabulary to critique arguments for repeal of the death tax. They reveal why private acquisitiveness untempered by the dictates of prudence, justice, and beneficence cannot be good for an individual or society. Together the two help to break the stranglehold of economic discourse surrounding the death tax, which depends mightily on absolutes to persuade.

THE CASE FOR GOVERNMENTAL INTERVENTION

Smith and Austen establish the dangers of avarice and the benefits of a life lived with prudence, justice, and beneficence as a guide. Their approaches to the promotion of public welfare escape the futile economic arguments that dominate the current debate about death taxes and demand a resolution that addresses the unavoidable tension between market and nonmarket sentiments. Both, however, stress voluntary compliance based on collective social controls, as opposed to governmental intervention, as the ideal.[67] In fact, Smith's virtuous social being provides the foundation for the successful laissez-faire economy he promotes throughout his writings.[68] The crucial question Smith and Austen leave us to consider is whether government, through some form of a death tax, can or should have a role in instilling prudence, justice, and beneficence into civil society.

The answer to this question depends on how we evaluate how close we have come to the ideal of voluntary compliance and whether governmental

---

sent them. It had always been evident to her that such an income as theirs, under the direction of two persons so extravagant in their wants, and heedless of the future, must be very insufficient to their support . . . (344).

For further discussion of Wickham and his marriage to Lydia, *see supra* note 56.
66. Georgiana, Darcy's younger sister, detects the alteration in spousal relations.

Georgiana had the highest opinion in the world of Elizabeth; though at first she often listened with an astonishment bordering on alarm, at her lively, sportive, manner of talking to her brother. He, who had always inspired in herself a respect which almost overcame her affection, she now saw the object of open pleasantry. Her mind received knowledge which had never before fallen in her way. By Elizabeth's instructions she began to comprehend that a woman may take liberties with her husband . . . (345).

67. *See* Rothschild, *supra* note 37, at 146, 158, 243 (showing how Smith's primary concerns with government is that it would provide regulation on behalf of those with political influence).
68. *See* Anspach, *supra* note 41, at 188–98; Jerry Evensky, *Adam Smith's Moral Philosophy: A Historical and Contemporary Perspective on Markets, Law, Ethics, and Culture* (Cambridge University, 2005), 213-42; Robert E. Prasch, *The Ethics of Growth in Adam Smith's* Wealth of Nations, 23 Hist. Pol. Econ. 337, 349–50 (1991); Tajima, *supra* note 40, at 589–90.

intervention to date has helped or hindered voluntary compliance. The state of the death tax debate suggests that selfishness, avarice, and individualism currently trump beneficence and communalism. What is more difficult to gauge is whether governmental intervention in the form of a death tax has engendered or placed a check on nonvirtuous conduct. For those most like Lady Catherine de Bourgh, the current death tax checks nonvirtuous conduct at the same time that it builds resentment toward governmental intervention. For those most similar to Elizabeth Bennet, it supports their antagonism toward social mores that pay undue respect to the wealthy, and it correlates with their commitment to a community's well-being. The tax neither engenders resentment nor detracts from the nonmarket sentiments they hold dear. The effect of the death tax on those who emulate Fitzwilliam Darcy is hardest to predict. They take great pride in their own virtuous conduct and may resent a death tax that presumes they would act in a manner contrary to the interests of a civil society. On the other hand, they, in contrast to the intransigent Lady Catherines, may come to see the benefits of governmental intervention. Given the current emphasis on market sentiments and the absence of sustained consideration of nonmarket sentiments, they may well agree that reliance solely on voluntary social controls is unwarranted.[69] Smith provides considerable support for this conclusion when he speaks directly to the "barbarous institution" of dead hand control.[70]

> But in the present state of Europe, when small as well as great estates derive their security from the laws of their country, nothing can be more completely absurd. They are founded upon the most absurd of all suppositions, the supposition that every successive generation of men have not an equal right to the earth, and to all that it possesses; but that the property of the present generation should be restrained and regulated according to the fancy of those who died perhaps five hundred years ago.[71]

What form of intervention should government take? To achieve the equivalent of Austen's experiment of melding economic men and literary women requires the repeal of the current death tax system and the introduction of a new tax intentionally designed to address the tension between market and nonmarket sentiments. That would allow for an approach that acknowledges the many benefits of capital accretion and entrepreneurship within a civil society that values prudence, justice, and beneficence. Whether policy makers could reconstruct the current death tax system, which over the last thirty years has had to withstand unrelenting attack, to moderate the undue emphasis on wealth and the accumulation of wealth seems doubtful. A new

---

69. *See* Samuel Bowles & Herbert Gintis, *Social Capital, Moral Sentiments, and Community Governance*, in Gintis et al., *supra* note 39, at 379, 395 (arguing that community governance, i.e., interaction among individuals, is more likely than the market and the state to accomplish tasks that "are qualitative and hard to capture in explicit contracts" and also arguing that "extremely unequal societies will be competitively disadvantaged in the future because their structures of privilege and material reward limit the capacity of community governance to facilitate the qualitative interactions that underpin the modern economy").
70. 1 Smith, *supra* note 33, at 385.
71. *Id.* at 384.

approach to death taxes equivalent to the once unimaginable marriage between Elizabeth Bennet and Fitzwilliam Darcy has the advantage of disrupting old habits of thought.

We don't have to go far to find alternatives. For over half a century scholars have promoted the advantage of an accretion tax, which is an excise tax on the receipt of a gratuitous transfer of property. Another possibility is for Congress to use the current income tax system to include receipts of gifts and bequests in the calculation of a recipient's gross income. The accretion tax alternative has the advantage of treating the acquisition of wealth through gift or inheritance as a unique transaction. The income tax alternative, on the other hand, has the benefit of having wealth transfers incorporated into a familiar tax system. Scholarship abounds concerning the operation and feasibility of both these alternatives and does not need further exploration here.[72] The attractiveness of both proposals is that they focus on the recipients of wealth. At the transitional ownership moment, either tax proposal reinforces the proposition that private wealth and public beneficence must operate in tandem. In the same way that the Bennet/Darcy marriage serves as a model for the couple's impressionistic younger sisters, these tax alternatives stand as evidence of our collective commitment not to allow avarice and economic growth to trump our other dearly held nonmarket sentiments.

CONCLUSION

Inheritance law contains a small number of far-reaching rules designed to temper a donor's right to testamentary freedom. The most important of these are the elective share, which prevents decedents from disinheriting surviving spouses in common law property states, and the RAP, which prevents donors from retaining control over their property for centuries upon centuries. The elective share periodically comes under attack in the scholarly literature as an unnecessary interference with donative freedom.[73] As of now, repeal of spousal protections has not gained much political appeal, probably because private arrangements can easily limit its import.[74] In recent years, in tandem with the accelerated interest in the repeal of the death tax, a number of state legislatures have succumbed to jurisdictional competition for trust dollars and pressures from the states' banks and estate planners. They have repealed or

---

72. *See, e.g.,* Joseph M. Dodge, *Replacing the Estate Tax with a Re-Imagined Accessions Tax,* 60 Hastings L.J. 997 (2009); David G. Duff, *Taxing Inherited Wealth: A Philosophical Argument,* 6 Can. J.L. & Jurisprudence 3 (1993); Task Force, *supra* note 11, at 171–203.

73. *See, e.g.,* Terry L. Turnipseed, *Why Shouldn't I Be Allowed to Leave My Property to Whomever I Choose at My Death? (Or How I Learned to Stop Worrying and Start Loving the French),* 44 Brandeis L.J. 737 (2006); Sheldon J. Plager, *The Spouse's Nonbarrable Share: A Solution in Search of a Problem,* 33 U. Chi. L. Rev. 681, 698 (1966).

74. *See* Restatement (Third) of Property (Wills and Donative Transfers) §9.4 (2003) (considering waivers of spousal rights).

substantially liberalized their state's RAP. Death tax avoidance powers the appeal for perpetual trusts.[75]

Death tax repeal placed in the context of the RAP bolsters the thesis of this article. The RAP represents a reasonable balance between the donative freedom of the current generation and the donative freedom of future generations.[76] Dead hand control, as well as wealth accumulation, has justifications and frequently leads to beneficial results, but not when left unrestrained and untempered by other values. The path back to moderation of avarice is not nearly as obvious as the accelerated path we have taken toward it. As unlikely as it may seem, the Solon–Croesus legend, Smith's *TMS*, and Austen's *PP* taken together change the nature of the current debate. All three highlight social relations rather than individuality. Solon's advice to Croesus severs the relationship of happiness to wealth and treats death as a moment to reckon a life well lived. For our purposes, Smith's insistence on moderation of avarice is as important as his focus on prudence, justice, and beneficence as he sets out the ideal virtuous social being. Austen's novel about young women, the dances they enjoy, and the local marriage market in a small Hertfordshire town also serves to disrupt the current political appeal of death tax repeal. She shows us just how radical and dangerous repeal can be. She also shows us that a discourse of moderation remains our best hope to build strong social institutions for future generations.

---

75. *See* Max M. Schanzenbach & Robert H. Sitkoff, *Perpetuities of Taxes: Explaining the Rise of the Perpetual Trust*, 27 Cardozo L. Rev. 2465 (2006); Robert H. Sitkoff and Max M. Schanzenbach, *Jurisdictional Competition for Trust Funds: An Empirical Analysis of Perpetuities and Taxes*, 115 Yale L.J. 356, 360 n.4, 381–82, 381 n.76 (2005).

76. *See* Mary Louise Fellows and Gregory S. Alexander, *Forty Years of Codification of Estates and Trusts Law: Lessons for the Next Generation*, 40 Ga. L. Rev. 1049, 1077–86 (2006).

VIII

INTERNATIONAL TAXATION

11

IS THERE A FUTURE FOR REDISTRIBUTIONAL NORMS IN INTERNATIONAL TAX POLICY?

Karen B. Brown, George Washington University Law School[1]

Economic efficiency has long held sway as the appropriate foundational principle of the U.S. international tax regime. Capital export neutrality (CEN), the efficiency model chosen, requires that the tax system remain neutral concerning a domestic corporation's decision to invest at home or abroad. The goal is to encourage location of investment in the country in which returns to capital are greatest. The expected payoff is maximization of worldwide welfare—a trickle-down-based premise under which all nations benefit when every multinational enterprise maximizes investment returns. A tax system is capital-export-neutral when it taxes worldwide income of resident businesses, affording a credit (designed to eliminate double taxation) for foreign taxes paid when activities are located outside the border. When rates are identical, the home country's tax will be exactly offset by the foreign tax. The home country's system remains neutral by removing the potential for double taxation, which is thought to erect a disincentive to shop for the locale supporting the highest level of productivity.

While maintaining support of capital export neutrality as a foundational principle, U.S. tax policymakers in recent years have curtailed reliance on the worldwide efficiency rationale in favor of another type of efficiency rationale—competitiveness. These proponents, advocates of capital *import* neutrality, contend that welfare is maximized when all companies compete in a given location on the same terms. This has led some home countries to forgo tax on certain types of foreign source income (usually in the form of a dividend exemption) in order to allow their multinationals to compete in low-tax regimes on an equal footing with firms from other countries.

---

1. Donald Phillip Rothschild Research Professor of Law, George Washington University Law School, All rights reserved, 2013. This chapter is dedicated in loving memory of Laverne Tillman and Leon E. Wynter.

The capital import neutrality principle has gained currency on the agenda of Congress as well as that of multinational firms and the general public. Even the Treasury Department has indicated that it would consider a move to a so-called territorial regime (tax exemption for foreign-source income), but only in the context of overall tax reform.[2] Multinationals have long claimed that critical to their success—that is, their ability to outperform foreign firms—is a regime that allows them to reduce tax liability. Some lawmakers have crafted proposals aimed primarily at reducing U.S. tax on foreign source income, such as those contained in various incarnations of a foreign dividend exemption proposal.[3] On the other hand, U.S. businesses operating across borders have supported arrangements that allow them to combine foreign tax liability reduction with ad hoc mitigation of U.S. liability, pushing the quest for competitiveness to an unanticipated extreme. These schemes combine abusive transfer pricing methodologies, favorable foreign no-tax or low-tax regimes, treaties, and creative use of treaties and foreign tax credit provisions, requiring no legislative seal of approval, to effectively undermine the imposition of even one level of taxation on income.[4]

In turn, recession-weary public opinion has called for any tax policy prescription depicted as a boost to the economy. There is widespread belief that reduction in the tax burden imposed on U.S. multinationals will result in continued loyalty to the domestic marketplace, increased productivity, and more U.S.-based jobs, an especially critical concern during any period of economic downturn. Experience gleaned from an experimental tax holiday–type provision enacted in 2004 suggests, however, that multinationals will not return tax savings to the U.S. economy in ways that will provide increased employment.[5]

At the international level, the antitax sentiment implicit in some reform proposals threatens to move tax policy perilously close to a no-taxation-for-multinational-enterprises consensus. Yet dramatic reduction in the obligations of multinational firms and the attendant reduction in tax revenues would compromise the infrastructure needs not only of the constituents of the richer economies of developed nations, but also those of poorer economies in the developing world. Absent from most prescriptions for reform is consideration of the importance of the tax policy choices of leading nations, such as the United States, to the viability of developing or emerging countries.[6]

The economic crisis resulting from the recession precipitated by fiscal events of late 2008 has debilitated not only the developed world, but also developing nations. Developing nations in the Caribbean region have been

---

2. Meg Shreve and Drew Pierson, *No Repatriation Holiday Without Tax Reform, Geithner Says*, 61 Tax Notes Int'l 496 (2011).

3. I.R.C. §965; Joint Committee on Taxation, JCS 02–05, 109th Cong., *Options to Improve Tax Compliance and Reform Tax Expenditures* (2005), at 186.

4. The Obama administration has opposed these schemes by supporting enactment of anti-abuse measures, such as I.R.C. §§909 and 901(m).

5. *See* Roy Clemons and Michael Kenney, *An Analysis of the Tax Holiday for Repatriation Under the Jobs Act*, 120 Tax Notes 759 (2008); Martin A. Sullivan, *U.S. Drug Firms Bring Home $98 Billion*, 42 Tax Notes Int'l 321 (2006).

6. *But see* Adam Rosenzweig, *Why Are There Tax Havens?* 52 Wm. & Mary L. Rev. 923 (2010) [hereinafter "Rosenzweig, *Tax Havens*"].

hard hit because their financial stability depends in large part on the health of the economies of the leading nations, including the United States. In a global economy, however, the health of every nation, especially in the developing world, affects the viability of all. Consequently, the United States and other leaders are challenged to acknowledge that it is in their self-interest to consider that the well-being of nations, such as those in the Caribbean area, that serve as consumers of a large portion of the goods and services they produce, when undertaking the business of tax reform.

This chapter examines the virtual absence in the policy debates relating to reform proposals of consideration of measures that accord importance to the development needs of poorer nations. Most tax reform options under discussion hold little promise because they seek either to tax multinationals too lightly or to ignore the burdens that rich-country policies place on poor nations. Proposals to move to an exemption-type system are destined to promote investment in highly developed countries (offering the benefits of attractive infrastructure) with low tax rates (such as Ireland and, more recently, Canada, Japan, and other nations), foreclosing the ability of developing countries to compete. On the other hand, a U.S. move to worldwide taxation without the possibility of deferring tax on foreign-source income would shut down strategies developing countries have employed to attract investment. One promising scheme—to institute worldwide formulary apportionment, by which net income of multinationals is allocated to taxing jurisdictions on the basis of selective factors, which would accord some measure of fiscal autonomy to developing nations—has been largely unexplored by legislators.[7] A second proposal, which would require high-income nations to acknowledge the roles their tax systems play in undermining the viability of developing-country economies, has not been embraced by policymakers.[8]

Indeed, efficiency rationales, either by reliance upon capital export neutrality (worldwide taxation with a credit for foreign taxes) or upon capital import neutrality (some type of exemption for foreign-source income), fall short when the limitations of efficiency models regarding the growth capacity of the developing world are not acknowledged. Yet consideration of the impact of international tax reform on the interests of the developing world is a moral and pragmatic imperative. Particularly for the United States, the time to consider strategic alliances with neighboring countries, such as those in the Caribbean region, has arrived. Despite recent fiscal setbacks, the United States, in its position as the dominant economic policymaker, is compelled to consider the needs of the poorer populations of the world. The economic decline marked by events beginning in late 2008 has been especially hard on the developing world. Like the vulnerability fund recommended by a World Bank head, amidst talk of economic bailouts, as a mechanism to assist those countries unable to afford budget deficits to support a safety net, construction of tax policy that will support economic growth of poorer nations is important to the

---

7. Reuven S. Avi-Yonah, *Globalization, Tax Competition, and the Fiscal Crisis of the Welfare State*, 113 Harv. L. Rev. 1573 (2000).
8. Rosenzweig, *Tax Havens*, *supra* note 6 (proposing unlimited credit for taxes paid to developing nations).

interests of all nations.[9] After exploring the ways in which current reform proposals fail to address developing-country concerns, this chapter sets parameters for reversing this dynamic.

Concern for the Caribbean economies is dictated not only by the proximity of that region to the United States but also by the potential for growth in a politically and fiscally united area (the Caribbean Common Market) that includes diverse economies (relatively successful ones, such as Jamaica and Barbados, as well as severely depressed ones, such as Haiti). As a practical matter, worldwide long-term interests are served only if the potential of those regions, both human and economic, is allowed to develop at a rate sufficient to sustain the growth of those populations. The second section of this chapter offers a critique of efficiency-based reform proposals, while the following two sections explore ways in which the needs of the developing world may be addressed.

CRITIQUE OF EFFICIENCY-BASED REFORMS

There are many stakeholders in the debates relating to the future of the tax system, including workers and other low- and moderate-income taxpayers, upper-income and other wealthy individuals, governments in serious need of revenue sources in a weakened economy, and domestic and multinational companies. The progression of international tax reform is a fraught enterprise in which U.S. multinationals, feeling there is much to gain or lose, dominate the input. The outcome of the discussions, most likely to be resolved in the aftermath of the 2012 national elections, will fashion a game plan for the future once political consensus to change can be measured. The stakes are cast in terms of competitiveness and productivity, with many commentators going so far as to consider the interests of business paramount, as well as separate from the interests of other marketplace constituents. By treating as marginal the interests of society in maintaining polities that offer a fair distribution of the tax burden under a regime that collects sufficient revenue to maintain an infrastructure to support an acceptable level of subsistence both at home and abroad, policymakers fail to consider values that are critical to the future viability of the global marketplace. Economic success in any country, including those with high incomes, depends upon a sufficiently strong network of treaty and trading partners in the remainder of the world.

This section describes five of the primary approaches to international tax reform. They are based on (1) a "pure" form of capital export neutrality, (2) an imputation-type system, (3) a hybrid form of capital export neutrality, (4) a tax exemption for foreign-source dividends from controlled foreign corporations, and (5) formulary apportionment. With the exception of the last alternative (formulary apportionment), proponents of these initiatives have not taken the opportunity to understand the way in which the tax systems of the

---

9. Robert B. Zoellick, *A Stimulus Package for the World*, N.Y. Times, Jan. 23, 2009, at A27.

United States and other high-income nations make it difficult for developing countries to sustain their own economies.

A "pure" form of capital export neutrality would correct flaws in the operation of the U.S. system, as it is currently configured, in two ways. It would eliminate "deferral," which is the ability of firms to avoid taxation of profits earned by wholly owned foreign subsidiaries until those funds are repatriated or returned to the U.S. parent. It would allow a credit for foreign income taxes paid by the subsidiary to alleviate double taxation, but it would not prohibit the offset of U.S. tax liability on worldwide income by foreign taxes computed at a rate higher than the U.S. rate. A true or "pure" form of capital export neutrality is built on the premise that removal of a tax impediment to moving offshore will produce maximum efficiency gains when the relocating business anticipates enhanced productivity. This would cause the U.S Treasury to refund to domestic corporations foreign taxes imposed at a rate higher than that of the United States or foreign taxes computed on a base that does not conform to the U.S. notion of net income.[10]

There are obvious critiques of the pure form of capital export neutrality. It would conflict with a "put the U.S. first" mantra that frequently dominates modern tax policy debate. At a time of mounting deficits, declining tax revenue, high unemployment, and economic hard times, few would support the burden on the U.S. treasury imposed by an obligation to refund out of its own coffers taxes imposed by a foreign government. Even in the best economic times, sacrifice by the United States of its own well-being in order to promote location of investment in another jurisdiction thought to offer more productivity gains, in an effort to secure enhanced worldwide efficiency, may be difficult to justify.

Even among efficiency advocates, there is little support for a move to this "pure" form of capital export neutrality, primarily because it has not been implemented by any other country and would place the United States outside of the international norm. A more important argument against capital export neutrality in its purest form is that it impedes the ability of developing countries to implement their own tax regimes as they work to attract foreign investment. The strategic use of low tax rates or a different-from-U.S. income (or other) tax base has no effect in face of a U.S. system that taxes the U.S. multinational at 35 percent and allows a credit for the developing-country income tax.[11] Moreover, as discussed more fully below in reference to recent proposals to move to an exemption system, businesses based in the United States and other developed nations have little incentive to establish subsidiaries in developing countries when low-tax developed-world countries, such as Ireland, the Netherlands, and Luxembourg, offer a more attractive infrastructure.

A move to a pure form of capital export neutrality also holds no benefit for developing countries because the foreign tax credit limitation operates to restrict the credit against U.S. tax liability for foreign income taxes imposed

---

10. This would occur if the foreign country tax rate were equal to or lower than the U.S. rate but is imposed on a base that is larger because the foreign tax laws deny deductions or other allowances accepted for U.S. purposes.

11. The maximum income tax rate of 35 percent is used here in order to simplify analysis. *See* I.R.C. §11(a).

at a lower-than-U.S. rate on foreign-source taxable income. A developing-country rate of 10 percent, for example, would fail to attract investment by U.S. multinationals, which would remain subject to a residual U.S. tax of 25 percent on the income. Even if the developing-country rates were identical, a credit might not be available if that country's income tax base were dissimilar to that of the United States. The absence of a developing-country tax base that is consonant with that of the United States could render a substantial part of its income taxes ineligible for a credit.

An alternative that ends deferral but minimizes the foreign tax credit issues just detailed is to move to a type of imputation system in which foreign corporations are treated as pass-through entities. This is a sophisticated and well-structured proposal by highly regarded tax scholars (Professors Peroni, Fleming, and Shay) to move to a pass-through system employing a partnership-type regime in which corporate income is attributed to shareholders. It has not captured the imagination of legislators, but it merits serious attention.[12] One commentator found the imputation model preferable to the Obama administration's budget proposals over a number of years, discussed subsequently, to remove advantages to U.S. firms that game the current system by moving production offshore to take advantage of low tax rates. He found that the administration proposals failed to address the flaw in the tax code that provides an incentive to "create a job in Bangalore, India, [because you pay lower taxes] than if you create one in Buffalo, New York." By contrast the Peroni–Fleming–Shay plan eliminated this incentive.[13]

Under that plan each U.S. shareholder (regardless of shareholding percentage) reports its pro rata share of all of the foreign corporation's gross income (expanded beyond the subpart F categories) and expenses. Losses flow through as well, but with limits. The character of all items (determined at the controlled foreign corporation (CFC) level) passes through to each shareholder. Foreign taxes paid are attributed to shareholders along with credit eligibility. While the imputation-type system would end deferral and remove the incentive to move offshore to lower tax regimes, it continues to rely on the foreign tax credit to eliminate double taxation and, in the ways just detailed, provides no support for developing-country efforts to attract foreign investment.

A third possibility, a hybrid form of capital export neutrality, has been advocated by the Obama administration and previous ones. In its 2010 and subsequent budgets, while not advocating an end to deferral, the administration offered three international tax innovations: repeal the check-the-box rules; suspend certain expense deductions (primarily interest and operating expenses, but not research and development (R & D) expenditures) until the foreign source income to which they relate are subject to U.S. tax; and end foreign tax credit abuse, such as that created by foreign tax credit generators (FTC generators) (arrangements that generate FTCs to be used currently, while

---

12. Robert J. Peroni et al., *Getting Serious About Curtailing Deferral of U.S. Tax on Foreign Source Income*, 52 SMU L. Rev. 455 (1999).

13. Samuel C. Thompson, *Obama's International Tax Proposal Is Too Timid*, 54 Tax Notes Int'l 579 (2009); *see also* Samuel C. Thompson, *An Imputation System for Taxing Foreign-Source Income*, 130 Tax Notes 567 (Jan., 2011) (noting that a move to a territorial system would not allow the United States to cut the top corporate tax rate to 28 percent).

the underlying income on which the tax is determined is taxable only in the future, if at all). These proposals would strengthen the current system and eliminate many abuses, but as Professor Samuel C. Thompson has indicated, they do not remove the advantages of moving offshore to minimize U.S. tax liability.

A fourth proposal, actively advocated by some multinationals and others (including legislators), is a move to some type of a (possibly temporary) territorial or exemption system (featuring reduction or elimination of U.S. tax on foreign-source income or on dividends paid by CFCs to U.S. parents). This reform model has developed in response to recent strategies of U.S. multi-nationals to park profits offshore in foreign subsidiaries strategically located in low-tax jurisdictions in order to defer U.S. tax on profits with the hope of bringing them back to the United States tax-free to take advantage of one or more "tax holidays" enacted by Congress. The Joint Committee on Taxation, members of Congress, tax reform commissions established by Presidents George W. Bush and Barack Obama, and others have urged a move to an exemption system.

The current U.S. system of deferral on the active income of foreign subsidiaries, failing to intentionally address the needs of the developing world, has inspired aggressive tax planning by U.S. multinationals that use devices such as the Dutch sandwich to reduce their effective rates drastically, sometimes below 5 percent. The investment in low-tax jurisdictions has gone to Ireland, the Netherlands, Singapore, Bermuda, and Switzerland, which have competed aggressively for investment capital, and not to the developing countries, some of which have been labeled as "tax havens" by the high-income member nations of the OECD for the self-protective strategies they have employed in order to raise revenue and to counter the effects of rich-country policies.

Yet the "tax haven" moniker is not to be linked solely to the developing world. In the name of competition, multinationals in every jurisdiction, whether developed or developing, have entered into the business of drastic tax rate reduction. All jurisdictions, including the United States, are mindful of this trend as they strategize to attract investment dollars through either rate reductions or a tax base susceptible to manipulation.[14] This movement by the developed world has not, however, accounted for the impact on the developing world. Without the infrastructure necessary to secure productive investment, developing nations are forced into enacting tax regimes that fail to secure the essential revenue needed to fulfill the needs of constituents. More often than not, their revenue-seeking strategies are depicted as "unfairly competing," "uncooperative," and "harmful" by high-income countries that exploit them (using them as a destination for exports of goods and services, for example, without recognition of a reciprocal obligation) for their own purposes. More likely it appears that these low-income nations are using these mechanisms only in an attempt to survive economically.

---

14. Charles Duhigg and David Kocieniewski, *How Apple Sidesteps Billions in Taxes*, N.Y. Times, April 29, 2012, at A1 (detailing the no-tax strategies of U.S. multinationals, especially in the high-tech sector).

As Fleming et al. indicate, some multinationals have no interest in a permanent move to a territorial system, because the current U.S. system is better than an exemption system.[15] Indeed, many multinationals prefer the combination of the current regime of deferral of U.S. tax on active income on profits of controlled foreign subsidiaries with temporary periods of exemption in order to permit them to bring low-tax offshore profits back to the United States at temporarily low rates.[16] This is a strategy designed to result in very low or no taxation of a substantial portion of profits of those businesses that can operate effectively offshore. Companies that can work this system to their advantage gain an advantage over those that cannot.

There are advocates of a permanent move to an exemption system. The Hines–Desai exploration of the principles of capital ownership neutrality and national ownership neutrality has furnished support for an exemption-type system.[17] They have found that Peggy Musgrove's CEN work fails to account for the benefits to domestic investment or production of increased foreign investment or production and conclude that in a world where all nations adopt an exemption system, there will be more efficiency gains. This results from the swapping of domestic assets for foreign assets and the effective real-location of ownership rights. While the effect on domestic revenue depends upon the productivity of the resulting ownership pattern, Desai and Hines anticipate efficient allocation of capital ownership under this model.

In an exemption system, however, either as an intermittent or permanent tax strategy, developing countries are the losers unless there is intentional consideration of their interests. Efficiency gains in the allocation of resources must take into account the special needs and vulnerability of developing-country markets. To succeed in efficient allocation of capital worldwide, as discussed subsequently, an exemption system is better founded upon mechanisms, such as treaty arrangements, that permit participation of developing nations in the structuring of regimes that enable them to satisfy the needs of their own populations.

The final important tax policy prescription for change is formulary apportionment. Of the many versions under consideration, the approach advocated by Professors Avi-Yonah, Clausing, and Durst seems very promising.[18] Under this plan, U.S. tax on multinationals is computed on the basis of a fraction of their worldwide income. Income of each group is determined on the basis of distinct groups of functions, or activities (i.e., each separate trade or business) of all related parties on a worldwide basis. Treating each activity separately,

---

15. J. Clifton Fleming Jr., et al., *Worse Than Exemption*, 589 Emory L.J. 79 (2009); see also J. Clifton Fleming, Jr., et al., *Designing a U.S. Exemption System for Foreign Income When the Treasury is Empty*, 13 Fla. Tax Rev. 397 (2012) (accepting the inevitability of the introduction of a territorial regime and offering prescriptions for implementation). Congressman David Camp, Chair of the House Ways and Means Committee, has proposed a territorial regime in which the maximum U.S. rate on dividends from CFCs would be as low as 1.25%.

16. *See* repealed I.R.C. §965 (providing a deduction equal to 85 percent of profits repatriated via dividends from controlled foreign subsidiaries, amounting to a 5.25 percent rate on profits brought back during a one-year temporary tax holiday, enacted in 2004).

17. James R. Hines Jr., *Reconsidering the Taxation of Foreign Income*, 62 Tax L. Rev. 269 (2009).

18. Reuven S. Avi-Yonah et al., *Allocating Business Profits for Tax Purposes: A Proposal to Adopt a Formulary Profit Split*, 9 Fla. Tax Rev. 497 (2009) [hereinafter "Avi-Yonah et al., *Formulary Profit Split*"].

income is computed by subtracting worldwide expenses from worldwide income. Resulting net income is apportioned among jurisdictions based on a formula that takes various factors into account. Of that net amount, routine income is assigned to each country by allowing it an estimated return on the tax-deductible expenses of the group in that country. Any additional income remaining after routine income, often termed "residual income," is assigned based on the group's relative sales in each country. Apportioning residual income on the basis of a fraction of worldwide sales places less emphasis on the location of property, payroll, and sales (currently used by certain U.S. states to determine their share of the income of a multistate operation) and reduces the incentive to shift these factors (such as location of assets or employment) from high-tax to low-tax jurisdictions. Place of sale would be determined on the basis of destination of goods (location of the customer), a factor not easily manipulated without loss of profits.

Among the advantages of formulary apportionment are the elimination of reliance on inadequate transfer pricing rules, elimination of the incentive to shift income to zero- or no-tax jurisdictions,[19] an increase in simplicity in the international tax regime, and the possibility of raising more revenue on a broader base, which could enable a rate reduction. While there are obvious critiques of the plan, including concern about the critical need to determine place of sale and expenses accurately, it holds promise to secure a larger role for the developing country in fashioning a tax system and appropriate rates that would allow it to cover its revenue needs. The advantage for developing countries is that:

> By reducing the ability of "tax haven" countries to attract income from other countries' tax bases, a formulary apportionment approach could help governments around the world set their tax policies more independently. The wishes of voters in each government would influence the ideal size of government, required revenue needs, and the allocation of tax burden among subgroups within society. Under the proposed approach, governments are better able to choose their own corporate tax rates based on their assessments of these sorts of policy goals, rather than the pressures of tax competition for an increasingly mobile capital income tax base.[20]

The next section discusses three ways in which reform of the international tax system may address the needs of the Caribbean region.

TWENTY-FIRST CENTURY SOLUTIONS

In the aftermath of the near collapse of the world economy in late 2008, the role of the United States and other leading nations in supporting the vitality of developing nations can only serve the long-term interests of all. The surge in

---

19. Avi-Yonah et al., *Formulary Profit Split, supra* note 18, at 511. The authors note that their proposal "eliminates the tax incentive to shift income through legal and accounting devices, such as licenses of patents and other intangible property, to subsidiaries in zero- or low-tax countries." They conclude that removing the incentive to shift employees and plants outside the United States "will also result in less tax-distorted decisions regarding the location of economic activity." *Id.*

20. *Id.*

economic inequality resulting from fiscal decline has led the Secretary-General of the OECD, Angel Gurría, to dispute the inevitability of inequality, suggesting that it is up to OECD policymakers, which include the leading economies of the world, to "build comprehensive strategies for inclusive growth and better wealth distribution."[21] One of his recommendations was use of tax and benefits systems to ensure equitable distribution of income as well as economic growth.

Robert Zoellick, former president of the World Bank, offered a similar observation when he noted that "[d]eveloped countries need to recognize their self-interest in helping developing countries get on a pathway to sustainable growth."[22] Zoellick's prescriptions for change included formation of international coalitions for both economic and social equality.

Discussions surrounding reform of the U.S. tax system have been concerned primarily with alleviating the tax burden on U.S. multinationals and attracting foreign investment to the United States. The political stakes are cast as a domestic struggle between the interests of business and wealthy investors on the one hand and the middle class on the other, while the impact of U.S. tax policy choices on the viability of the economies of developing countries is largely ignored. Proposals are put forth to reduce the top rates of corporate tax and to retain the already-low rates on investment-type income, such as dividends and capital gains, as an inducement for economic growth. They are founded upon the notion that reduced taxation removes a disincentive to holders of capital to engage in economically productive activity. Opponents point to the absence of real evidence that lower taxation will result in higher production and more jobs. They urge increased taxation at the higher income level and increased spending on social welfare and other entitlement programs so as to pump up revenues in order to support a certain amount of redistribution to the middle and lower-income sectors.

Given the influence of the U.S. economy on the fiscal well-being of the developing world, meaningful innovation requires policymakers to adopt reform of the international tax system that takes the interests of the developing world into account. Three of the many possible options are discussed here. They include a tax treaty solution, serious consideration of a move to formulary apportionment, and use of a per-country foreign tax credit limitation that would favor developing countries.

TAX TREATY

The tax treaty option would provide exemption of active foreign income (when repatriated as dividends from the controlled subsidiary to the parent) derived from investments in developing countries that have entered into a special treaty with the United States. It would be negotiated between the United States and a regional association of countries. This multilateral treaty would be negotiated mindful of the particular needs and interests of the represented countries and could include — in addition to agreements concerning tax rates, transfer pricing, source and expense allocation rules — provisions

---

21. Angel Gurría, *Tackling Inequality*, OECD Observer No. 287 Q4 2011 at 3.
22. Robert B. Zoellick, *Beyond Aid*, speech delivered September 14, 2011, at George Washington University, text in http://web.worldbank.org.

relating to environmental, labor, development, and other topics. The pressures that a move to an exemption system would place on transfer pricing, source, and expense allocation rules would be considerable under such a system, but they would not be insurmountable. Potential problems in implementation would be justified as a device to offset the incentives in the current U.S. regime to use developing countries as a prop to achieve to minimize or avoid tax on revenues derived from production in other countries.

The existence of CARICOM (Caribbean Community), an economic and political association of countries in the Caribbean region, would facilitate the conclusion of a mutually beneficial treaty with the United States. CARICOM has adopted best-practices guidelines and has a leadership structure in place that would serve to guide negotiation of a treaty process mindful of the interests of the nations of that region. The diversity of the area, consisting of fifteen nations, including some of the richest and poorest in the Western Hemisphere, makes it an ideal region for this initiative.[23]

FORMULARY APPORTIONMENT

The second option is serious consideration of a U.S. move to formulary apportionment. Avi-Yonah et al. demonstrate, as noted in the previous section, that income apportionment approximating transfer pricing's profits split method would enable developing countries to set tax policy, including rates, at levels that would sustain their economies. It would eliminate the incentive for multinationals to shift income unilaterally without providing any benefit to the lower-tax jurisdiction. In a world in which all nations adopted this method of income allocation, each location in which a multinational operates would be apportioned its fair share of the income (tax liability would be based on total world income plus a share of the company's sales occurring in the jurisdiction), which it would be free to tax at whatever rates it deemed appropriate.

PER-COUNTRY FTC LIMITATION

A third option, proposed by Professor Adam Rosenzweig, is a move to a per-country foreign tax credit system with an unlimited credit allowed for taxes paid to a developing country. Rosenzweig demonstrates that this shift from the current system would place pressure on developed countries to reduce their rates (but presumably not lower than sufficient to meet spending commitments) and on developing countries to increase their rates to sustainable levels. Pressure would be placed on developing countries to raise their rates solely to free up tax credits that could be used to offset U.S. tax. Under this system:

> [B]y unilaterally amending the basket rules for the foreign tax credit, the United States can dramatically change the incentives of U.S. capital, and consequently, tax competition for capital. This would reduce the incentives for poorer countries to engage in tax competition. Rather than serve to "reward" bad behavior, or insist on a harmonized world regime, or surrender to the

---

23. The CARICOM members are Antigua and Barbuda, Bahamas, Barbados, Belize, Dominica, Grenada, Guyana, Haiti, Jamaica, Montserrat, St. Kitts and Nevis, St. Lucia, St. Vincent, Suriname, and Trinidad and Tobago.

inevitability of tax competition, the law in this manner could internally har-
monize its moving parts solely on its own terms (with respect to incentives it
creates), regardless of how or whether other countries react.[24]

POTENTIAL FOR GROWTH IN THE CARIBBEAN REGION

The Caribbean is a diverse region consisting of a range of countries presenting a
divergent set of circumstances. An inaccurate picture paints the area as one
harboring tax havens that disrupt the operation of legitimate taxing jurisdictions. Some nations adopted no-tax regimes and bank secrecy rules in the
1980s in response to specific recommendations by world bodies, such as the
World Bank and International Monetary Fund, and as a mechanism to compete for capital in world shaped by the CEN policies of the developed world.
Most, however, have not even been in a position to offer tax-competitive
regimes. As a result of what has been described as the CEN paradox, in a
world in which rich countries adopt CEN, poor countries "have an incentive
to engage in tax competition because they are otherwise unable to raise sufficient revenue to meet their minimum needs."[25] The incentive is for developing countries to use their own tax laws to attract capital by exploiting policies
adopted by wealthier countries in the name of worldwide efficiency.

As discussed in the next paragraph, the Caribbean region has made vital
contributions to U.S. economic success. Therefore, the United States has a
responsibility to disrupt this dynamic and to add discussion of the options
described in the previous section as it moves toward international tax reform.
Consideration of affirmative efforts to build a modern tax system that would
open a path for Caribbean nations to develop tax regimes meeting their needs
is a moral imperative for the United States.

The Caribbean region was the eighteenth largest market for U.S. exports in
2010. Total 2010 exports to the region were $18.5 billion. Total 2010 imports
from the region were $10.1 billion.[26] While aid to the region has declined, a
series of natural disasters in recent years has placed some countries in the
region, such as Haiti, in economic decline. With a range of countries, from
Haiti, with a very low per capita income, to Barbados, with a moderate per
capita income, implementation of any of the options discussed in the preceding section has the potential to support growth in the region. Given the U.S.
commitment, beginning in the early 1980s, to support economic development
in the area through the Caribbean Basin Initiative and its reliance upon the
area as a destination for U.S. exports (creating a favorable trade balance),
reform of the international tax system must embrace strategies that will not
disadvantage the region and, more importantly, will support it in its effort to
move toward economic stability.

---

24. Rosenzweig, *Tax Havens, supra* note 6, at 992.
25. *Id.* at 951.
26. Office of the U.S. Trade Representative, Exec. Office of the President, *Ninth Report to Congress on the Operation of the Caribbean Basin Economic Recovery Act* (2011).

CHAPTER 12

INTERNATIONAL DYNAMICS OF INTERNATIONAL TAX

Diane Ring, Boston College Law School

Design of successful and comprehensive tax policy requires attention to more than the traditional concepts and goals of neoclassical economic analysis and its efficiency implications. Or, put another way, failure to consider a fuller vision of tax policy extending beyond economic analysis produces policies of limited scope and less than maximum benefit. This chapter starts with the assumptions drawn from Brown's chapter (that appropriate tax policy goals extend beyond efficiency) and adds the corollary that the relevant actors extend beyond the nation-state. The reality of other players significantly influencing tax policy (other states, multinational corporations, international organizations) must directly shape a country's design of its own international tax policy. Current dialogue and rhetoric in the United States on international tax often fail to adequately wrestle with this feature of the global tax system. Countries need an overarching policy shift to accommodate this expanded understanding of these forces in international tax.

As the first two sections in this chapter document, there are two compelling realities of modern international tax that must guide the development and pursuit of a state's international tax policy goals. The first reality is the importance of bilateral and multilateral measures for the resolution of current tax problems. The second reality is that this essential cooperation and interaction is not exclusively among states; nonstate actors of all stripes actively construct international tax policy.

The first section explores the use of unilateral action in international tax, considering both its advantages and its disadvantages. The second documents the increasingly active role played by other actors in shaping international tax policy and identifies the questions that must be answered in order to assess their impact. This discussion draws upon the recent efforts to incorporate work from the international relations literature into tax policy. The final section concludes by articulating why understanding the forces *behind* the formation of international tax policy will be just as crucial to states as identifying their desired tax policy.

A UNILATERAL PATH IN A MULTILATERAL WORLD

The fiscal crisis continuing through 2013 has only increased the scrutiny given to international tax. The fiscal effects of tax policy bear directly on revenue and the economy. For scrutiny of the tax system to be valuable, it must draw upon an accurate assessment of the realities of international tax. One crucial observation is that all international tax policy choices have cross-border repercussions, including those made by more dominant economies such as the United States. This is true even where the execution of such policy can be achieved through unilateral legislation. Two examples from the United States illustrate this point. First, consider the earnings-stripping rules of section 163(j), which target a foreign parent's attempt to extract profits from the United States without taxation. If a U.S. subsidiary pays interest to its foreign parent, the interest generally would be deductible by the subsidiary in the United States under sections 162 and 163(a) and taxable to the recipient foreign parent as U.S.-source income, thereby preserving one level of U.S. tax on debt capital employed in the United States. However, depending on the income tax treaty that may apply, the interest income earned by the foreign parent could avoid most or all U.S. withholding tax. The result would be no U.S. income tax on the business profits generated by the U.S. subsidiary and paid out as interest to the foreign parent.

The earnings-stripping rules (section 163(j)) step in to ensure that the foreign parent does not capitalize the subsidiary through excessive parent-subsidiary lending. If the U.S. subsidiary has too much debt (according to a multistep formula), a portion of its interest paid to untaxed (or low-taxed) related parties such as the foreign parent is not currently deductible. These earnings-stripping rules serve as a brake on a foreign parent's plan to fund its U.S. subsidiary virtually entirely with debt. Not surprisingly, some treaty partners strongly objected to the enactment of section 163(j), which essentially overrode U.S. treaties granting reduced withholding on interest income. In the years following the introduction of section 163(j) in 1989, there was discussion both inside and outside the United States considering whether the provision violated the nondiscrimination provisions of U.S. bilateral tax treaties.

The European Commission's annual reports (for example, the 1999 Report and the 2002 Report) on U.S. barriers to trade and investment regularly identified section 163(j) as problematic. Other commentators — some academics, some from the business community — suggested that the U.S. stance on section 163(j) (that it did not violate the nondiscrimination provisions in U.S. treaties) created two basic problems for the United States. First, it would be harder than it had been previously for the United States to lodge effective complaints that a given country (e.g., Japan) was effectively discriminating against U.S. businesses operating in the other country by treating them more harshly than their local competitors.[1] Second, the provision raised the specter of retaliation and/or reduced investment in the United States. A letter to the then-Secretary of the U.S. Treasury, Lloyd Bentsen, from the Confederation of British Industry argued that section 163(j) and the revisions that

---

1. *See* Kees Van Raad and Richard Doernberg, *The Legality of the Earnings-Stripping Provision Under U.S. Income Tax Treaties*, 2 Tax Notes Int'l 200, Feb. 1990.

Congress was then contemplating in 1993 would lead to retaliation as trade partners leveled the playing field. Despite these risks, however, the provision itself is unilateral in operation and requires no cooperation from U.S. trading partners. To the extent the United States seeks to discourage significant leveraging of U.S. subsidiaries with debt owed to foreign parents, this domestic code provision achieves that step. Whether it is a desirable policy is a relevant but different question.

Before considering how a country might assess that calculus of benefit and risk, consider another high-profile U.S. rule, the branch profits tax of section 884, which has similarly provoked strong reaction from U.S. trade partners. The branch profits tax aimed to secure the implementation of two levels of U.S. tax on corporate equity investment in the United States conducted through branches. The two levels of tax would be consistent with the classical tax system reflected in U.S. rules: income is taxed once when earned by a corporation and then a second time when the income is distributed as a dividend to the owners of the corporation.

If a foreign corporation conducts its activities in the United States through a U.S. subsidiary, then under U.S. domestic tax law, the equity investment bears two levels of U.S. tax: first at the subsidiary level, and second at the parent shareholder level when a dividend is paid. The two levels of tax occur because there is no subsidiary deduction for the dividend, and because the dividend is taxable U.S.-source income for the recipient parent (although a governing treaty could reduce or eliminate the U.S. tax imposed on the parent's receipt of the dividend).

If, however, the foreign corporation operates in the United States through a branch, the U.S. income is taxed once to the branch (as a trade or business/permanent establishment), but the subsequent repatriation of profits to the home country office would trigger no additional tax under the basic rules because it would constitute an intra-taxpayer transfer, not a taxable dividend. In theory (and under prior law), a later dividend paid by the foreign corporation to its foreign shareholders could be subject to tax under U.S. rules, but in practice the provision has proven completely unadministrable.

The 1986 branch profits rule guarantees that a "withdrawal" of profits from the U.S. branch to the home office triggers a second level of U.S. tax corresponding (although not identical) to the tax that would be due on a dividend distribution by a U.S. subsidiary to its foreign parent. All of this was possible without any specific action or coordination on the part of other states. Once again, however, the foreign reaction was not positive, and treaty partners considered the U.S. action to constitute a treaty override. In his statement to the Senate Committee on Foreign Relations in June of 1990, the then–assistant secretary (tax policy) for the Department of the Treasury, Kenneth Gideon, expressed concern that the "benefits of a broad U.S. treaty network" would be "eroded if Congress made a practice of overriding significant U.S. treaty obligations."[2] Gideon identified specific ramifications from the 1986 Tax Act overrides:

---

2. Kenneth W. Gideon, Assistant Secretary (Tax Policy), Department of the Treasury, Statement to the Committee on Foreign Relations, United States Senate, Washington, D.C. (June 14, 1990), 90 TNI 25–64.

Our treaty partners have voiced strong objections to treaty overrides in both bilateral and multilateral fora. Several major U.S. treaty partners have recently suggested in the course of treaty discussions that they may insist on reserving in a new treaty the right to retaliate automatically against any United States overrides. More importantly, it is becoming increasingly difficult to negotiate reciprocal concessions when the foreign government fears that the United States may unilaterally reverse the bargain by legislative action.[3]

The conclusion, therefore, is that even for cross-border tax policy choices capable of unilateral implementation, such as earnings-stripping and branch profits taxes, the rules are likely to draw the attention if not the ire of foreign countries attentive to the impact on their own resident taxpayers. Why would the United States care about the foreign reaction to these policies if the U.S. goals can be achieved unilaterally? The reactions identified above to the U.S. unilateral actions on earnings stripping and branch profits suggest that direct retaliation and impaired treaty negotiations are possible risks.

Does this mean that a country such as the United States cannot or should not act against the consent of its treaty or trade partners when enacting domestic tax laws on cross-border questions? Certainly not. Policy decisions reflect a constant weighing of risks and benefits, both short- and long-term. Moreover, the precise nature of the unilateral effort may be relevant—for example, a clear treaty override may look quite different from a new rule that simply adopts a strong stance on source or residence taxation. The benefits to the United States from trying to implement quickly and decisively a firm position on U.S. taxation of foreign investment in the United States could be worthwhile, particularly if the U.S. bargaining position in the international arena remains strong. The more relevant question is how those benefits compare to the degree and nature of costs incurred by staking out a unilateral path. The fact that the U.S. action in both of the above cases was unilateral tax policy does not insulate it from the need to account for the international response, especially as we consider that many other U.S. policy goals, such as those considered subsequently, likely require some measure of cooperation and outreach. As more of our tax goals cannot be achieved unilaterally, the support and involvement of other states and actors become essential. The real dynamics of international taxation have started even though the rules at issue could be successful on a unilateral basis.[4]

Perhaps in the past the value placed on fostering a cooperative approach in international tax was less pressing, at least for the United States (although even 20 years ago, the Treasury Department was concerned about the ramifications of unilateral action). Regardless, many of the important international tax issues on the U.S. agenda today do depend on assistance, coordination, or

---

3. *Id.*

4. It is interesting to note that the predecessor of the branch profits tax rule, the resourcing rule for dividends paid by foreign corporations with a certain amount of U.S. trade or business income, was considered ineffectual, especially without additional assistance from foreign governments in identifying the existence and amount of such dividend payments from foreign corporations to their foreign shareholders. The more recent change in withholding rules (which provide that resourced dividend payments made by a foreign corporation to its foreign shareholders will no longer be subject to withholding) was a final and direct acknowledgment of the failure in that earlier approach.

cooperation from other states and cannot be best resolved unilaterally. The tax literature has devoted significant attention to many of these policies, including tax competition, cross-border tax arbitrage, permanent establishments, transfer pricing, tax compliance, and tax evasion. The nature and degree of need for coordination and cooperation varies depending on the issue.

For example, cross-border tax arbitrage presents three basic tax policy responses. First, a state can simply ignore the existence of the arbitrage opportunities. This position is advocated by a number of tax analysts on the grounds that arbitrage is inevitable in a multijurisdictional system with a wide range of both formal rules and informal enforcement practices. Alternatively, a state can make unilateral changes to its rules to eliminate the arbitrage opportunity. This path bears a number of drawbacks, including concerns that the state taking the unilateral action may disadvantage itself or its taxpayers, that the state will de facto have to match its tax rules to the other state or states with whom there are arbitrage opportunities, or that the other states will react with legislation that puts taxpayers in a position of double taxation (if, for example, both the United States and the other state were to deny any deduction for a transaction in response to a double deduction arbitrage).[5] Recent examples of arbitrage, such as the potential for dual consolidated losses between the United States and the United Kingdom, illustrate these tensions. Finally, a state might seek to work out a coordinated plan with one or more states to eliminate the arbitrage opportunity, either at the outset or following a less than successful series of unilateral actions.

Other cross-border tax problems offer only very limited unilateral solutions, with the most promising responses being bilateral at a minimum. Perhaps one of the most widely considered is tax competition. Although the Organisation for Economic Co-operation and Development (OECD) project on harmful tax competition identified a number of unilateral steps that nations could take to limit the effects of such competition (e.g., the implementation, or improvement, of controlled foreign corporation rules), the dominant thrust of the project took aim at the behavior of the tax havens it identified. To the extent tax competition is broadly conceived of as any effort to use the substantive, procedural, and administrative rules and practices of a country's tax system to facilitate the earning of income with little or no taxation, then it becomes apparent that if one country tightens its rules, any mobile income, activity, or flows can and often will migrate to another country with a more "forgiving" or "flexible" approach. Efforts by one country, let alone a few, would likely prove highly ineffective at curbing this competition. Some observers have even suggested that a single holdout could essentially undermine an entire multilateral plan to limit tax competition because the remaining holdout either garners all income, activity, or flows or causes a sufficient number of plan participants to doubt the success of their plan and ultimately back out.

In addition to tax competition, which highlights the coordination/cooperation question from the government perspective (i.e., the governments and

---

5. If, for example, the first state attempts to address the cross-border arbitrage opportunity by denying arbitrage deductions in certain circumstances, and the second state later responds with a similar rule, then the result is that the transaction that was in theory "entitled" to one deduction (but not two) now has zero deductions.

their fiscs are generally the perceived losers from tax competition, at least "harmful" tax competition), transfer pricing presents another important arena for coordinated tax action. Here, taxpayers can lose from inconsistent positions taken by two countries, each claiming income has been earned in its jurisdiction. Of course, governments themselves are frequently on the losing end as taxpayers pursue aggressive transfer pricing and income-shifting strategies. The international tax community has taken a variety of steps over recent years to mitigate these negative repercussions from transfer pricing. These steps include common transfer pricing practices promulgated by the OECD, bilateral treaty provisions with competent authority mechanisms for resolving conflicts between countries, and bilateral and multilateral advance pricing agreements (under which two or more countries agree, along with the taxpayer, to a plan of action for the pricing of a series of specified related-party transactions involving both jurisdictions). Although transfer pricing remains a serious problem, with serious administrative and conceptual challenges from both the taxpayer and government perspectives, a significant degree of consensus exists over the communal nature of the problem.

Consideration of just these examples demonstrates that there is no single model of the possible or necessary interactions among states on cross-border tax issues. What it does emphasize is that no course of action on taxing cross-border activity is free from international ramifications. Furthermore, although each decision to pursue unilateral or bilateral/multilateral action requires a weighing of costs and benefits, for the high-profile issues of today the balance is shifting toward bilateral and multilateral action. Thus, the *first tax reality* of the current global economy is the interconnected nature of our tax rules and the importance of cooperation among states to fully realize desired tax policy.

However, a deeper examination of some of the foregoing examples would reveal the *second reality* shaping modern international tax policy: not only must we turn our attention more closely to other states as we seek cooperation and coordination, but we must also acknowledge the powerful and complicated role played by a wide range of *nonstate* actors, including multinational corporations and international organizations. For example, the Advance Pricing Agreement (APA) program (originating in the United States in 1991 but now widely in place around the world) is premised on the idea that a taxpayer, typically a multinational corporation, will voluntarily come to the Internal Revenue Service (IRS) to discuss the appropriate methods for analyzing and pricing its future cross-border transactions with related parties. Discussion of this question in advance of the actual transactions is expected to reduce conflict and facilitate agreement between the taxpayer and the country (or countries) and enable them to sign an APA memorializing their agreement on these highly controversial questions of fact and law. However, initiation of the APA process requires the taxpayer to voluntarily disclose a significant amount of information to the IRS. Essentially, the success of the government-structured "solution" to transfer pricing requires the support of the business community. When the APA was initially introduced in the United States in 1991 with the announcement of an already completed APA, the general reaction of both multinational corporations and many foreign countries was not positive. At a minimum, critics argued that a business would have to be crazy to unveil itself so fully to the IRS. At the more extreme end, some governments considered the program a ploy by the United States to capture a larger portion of cross-border revenue through the pricing in the APAs. Ultimately, many taxpayers and countries came to view APAs as a viable path (even if it was not suitable for all companies). Multinational corporations, of course, have played other, arguably more aggressive, roles in shaping international tax policy. Either directly or through trade groups (such as the National Foreign Trade Council), they advocate for or against tax proposals, draft desired tax language, comment to Treasury and IRS on proposed rule-making, and lobby governments around the world. Depending on the size, wealth, and political structure of the country in question, the influence of multinational corporations may be quite strong.

Other kinds of international organizations actively mold the path of tax law. For example, in the area of taxation of permanent establishments, the OECD has played a sustained and prominent role in establishing the model treaty and commentary and, in more recent years, pursuing a series of reform projects related to specific types of permanent establishments and to the attribution of profits to those establishments. An active part of the OECD reform projects involves the solicitation of comments from taxpayers, especially multinationals and their representatives.

Still other kinds of international organizations influence policy through the research and analysis they sponsor (e.g., the European Association of Tax Law Professors) or through the dissemination of tax planning knowledge among a community of taxpayers (e.g., the International Tax Planning Association). These examples serve as only the barest indication of the range of players, practices, and purposes at work in the world of international tax policy formation.

But this intricate web of participants in designing international tax policy is no surprise to observers of international relations. They would immediately recognize that even in an area such as taxation, where state actors have a particularly dominant role,[6] the path and shape of policy design cannot be understood and explained by reference only to the state actors. International organizations and multinational corporations also wield notable power. The real question is not whether these nonstate actors are relevant, but rather whether the confluence of state and nonstate forces can be predicted and understood on a systematic basis. This is not just a question of academic interest. Given the established importance of cooperation and coordination in much of international tax policy, every state should be deeply interested in how the dynamics of international tax relations pertain to its tax policy agenda. Just as states devote extensive attention and study to the economic implications of existing and contemplated tax policy choices, states should consider the study of international relations in tax to be a

---

6. To appreciate the potentially dominant role of states in tax policy, contrast that topic with environmental law. States can impose environmental regulations, or businesses can implement industry standards. Potentially both could produce the same environmental outcome. However, in the tax arena, the tax rules are set by the state and the revenue is collected by the state. Other than a plan of voluntary contributions by taxpayers to the fisc, there is no readily identifiable tax parallel to the setting of standards by an industry in the environmental context.

necessary complement to their current efforts to design, develop, and implement their desired tax policy.

Certainly, the Treasury and IRS consider themselves in the business of doing more than drafting and implementing tax rules. They seek, in concert with Congress, to frame an international tax policy that reflects a sophisticated understanding of these complications. To date, the focus, however, has been on the *economic* ramifications. IRS and Treasury periodically generate a variety of studies, reports, and white papers, but the general scope and mission of these analyses has been on the economic (including investment and competitiveness) implications of different options. The next step in advancing the international tax policy agenda should be to develop a sophisticated knowledge of the international relations of tax policy. The following section examines the kinds of questions that need to be answered and the kinds of analyses that may provide these answers.

ASSESSING THE COMPLEX INTERACTIONS BEHIND THE CREATION OF INTERNATIONAL TAX POLICY

The roadmap for a revised international tax policy agenda should include travel down three separate but very connected lines of inquiry: (1) understanding the distinctive role of international state-based organizations and bodies; (2) understanding the nonstate actors (including multinational corporations and tax experts); and (3) understanding the networks of tax administrators and bureaucracies. Work on these three lines of inquiry would not be in uncharted waters. International relations scholars have been developing these areas for years, and some tax observers have already begun investigating segments of these questions. The goal is to unite these questions explicitly under a coherent analytical and investigational framework that directs and supports tax policy. This section outlines the research and the questions that can form the foundation of the three initial lines of inquiry listed above (international organizations, nonstate actors, and administrator networks), as well as some examples of where and how that knowledge would be valuable for tax policy.

INTERNATIONAL ORGANIZATIONS IN INTERNATIONAL TAX

The United States continuously interacts with a wide range of international organizations on tax matters, including some of which it is a member (e.g., the OECD and the United Nations), and some of which it is not (e.g., CARICOM, ASEAN). What is the role (or roles) played by a state-based international organization? How does its agenda become established? When is an international organization likely to be influential or powerful? Are international organizations a positive or negative force on the development of tax policy? Are there particular characteristics that would be desirable to encourage (or discourage) in the operation of an international organization?

Full resolution of these important and complex questions is beyond the scope of this chapter. However, what this chapter can do is develop the framework of important questions and areas of research, and provide some concrete applications from international tax. As a starting point, probably one of the most globally significant international bodies involved in the tax field is the OECD. In addition to providing one of the dominant model treaties and accompanying commentary, it also affords an opportunity to member states and others to debate the continuing interpretation and application of standardized provisions and to study (through formalized working groups) major international tax questions of the day, ranging from transfer pricing to permanent establishments to electronic commerce. What do we know about the OECD and how it impacts global tax policy? The effect of the OECD on global tax policy turns on (1) its membership, (2) its goals, and (3) its institutional structure. A brief review of these features will lay the groundwork for answering the larger tax policy questions.[7]

A Look at the OECD

The OECD's predecessor organization, the OEEC (Organisation for European Economic Cooperation), emerged from the aftermath of World War II and the Marshall Plan recovery efforts. The OEEC's projects encompassed commodities production, provision of services, tariffs, currency, and worker mobility. The Fiscal Committee of the OEEC began in the 1950s to examine core questions of cross-border taxation (including permanent establishment, fiscal domicile, and tax discrimination).[8] By 1960, the OEEC members sought to shift the organization's focus away from and beyond its post–World War II European roots, expanding its vision and membership, to reflect the changing economic environment. The new organization, the OECD (formed Sept. 30, 1961), comprised many European nations (including Austria, Belgium, Denmark, France, Germany, Greece, Italy, Spain, Switzerland, and the United Kingdom) and some non-European nations (including the United States and Canada). OECD membership has continued to grow with the addition of states such as Australia, the Czech Republic, Hungary, Japan, Korea, Mexico, New Zealand, and the Slovak Republic.

According to Article 1 of the OECD convention, the OECD aims to promote sustainable economic growth, employment, financial stability, and rising living standards in member countries. The OECD also maintains a commitment to economic development beyond the borders of its member states, expressing a commitment to policies that "contribute to the development of the world economy" and "contribute to the expansion of world trade on a multilateral, nondiscriminatory basis in accordance with international obligations." This far-reaching agenda resulted in the OECD pursuing not only strictly matters of trade and financial policy but also a full range of taxation

---

7. For a more extensive consideration of some of these questions, *see* Diane Ring, *Who Is Making International Tax Policy? International Organizations as Power Players in a High-Stakes World*, 33 Fordham Int'l L. J. 649 (2010).

8. *See, e.g.*, J. L. L. Wisse, *The Organisation for Economic Cooperation and Development* (Apr. 2007), copy on file with the author.

issues (e.g., tax conventions, taxation of multinational enterprises, tax avoidance, and consumption taxes). As a result, the OECD built a tremendous body of tax work in the form of research, model language for tax instruments, and reports. Moreover, the OECD developed an acknowledged expertise in taxation and established itself as a significant player in the international tax world. However, when we speak of the OECD's work and accomplishments in this way, to whom and to what are we specifically referring? What institutional structure lies behind this output, expertise, and influence?

At the top of the OECD organizational chart is the Council, a plenary body with representation of all thirty-four member states by their minister or permanent representative. A number of nonmember states and international organizations have "observer status." The precise composition of the group of observers depends on what level and topical area (e.g., taxation, trade and agriculture, education, environment) of the OECD is involved. Observer status grants the opportunity to participate in discussions but not to vote. In addition, one entity has been granted a role between observer and member. By virtue of a supplementary protocol to the OECD Convention, the Commission of the European Community became entitled to "participate" in the work of the OECD. This special role extends beyond observer status and affords the EU what the OECD characterizes as "quasi-member status." OECD membership expanded in 2010 with the addition of Chile, Slovenia, Israel, and Estonia. The OECD offered "enhanced engagement" to Brazil, China, India, Indonesia, and South Africa. Although not precisely an accession to membership path, this relationship with the OECD could serve as a prelude to formal membership.

The Secretary-General of the OECD serves as the Chair of the OECD Council and has a staff to assist in the performance of the Secretary-General's oversight and executive functions (approximately 2500 staff members serve in the Secretariat in Paris, including economists, scientists, and lawyers). The bulk of the OECD work is undertaken by its subsidiary bodies established by the Council. The Committee on Fiscal Affairs (CFA) is the plenary subsidiary body formed by the Council and charged with the responsibility of studying and reporting on tax issues. In addition to its plenary membership, the CFA has formal observers, including Argentina, China, India, Russia, South Africa, the International Monetary Fund, and the World Bank. Under the CFA are several topical "working parties," at present (1) Working Party 1: Conventions and Related Questions; (2) Working Party 2: Tax Policy Analysis and Tax Statistics; (3) Working Party 6: Taxation of Multinational Enterprises; (4) Working Party 9: Consumption Taxes; and (5) Working Party 10: Cooperation to Minimize Tax Evasion and Avoidance. The most well-known output from these subsidiary bodies is the OECD Model Treaty and Commentary, developed by Working Party 1 and approved by the Council. Other subsidiary bodies under the CFA include the Forum on Harmful Tax Practices and the Forum on Tax Administration. The various formal actions that the OECD can take (ranging from resolutions and recommendations to decisions and formal agreements) require unanimity (unless a member state chooses to abstain).

Although the formal OECD structure relies on sovereign states (both members and observers) and some international organization observers (such as the

World Bank), the OECD contains the seeds of its own direct contact with the business community. In 1962, following the creation of the OECD, BIAC (Business and Industry Advisory Committee to the OECD) was founded as an independent entity to provide the voice of business to the OECD. According to BIAC's 2011 Annual Report, its mission is to ensure that "business and industry needs are adequately addressed in OECD policy instruments . . . which influence national legislation" and that OECD positions "assist private sector growth and prosperity and, thereby, contribute to the global economy." Moreover, the various subsidiary bodies of the OECD that are active in research and the development of proposals solicit input from beyond the OECD community. For example, when the OECD released its new draft update of the model income tax treaty in April 2008, comments were invited to be sent to the OECD Centre for Tax Policy and Administration (which provides technical expertise to the CFA). As of the closing date for comments, the OECD reported receipt of position statements from not only BIAC, but also (1) the Treaty Policy Working Group (an association of multinationals focused on permanent establishment related issues), (2) Qantas, (3) KPMG, (4) Siemens, and (5) the Software Coalition.

The extensive OECD operations are funded by a budget, which, for 2012, was €347 million. Funding comes from the 34 member states, with the individual national contributions determined based on a formula accounting for the size of the member's economy. The United States is the largest contributor, at nearly 22 percent of the budget, followed by Japan. In addition to these formal contributions, individual nations can, with Council approval, provide additional voluntary funds to special programs outside the main budget.

How does membership shape the OECD's work?

Clearly the OECD has a significant apparatus that it can bring to tax research, drafting, and policy. The preceding examination of the OECD's operations prompts a number of important questions, but perhaps the most essential is "How does the composition of the OECD's membership mold its actions?" In particular, how does membership influence (1) the topics selected for extensive examination and recommendations by OECD bodies; (2) the OECD's policy perspectives threading through its output; (3) the nature of the OECD's persuasive powers; and (4) the OECD's future role? Although the expansion in OECD since 1961 has been significant and brought on board a growing variety of nations, the OECD nonetheless retains a reputation and identity as a rich countries' club. One might expect that an organization's focus and perspective would reflect the concerns of its members. Although those concerns need not always be in direct conflict with nonmember nations, the economic differences between most members and most nonmembers suggests that some tension should be expected. The story of the OECD and tax competition illustrates the complicated effect of membership on OECD action. Moreover, the tax competition story, which starts with the first reality of modern international tax policy (that many important issues require more than a unilateral response), quickly reveals the relevance of the second reality (that there are multiple actors beyond the states who directly and successfully act to shape international tax policy). If we do not understand how these players interact, we limit our ability to effectuate desired tax policy.

As described in the first section of this chapter, the term "cross-border tax competition" refers to situations in which one country uses its tax system to attract investment, business activity, or capital from other countries. The competing jurisdiction becomes attractive through a regime of no taxation, little taxation, and/or limited disclosure of information to other governments. Competing on the basis of taxes is not new. But, international tax competition became a more significant concern in the 1980s with the increased mobility of capital, general globalization, and rapid developments in communication and technology. Some OECD members expressed concern with what was ultimately characterized as the "harmful" effects of tax competition. In 1996, at the urging of some of its members, the OECD agreed to study this issue. Over the following two years the CFA (through its subsidiary bodies) studied tax competition and organized three regional seminars to institute a dialogue with nonmember states on these issues. The first seminar took place in Mexico and was attended by Argentina, Bolivia, Brazil, Chile, Colombia, Jamaica, Peru, and Venezuela. The second seminar took place in Istanbul with participants from Albania, Azerbaijan, Estonia, the Former Yugoslav Republic of Macedonia (FYROM), Georgia, Latvia, Lithuania, Moldova, Mongolia, Romania, the Slovak Republic, and Ukraine. The third seminar was held in cooperation with the Asian Development Bank in Singapore, with China, India, Indonesia, Malaysia, the Philippines, Singapore, Sri Lanka, Chinese Taipei, and Thailand attending.[9]

Finally, in 1998 the OECD released its now famous report, *Harmful Tax Competition: An Emerging Global Issue.* The Council approved the report (Luxembourg and Switzerland abstained) and adopted a recommendation to its member countries to "implement the recommendations [of the report], including the Guidelines for Dealing with Harmful Preferential Tax Regimes." The Council also instructed the CFA to establish a "Forum on Harmful Tax Practices," to continue the additional work outlined in the Appendix to the Report," to report periodically to the Council, and to develop a dialogue with nonmembers on the analysis, conclusions, and recommendations of the report. Over the next two years, the OECD notified a range of countries regarding their potential characterization by the OECD as a "haven" jurisdiction. Some countries agreed to cooperate with the OECD and implement tax reform in order to avoid being listed by the OECD. Ultimately, in June 2000, the OECD released a report blacklisting 35 nations, none of which attended the earlier OECD regional seminars. Among the listed nations were Andorra, Anguilla, the Bahamas, Guernsey, and the Netherlands Antilles. An additional 17 countries avoided the list (including Bermuda, the Cayman Islands, and Mauritius), apparently through a commitment to cooperate with the OECD. At the end of June 2000, the OECD sponsored a symposium with thirty non-OECD members in attendance (some had attended the earlier OECD regional seminars and some had not). An OECD representative characterized the event as the first substantial effort on the part of the OECD to work with nonmembers on the tax competition issue.

---

9. OECD, *Harmful Tax Competition: An Emerging Global Issue* (OECD, 1998), 10, available at http://www.oecd.org/tax/transparency/44430243.pdf .

By late 2000, however, resistance to the OECD tax competition project increased both in the havens and in the United States. Resistance in the United States was directed substantially by the Center for Freedom and Prosperity (CFP), which had been organized in October 2000 which a mission to preserve "tax competition, sovereignty, and financial privacy." The CFP lobbied Congress, including specific efforts to lobby the Congressional Black Caucus on the grounds that efforts to stop certain tax competition would be harmful to poorer nations, including those in the Caribbean. A paper trail of their success in persuading many members of Congress that it was a bad idea to limit even "harmful" tax competition appeared in the form of letters to then–Secretary of the Treasury Paul O'Neill outlining their objections to U.S. participation in the OECD project. Their stated objections sometimes reflected concern for haven countries and in other cases reflected a concern for American taxpayers as well as a view that the United States itself might serve as a haven in some contexts — and that such profitable status should be preserved.

At the same time that the CFP targeted Congress, it also encouraged and structured the fermenting rejection of the OECD approach among haven states. The CFP founders attended the December 2000 Annual Conference on Caribbean and Latin American Economies, then shortly thereafter sponsored a symposium in Barbados on the OECD tax competition efforts. Ultimately, the CFP even persuaded Antigua to designate the CFP leaders as the representatives of Antigua at the January 2001 OECD summit with Caribbean tax havens.

The CFP's strategy ultimately resulted in O'Neill announcing in May 2001 that United States did not support the OECD's tax competition project — a complete reversal of its active, supporting position of the prior year. Eventually this stark position, which reflected misunderstandings of the scope of the OECD project, was moderated, but its impact remained. Although the OECD work on tax competition has continued to the present, U.S. participation and the scope of the project were tempered as a result of this negative pushback. The project shifted direction to focus more extensively on transparency and information sharing.

What does this story reveal about the impact of OECD membership on topic selection, perspective, persuasion, and the future? Clearly the OECD attention to tax competition reflected the interests and concerns of more developed economies, which sought to secure a solid tax base to fund their social welfare systems. This perspective is not surprising for an organization often characterized as a "rich countries' club." Although there is considerable discussion in the literature and public sphere regarding the idea that tax competition might not be good for havens and developing economies and may fail to deliver on its promises of employment and investment, the havens were not the states arguing against tax competition. Rather, it was the developed, non-haven economies. There is nothing wrong with an organization having a cohesive membership or with an organization advocating the interests of its members. From a tax policy perspective, though, it raises interesting questions regarding which issues will receive serious attention and how successful the organization will be in pressing its goals in a more global arena.

An organization of developed economies likely will focus on concerns salient to its membership. Tax competition certainly falls into that category, as do many other major tax issues covered by the OECD such as transfer pricing, electronic commerce, and permanent establishments. To the extent that the OECD can develop a focused approach to important issues of international taxation, it may be able to marshal its resources better for both research and advocacy. However, the shared perspective of its members that initially orients the OECD's work could prove a more limiting factor as the OECD seeks to develop a broader international consensus. Where OECD projects require, or at least benefit from, cooperation beyond the universe of developed economies, this question of persuasion is important. In the case of tax competition, although the OECD operated the initial regional seminars for nonmembers, these seminars did not constitute an extensive dialogue and did not include the nations that ultimately appeared on the uncooperative haven list.

There is no guarantee that earlier, more extensive conversations with countries such as Anguilla or the Netherlands Antilles would have resulted in a cooperative outcome. But it is not implausible that more extensive consultations earlier in the process might have forestalled and muted the resistance on the scale that eventually emerged. Essentially, once the OECD decided to confront tax competition, which frequently though not exclusively brought it into conflict with nonmember havens, the question was whether the OECD would have more success by adopting a harsh stance, an open engagement approach, or a multistep process where stronger statements are followed by more conciliatory dialogue and the concession of some initial positions. The OECD itself considers its work in tax competition to be a learning process in which it began to move toward a more cooperative and "forward-looking" approach in its relations with havens. It is possible that the stronger stance of the 1998 OECD report against havens may have generated heightened attention to and awareness of the organization's deep concerns about tax competition — and provided an essential impetus for any real action. Regardless, even this international organization, which itself was a primary player in shaping the international tax agenda, realized that the universe of relevant actors was becoming more complicated. Fruitful tax policy work would demand increasing attention to the multiple players and intersecting interests.

Part of the complication in understanding the forces at work in shaping international tax policy derives from two important observations. The first is that state-based international organizations such as the OECD are not simply agents of their member states. Although ultimate policy choices will reflect the underlying interests of the members, there is variation among OECD members, and there is independent influence at the organizational level. Recall that the OECD itself has a sizable permanent staff that engages in research and policy formation. One would anticipate that some of the staff effectively serve as tax policy leaders with influence to help direct and contour membership agreement on an issue.

The second important observation is that membership is not an exclusive status. Nations (and other groups) frequently hold membership in more than one relevant organization simultaneously. What is the impact of this cross-membership on the member's own strategizing within each organization and on the actions of the organization (bearing in mind that typically the membership rolls across two organizations will not be identical, even when there is some overlap)? A classic example from international tax looks at the OECD and the United Nations, where OECD membership is a subset of the U.N. membership. Although the OECD has a deeper involvement in tax issues, both organizations play a role in tax policy, and each offers a model double taxation treaty. Traditionally, the U.N. model treaty has been hailed as more sensitive to the needs and circumstances of developing economies. In contrast, the OECD model is generally characterized as favoring developed, capital-exporting nations. Given the high degree of similarity between the models, and the reality that the U.N. model consciously relied on the OECD model as a starting point, distinctions between the two should not be overemphasized. Still, there are differences. Does that mean that the developed economies forming the basis of the OECD were outvoted in designing the U.N. model? Or did they share in the consensus that another vision of tax treaties was appropriate to reflect the needs of developing economies? Or was the treaty in the U.N. part of some broader package of work brokered by the organization to which all members were willing to agree? Answers to these questions would illuminate the impact of members, cross-membership, and membership strategy on the trajectory of international tax policy.

The OECD's membership may prove a critical factor in determining the organization's role in the future. The increased variety and quantity of international tax conflicts have prompted contemplation of a more enhanced cooperation among states over international tax. Typically this idea envisions a lead organization through which the coordination could take place. Some would argue that the OECD's extensive technical and historical expertise in taxation (and in trade and economics more broadly) make it a sensible focal point for coordination efforts. Others contend that the OECD's history as an organization for developed countries makes it unable to reach out to and garner support from developing economies. Which scenario is more plausible? Why? Can the OECD's long-standing reputation be offset by its increasing efforts (both in the tax competition area and beyond) to connect with nonmember nations, as it has done with the Global Tax Forum? What in fact are the most critical factors for an institution to succeed in being *the* global leader, *the* global body? Contemplation of these questions leads us to two additional issues we need to understand better regarding international organizations and their potential influence: how might the framing of the organization's mission be significant, and how does the choice of structure for the organization impact its operations and output?

How does an organization's mission fashion its place in international tax?

This broad inquiry points to a number of more targeted questions. First, what is the relationship between membership and the stated mission of an organization? If, for example, the OECD membership is predominantly wealthy countries, can it profess a commitment to broader social and economic goals and correspondingly increase its credibility? Article 1 of the OECD Convention states that its "aims . . . shall be to promote policies designed to: (a) achieve the highest sustainable economic growth and employment and a rising standard of living in Member countries, while maintaining financial stability, and thus to contribute to the development of the world economy; [and] (b) to contribute to the sound economic expansion in Member as well as non-member countries in the process of economic development." What is the effect of a mission statement such as that of the OECD, which professes a primary commitment to Member countries but includes a more comprehensive goal of universal economic development? Does the standard image of the OECD member as a wealthier nation, combined with language stressing the support of member states, significantly impede OECD efforts to reach beyond its membership? Would the OECD be viewed as less narrowly self-interested than an individual nation but more self-interested than, say, an aid organization whose members obtain a much more attenuated benefit from the work of the organization? Is it easier to believe that an organization with more elite membership is working toward a broader good when the subject matter is less directly "economics"? Or can an international organization such as the OECD use both its mission statement and its conduct to expand its reputation beyond the immediate boundaries of its members? Again, research on the work of international organizations, the role of knowledge and expertise in international relations, and the process and impact of norm building by communities and organizations would all bear directly on these questions.

Second, although an international organization's mission can fall anywhere on the spectrum from narrow to extremely broad, what are the implications of that choice? It might be easier for an organization with a clear, concise focus to develop its own analysis and then attempt to hash out a final position with a competing organization, entity, or state. Alternatively, an organization with a broader mission has the opportunity to facilitate horse trading. For example, the organization can present recommendations on tax as part of a full package of reforms covering multiple subjects; although the package might not be ideal in all aspects for any single member, it nonetheless offers enough to each member to gain its support. Had the organization been limited to discussing only tax, its range of negotiating points would have been considerably lessened and the prospect for consensus more limited. Related to, and often intertwined with, the scope of the organization's mission is the scope of membership. Although narrow membership can make agreement easier, a broader membership can enable the organization to develop its position, fully cognizant of the views of those most likely to dissent, and to build support from potential naysayers before positions become entrenched.

Translating this to the world of international tax, we can again directly compare the OECD and the United Nations (other organizations may provide an even sharper contrast in terms of narrowness of mission, but the high degree of familiarity with these two facilitates a quick review). The OECD is more focused than the UN, in both membership and mission coverage, despite its array of activities including environmental, tax, and financial markets. The UN works across many topics including global security, humanitarian action, human rights, drug trafficking, and refugees, in addition to taxation. What is the effect of the OECD's narrower (though hardly limited) agenda? When is a narrower focus more desirable? Does it create expertise? Does it reduce spillover effects from other contentious issues? When is it less desirable? Does it render the institution less sensitive to the connections among policies and issues? This point frequently surfaces in discussions of tariffs and taxes, as observers comment on the ability of both mechanisms to achieve similar effects. Should the two subjects always be approached in tandem? Or are there important ways in which taxation and trade differ, and thus their mediation through an institution cannot and should not be identical? The real-life version of this question can be seen in the inquiry into whether it would make sense for the World Trade Organization (WTO) to seize a more prominent position in global tax policy coordination because of its leading role in trade matters combined with its membership, which has been historically broader than that of the OECD.

In what ways does the institutional structure of an organization predict its action and influence?

In addition to membership and mission, just outlined, the structure of an organization is an important feature in determining how the organization functions and what the organization does. Asking about structure is really asking several distinct questions. First, how do specific choices and decisions get made in the organization? This inquiry includes but extends far beyond the basic voting rules of the organization. Unanimous voting ensures that the organization acts with consensus and broad support, but it significantly limits the ability of the organization to act at all. The operation of the European Union on matters of taxation demonstrates this limitation quite clearly and intentionally (although the EU is not an international organization in the same mold of the UN or the OECD, it nonetheless has enough similarities to provide useful insights). The EU members explicitly sought to retain most direct taxing powers to themselves. Thus, the EU continues to list direct taxation as one of the subjects requiring unanimous support for EU action. As a result, the EU has moved very slowly (outside the European Court of Justice) in directly shaping tax law in the EU.

In addition to making it difficult for an organization to produce any recommendations or positions, unanimous voting requirements increase the likelihood that any resulting positions are sufficiently limited or watered down so as to appease all voting members. The role of unanimous voting, however, is further complicated where there is a possibility of abstention. The availability of the abstention option can be useful in allowing a country to express its disagreement without going so far as to block what might otherwise be an essentially unanimous outcome. The real effect of abstention, though, can be appreciated only in the specific context, taking into account the nature of the decision from which the country abstained (Was it binding on all members or only participating members? Was it advisory? Did it provide for alternative compliance possibilities?) and taking into account the broader meaning of abstention in that organization.

Moving beyond formal voting, how is the organization's agenda established? How does it decide which issues to explore and prepare for policy recommendations? Is that a decision of a plenary body? Is it the decision of a more specialized and limited subsidiary-level body? What is the process within the organization for encouraging dialogue? Are discussions conducted in open sessions, or closed ones? What is the policy on the inclusion of nonmembers? In the case of the OECD, both the Council and the primary subsidiary tax body (the CFA) are plenary bodies. Other subsidiary bodies are not plenary in nature; how is their membership determined, and what power do such bodies possess in shaping choices, ideas, and information brought before the plenary bodies? In addition to the explicit involvement of members in the consultation, discussion, and decision making, the OECD maintains an established role of nonmembers, as well as other types of entities and parties in the process. The OECD has observer nations at both the Council and the subsidiary body levels. Other organizations, such as the World Bank and BIAC, also function as observers or advisers to the OECD.

The formal structure of the OECD, with plenary participation at the Council level and unanimous voting on OECD positions, would suggest that member states are fairly equal in their power. Does the reality of OECD operations reflect that formal picture, or do the functioning of the nonplenary bodies and the de facto practices of the organization invoke the real-world differences among states in terms of resources, power, experience, and leverage? For example, how are important individual posts within the OECD, such as the Secretary, filled? Is there an implicit alternating pattern? Research looking at a range of international organizations has suggested that informal understandings determine the rotation of many significant leadership positions in international organizations. Informal practices offer significant insight into an organization and its operation. Once selected to a leadership position, how significant are the individual's leadership skills and personal relations in moving the organization's agenda? International relations work outside of taxation has documented ways in which individual leadership skills may be an essential component to reaching agreement and establishing a "regime" on a particular tax problem or set of issues. What are the impact and role of the OECD's own professional staff in the process? As argued earlier, the OECD is more than an aggregation of the member nations. Although the voting takes place through the Council with formal representation for member states, the OECD professional staff, which is deeply involved in the research and execution of projects pursued by the organization, constitutes a relevant force within the organization. As yet, these questions remain unanswered. Although some work is now focusing on understanding the operations inside important international organizations, such as the OECD,[10] much more remains to be done.

This section has primarily focused on the OECD as the example of a state-based international organization, yet the OECD is by no means the only relevant organization. Other organizations also mentioned above warrant comparable scrutiny, including the UN and the WTO. Moreover, many other organizations should be added to the list, particularly those that may be regional, topical, or more tangentially related to tax (such as the World Bank). One would expect that many of the same questions need to be answered for each organization. However, one would also expect that not only would the answers vary, but perhaps some additional questions would also come to light.

---

10. *See, e.g.*, Allison Christians, *Networks, Norms, and National Tax Policy*, 9 Wash. U. Glob. Stud. L. Rev. 1 (2010); Diane Ring, *supra* note 7, at 649.

Additionally, the multiplicity of organizations is itself significant as we explore the interactions among various international tax actors. A sophisticated understanding of the specifics of each international organization and player, along with a theoretical framework for evaluating international relations, will advance our ability to dissect current events and look to the future.

NONSTATE ACTORS

Although nations and state-based international organizations may be the more readily observed actors making international tax policy, they are not the only ones. Certainly nations impose and enforce tax laws, and the major state-based international organizations provide the "universal" tax documents, such as the UN Model Double Taxation Treaty and the OECD Model Treaty with Commentary. However, other forces work through, with, and beyond both the states and the international organizations in ways that concretely and more indirectly influence tax policy. These nonstate actors have not traditionally received as much analysis and scrutiny as the formal state-based international bodies, but the growing focus in international relations on the role of the nonstate actor signals their significance.

Who are these nonstate actors? They include large multinational corporations and their representative organizations; tax experts (a broad category of individuals with extensive knowledge about tax law who are often called upon by governments to provide information, guidance, and commentary); and issue-based groups. Consider for example, the impact of the CFP on the course of the OECD tax competition project. This issue-driven organization likely had business backing, but its support base is not public, in contrast to many other trade or business organizations operating on behalf of an identified industry or set of businesses. What is clear is that the impetus for the organization sprang from U.S. and OECD efforts to curb tax competition. The CFP has actively urged its position on these questions for almost ten years through conferences, papers, and lobbying. Even if the CFP lacks extensive membership rolls, it has been able to crack into the world of tax policy formation.

Multinationals

Taxpayers can and regularly do influence tax policy. Multinational corporations, in particular, have both the resources and the leverage to exert substantial and effective influence. They affect policy through a series of formal and informal paths, often conscious of and carefully marshaling their power. We see their efforts at formal dialogue both as individual corporate taxpayers and as organized groups of taxpayers. Multinational corporations by definition face taxation in multiple jurisdictions. Thus, an increasingly important part of their business agenda includes careful assessment and management of these potential tax burdens. Multinationals interact with states on an individual level through audits, through lobbying of government (both legislative and administrative), and through contract negotiations with sovereigns. Although the audit interactions typically do not generate widespread reform, they can effectively determine the true operation of the system. If a multinational's taxation in a country is a function not of published rules but rather of private negotiations,[11] then the country's real tax policy is something other than the enacted rules, and the multinational's role in crafting its own tax rules is hidden. Whether this interaction should be understood as "influence" by the multinational or system design on the part of the country likely varies depending on the context. Undeniably, though, the informal, secretive nature of the process raises the potential for the exertion of influence. The pressure on developing economies can be particularly strong: "In many poorer developing countries, a few large transnational corporations provide a large portion of the more accessible potential tax bases. They have strong incentives to negotiate individually with government and to influence both tax legislation and its application by the tax administration."[12] For these and related reasons, tax reformers have frequently advocated transparency in tax systems and tax rules.

Multinationals individually lobby the legislatures and tax administrative agencies with respect to law and regulations that they seek to eliminate, add, or modify. Not only developing countries are susceptible to such influence. The tax history in the United States is replete with stories of major U.S. corporations lobbying for particular rules that benefit one or two taxpayers. In some cases, multinationals can combine both the sovereign's role in owning natural resources with the sovereign's right to impose tax. If a multinational is contracting with a country regarding the right to exploit a natural resource, the negotiations may also include agreements on the taxation of those activities. For example, when Bolivia agreed to privatize its oil and gas industry (at the encouragement of the International Monetary Fund and the World Bank) in 1996, the deal granted the multinational oil and gas developers control over the natural resources and a break from taxes in return for a royalty of 18 percent. The deal was justified as a way to increase overall oil and gas production in Bolivia to such a degree that the decreased tax taken by the country could be rationalized. Production did improve, but the anticipated revenue growth in the country did not.[13]

Much of the influence exerted by multinationals on tax policy is exercised through industry associations, business groups, or other joint lobbying projects. For example, in the United States, the National Foreign Trade Council (NFTC), which was founded in 1914 by American businesses (the first president was the head of U.S. Steel), focuses its attention and resources on issues related to international trade. The NFTC, with approximately three hundred member businesses, describes its role as follows:

> Leveraging its broad membership, expertise and influence, the NFTC is the only national business organization that exclusively advocates the international and public policy priorities of its members. From international trade,

---

11. The private negotiations envisioned here extend beyond the classic settlement based on an assessment of the rules, the facts, and the hazards of litigation.
12. Mick Moore, *How Does Taxation Affect the Quality of Governance?*, 47 Tax Notes Int'l 79 (Jul. 2, 2007).
13. Daphne Eviatar, *Bolivia Steps on the Gas*, The Nation, May 29, 2006; *IMF Approves Second Annual Loan for Bolivia Under the ESAF*, IMF Press Release Number 96/12, Mar. 25, 1996, available at http://www.imf.org/external/np/sec/pr/1996/pr9612.htm.

investment, tax, and export finance to human resource management, the NFTC's services and advocacy are a critical link for U.S. companies.[14]

The International Tax Committee of the NFTC seeks to "reduce the economic costs and restrictions produced by governmental tax policies that burden the cross-border trade and investment of NFTC members."[15] Four working groups operate under the Tax Committee and study a variety of issues. In 2001 the NFTC released an extensive study titled "International Tax Policy for the 21st Century." The report, which has been characterized as "scholarly" (and which had a respected tax academic as the Special Consultant to the Drafting Group), established the foundation for the tax lobbying campaign that emerged following the WTO's declaration in 2002 that U.S. export tax rules violated its treaty obligations.[16] According to one account, the NFTC's 2001 study, in which General Electric Company (GE) among many others had input, "helped lay the groundwork for the [tax] provisions that GE [later sought]."[17]

The NFTC also conducts an annual survey of members' views on tax treaties. Members identify which countries and which issues present the most pressing problems from their perspective. The NFTC views the surveys as "an important tool for NFTC members to communicate their tax treaty wish list . . . to the [government], and provides the 'cleansed' information from the survey to the U.S. Treasury and IRS officials working on tax treaties."[18]

In 2010, at the Fall Tax Meeting of the NFTC Tax Committee, several significant government tax policymakers participated as panelists or speakers, including (1) Chief Tax Counsel from the House Ways and Means Committee minority staff, (2) Tax Counsel from the Senate Finance Committee majority staff, (3) International Tax Counsel (Treasury), (4) Chief Counsel (IRS), and (5) Director, Tax Treaty Administration and International Coordination (IRS). The presence of these government officials at this tax meeting, and many others sponsored by a variety of institutions and organizations across the country, represents a legitimate and desirable mechanism by which the government can increase *its* understanding of the business perspective, concerns, and realities relevant to crafting successful and desirable tax policy. At the same time, it clarifies that multinationals are not passive recipients of tax rules from on high, but rather are engaged regularly in "educating" policymakers and shaping discussion.

The NFTC does not limit its activities to U.S.-based rules, regulations, and policies. For example, in May 2008 the NFTC sent a letter to the Dutch finance minister and the Dutch secretary of state urging the Netherlands not to adopt restrictions on interest deductions similar to those implemented in Germany a year before, noting the likely negative repercussions. The letter concluded with the following observation: "We would urge you not to risk your hard-won reputation as a stable, welcoming environment for multinational business

---

14. National Foreign Trade Council, *About Us* (2013), http://www.nftc.org/?id=225.
15. *See* NFTC, *2010 Fall Tax Meeting*, http://www.nftc.org/default.asp?Mode=Directory Display&DirectoryUseAbsoluteOnSearch=True&id=270.
16. Jeffrey H. Birnbaum and Jonathan Weisman, *GE Lobbyists Mold Tax Bill*, Wash. Post, July 13, 2004, at A1.
17. *Id.*
18. NFTC, Council Highlights (June/July 2008), at 11–13.

and investment, developed over decades. You would do this by a hasty adoption of an interest restriction regime which, in the German case, has already proved complex and discouraging. Our members would be more than happy to meet with you and your officials to discuss this further."[19]

The activities of multinationals, both individually and through organizations, includes not only study, analysis, and lobbying, as outlined above, but also political contributions. The issue of campaign contributions and their impact on government is pervasive and important. In some corporations, shareholders have pressured the corporation to disclose political donations (perhaps even their trade association dues) on corporate websites.[20] As a specific example of lobbying, consider the reaction in 2007 as Congress explored increased budgets and tax cuts (both of which would require a corresponding increase in tax revenue under the "pay-as-you-go" system in the legislature). Corporate taxpayers surged into action to avoid being a casualty of the balancing of increased spending and offsetting revenue raising. Congress contemplated limiting the rapid tax deductions available to sports utility vehicles (a move that would generate $2.2 billion over four years). Lobbyists for foreign and domestic automakers began their campaign to save the rapid deductions. Congress also turned to the international tax rules to find additional revenue. Once again multinationals responded: "Forty of them have banded together to form the Coalition for Analysis and Study of Territorial Taxation under the aegis of the accounting firm PricewaterhouseCoopers. The companies' tax executives meet regularly with academic economists to contemplate better tax systems, but their work would be useful in the short term if the pay-as-you-go knife falls."[21] This chapter simply notes that it is not possible to fully understand the shaping of international tax policy without careful consideration of the impact of campaign contributions and lobbying by business.

Assessing the role of the multinational in formulating international tax policy does not require that the multinational be pilloried. The goal is to identify and examine the forces critical in producing the global tax world we see today. The fact that multinationals in many circumstances have great influence does not tell us whether that impact is valuable. Moreover, if we are to understand the internal workings of influential parties on the global tax stage, it is important to recognize the growing role of taxation within a company's corporate governance. Tax directors have observed for some years that corporate management increasingly has focused on the entity's effective tax rate and how that compares to those of other businesses deemed relevant competition. Directors have reported being called on the carpet shortly after competitors reported lower effective tax rates. Intertwined with this focus has been the emerging role of the corporation's tax department as a "profit

---

19. Letter from William Reinsch, President of the NFTC to Wouter Bos, Netherlands Minister of Finance, and Jan de Jager, Netherlands, Secretary for Finance, May 27, 2008.

20. Jonathan Peterson, *More Firms' Political Ties Put Online*, LA Times, March 20, 2006, Bus. Desk, Part C, P. 1. *See generally*, Shayla Kasel, *Show Us Your Money: Halting the Use of Trade Organizations as Covert Conduits for Corporate Campaign Contributions*, 33 J. of Corp. Law 297 (2007).

21. Jeffrey H. Birnbaum, *New Math on Hill, Scramble on K Street*, Wash. Post Fin., March 13, 2007, at D1.

center." A variety of forces produced this new status, but with the combination of explicit attention to effective tax rates by top management and the opportunities afforded by business mobility at the end of the twentieth century, we should not be surprised that multinationals actively maximize their ability to shape their tax world.

Beyond their own, self-initiated involvement in tax policy, multinationals frequently are drawn into formal dialogue by international organizations and by governments, thereby blurring the lines among actors. Not only does the OECD have an affiliated business advisory group mentioned earlier, but the OECD itself calls upon businesses to assist in some of its tax projects. The OECD Centre for Tax Policy and Administration included selected business representatives at its January 2005 Roundtable regarding the Business Restructuring Project. Following the Roundtable, an OECD working group was formed and business representatives from more than 10 OECD countries and non-OECD countries were invited to compose an ad hoc business advisory group to assist the OECD working group in its preliminary stages.[22]

Although the specific power and influence of multinationals likely varies across settings and issues, their active presence in tax policymaking circles merits the examination of both their individual and their collective efforts to shape tax policy. In many cases, this input may be a valuable opportunity for policymakers to anticipate some of the likely business ramifications of tax design options. Governments and nations do not benefit from tax policies that are ill-considered or inadequately informed. Just as it would seem folly to design regulations governing hospital surgical standards without consulting medical professionals, crafting international tax rules without hearing the perspective of business could result in rules that either are ignored or stifle desirable conduct. Certainly multinationals are not disinterested commentators and advisors, but they can be well-informed ones under the mantra of "listen and verify." Of course in other settings, the influence may be viewed as insufficiently public and undesirable in a democratic process. Regardless, a more thorough understanding of their role domestically and globally is essential.

Tax Experts

Another group of nonstate actors that influence tax policy can be characterized as "tax experts." The identification of this set of actors draws upon the work in international relations examining the importance of experts in shaping the goals, techniques, and frameworks employed by states in responding to problems of a technical nature. This research reflects both a broad and a narrow conception of the impact of the expert. First, responding to a traditional premise in international relations (IR) theory that states are *the* major players pursuing strategies based on self interest, some IR theorists (cognitivists) have asked, "How do the states *know* what they want?" Self-interested policies are not always self-evident, particularly in technical matters. Even if it were agreed that each state seeks to promote its self interest, how does it establish

---

22. Available at http://www.oecd.org/document/6/0.3343.en_2649_37989760_34535302_1_1_1_1.000html.

what that interest is? According to the cognitivists, the state often relies on experts (inside and outside of government), with the result that knowledge holders can have a notable impact on state policy.

A second, more focused examination of experts emerged from the IR literature seeking to understand what factors increase the likelihood that states will reach agreement on a problem. This work, drawn in part from environmental case studies in IR, suggests that when scientists around the globe can reach a general consensus on an environmental problem, the countries themselves find it easier to reach a consensus. Why? The rationale is that to the extent that the issue involves expertise, the government will consult its local experts to help it understand which paths seem to be in the country's best interest. If each of these experts consulted by his or her own country shares in the general global consensus on some of the issues, then each will likely transmit to the government a common view of both the problem and the range of plausible solutions. This narrowing of the debate landscape, then, increases the ability of the nations to reach some type of agreement.

Moving to the tax arena, where do we find experts playing a special role in influencing tax policy? There are several different situations where tax "experts" can influence the law, including (1) tax lobbyists interacting with legislatures; (2) government commissions and studies with outside, "expert" input, such as President Bush's Advisory Panel on Tax Reform (formed in 2005, which produced its report in November 2005) or President Obama's Economic Recovery Advisory Board (formed in 2009, which produced its report in August 2011); (3) organized efforts to transform lobbying position papers into respectable studies by working with respected academic advisors;[23] (4) international organizations of tax professionals, such as IFA (the International Fiscal Association), which engages in regular analysis of active and current issues; (5) the U.S. Joint Committee on Taxation, which for many years had a particular niche role in providing nonpartisan analysis of tax issues to Congress; and (6) selected professional organizations that have developed a reputation for generating analyses and comments that are more than pure advocacy on behalf of their clients (for example, the New York State Bar Association and its regular reports on major tax issues and reforms of current interest).

Identification of these sources of influence by "tax experts" on international tax policy does *not* claim that such experts (1) always have influence, (2) have influence that is either inherently good or bad, (3) have influence that is equivalent, or (4) are neutral and without bias.[24] The point is that they do constitute another relevant force, sometimes used in combination with multinational corporations or international organizations. In addition to considering the source, nature, and level of influence of tax experts, it is relevant to consider the "limits" on the expert's effect. Some questions in tax policy are susceptible to ready characterization as

---

23. An example here is the decision of the NFTC to seek some recognized outside tax experts as advisors to their 2001 report on international tax policy in the twenty-first century.

24. Certainly there might be differences between someone hired by a corporation to explain and argue a point and an academic preparing an independent paper, but that latter category itself can have many versions, is never "free" of bias, and may meld into hired papers.

questions of expertise, but other questions may be more clearly distributional concerns, which are inherently "political" questions and not the exclusive domain of the tax expert, although the tax expert may be important in identifying and highlighting the existence and implications of the distributional issues.

Networks of Bureaucracies

Another set of nonstate "actors" we might identify includes the networks of bureaucrats and tax administrators. Separating these networks from discussions of states as actors may seem a little odd, and if someone chose to analyze these networks as part of a deeper discussion of *how* states create international tax policy, the core point would be made as well. Increasingly, through formal and informal arrangements, tax administrators around the globe are sharing some of their experience, knowledge, and perspectives. Prominent examples include the Joint International Tax Shelter Information Centre (JITSIC), which was organized in 2004 by the tax administrations of the United States, Australia, Canada, and the United Kingdom (and now China, Japan, South Korea, France, and Germany) with a goal of combating tax shelters and abusive transactions with real-time information. Other formal organizations exist along regional or topical lines. Additionally, increased interactions among tax administrations more generally (sometimes on simply a bilateral basis) can facilitate coordinated action and shared perspectives. Although similar relationships and networks have been explored outside of tax, more research is required in taxation.

BEYOND EFFICIENCY, BEYOND A SPECIFIC TAX POLICY AGENDA: THE FUTURE OF INTERNATIONAL TAX THROUGH ITS INTERNATIONAL RELATIONS

Two important realities now shape international tax policy—both its multilateral dimension (cooperation among states can be essential to the full realization of desired tax policy) and its multiactor dimension (states are not the only active and significant forces in international tax policy). This means that we can no longer rely on traditional tax policy analysis as the exclusive inquiry for setting a tax policy agenda. Not only must we identify our preliminary vision of good tax policy (which itself extends beyond economic inquiry), but we must also examine the universe in which we seek to pursue that policy. By comparison, consider the following question: Would the Department of Defense or the State Department develop its policies and positions for national defense without exploring in detail the interactive environment in which these policies play out and the complex interactions among all relevant parties? If the answer is no, then why would we anticipate that the IRS and Treasury should proceed differently?

An effective and comprehensive research agenda in international tax would study the full scope of actors influencing international tax policy and would aim to understand the ways in which influence is exercised and in which views are shaped. Are the outcomes different depending on the underlying issue (e.g., enforcement, transfer pricing, electronic commerce)? Does it matter who raises an issue first? How effective are parties at operating through several different organizations at the same time on a given issue? How frequently do parties attempt to trade tax issues? Do they trade tax and nontax issues? Existing research on the dynamics of international organizations and on modeling the interactions among organizations and states can help frame these inquiries and provide additional insights. But the first step begins with the recognition that the international dynamics of our international tax policy have become just as important as the policy itself.

INDEX

Notes and tables are indicated by "n" and "t" following the page numbers.

Qualified residence interest
(QRI) deduction (*continued*)
religious effects, 171
sexual orientation effects, 170–171
standard deduction, proposed as
add-on to, 176
tax credit, proposed conversion to,
177–179
as upside-down subsidy, 169–170

Race
critical race theory. *See* Critical race
theory
public housing and, HUD study on,
168
QRI deduction, effect of, 168–170
Racism, critical race theory and,
91–92
Rahdert, George, 97–101
Rawls, John, 54–60
Rawlsian doctrine, 54–60
difference principle in, 57–58
equality in, 58–59
natural primary goods in, 57
original position in, 55
overview, 62
redistribution in, 59–60
revenue-raising in, 59–60
social contract in, 54–55
social primary goods in, 55–57
taxation and, 59–60
REA (Retirement Equity Act of 1984),
203n68
Reagan, Ronald, 172
Real property tax. *See* Property tax
Rectification principle, 41–42
Redistribution
as goal of taxation, 184
individual income tax, use of, 190
in international taxation, 243–254.
See also International taxation
in Nozickean model of
entitlement theory, 41–42
in Rawlsian doctrine, 59–60
social welfare function and, 53
taxation and, 37n65
Regressivity
of employer-sponsored health
insurance and, 111–112
of property tax, 74–79
appreciation, failure to consider,
77–78

benefit theory and, 76–77
capital value theory and, 75–77
consumption theory and, 75–77
homestead exemptions and, 78,
83
individual income tax compared,
83
sales tax compared, 83
of VAT, 189
Regulation
corporate income tax, use of, 190
as goal of taxation, 184–187
Regulatory taxes, 183–190
allocation of specific goals, 188–189
bank tax (proposed), 189–190
carbon tax, 185–187
climate change and, 185–187
corporate income tax, efficacy of,
187–188, 190
health care tax, 189–190
individual income tax, efficacy of,
187–190
overview, 183–185
PPACA mandate as, 132–133, 183
regulation as legitimate goal
for taxation, 184–187
types of taxes best suited
for regulation, 187–188
VAT, efficacy of, 187–190
Religion, effect of QRI deduction on,
171
Renter deduction for property tax,
78n46
Republican proposals regarding
health care, 107, 127–128
Resourcing rule for dividends, 258n4
Retirement Equity Act of 1984 (REA),
203n68
Retirement plans
characteristics of, 195–197
defined benefit plans, 197, 200–201
defined contribution plans, 198
401(k) plans. *See* 401(k) plans
404(c) "safe harbor" plans, 204
IRAs
home ownership, use for, 180
HSAs compared, 116
mutual funds, 214–215
nondiscrimination rules, 196n15
overview, 193–195, 215–216
pensions, 196–197
qualified plans, 196n16